29. 10. 84.

The Odyssey of
C.H. Lightoller

The Odyssey of C.H. Lightoller

PATRICK STENSON

WITH AN INTRODUCTION BY
WALTER LORD

W.W. NORTON & COMPANY
NEW YORK   LONDON

First Edition

Library of Congress Cataloging in Publication Data

Stenson, Patrick.
    The odyssey of C.H. Lightoller.

    1. Lightoller, C.H. 2. Shipmasters—Great
Britain—Biography. I. Title.
VK140.L57S74   1984   387.5′092′4 [B]   84–18907

ISBN 0-393-01924-1

W.W. Norton & Company, Inc., 500 Fifth Avenue, New York, N.Y. 10110
W.W. Norton & Company, Ltd., 37 Great Russell Street, London WC1B 3NU

1 2 3 4 5 6 7 8 9 0

CONTENTS

LIST OF PLATES

For my American cousin,
John Hancke

ACKNOWLEDGEMENTS

Many people have given me great assistance during the preparation of this book. Almost everyone I approached did their utmost to help me in whatever way they could. Initially in these acknowledgements I was going to single out certain people for special mention because of the large contribution they made, but then I felt that would perhaps be unfair to those whose contribution in quantity may not have been as great but who were no less keen and willing.

For this reason I have simply put down the names in alphabetical order of those people, companies, institutions to whom I am greatly indebted for the help they have given me. I thank them all:

Captain Gerry Ashcroft
Mr. Jack Bailey
Miss Alison Beer, Adelaide Library
Mr. John Bennett
Mr. George Birtill
Mr. Stafford Bourne
Mr. Erwin D. Canham
Chorley Public Library
Mr. Maurice Cocker
Mrs. Mildred Cooper
The Dunkirk Veterans' Association
The Dunkirk Little Ships'
  Association
Elder Dempster of Liverpool
The Fleet Air Arm Museum,
  Yeovilton
Mr. Dennis Fowler
Mr. Alexander Fullerton
Captain and Mrs. A. R. B. Gillespie
Professor Robert M. Grant
Greenshields, Cowie of Liverpool
Harland and Wolff
Miss Iris Huckstep, Ramsgate
  Library
The Imperial War Museum

Mr. 'Ziggy' Jacobsen
Mr. George Jenner
Mr. Ron Lemthorpe
Mrs. Betty Lightoller
Commander Timothy Lightoller
Mr. Walter Lord
Mr. A. J. McMillan
Mr. Geoffrey Marcus
Mr. Simon Martin
Merseyside Maritime Museum
Mrs. Elsie Miller
Mr. Kenneth Miller
Captain Ian Mitchell
Mrs. Hilary Moorhouse
The Ministry of Defence
The National Maritime Museum
The Nautical School, Liverpool
The Naval Historical Branch,
  London
The Navy News
Mr. Laurence Parsons
Mr. James Reeve
Mr. Tom Rice
Mr. David Roberts
Dr. Douglas Robinson

ACKNOWLEDGEMENTS

Captain Gerald Rowe-May
Mrs. Sharon Rutman
Mr. Donald Sattin
Mr. John Sapsford
Mr. Jack Smith

Southampton City Archives
Mr. Mike Stammers
Mr. Edward Watson-Davis
Mr. Bert Webb

The excerpt from 'McAndrew's Hymn' is reproduced by kind permission of The National Trust and Macmillan London Limited.

I would also like to make an extra thank-you to Mrs. Betty Lightoller, Captain A. R. B. Gillespie, Mr. Stafford Bourne, and Harland and Wolff for kindly lending me photographs for publication in this book.

Patrick Stenson,
Altrincham,
Cheshire.

INTRODUCTION

The date was April 15, 1932. The headline said, HERO OF TITANIC NOW ILL AT POOR FARM. The story in the Baltimore *Evening Sun* told how Charles Herbert Lightoller, Second Officer of the lost liner, had been forgotten by the hundreds he helped save twenty years earlier. 'Today, Lightoller, friendless and alone, is a patient at the Sonoma County (Cal.) Hospital and Poor Farm, suffering from paralysis, which has rendered helpless his right arm and side.' The story seemed certain to teach me, an impressionable 14-year-old, a lasting lesson about the ironies of life.

Actually, there was a lesson to be learned, but it was not about irony. It was about sham. The destitute old sailor at the poor farm turned out to be not Herbert Lightoller at all, but an engaging old mountebank hoping for sympathy, and perhaps something a little more tangible, by posing as the *Titanic*'s heroic second officer.

The real Lightoller was happy and well, living in a suburban cottage near London with his charming wife Sylvia and five devoted children. I never had the privilege of knowing him personally—he died several years before *A Night to Remember*—but I did get to know Sylvia. I occasionally visited her at the cottage (with the quaint address, '1 Duck's Walk'), and spent many hours sipping tea in the late afternoon sunshine, listening to at least second-hand stories about the *Titanic*.

Later I learned of Lightoller's remarkable exploits at Dunkirk, when he took his cabin cruiser *Sundowner* across the Channel and brought back 130 British Tommies. It seemed incredible that one man could have played such a spectacular role in two such diverse events, 28 years apart.

I didn't know the half of it. Not until I read this beautifully crafted biography by Patrick Stenson did I fully appreciate all the amazing things 'Lights' had done over his adventurous career. He survived four shipwrecks; he triumphed over a bad fire at sea; he was marooned on a desert island; he mined for gold in the Klondike, punched cows in the West, and rode the rods back east, hobo-style. He also rammed and sank a German U-boat with his destroyer in the First World War, and just before the Second War, he even went on an espionage mission reminiscent of *The Riddle of the Sands*.

Some of these events he described himself in his own memoirs, published in 1935 but soon withdrawn for legal reasons. He was simply too outspoken for the lawyers. I bought the book at the time, but did not pay much attention to the early chapters. They were mostly about sailing ships, and for me Lightoller's story began on page 214—the part about the *Titanic*.

Now I see what I missed. But Patrick Stenson's biography is no mere rehash of the memoirs. He ranges far beyond Lightoller's own adventures, bringing to life the whole era of merchant-ship sailing: the routes, the hazards, the characters, the customs, the way the ships were run. We see 'Lights' in this world; we live, suffer, and frolic with him as he slowly climbs the ladder, ultimately moving on to steam and the crack Atlantic run.

Lightoller never quite achieved the rank or fortune he somewhat wistfully sought. He was too much the romantic individualist . . . too likely to say what he thought. The one time he played the 'company man' was at the official inquiries into the *Titanic* disaster. In current parlance, he more or less 'stonewalled it', but for all his pains, his employers side-tracked his career. No matter how loyal or how brave he may have been, it was fatal for a White Star Line officer to have been associated with the *Titanic*.

Lightoller took his fate philosophically—he was always good at bouncing back—and went on to new endeavors. For a while between the wars he even raised chickens—an odd change of course for an old sailor.

And so to Dunkirk. He was now 66—a little old to be dodging German Stukas—but naturally he took *Sundowner* over himself. It was a harrowing ordeal, but he was no stranger to disaster. A letter he wrote a week later shows the unquenchable spirit he always managed to summon up when the odds were against him. It ends:

> There's one thing you can rest assured on, and that is that this country will never give in. If they bomb us out of England, we'll come over to Canada and fight from there . . . We've got our tails well up and are going to win no matter when or how.

This heart-warming hero deserves a sparkling biography, and Patrick Stenson has written it.

WALTER LORD

PROLOGUE
[1940]

'This is the BBC Home Service. Here is the first news for today Saturday the first of June . . . Men of the B.E.F. are still getting back to England in large numbers—tired men, hungry men but men who are still in great heart and magnificent fighting spirit, only anxious to get back quickly and fight again the enemy who brutally bombs innocent civilians as part of his war method . . .'

As the motor-yacht *Sundowner* left the Thames estuary, rounded Foreness Point and passed beneath North Foreland light early on that Saturday morning, from over the calm and windless sea could be heard the continuous thunder of bombing and shellfire pinpointed by a sinister pall of black smoke rising into the otherwise clear blue sky.

Peering ahead from the wheelhouse, *Sundowner*'s owner could see that the Channel was noticeably busier today, far busier than he had ever known in his many years' experience of it; scores of vessels worked feverishly to and fro, reminiscent of a colony of ants. Soon he knew he would be one of them, yet he looked for all the world as though he was setting forth on just another pleasure cruise to add to the many he had already made across that stretch of water, attired as ever in the baggy grey flannels, shirt-sleeves and carelessly perched yachting cap concealing a steadily balding head.

Back at the Chiswick yacht basin an Admiralty Requisitioning Officer had come aboard to tell him his yacht was to be taken over and manned by a naval crew. 'If anybody's going to take my boat to Dunkirk it will be me and my son!' had been his belligerent reply. There was something about this broad-shouldered old sea-dog with the weather-worn face and deep nautical drawl that one obviously didn't trifle with, and certainly not if one was some clipboard-toting popinjay from the Royal Navy aboard the owner's craft, his cherished *Sundowner*, exclusive property of Commander Charles Herbert Lightoller DSC and Bar, RD, RNR (Retired). The part in brackets was to be tossed aside forthwith.

'In that case, go to it!' the official had said, with a laugh more of relief than of amusement. Anyone willing to take his own vessel across was more than welcome to go. There were owners who had shown themselves not so willing and others who could not be contacted in time. Their boats were taken anyway. Now there was a shortage of crews. As for the owner of *Sundowner*, it would have been utterly unthinkable that anyone else but he should take her on this of all trips.

At first he had not been fully briefed on why they wanted *Sundowner* though he had a good idea. His suspicions were not long being confirmed, and now he knew exactly what was happening over the Channel and what fearsome hazards were awaiting there for his precious boat. But if she had to go then her best chances were with him, the man who knew her and understood her better than anyone. In her own way she was as dear to him as the wife and grown-up family to which he was devoted. He had helped to conceive *Sundowner*, somehow managed to scrape together the cash to turn an inspired idea into a magnificent reality, following eagerly every minute stage in her progress taking shape on the wharf, to watch excitedly as she slid down the slipway on that memorable spring morning. When he first took her for her sea trials, she surpassed all hopes. *Sundowner* was a mighty fine boat and everyone said so. But for her new owner *Sundowner*'s greatest gift was to return him to the true joy of the sea which he had sorely missed for such a long time. If now she could be destined to be blown to pieces, then it would be only with him in command. The sea had never claimed him yet—and God knows, it had been given enough chances!

Sundowner slipped by the ever peaceful Dickensian seaside charm of Broadstairs and headed for the entrance to Ramsgate harbour where she had been instructed to put in for her orders. As he approached the harbour entrance on that morning the little Kentish port was presenting a very different picture from the one he remembered in the past.

The strict rule of the road that only one vessel at a time could pass in or out of the harbour had gone completely by the board. Boats seemed to be coming and going at will and a motleyed collection they were at that: fishing boats of various origin from North Sea drifters to Brixham smacks, channel trawlers to oyster catchers. Then came the tug boats with barges in tow, the colliers, the pleasure steamers including a couple of paddlers, smaller pleasure craft like his own 60-

foot *Sundowner*, lifeboats, minesweepers, Thames hopper barges that usually carried sludge, and even a dredger and a Thames sailing barge. Many carried the marks of the cruel incessant beating being taken over the Channel—and on much of the route there and back. It was a brave and glorious effort in the face of a determined ruthless enemy to fetch 'the chaps' and bring them home; boats were crammed to the limit with their dishevelled cargoes of khaki, men on their last legs and so thankful to be out of it at last.

Ramsgate harbour, a buzzing hive of boats and men, was under the control of the Royal Navy. Here they were handling the smaller craft engaged in the Dunkirk evacuation. The bigger transports, the cruisers, the destroyers and troop carriers were working out of Dover further down the coast from where, beneath the town's famous castle, the overall Dunkirk operation—'Operation Dynamo'—was being directed. Other harbours along that Kent coast were involved. The large number of small craft coming and going at Ramsgate was obviously making for a tricky co-ordinating job. An officer, directing traffic with a loud-hailer from a navy launch, told *Sundowner* to lie off the harbour entrance until given the word; eventually she was directed to tie up alongside another couple of vessels.

It was then that the appalling significance of the situation was brought home to Lightoller. So these were the undefeated men who had come back in glory with morale 'as high as ever', and who were anxious to be back soon 'to have a real crack at Jerry'. As he looked at the endless queue of men all round the harbour waiting to board the buses lining the seafront, many seemed hard put to stand, let alone to fight; soldiers without their helmets, their rifles, and others in an even greater state of undress, missing boots, shirts, and tunics all long since discarded at the sea's edge in the desperate struggle to escape the guns and bombs of the Hun, to get away from the 'Hell of Dunkirk'. In company with the buses was a fleet of ambulances operating a constant shuttle-service for the casualties, among them the many who had undoubtedly taken their first and last 'crack at Jerry'. And then there were the splendid women of Ramsgate beavering away without pause on the serving tables that had been hastily lined up beneath the Pavilion balcony. As the men kept arriving in their hundreds, their thousands, there would be a mug of tea from the urns and a wad for every single one.

Royal Navy headquarters was set up in a building that had known considerable contrast in use during its lifetime. Nestling at the foot of the cliffs overlooking the town it had originally been the railway station which offered the trippers the unique facility of being able to step off the train and straight onto the beach. Later it was turned into a ballroom and amusement centre cheerfully christened '*Merrie England*'. And then came the war and the Royal Navy. *Merrie England* was now H M S *Fervent*, and whoever chose the name seemed to have foresight. When Lightoller arrived there for his orders that morning it was certainly living up to it.

As he stepped inside and made for the hub-bub of the main operations room he found himself among an assorted bunch of skippers, boat-owners, some of whom he knew, and other miscellaneous Merchant Service and Royal Navy personnel. Some, like him, were about to go across for the first time while others had just returned and were about to go in again. There was talk of the 'unmitigated hell' to be found over there, with grisly stories of how boats had met their end, often with severe loss of life, as the waves of whining Stukas dived down again and again. Then there were the tales of men being rescued from one wreck only to find themselves back in the water again when the craft which had plucked them to safety met the same fate. But always there was the one angry burning question, 'Where's the bloody R A F?' The Royal Air Force was there all right, but not exactly in force. Their numbers were so limited that in the hours that passed between sorties by the few squadrons of Spitfires, Hurricanes and Defiants, the Luftwaffe controlled the air and was taking full advantage of it.

Since the evacuation began in earnest five days previously it was apparently the worst day so far. Goering was obviously determined to prove once and for all to his Führer that the Luftwaffe could put paid to the exodus. So too were his counterparts on the ground. The Allied-held territory around the perimeter of Dunkirk was rapidly shrinking under heavy enemy pressure. The German panzers were on the verge of breaking through. The British rearguard had done all that could have been asked of them and now their turn must come to pull out and make a run for it.

One last supreme effort was required of the Dunkirk 'Armada' but that morning their losses had been catastrophic, not least for the Royal Navy. Six destroyers had been knocked out, either sunk or severely damaged, as had a score of other vessels ranging from two large troop transports down to little ships like *Sundowner*, there one second, gone the next—so much floating matchwood.

Thousands of men were getting away, but there were many who were not, among them ordinary civilians who might have been seated at an office desk in the City the day before when the summons came from the Admiralty to get their boat ready. Their wives and families would still be wondering where they'd got to . . .

Despite the weather, Lightoller had put on a black tie and his old RNR Commander's jacket complete with gold rings and medal ribbons, still smelling of mothballs; he meant to look the part as much as possible. But he need not have troubled. The officer in *Fervent*'s operations room was only too grateful that this owner was all set to go himself. If the official had wondered about the old man's age he did not show it as he casually gave Lightoller his orders. They were the same as everyone else's:

'PROCEED TO DUNKIRK FOR FURTHER ORDERS.'

That tickled his dry sense of humour, though it wouldn't be quite all. There was a recommended route to take where the least enemy hostility might be encountered, except that by now there was no such route. Lightoller knew Dunkirk harbour. He had been there in another war. Bombs had dropped on it then, but in comparison to the present blitz, that was peace-haven. In subsequent years he had called in with *Sundowner* during pleasure jaunts across the Channel with family and friends. This time would be different.

He was concerned about his charts which were, as he pointed out to the man behind the desk 'somewhat antiquated' and asked for a new set. But the trouble with charts for those waters in the days of May/June 1940 was that the sea-bed off Dunkirk was changing from hour to hour—the enemy saw to that. He was given his new charts displaying a heavy amount of additional pencil work round the Dunkirk stretch of coast where, as far as was known from sources returning, new wrecks were lying but it was impossible to pinpoint them all. Even in the last hour the number of sunken vessels had been considerably added to. And then there were the mines. Minesweepers had been hard at work constantly over the last few days but 'Can't give any firm guarantees on that score, old boy,' he was told.

A meaty thumb went to *Sundowner*'s starter button. There was a violent bang of air, the starter system turned and whined and the Gleniffer 72 HP diesel rumbled into life. *Sundowner* was unhitched by Gerald, the young sea-scout who with the two Lightollers—father and son—made up the whole crew. She was fended clear of the fishing vessel that had been her temporary dock during this brief pause in her mission. She swung round in a tight arc and, filtering in among a procession of other craft bound for the same destination, headed out through the harbour entrance and into the English Channel.

The time was 10.00 a.m. by *Sundowner*'s clock—the ship's clock which once upon a time dictated the hour-by-hour, watch-by-watch life at sea of a very promising young Western Ocean mailboat officer. There were the times when he had loathed and cursed that clock and yet here it was decades later still watching over him aboard his own little craft, serving as a symbolic reminder of time long past, how life once was and how it might well have continued but for a cruel turn of fate.

As *Sundowner* cleared the harbour the brass throttle lever to the right of the helm was eased forward as far as it would go. The deck of the wheelhouse began to reverberate more vigorously under her skipper's feet to the increase in engine revolutions . . . 700 . . . 750 . . . 800 . . . 850 rpm. She was flat out and cutting through the smooth water at just a little over ten knots. The chaos of Ramsgate harbour, the town and its backcloth of white cliffs began to shrink astern while before them that tell-tale tentacle of blackness, still reaching way up into the sky, an unsightly disfiguring dark smudge, already felt closer. Mingled with the chatter of the diesel, the swish of water spreading back from the bows, and the cries of the scavenging sea-gulls came the unmistakable noises of war.

PART ONE
LEARNING THE ROPES

Though the gales should lash and harry,
Pile on all the rags she'll carry,
Listen to the reef points drum,
And tautened back stays drone.
Up and down the 'Old Man' paces,
'Keep the padlocks on those braces!'
So keep them on you bullies—keep them on!
Though the gales should rip and tear you,
And the toil and moil should wear you,
Crack it on! Crack it on!

Tom Manners

1

From the very first day that young Herbert Lightoller laid eyes on the port of Liverpool his mind was made up. It was not just the sea and all things connected with it that took his fascination. It was also a way of escape.

The family were in cotton and had been for generations. It was his great-grandfather Timothy who first introduced cotton spinning to the Lancashire town of Chorley when he moved there from neighbouring Rochdale at the turn of the nineteenth century.

The business grew and flourished and the Lightollers became wealthy and important people in the town. Their giant five-storey stone mill on the corner of Standish Street and Lyon's Lane dominated the skyline for many miles around and they had a standard of living to match. The family home of Yarrow House on the southern edge of the town was an impressive residence indeed.

They were liked and respected as much as any employers could be in the hard uncharitable world of the Lancashire cotton industry of those times. It was the Lightollers who gave Chorley its first street lighting. Five lamps in Standish Street were erected by the Lightollers and lit from the gas plant in their mill. They believed in living up to the family motto *'Lux Vestra'* — 'Let your light shine'.

The mill that was built up by Timothy went on to prosper under sons Richard and Henry. Then came the American Civil War and the cotton industry was never quite the same again for the Lightollers. The prospects at the mill for Charles Herbert, born on March 30th 1874, were considerably less promising than for previous Lightoller sons.

His mother died a month after he was born, followed within a year by a sister, and then Grandfather Henry, which meant that his father was now in charge of the mill. But the damage to the business was irreparable and too much money had been lost—too much certainly for Herbert's father, who one day simply upped and left for New Zealand with a new wife, leaving Herbert and his sisters in the care of an uncle and aunt. For that his son would never forgive him.

Life bereft of normal family affection seemed to be dominated instead by religion, discipline and a perpetual shortage of pocket money. He had to get away—away from the strap and away from

3

those repetitive reports from school which always said he could do much better if he applied himself. The boy knew he could do better but not at Chorley Grammar School and it was evident that the school had reached the same conclusion. And so he resolved, at the mature age of thirteen, to go to sea.

On those visits to Liverpool to see the Cotton Exchange and its workings in preparation for the day when he would follow in family footsteps, he found himself irresistibly drawn to the docks. These were the days when Merseyside was in its prime. Whatever the time of year, there would seldom be any less than a hundred vessels tied up in Liverpool from the humblest ketch loading coal for the Isle of Man in Canning Dock to the most glamorous transatlantic steamship at the Princes Landing-stage, taking on passengers for New York.

Then there were the thousands of sailors, tradesmen, and stevedores to be seen hard at work in and around the vessels alongside the quays overhauling the running gear, chipping and 'painting ship', taking in stores, or unloading cargo brought in from some distant port.

Steam was slowly creeping up on the monopoly of sail, but when it came to trading across the oceans, sail still held the upper hand, mostly in the shape of the big square-sail three- and four-masted barques. These were the ships that beckoned to the boy at a time when Liverpool's skyline more than ever was dominated by a 'forest of masts'. The day a friendly mate invited him to come aboard a sailing ship for a look round and even climb into the rigging, his mind was made up. The thought of sailing away across the oceans in one of these magnificent windjammers to lands distant and new thrilled the boy to the marrow.

His request was readily granted, almost a little too readily perhaps, but then he was far too excited to care that his uncle was more than glad to get him off his hands: 'Might do the boy some good . . .' 'Knock some sense into him . . .'

His 'chum' sister Janie was not so pleased about it. The lack of mother and father had drawn them close to one another. She was going to miss him and she would worry about him too.

One bleak February day in 1888 Charles Herbert Lightoller, a rather undergrown boy rising fourteen, signed on as a brass-bound apprentice aboard the *Primrose Hill*. He was fully outfitted with pilot coat, heavy trousers, two shore-going uniforms with cap, two pairs of overalls, heavy underwear, sea-boots complete with sea-boot stock-ings, a full set of oilskins with stormcap, knife and spike and straw mattress all neatly packed in a sea-chest. The vessel was a steel-hulled four-masted barque and three-skysail-yarder of 2,500 tons belonging to William Price and Company of Liverpool. There was a distant cousin who was Third Mate in a ship of the same line, so it was agreed this would be the most suitable company for him to join.

The £40 surety for his apprenticeship was willingly paid over and, from the moment of signing the 'Articles of Agreement' (including a pledge not to frequent taverns or alehouses, to keep the Master's secrets and not do any damage to him), he was bound to the company for the next four years. He would not receive any pay. He would after all be getting the benefits of a full training at sea.

He was now a member of the half-deck crowd of the *Primrose Hill*, the half-deck being the part of the ship where the 'young gentlemen' were quartered. But for him no roomy cabin or comfortable saloon to relax in. It was a small evil-smelling den towards the after end of the ship, reached by descending a steep ladder leading from the fore part of the poop deck. Round its perimeter were the bunks where the boys slept, and in the middle a crude table with a grimy oil lamp slung above it. There were no such refinements as seats. You sat on your sea-chest. So here would be his home for the years of servitude to come—a home which he would discover was wet more often than it was dry. The half-deck boys were treated no better than the ordinary deck-hands—but they had a great deal more to learn. However the boy, at this stage, had never for one moment paused to consider the hardships that were awaiting him as he embarked on his chosen career.

'Stand by the halliards! . . . Loose all sails! . . .' As the dock cranes, the warehouses and the forest of masts that was Liverpool began to diminish in the haze astern, the steam tug that towed the *Primrose Hill* out of the Mersey and into Liverpool Bay tooted her cheery farewell and the sailing ship began to come to life.

'Set the headsails! . . . Sheets to starboard! . . .'

'High ho she rises boys and we'll all sling slush at the cook!' sang the crew as they manned the halliards. A small pair of hands unaccustomed to hauling on rough prickly ropes were already getting blistered and raw. 'Salt water boy, that's the best cure for that!' But what cure for the puny muscles that still ached from the torturous work back in port, humping endless crates of provisions aboard and hauling heavy sails around the decks?

'Armstrong's Patent, that's the medicine!'

Thirty-odd hands on deck and aloft, each one of them familiar with the ship and his job in it responded unhesitatingly to every command that boomed from the bearded one pacing the poop deck with four gold rings on his sleeves.

'Haul round the foreyards! . . . Shift over the jibs! . . .'

She began to gather way, her great spreads of canvas cracking like thunder at the first feel of the freshening wind. Gently she heeled over and began to build up speed . . . seven knots . . . eight . . . nine knots . . . ten . . . and now with every one of her milk-white sails set the *Primrose Hill* was gliding along with the grace and speed for which she was famous. Every now and again she dipped her lee rail under and the sea would come gurgling through the scuppers and washports and swish about the deck.

It was a wonderful feeling just then for a young first voyager, but no matter how thrilled a boy might be about the prospect of going to sea there would always come that moment of regret over the folly of his decision. For the young Lightoller it came as the *Primrose Hill* sailed into the teeth of a gale. As the ship pitched and rolled in the heavy seas that surely must swamp her at any moment the boy became convinced his stomach was going to turn inside out. The sea was wasting no time about giving this young upstart his first lesson on who was mistress. He would only too willingly have swopped it for a whole week of Latin lessons just for the miracle of being transplanted back onto the firm dry streets of Chorley—but it was too late. 'Tie a piece of pork fat to a length of string, keep swallowing it and pulling it up. That'll put a stop to it!' That was one piece of seafaring remedial advice which he would decline to take.

And yet once the young apprentice was totally resigned to the unrelenting misery of seasickness, he found his viciously churning insides beginning to subside. After three days his complexion lost its ghastly pale green, pasty look and returned to something of its normal hue. He was finding his sea legs. Perhaps he had been too hasty in his regret.

'Now then boy, up aloft with you and stop the main skysail buntlines!'

As was the usual custom, apprentices got their first 'feel' of being aloft while the ship was in port, but once at sea Lightoller would discover that going aloft took on a completely new meaning. The apprentices worked under the watchful eye of the Third Mate who was their tutor and mentor and Lightoller learnt that when he said 'Up!' up you went without the slightest hesitation, else it was a rope's end across the backside or a swift backhanded crack across the jaw to send you sprawling across the deck. 'Growl you may, go you must!' a maxim which was law aboard the *Primrose Hill*, where he found those buntlines would soon become a familiar acquaintance. The buntlines on a square-rigged ship were the lines which led from the sails to the deck for gathering the belly of a sail up to the yard for furling. When the sail was unfurled and set, the buntlines, which then hung unchecked, had to be 'stopped' or else they might rub against the canvas and eventually hole it. To stop buntlines (and ensure they remained slack) meant climbing aloft armed with short lengths of twine called 'stops' and securing the looped ends of the buntlines to their correct and appointed places on the running gear. Lightoller's principal responsibility as a first-voyage apprentice in the *Primrose Hill* was the skysail buntlines, where he would become only too well acquainted with the true significance of a 'three-skysail-yarder' which he had so proudly boasted about to envious school chums back at the grammar school when he nonchalantly announced he was leaving and 'going to sea'.

The skysails on the *Primrose Hill* made her just that little bit more special than the average windjammer. The standard barque of her size tended to carry no more than six sails on each of her square-rigged masts, the lowest and largest sail being the course, then up to the lower and upper topsails, next the lower and upper t'gallants, and then the sixth and usually the uppermost sail of all, the Royal. But the *Primrose Hill* went one better. Above the Royal on each of her three square-rigged masts she carried a seventh spread of canvas . . . a skysail. Most ordinary barques did not carry them, as many owners considered skysails more ornament than use and hardly worth the extra bother or manpower to handle them. But there were those, such as William Price and Company, who stuck to the theory that skysails gave a ship that extra turn of speed, and after all, in such times of increased competition with steam, a sailing ship needed all the speed she could muster to stay in the race. Certainly they added something to the appearance, if not necessarily the speed, of the *Primrose Hill*. That seventh sail also gave her the distinction of being one of the tallest ships afloat, a distinction which found her easy to pick out from amongst a multitude of masts in port. From deck to skysail yard she measured approximately two hundred feet, an awfully long way up for the young first voyager making his first nervous steps aloft.

The initial stages of the climb he found relatively easy. There were ratlines as far as the Royal yard, about 180 feet, but then there came the last stage of the journey to the skysail yard which presented a novel obstacle. At this point the ratlines stopped and the only means of scaling the remaining twenty feet or so was by shinning up a wire backstay. It was a perilous enough assault course in calm conditions, but young Lightoller at the age of fourteen, and small with it, would be expected to tackle it day or night without question, no matter how much the ship might be heaving and wallowing beneath him while gale force winds, driving rain, and wildly flapping canvas all conspired to reduce his chances of clinging on for survival—and with nothing more than a slender footrope supporting him. 'One hand for yourself and one for the owner' was the maxim in those circumstances, but nobody yet had ever managed to furl a sail with one hand. Many a boy on his first voyage in sail went to his doom through falling from aloft, either to smash onto the deck or plunge into the sea whichever way his downward trajectory took him.

Eventually he would come to resent those skysails, but not because of fear that he might fall from them. They simply amounted to one infernal nuisance because it was so much hard work getting up to them. He would in fact conquer all fears of the height very early on to show a natural instinct for work aloft. And he had to admit that once up there it was a wonderful heady sensation to stand out on the skysail yard with the wind blowing in his face and survey the great spread of canvas stretched out beneath him. For a time he found it hard to understand how that thin sliver of deck that lay so far below somehow managed not to tip over under the height and weight of all that steel and canvas it supported.

There was so much to learn. The so called 'training' was virtually non-existent and in the main he had to learn for himself, the incentive being that if he did not understand an order when it was given, a flint hearted mate would soon teach him the hard way. Consequently Lightoller's early days of apprenticeship at sea were purgatory until he knew every sail, rope and element of running gear that existed in the ship. The *Primrose Hill* carried a total of thirty-six sails consisting of twenty-one square sails, the jibs at her bow, the staysails that 'flew' on the stays between the masts, and bringing up the rear on the jigger mast, the gaff topsail and spanker. To control these sails there were more than five hundred ropes and Lightoller had to learn every one of them and what each one controlled, and know them not just by sight, but by feel, because at night a seaman had no lights of any kind to work by. He had to find the rope he wanted by instinct. Learning the ropes was no figure of speech, except that he discovered they were rarely called ropes. There were braces, sheets, lifts, buntlines, clewlines, leachlines, downhauls, halliards, robands, gaskets, stirrups, shrouds, ratlines, hawsers, springs, warps, painters and still many more to learn. The boy got to know some fancy knots as well; bowline on a bight, sheet bend with toggle, round turn and two half hitches, as well as the rolling hitch, fisherman's bend and Flemish loop.

But then no sooner might he be congratulating himself on some new piece of maritime knowledge or expertise acquired than he would fall victim to one of those humiliating traps always laid for the unsuspecting first voyager. The favourite one was to send a boy to get green oil for the starboard lamp and red oil for the port; then there was the order to go to the 'donkey engine' and get a bucketful of blue steam from the donkeyman. 'Fill 'er up yerself,' said the donkeyman, pointing to the valve. One day he might be hauling for all his worth on a rope behind a line of seamen who had secretly been gathering up slack and holding it taut. At the right moment the rope was released to send one startled boy sprawling across the deck.

It was all part of his initiation into a way of life that would not be long in transforming him from a naïve stripling to a hard-headed young buck.

The *Primrose Hill* was what the Americans called a 'Lime Juicer' —Limey for short—because of a Board of Trade regulation which laid down that the crews of British deep-water sailing ships should receive daily a pannikin of lime juice. To comply with the rule, lime juice was dutifully served up on the *Primrose Hill* every day at noon. It was a custom that dated back to the days of Captain Cook, who discovered that lemons were a very effective preventative of scurvy—the disease common in sailing ships due to long spells on salted meat without fresh fruit and vegetables. Lime was substituted for lemon because it was cheaper, although it would later be found that lime had none of the anti-scurvy properties of lemon.

The salted meat, usually horse or pork, was carried in barrels from which the pickle had often long since leaked out leaving the meat dry and hard like cement as it rattled around inside. When it produced scurvy the body broke out in large evil looking sores accompanied by a putty condition of the flesh. As for young Lightoller, it was a case of eat it or starve. When he did get used to eating 'salt junk' he found there just was not enough to keep body and soul together. This was a hard way of life that made for a big appetite, but 'Yer fair whack and nai mair' was the rule in the galley. Lightoller found his 'fair whack' anything but fair, and from that moment on his priority was that of every other apprentice who ever went to sea . . . food. He was forever hungry and the only way round the problem in the end was to thieve. Stealing food became a religion as it was to everyone in the half-deck. They would go to any lengths to pinch a piece of the skipper's pie from the pantry, anything to supplement that revolting diet of salt horse or pork—or on a slightly better day, cracker hash, a kind of pie containing the same salt meat, but minced up with 'Liverpool pantiles', the not so affectionate nickname for ship's biscuit. Even when the prospect of green rotten pork was heartily welcome after a few gruelling hours aloft it came in a portion so paltry that it would hardly satisfy a mouse.

As far as the ship's steward was concerned the apprentices were to be looked upon as nothing but an evil gang of little scavengers who would never miss an opportunity to raid his domain if he should relax his guard for a moment. Occasionally he would attempt to set a trap for them but nearly always 'those cunning young imps of Satan' were far too clever to be caught. The real crime was not in the stealing —but to miss an easy opportunity when it was there. It was the only way to survive.

2

They were headed south, bound for San Francisco by way of Cape Horn with a cargo of railway lines. These were the days when England supplied the world with rails. A good start from a Nor' Nor' Wester had seen them into the Trades—the North-East Trades and 'good old flying-fish weather' where young Lightoller discovered that fish really did fly, sometimes two or three hundred yards.

The weather was glorious, the first really hot sunshine the boy had ever known as heavy overalls were cast aside for lighter wear and everyone went about the ship in their bare feet. For once the sails needed little tending, but there was always work do to aboard a sailing vessel, holystoning the decks, 'painting ship', or polishing its 'bright work'. On Sundays it was not only the *Primrose Hill*'s fair-weather suit of canvas that billowed in the warm fresh breeze: this was wash-day, when the decks became a crazy confusion of clothes and bedding hanging out to dry. Meanwhile a man might get on with his mending, sewing and darning. Lightoller was taught to keep his clothes clean and in repair and the importance of always being neat and tidy.

In these tropical seas the porpoises would remain with them for hours, jumping in and out of the sea and playing all sorts of strange games amongst themselves, before taking up position beneath the bowsprit where they kept in perfect formation with the speed of the ship. They liked to fling themselves out of the water and through the air in a sort of sideways twist before landing flat on the surface again with a resounding thwack like an explosion.

This was where Lightoller had his first introduction to the skills of one of the 'Dutchmen' in the *Primrose Hill*: that was what all North Europeans were called who sailed in British deep-water sailing ships. The 'Dutchman' in this case was a Dane called Knut. He'd been a skilled harpoonist in a whaler, and there was no doubt that Knut's harpoon came in very handy when the porpoise and dolphin were around, and a welcome change they made to salt-horse which the heat was turning even more rotten in its casks. Occasionally flying-fish attracted by the lights of the ship at night would accidentally land on board. It seemed a shame to make a meal of such beautiful specimens with their slender silver bodies and delicate gossamer wings but they were good to eat—and hunger leaves no room for sentiment.

Even the steward seemed friendlier these days and if the boys gave him a hand around the galley with some washing up, cutlery cleaning, floor mopping and the like, A N D promised to do no thieving, he just might find a pinch of ginger from somewhere and show them how to make Dandyfunk.

For the uninitiated this much loved traditional confection of sailors meant first of all making a canvas bag into which 'Liverpool Pantiles' were placed — having made sure any weevils in the biscuits were well and truly ejected. The bag was then soundly battered with a suitable implement (a belaying pin would do nicely) until the contents were converted into what was termed 'flour'. The flour was then tipped into a square shallow baking tin and mixed preferably with margarine, but as there was none left it would have to be grease, the grease used on the masts. Then in went the most essential ingredient of all, the ground ginger, and finally after the addition of a little salt water the resulting 'dough' that had been lovingly mixed by the boys was flattened out in the baking tin until 'nicely brown'. When done it was tipped out of the pan and onto the deck to be carefully measured and divided into equal squares for each apprentice to get his 'fair whack'. No person's piece could be the tiniest fraction larger than another's or bitter jealousy would ensue. The portions had to be measured to a hairsbreadth. So Lightoller got his first sampling of Dandyfunk.

It was always the custom for the half-deck to have an instrument of some kind. On the *Primrose Hill* it was a banjo. From that rare idle moment when Lightoller first picked up the instrument and began tentatively plucking at its strings he showed a natural flair, and before long his newly discovered talent was in demand . . .

'C'mon "Lights" — give us "Stormalong" ' . . .

> 'O Stormy's dead and gone to rest,
> To my way, you storm along.
> Of all the sailors he was best.
> Ay ay ay, Mr. Stormalong' . . .

As they reached further south and the sun got higher, the deck became hotter and whiter and the pitch began to ooze out of the deck seams and stick to Lightoller's bare feet. Still tender, they blistered easily — but the skin would soon harden.

He was to discover that the heat brought other movement out of the woodwork — rats and cockroaches. Once he had got over his horror and disgust at them he became quite adept at killing rats either by a lusty blow with a belaying pin if one was handy, or eventually just stamping on them with his bare feet. The only trouble was that the rats had a habit of coming to visit him at night while he slept in his bunk and make a meal of the blistered flesh on the soles of his feet. He would not know anything about it until he stepped out on deck and into salt water. The little beasts would be heartily cursed then. As for the cockroaches they were by far the biggest insects he had ever seen. Some of them were two inches long, but he learnt to deal with them just as effectively. When one came to settle on his body a quick dab with a brush dipped in strong caustic soda soon 'settled their hash'.

One day the healthy breeze which seemed as though it would carry the *Primrose Hill* on forever suddenly left her. They were in the doldrums, or, as sailors called them, the 'Horse Latitudes'. This was where they had to 'work like horses' pulling the yards from port over to starboard, starboard back to port, back and forth, back and forth in an effort to catch every faint wisp of wind and get the vessel through this windless belt of the equator. Sometimes it could take weeks of 'pulley-hauley' under the baking sun to work a sailing ship over these four hundred or so miles of sea.

As the ship lay becalmed in this oily barren waste the 'Old Man' pounded uneasily to and fro across the poop deck, every now and again gazing anxiously aloft in hopes of some sign of wind in the sails that hung listlessly at the yards. Occasionally he might whistle for the lost wind as though for a lost dog. His mood was not good and Lightoller and the rest of the half-deck boys were warned by Hughes the Mate to steer clear of him. Lightoller was in total awe of Captain Anderson as he paced his lonely beat up and down the poop deck with that deep-sea roll the boy had been trying so hard to imitate.

Every now and again the skipper would bark out a string of commands when he sensed the slightest breath of wind in the sails . . . 'Port tack! . . . Shift over the jib!' Hard work under the relentless sun. But every so often the sky would become overcast and dark and then without warning the black clouds opened and down came the deluge. Occasionally these tropical downpours would be accompanied by a violent thunderstorm. Instantly everything that could conceivably hold water aboard the ship from spare sails, tarpaulins and awnings to buckets and cooking pans was arrayed out across the deck to replenish their dwindling supply of souring Liverpool water. Such downpours also brought a much needed natural bath for all the crew.

They inched their way across the line and then, behold, a flutter in the sails: as quickly as the wind had been lost, it had returned. They had found the South-East Trades. The *Primrose Hill* was on her way again. For the next couple of weeks the weather conditions returned to near perfect as the barque, following a course roughly parallel to the coasts of Brazil and Argentina, pressed on deeper into the South Atlantic in the direction of Cape Horn. As they left the Tropics their shadows gradually began to lengthen and Lightoller observed how the clear blue sky that had not shown the faintest speck for days on end was becoming more and more smudged by clouds. As the air became cooler and the sky more overcast he was to discover that as surely as he had enjoyed the most ideal sea conditions which the globe could offer, he was about to experience the very worst. The *Primrose Hill* had crossed latitude 40 degrees south and was into the Roaring Forties when it struck her . . . 'All hands on deck! . . . 'Shorten sail! . . . Clew up the skysails!'

. They had run into a vicious Westerly gale. The seas became horrendous as the ship danced wildly from the summit of one mountainous wave to the next. No sooner had she conquered one grey-bearded peak than she was plummeting on down into a deep valley of green towards another great mountainside rolling up to meet her. When it did, tons of water cascaded across the decks and over men clinging for their lives to the nearest rope or stanchion. Relax your grip for a moment and you were overboard, and nothing could be done to save you. Sometimes when the ship went down under the weight of a particularly heavy boarding sea the delay was agonising, waiting for her to come up. But then sure enough the *Primrose Hill* shook herself clear of the sea that was trying to smother her and rose to meet the next challenge. That first experience of 'rough sea' as they were leaving English shores which had made Lightoller so seasick now seemed like a millpond compared to this. These were times when more lives were lost in the region of Cape Horn than in all the other oceans put together—and not just through falls from aloft and mishaps overboard. In these hungry seas ships were regularly being 'lost with all hands' leaving no trace of how they had actually met their fate. They had simply sailed away from port one day and never returned. It was assumed the Horn had claimed them. When the command was given, Lightoller somehow managed to shin up that last remaining leg of the journey to the skysails, clinging on for dear life while the ship tossed around like a cork beneath him in the immense seas. 'Growl you may . . . go you must' he had already learnt, but this was an emergency and he was not growling now in his haste to reach those skysails and get them in before they were blown to rags by the rioting storm which was threatening to rip sails, masts and everything out of the ship. Perilously perched on the yard in the driving wind and rain the boy desperately clawed at the thrashing canvas with only the sagging footrope between him and certain death. In the days to come it would be commonplace for Lightoller to be aloft for anything up to eight hours at a stretch gathering in just one sail to its yard. The sails meanwhile were getting harder and harder as the cold grew more intense, so that fingernails on hands blue and frozen were ripped back leaving his fingers raw and bleeding. As for his oilskins he found that they were of little protection in this kind of weather. It did not matter how many lengths of rope yarn he used and how tightly he tied them around his waist, wrists and tops of his boots to seal himself up and keep the sea out, it always found a way. It was not long before he was drenched to the skin, oils blown to tatters and his boots full of water. But he must stay up there until the job was done, and that could be many more hours.

How welcome it would have been, after all those gruelling, dangerous hours aloft, to descend to a good hot meal and a steaming hot drink, followed by a good sleep in a warm dry bunk . . . except that the boy had no such comfort to look forward to. Instead he would come down to find the galley invariably washed out and nothing more to eat than a weevily biscuit. As for that hot drink, more often than not the water pump was frozen up so there was nothing to drink of any kind. But at least there might be the consolation of rest once he had waded through the ankle-deep water swilling around the half-deck quarters and slumped onto his sodden bunk. Despite all efforts to batten down the ship and seal every vent, keyhole and hairline slit the sea somehow always got in while the atmosphere in those closed up quarters got so thick it could be cut with a knife. In the end all he cared about was sleep; but no sooner would he be on the verge of achieving that modest enough ambition than the door of the half-deck would be flung open and there would be the Third Mate. 'Up and look lively you boys . . . all hands on deck!' The wind had changed and he had to get aloft again and tug with all his flagging strength on those iron-hard sails while his small young hands got more raw, battered and bruised, the only relief from the pain being numbness from cold.

As though that was not enough, he now had to endure one of the more unpleasant physical discomforts of labouring in those conditions—salt-water boils; sores on the arms and wrists with cores the size of a sewing thimble caused by the constant chaffing of wet oilskins on the flesh. They were excruciating. No human being should have been expected to carry on with such a painful handicap, but he had to. It was a case of bandaging them up as best he could and battling on. Lightoller was learning that in a sailing ship you had to be virtually on your death-bed before being deemed unfit for work . . . particularly in these circumstances.

That is how it was for the days that ran into weeks as the *Primrose Hill* was driven further and further south from the Roaring Forties, through the Shrieking Fifties to Cape Horn—or Cape Stiff as sailors called it and now the boy knew why. This was the South Atlantic in winter, where day was barely distinguishable from night in conditions which any seamen would say had to be experienced to be fully appreciated. For six long weeks they battled in that wilderness of boiling sea . . . but it was a battle in which they were losing ground all the time as the ship was driven ever south, way beyond the Horn.

And then one night without warning the wind and the sea that had battered them so mercilessly day after day began to subside. A welcome enough respite, except that, having grown so accustomed to the incessant beating of the elements, they were all mystified by this unexpected change in the weather—even the skipper treated it with considerable mistrust. Lightoller began to sense an even sharper, more piercing cold filtering through the night air that seemed to cut right through him as the speed of the ship slowed to a crawl on the glassy sea. The atmosphere around developed a strange eeriness as though there was some kind of presence close by. It was midnight and as the look-out watches changed over he observed how one of the aging salts taking over walked to the bow of the ship and stuck his nose in the air as though sniffing for something.

All ships carried at least one old shellback like this fellow whose experience from a lifetime at sea often proved invaluable.

All of a sudden he wheeled round. 'Ice right ahead, sir!' The old boy had not seen ice at that point. He had smelt it.

The vital questions now were 'How far away was the ice? On what bearing? How extensive was it?' It was pitch dark and although the ship was burning flares, visibility was only a few hundred yards. The man at the helm could not see very much from his position way back on the poop where his view was obstructed by sails.

To these sailors there were more dangers in one iceberg lurking in their path than in all the storms of the Horn. Once a sailing ship found herself in amongst ice it would take all the skipper's skills in ship handling to get her through it safely, knowing that the slightest unexpected gust of wind in the wrong direction could drive his vessel onto a berg and that would be the end of her, and almost certainly with all hands. Survival in that killer cold was hard enough on board ship, let alone in an open boat.

The *Primrose Hill* had sailed from one crisis straight into another and a potentially far more hazardous one, which Lightoller the apprentice was realising called on a whole new set of skills in seamanship if disaster were to be averted. To encounter ice in broad daylight was dangerous, but now the *Primrose Hill* was in amongst it in darkness and with no moon which meant no chance of 'ice blink', the glinting effect produced by ice when reflecting moonlight. Added to that, the more calm the sea became the less chance there would be of spotting a berg by the usual tell-tale foam that fussed round the base. There was also the risk of encountering the kind of ice hard to see in any circumstances at night—that which might have recently overturned and be exposing only a dark surface. And then there was the dreaded growler, the most feared species of iceberg because of the way it floated deep in the water, which made it the most difficult of all ice to pick out.

So this was Lightoller's first night-encounter with ice, and in the worst circumstances: no moon, no wind and the sea calm. He would encounter them again one night many years into the future.

'Put your helm hard up, sir! The ice is to windward!' The old man had finally seen it but his advice was risky to take as there could be more ice in the direction they turned. Then they all saw it and sure enough it was to windward . . . a great mountain of ice looming up at them from out of the darkness and dwarfing the ship. Now they knew what it was that had taken the wind from their sails. Anxiety was increased by the possibility that a protruding edge might be jutting out unseen below the waterline waiting to hole the ship.

Slowly but surely with what faint breeze there was they drew clear and the skipper decided to heave to until morning when he would be able to get a fuller grasp of the situation.

The cold was unbearable. Everything on the ship was by now

frozen up; pulleys, blocks and lines solid with ice and the sails like concrete. Even the very clothes on their backs were frozen stiff. It took a lot of hard work with belaying pins wielded by hands numb with frostbite to snug the ship down that night.

When daylight came, such as it was in those latitudes, and Lightoller stepped out on deck it was to be confronted with an incredible sight. They were alongside a towering cliff of ice that seemed hundreds of feet high in parts and stretched as far as the eye could see ahead and astern.

They were on the edge of the Antarctic.

The big problem facing them now was how to get round this gigantic frozen mass that lay before them because it was blocking their way northwards. Men and boys struggled again with the iron-hard sails and frozen-up running gear to get the ship under way. Slowly but surely the *Primrose Hill* did begin moving sedately along beside that spectacular icy cliff with all its wondrous shapes and forms: yawning caverns, canyons and ravines, bays and fjords with some of the inlets traversed by bridges that seemed to young Lightoller as though they had actually been designed and built by expert engineers. Sometimes the ice would grow into a whole town that took on a kind of weird oriental appearance with its mosques, minarets and pagodas. But nobody in the ship including himself at this time was quite in the mood to appreciate its beauty. This wicked frozen wilderness seemed to go on forever and was holding them prisoner.

When night fell again they realised there was not only the risk of hitting a berg but of unwittingly running into a bay and getting trapped for good while the wind played tricks on them. However, fortune was to smile on the *Primrose Hill*: two days later they had worked their way round the edge of the ice-barrier and there lying before them to the North-West was the open sea.

So Herbert Lightoller experienced his first rounding of the Horn. He had stood up to it bravely and done all that was asked of him willingly when it mattered. The hardships he had suffered defied description and yet he had borne them without a whimper—at least as far as anyone knew. If he could go through that and still come up smiling then he could take anything. He might still only have been a boy—and a rascally young devil at that, as the steward might testify—but in spirit he had the makings of a seaman, and an exceptional one. The sea had already found its way into his blood.

It was a happy bunch aboard the *Primrose Hill* that leapt aloft with

18

renewed vigour and enthusiasm to set the sails for the fair wind that would whisk them back up to 'good old flying-fish weather'. They would have some friendly sunshine on their backs again before too long, but this time in a new ocean, the Pacific, as they 'cracked it on' for 'Frisco.

3

San Francisco in the 1880s enjoyed the reputation of being the most lawless seaport in the world; as the *Primrose Hill* slipped through the mist-shrouded Golden Gate and into San Francisco Bay the temptations, pitfalls and misfortunes waiting to trap her unwary sailors were numerous. Almost six months had passed since they had bade farewell to the Mersey estuary and men who had not seen land, let alone set foot on it for so long, could be easy game for the ruthless vultures that were waiting to swoop down upon them as soon as they arrived. Even before the ship had tied up at the quay they pounced —the wretched crimp's runners. On to the *Primrose Hill* they swarmed and there was nothing the skipper and the mates could do to stop them. They would leap over the rail and join in with the men heaving round on the capstan and pulling on the halliards, then sneak off and hide in the fo'c's'le waiting for the opportune moment to make their proposition: after plying their victim with drink from the bottles they carried with them (often doped), they tried persuading him in his half drowsy state to desert ship with tempting offers of a good time ashore. The easy-going seaman who was simple and gullible enough might fall for it, but the pleasure would be short-lived. The business of the crimps was flesh and blood: sailing-ship crews were becoming more difficult to recruit and many a skipper was reduced in the end to paying the crimps for men needed to make up his crew.

Once a man had been lured into deserting his ship he would be spirited back by the crimp's runners to their master's lair, the 'boarding house', to anticipate a night of pleasure with all the drink and women he might desire. But then almost certainly he would wake up the next day and find himself sprawled across the deck of a ship bound for somewhere in Asia, having been doped senseless and sold for fifty dollars to a skipper short of men. The fee would be deducted from the unfortunate sailor's pay at the end of the voyage.

As for the police in San Francisco, so long as they got their cut from the proceeds, the crimp and his boarding house, whether he be Shanghai Brown, Shanghai Kelly, Black Bob or Red Jake —whichever one happened to hold the monopoly on the waterfront at the time—was left alone to prosper.

The skipper of the *Primrose Hill* had to be philosophical about it. He could hardly refuse everyone shore leave. He just had to accept the situation and hope that he would not lose too many of the crew. In fact he was more than fair with them. As soon as the ship was tied up and the crimps who had leapt aboard were forcibly dispatched by the mates, he doled out money from his own pocket to all the men as an advance on their pay. He told them to go ashore and enjoy themselves but with one earnest piece of advice: 'For God's sake, men, watch out for those damn crimps!'

Young Lightoller and the boys of the half-deck were given a dollar pocket money and left to their own devices. It did not seem of all that much concern that a small boy stepping off a ship in his smart uniform was even more vulnerable to the menace that lurked around every dark corner of this dangerous waterfront. A youngster wandering alone was the easiest of targets. Even if he had no money, just his clothes were worth taking and even worth killing him for. There was many a story of an apprentice who had mysteriously disappeared from his ship never to be seen again—unless his body happened to be found days later naked and mutilated, floating down the Sacramento River.

San Francisco might be dangerous, then, but it was certainly fascinating, as young Lightoller discovered, with its medley of races —Chinese, Spaniards, Italians, Negroes all living in their own neighbourhoods. The boy from Chorley, Lancashire, had never seen any of these colours and creeds before except in books.

Nowhere did he find them more crammed than in Chinatown, the quarter of the city he had been warned, above all others, to keep clear of, but that only made the adventurous boys of the *Primrose Hill* all the keener to go exploring. Lightoller found the world of 'John Chinaman' an intriguing one: the Chinese food and provision stores with everything printed and written in their language, the curio sellers, the multitude of cafés and restaurants with their typical odours of Cantonese cooking, and all those laundries which steamed away day and night. Then there was the other side of it—the opium dens, the gambling haunts, the bawdy saloons and the whorehouses where a steady traffic of men, mostly seamen, some staggering from the effects of drink, came and went through the crimson-lit doorways. This was the heart of 'Devil's Acre' where pickings were richest for the thieves, cut-throats and crimps who went about their wretched pursuits with impunity, in daylight as in darkness.

As the days passed the novelty of it all for Lightoller would gradually begin to fade—and hunger made a nagging companion. In port, the food situation was no better than at sea, a state of affairs made all the more frustrating because he could now actually see and smell the food in the stores and restaurants—mouth-watering food which his funds were not sufficient to buy. He found some consolation in one certain 'Frisco delicacy that was tasty and cheap and for a time the answer to his dilemma. It was a kind of batter cake served up hot and smothered in butter and maple syrup: waffles. He found he could get a good few of these for ten cents or so at most restaurants on the waterfront and with a good cup of coffee to wash them down. But even the good value to be found in the waffles had its limits on pocket money of a dollar a week.

It seemed as though he was destined to be forever hungry he thought as he wandered the streets broke and thinking if only he had a dollar in his pocket what great things he could do for his pining stomach. It was getting late and night was coming on as he stood alone and looked longingly through the window of a restaurant imagining what wonderful things he would have to eat if he had the choice, when a shadow loomed up behind him. Instinctively he turned to confront a giant of a man in rough clothes glaring down at him from a great height—surely the biggest man he had ever seen. So far he had been blessed with good fortune but it looked as though he was about to pay dearly for his casual attitude towards the dangers of the waterfront. His luck, it appeared, had run out. What dreadful fate could be in store for him now as he craned his neck aloft and gazed into the big bearded face on this colossal man who it would be pointless to try and resist . . .?

'Could you go a feed, sonny?'

At first Lightoller could not believe his ears. Here was somebody, a total stranger, offering to buy him a meal! The boy did not spend too long thinking about it. He was far too hungry to be concerned about the risks he might be taking. This was an offer that was much too good to refuse. He just nodded and into the restaurant they went, the small boy dwarfed by his magnificent benefactor.

It turned out that the man was a miner up to town on business and being a man with a heart to match his stature, had taken pity on a small pathetic boy who looked desperately in need of a good meal inside him. And what a feed it was: a great mound of ham and eggs followed by apple pie and cups of thick chocolate to wash it down.

Right at that moment it was the most wonderful meal the boy had ever eaten in his life. As for the one whose generosity made it possible, he got just as much pleasure and delight watching the heap of food disappearing off the plate as the one who was eagerly devouring it. The big miner was overcome with sympathy for Lightoller and his half-deck mates when he was told of the tough life an apprentice had to endure aboard a sailing ship. When the plate was empty he implored the boy to eat some more. 'Just one more piece of apple pie?' but no, he was full fit to explode and could not manage another crumb.

As Lightoller bade farewell and returned to the ship, that was not to be the last he saw of his generous giant. The next day he came down to the quay with pockets full of apples for Lightoller and his fellow apprentices, having been unable to sleep all night for worrying about the poor hungry boys of the *Primrose Hill*!

Finally sailing day came. The *Primrose Hill*, loaded with her homeward cargo of grain, sailed out through the Golden Gate, to a farewell chorus of barking sea-lions and the famous foghorn, and headed back to the Horn. By the time they got down there it would be well into spring and the return passage round would be a very different experience from the hell they had endured on the way out. To Lightoller it seemed like a pleasure cruise in comparison.

By the time the *Primrose Hill* arrived back in the Mersey estuary she had covered some 30,000 miles and been away almost a year to the day.

Meanwhile aboard was a certain young apprentice coming to the end of his first voyage who could not wait to get home to Chorley to tell everyone about it—and stick his feet up on the table, the right of every sailor who has been round the Horn.

4

If there was one single quality a sailing-ship commander prided himself on above all else it was his reputation for carrying sail, and there was no skipper sailing out of Liverpool in the 1880s with a better known reputation for that than the celebrated George 'Jock' Sutherland, who many argued was the 'most daring cracker on' ever to sail from the port. Jock was the embodiment of everything one could ever expect in the typical sailing-ship commander; a big bluff, hearty Scot with luxuriant grey beard that made him instantly recognisable wherever he went in the port. It was immediately obvious what ship Jock Sutherland commanded: she was clearly distinguishable by the figure pacing the poop, barking out his commands, and by the way she was laying her rail well under in 'half a gale of wind' with all canvas set right up to the skysails.

'Aye, it's the *Holt Hill* all right!' And if your ship happened to be sailing the same course as the *Holt Hill* you could be sure she would not stay in sight for long, because Jock had one famous boast: 'I'll never let another ship overtake me while any of my sails are furled!'

That was a principle he stood by more resolutely than ever when it came to steam ships. Jock had utter contempt for steam, a mood that became more and more aggressive as they cut deeper and deeper into the trade routes of his beloved windjammer. Jock was determined to prove that the only true ship was a sailing ship and that those ridiculous floating smoke-stacks should be cleared from the seas once and for all. As far as he was concerned anyone who left sail and went into steam had given up the sea. Meanwhile he became more and more daring with his 'cracking on', and his good fortune continued to hold. Jock's attitude was one that gave cause for constant anxiety on the part of William Price and Company, his employers, but apart from the odd minor mishap such as an occasional tattered sail or stove-in plate, Jock always made his passage and, it had to be admitted, always in excellent time. He seemed to be a skipper who knew to the last stitch exactly how much sail his ship would carry in every kind of weather. It was simply that he tended to cut his safety margins a lot finer than most other skippers.

For his second voyage Lightoller was transferred from the *Primrose Hill* to her legendary sister ship the *Holt Hill*, to serve under the notorious Jock. The boy had heard before joining the ship all kinds of salty stories about his new skipper, but instead of being apprehensive about the prospect he was looking forward to it. Was it really true that once during a heavy storm when Jock refused to shorten sail he got so angry with his frightened, protesting crew that he went below and returned with a revolver, threatening to shoot the first man who so much as moved towards halliard or sheet? It was true.

But while the commander of the *Holt Hill* proudly basked in his reputation, a certain brand of notoriety had grown up round his apprentices—that of being the wildest, most unruly bunch of young savages ever to come out of a half-deck. 'Jock's Boys' seemed to have the knack of causing havoc in every port they visited. When Lightoller joined the 'wild crowd' of the *Holt Hill* he soon fell into the way of things—indeed, he became one of the ringleaders.

This time they would not be rounding the Horn. They were bound first for Rio de Janeiro, and with the most mundane of all cargoes—coal. The voyage seemed dogged with ill luck right from the start. They were not many days out of Cardiff when a man was lost overboard, one night of filthy weather, as the *Holt Hill* was being driven to her limit in customary Sutherland fashion, beating through the mighty seas under twice as much canvas as any self-respecting textbook on seamanship would ever recommend. The man was caught by a particularly heavy boarding sea that he was not expecting, and before he had time to grab for a rope or stanchion he was over the side and gone. The skipper nearly ripped the masts out putting his ship about, but even though they succeeded in putting a boat away, there was no hope of finding the man on such a dark night in those conditions.

There was no doubt that if the *Holt Hill* had not been pounding along the way she was the accident would not have happened, but every seaman, the skipper would argue, should be constantly alive to the dangers of seas coming aboard.

Despite such an incident not for one moment would Jock consider the wisdom of shortening down. On and on he pushed the *Holt Hill* and certainly if the crew were muttering as usual against Jock and his reckless attitude, Lightoller and the boys were loving every moment of it. To them it was a wonderful thrill to feel the ship heeling in the wind to the chorus of groaning yards and cracking ropes as everything strained to the limit, while the sea thrashed continuously over the decks.

25

But it was not to last. Whether what happened next was down to sheer bad luck due to a sudden change of wind, or to downright bad seamanship on the part of a skipper who had become altogether too over-confident in his sail carrying prowess would never be known.

There was a sudden deafening crack, and the thundering of wildly flapping sail that reverberated right through the ship. Lightoller was off watch at the time, and as he and the rest of his half-deck mates scuttled topside to see what had happened, they were confronted with the sight of the upper sections of two of the *Holt Hill*'s lofty masts crashing down across the deck complete with sails, yards, running gear and all. Lightoller thought the whole thing was a great joke despite nearly having his head taken off by a falling yard that landed across the deck a few feet away from him. But there the joke ended as the ship started to flounder helplessly in the freshening gale.

It was a miracle that no-one was injured as those tons of wood and steel came clattering down onto the ship. At least it meant that every hand aboard was fit to go to work in the race to save the *Holt Hill* before the storm finished her for good. That day and the next night every man aboard laboured without pause for food or rest in the back-breaking effort to get the ship into some sort of seaworthy shape while she tossed helplessly in a full-blown Atlantic gale. A man did not appear to need telling more than once what he had to do. They all just seemed to know instantly what was required of them, each man realising that his life depended on their common effort. They could grumble all right about Jock, but the damage was done, and all that mattered was to save the ship and themselves. Despite being almost totally out of control at the mercy of the vicious storm for hour after hour, she rode it out bravely and long enough for the wreckage of masts, yards and other broken running gear to be cleared up, and what was useless thrown overboard, while sufficient makeshift repairs were made to get the ship moving again. From then on, however, it would take two men to handle the wheel.

The one blessing was that when the accident happened they were just off Cape Frio and within a day or two of completing their passage to Rio de Janeiro. It was a relief to all when the mountains of the Brazilian coast hove into sight, among them the famous Sugar Loaf mountain, the landmark standing sentinel at the entrance to Rio harbour. The *Holt Hill* limped ingloriously through the gap in the mountainous coastline that signposted the route in; on the port side, the smooth-sided granite peak of Sugar Loaf rising steeply to its thousand-foot summit, and to starboard, an impressive stretch of cliffs dotted with palm trees and the rich green of other products of the tropical soil. Once inside this imposing gateway, the harbour opened out before them into a huge bay stretching some twelve to fifteen miles ahead and up to eight miles at its widest point, dotted with countless tiny islands and surrounded by high mountains. The faint breeze across the bay seemed to bring a strange mixture of aromas; the sweet rich smell of pine and wild spices and fruit from the mountains, and the more distasteful odours from the streets of a city with bad sanitation and drainage.

When the *Holt Hill* was towed to her berth it was not beside a quay in some cluttered dockland. In Rio ships lay at anchor offshore, scores of them dotted all over the bay. Windjammers like the *Holt Hill*, mostly British or American 'Down Easters', were spread across the middle. Close by there was a roadstead allocated to warships of all nations, including two small cruisers of the British Navy, and then in another area of the bay was a huddle of smaller coastal vessels nearly all with white hulls making them more reminiscent of the moorings at Cowes, than of a busy commercial port.

The *Holt Hill* dropped her anchor. Almost immediately a steam pinnace was alongside and up onto the *Holt Hill*'s deck clambered a mean-looking bunch of the local military wanting to know all about the ship . . . where from? What cargo? The *Holt Hill* had apparently arrived in Rio during a revolution: Dom Pedro II was in the process of being unseated by a military coup and anything that arrived in port during this crisis was treated with extreme suspicion. The soldiers were eventually convinced that Captain Sutherland's mission was purely peaceful and in the interests of trade, but there was one rule in force which everyone had to adhere to: no-one was allowed on the water after dark.

A revolution was problem enough, but Rio was at the same time beset with another: a particularly bad epidemic of small-pox, with deaths ashore averaging more than two hundred a day. Many of the windjammers anchored around the *Holt Hill* were completely deserted because whole ships' crews were being struck down with the plague.

Some vessels had been marooned at the port for months because the crew had gone down sick to a man. Ambulance vessels—or 'Dead Boats' as they were depressingly called—continuously toured the harbour collecting sick cases from ships . . . sometimes alive, sometimes dead. When there was a case aboard a ship, the national flag would be immediately hoisted on the foremast to draw the attention of a Dead Boat, which would then come and take off the stricken man. Meanwhile Lightoller and the boys of the *Holt Hill* half-deck could not have cared less about the threat of small-pox or for that matter of any revolution or curfew. They wanted to get ashore to see the sights and have some fun.

They had already spotted that while the Dead Boats patrolled the bay going about their own grim trade, there were other vessels devoted to a much more cheerful kind of business—little floating shops that went visiting the ships at anchor, filled with all kinds of gastronomic delights to tempt a hungry boy. These Bum Boats, as the American sailors had christened them, were a well-known attraction of Rio harbour as they sculled from ship to ship. And it did not matter if the prospective buyer had no money. A good article of clothing could secure any amount of merchandise from a sackful of bananas, oranges and pears to livestock such as monkeys, marmosets and parrots. It was easy to part with clothing meant for cooler climes in that warm sunshine, but many an apprentice had come to regret it later as his ship headed out of Rio bound for a winter passage round Cape Horn.

It did not take long for the *Holt Hill* apprentices to signal their arrival in Rio. Their first little game was to break the curfew, which led to a rowing match between the *Holt Hill* gig, a very light fast craft for six oars, and a rowing boat crewed by the police. Despite their strenuous efforts the police boat could not keep up with their quarry as it darted in and out of ships at anchor dodging the shots being fired. In the end the strong young muscles of the *Holt Hill* won the duel and the police had to give up in total exhaustion. They never did manage to find out what ship they came from.

Lightoller had discovered 'Old Jock' was a good sport with a twinkle in his eye. He might have been a strict disciplinarian in his ship but he took a different attitude ashore—a policy which undoubtedly contributed to the regularly wayward behaviour of *Holt Hill* apprentices when the ship was in port.

In daylight hours the boys' pursuits were a little less innocent; they took every chance they could to lower away a couple of boats and get ashore, sometimes with the Mate's permission, more often without . . . and with total disregard for the heavy risk of catching cholera or small-pox.

The most popular escapade was to venture off on food-stealing expeditions to the market-place. But the stall-holders learnt quickly, and the day came when they were ready and waiting to deal with these wretched young terrors from the sea. As the large gang of apprentices from ships in the harbour, with the *Holt Hill* boys as usual to the fore, descended on the market-place for another raiding spree, they found a reception committee waiting for them with knives drawn. A vicious brawl ensued that threw the market-place into chaos, with stalls flying and merchandise cascading all around, while the more peace-loving citizens of Rio scattered for safety to the chorus of screams from hysterical womenfolk.

In the midst of the pitched battle Lightoller took a couple of cuts about the body including a deep nick out of his hand as he fended off an attacker thrusting a particularly evil blade at him. Inevitably the police arrived, including a squad from the mounted division, and then it really was time to run.

When word filtered back to the ship, the boys realised that Jock, sport though he was, had his limits. The boys would not be going ashore again for a while, the British Consul was assured. His apprentices would be taught to live up to the best image of the British merchant marine.

For one such as Lightoller, in the early days of his sea career, this was a predictable phase he would go through on the first steps of the climb to command, simply because of the sheer hardness and deprivation of the life that went with training in sail. This was still the only recognised way to qualify for a ticket, despite the rapid advancement of steam. As for the sailing-ship owners it was a system that suited them perfectly. The boys in training were a ready-made supply of cheap labour. So long as they were just sufficiently fed to keep them strong enough to work they would need no more. Some might have said it was total exploitation, but nobody could blame the owners for merely complying with all that the Board of Trade asked of them, and after all that is how it had always been for every boy that ever went to sea. But then there was another side to it. Although the hardship was at times bringing the young devil out in Lightoller, there would come a time when this crude spartan grounding would go towards bringing out the best of him as a seaman worthy of promotion to officer.

*

29

Her cargo of coal by now discharged and repairs to the masts and running gear completed, the *Holt Hill* was ready for sea again—at least as ready as they could possibly make her. They had found in this port harassed by revolutions and ravaged by plague, it was imposs-ible to get the necessary gear to restore the ship to her former skysail-flying glory. The days were past when crews could re-rig ships themselves after dismasting and replace their own spars and masts. It was really a job for the shipyard. In the end they had to be satisfied with a makeshift arrangement that reduced her to only two thirds of her normal sail-carrying capacity.

Adding to the problems the replacement spars which they did manage to get were abortive misfits and the new sails felt, to Lightol-ler, more like rhinoceros hide in his grip than the good British fair weather canvas he knew. In fact the whole effort to improvise had resulted in an unsatisfactory lash-up. But it would have to do. They were bound for Calcutta for further orders. In the meantime for a somewhat bad-tempered Captain Sutherland, 'cracking on' just would not be quite the same.

At least there was one favourable result from their call at Rio; nobody appeared to have caught the dreaded small-pox. Certainly as far as the boys were concerned they gave it every chance while they wandered freely around the streets and markets, not forgetting that one occasion when they mixed with the local inhabitants more than they ought to have done.

As the tug towed them out of that picturesque harbour, the feeling of 'good riddance', Lightoller reflected, was definitely mutual.

5

The *Holt Hill* was difficult to handle under her improvised sail arrangement. She had been painstakingly designed for achieving the best in performance and speed, a sleek thoroughbred, built at a time when sailing vessels had reached the peak of scientific perfection. But now she twisted and griped under this uncomfortable and odd-looking rig: her mizzen mast carried its full spread of canvas up to the skysail—this having remained intact—while the two remaining square-rigged masts were mere stumps.

Two men were constantly needed at the wheel to keep her steady and on course. In a freshening wind she would threaten to heel right over on her beam ends—all the worse because she was riding high and in ballast on this next leg of her voyage, from Rio to Calcutta. Her ballast comprised about a thousand tons of granite lumps which the crew had manhandled on board from lighters back in Rio. Because of the time and back-breaking effort involved humping them onto the ship and down into the holds the skipper had decided to call a halt at a thousand tons. He realised now it was nowhere near enough to keep her stable.

So in the end Jock was faced with the decision that for him was truly a bitter one to make: he would have to shorten sail. From then on the behaviour of the *Holt Hill* improved markedly, and under the wing of a friendly Westerly that carried the ship along at a healthy nine or ten knots, despite her makeshift condition, they stretched away for the Cape of Good Hope.

The wind held and they continued to make good time, reaching the Cape in just a little under three weeks of leaving Rio. At this stage of her passage instead of turning north-east in the natural direction of their destination they carried on eastwards, working just a little to the south to 'run their easting down', a course followed by all sailing ships heading for India and the East Indies from the Cape of Good Hope. They would continue to take full advantage of the good Westerly winds and aim for the island of St. Paul, a small lonely outcrop poking out of the Indian Ocean roughly midway between Cape Town and Perth. On reaching St. Paul or thereabouts the *Holt Hill* would then turn north and head directly for Calcutta.

It was in the afternoon of November 13th 1889, as the *Holt Hill* was nearing St. Paul that another sailing ship of about the same size came rapidly up astern and overtook her. Jock was beside himself with rage.

'I've never let another ship pass me with any of my sails furled yet and I won't start now!' he fumed to his Chief Mate, James Williams. 'Set everything!'

The order was duly carried out and the *Holt Hill* began to surge forward heeling dangerously, almost broaching to while two men desperately fought with the helm to keep her steady and on course. Many times Lightoller thought she was going to go right over but for some reason she did not, as that four-masted barque that had the audacity to try and overtake Jock Sutherland and the *Holt Hill* was left far astern to become a dot on the horizon.

The *Holt Hill* was in no condition for cracking on and yet despite having made his point Jock refused to ease off and shorten sail. He just 'let her go' as he walked up and down the poop with the burly Cornishman Williams, a loyal Mate who always stood by Jock. Lightoller however got the impression that both men wanted to suggest shortening down right now but neither would give in to the other. Meanwhile the *Holt Hill* ploughed recklessly on into a steadily worsening gale.

Eight bells sounded, which was the signal for the watches to change and for Williams to be relieved by Bob Mowatt, the Second Mate. No one was happier about that than Williams. The matter was out of his hands now and it would be up to Mowatt to take in the canvas. Lightoller heard Williams tell Mowatt to keep a sharp look-out for land ahead as he knew they were nearing St. Paul. The *Holt Hill* was by now reeling off thirteen knots and she had become almost impossible to steer.

As Mowatt relieved Williams, Lightoller heard the new man shout through the howling wind, 'Just as soon as you get below I'm for having some of these sails in!'

'Just as you like, and the sooner the better,' Williams yelled back as he went below.

As Lightoller also went below off watch he could see in the gathering darkness ahead a heavy squall of thick rain developing.

The boys of the half-deck were turning in and about to put their lamp out when suddenly they heard the heavy clump of Mowatt's boots galloping across the deck above them followed by the dreaded cry, 'All hands on deck!'

Lightoller hurriedly got his clothes on and rushed up on deck in answer to the call. When he arrived it was not this time to be greeted with masts, spars and sails plummeting down to meet him. It was far more horrifying than that.

There before him stood a great rocky mass towering above the ship and they were racing straight towards it. The watch on deck had not seen it sooner because of the poor visibility in the rain squall. But then it had cleared revealing, to the Second Mate's horror, land dead ahead and at the speed the ship was moving, only minutes away.

He had panicked and ordered the helm 'hard down' in his desperate bid to steer clear of the obstruction, but as soon as Jock arrived on deck and sized up the situation he countermanded the order. 'Hard up!' he barked, realising that there was more sea-room if he turned the ship the other way. But either way it was already too late.

As the ship began to swing back again in response to the skipper's new order valuable seconds had already been lost. Jock could now see the terrible truth of the dilemma. He could either continue to try and swing the ship clear but run the risk that she might finish up smashing sideways on into the jagged rocks with the almost certain loss of all hands, or he could simply drive the ship ashore in the hope that she might lodge herself firmly aground and give everyone a chance to save themselves. No skipper could ever have had a more agonising decision to make.

Meanwhile Lightoller just gaped transfixed at that evil mountain of rock looming closer and closer waiting to claim its prize. Then through the screaming gale he heard Jock give his command: 'Steady the helm. Put her straight at it. Steady as she goes. Belay everything.'

Not since the early days of his first voyage had Lightoller felt such fear inside him, but the boy was determined to hold himself together as the ship careered towards her doom.

The *Holt Hill* was now beginning to toss around frantically in the rolling breakers that were eagerly helping to speed the ship on her journey to destruction. As for Jock, Lightoller could not help feeling pity for him as he stood there on the poop erect as ever, waiting helplessly like the rest of them for the crash to come.

The boy was surprised at the casual way he just said to Williams, 'Well she's in the breakers now. She won't be long before she bumps.'

But it was obvious to see that inside it was churning old Jock up to do this to his ship . . . the ship that had been with him since she was

33

launched, giving birth to a famous partnership that had earned him his label 'The Most Daring Cracker-on out of Liverpool'.

Now it looked as though Jock's luck had run out and that the reputation coveted with such pride had finally, and perhaps inevitably, come home to roost; smashed on the rocks of an island in the middle of the Indian Ocean. 'But what of me?' the boy thought to himself. Not yet sixteen, with so much of life left to live and a budding sea career that looked so promising. Was it really all meant to end so soon?

The skipper and his thirty-two men and boys stared silently ahead at the gigantic black mass that was growing larger and larger in front of them. Nobody spoke, nobody moved; they just stood rooted to the deck of their doomed ship, clinging to the most secure thing that came to hand to steady themselves while she was picked up by the huge seas that were battering the base of those rocky cliffs.

Lightoller felt an eerie sensation during those brief and yet interminable moments when he waited to know what card it was that fate was to deal him. For most people death rarely ever gave them a chance to think about it. Even after a long illness the end, when it finally came, was sudden. But here he was, a mere youngster, facing up to a terrible reality that within the next few minutes he might be dead—and unbelievably, this was more than likely.

'Stand aft under the break of the poop!'

At the word from Jock everybody rushed aft to be in the safest place to be clear of falling gear when she hit. The experience of that earlier break-up, which all seemed such a long time ago, would be nothing compared to the avalanche of masts and running gear that might topple on them any moment now.

'Every man for himself!'

The last command of all. The suspense seemed to go on and on. For a moment it felt as though time was almost standing still. And then she finally struck.

The first contact was with an invisible outcrop of rock which she hit with such crushing force that the whole ship trembled. But the agony had just begun as the *Holt Hill* was driven on by the wind and sea over the deadly rocks which ripped through the plates of her keel, gouging the guts right out of her with a rending, grating sound that made the boy sick. It was a ghastly sensation to feel and hear the ship being torn apart beneath him.

The big question now was would she hold together sufficiently for them to have a chance of saving themselves, or would she immediately break up in pieces and throw them all to the mercy of the rocks and the vicious seas, in which case there could be no hope for anyone.

But the sea, even in its most ruthless moods, can have a way of inadvertently throwing out a lifeline. For the *Holt Hill* it came in the form of a huge wave which took hold of her, hoisted her up and carried her bodily towards the cliffs with such force that Lightoller thought for a moment she might sail right on up the cliff face. Instead, with almost uncanny precision, the *Holt Hill* came to a grinding and abrupt halt at the foot of the cliffs with her bows neatly planted in the pincer-like grip of two large pillars of rock which held her fast, and now prevented her from sliding back into the sea.

It was time to abandon ship because she would not be in one piece for long as the sea went hungrily to work, starting with the stern which was already disintegrating. Even in this life-and-death situation Lightoller could not help thinking how ridiculous the *Holt Hill* looked, lodged there, immovable, with everything still in its place on deck as it should be; her lamps still burning, and her sails, in all their billowing magnificence, still set; the sails which the unfortunate Mowatt never did have time to take in and for some inexplicable reason had remained perfectly intact . . . but they surely could not for much longer. Then everything went black.

When he came to, the first thing Lightoller was aware of was an incessant cackling in his ears . . . It was the captain's hens going hysterical in their crate, adding their contribution to the mayhem. As the boy looked around to recollect his senses he found himself surrounded by a tangle of fallen gear which was obviously what had knocked him out. Once again it had been a lucky escape. Whatever it was that had come down on his head could only have just clipped him, otherwise his skull would have been in pieces for sure. But there was no blood, only a headache and a slight singing in his ears. It was now almost dark and nobody had noticed him as they were all too busy up at the bows preparing to abandon ship. Through the lifting haze of giddiness, instinct told him he should be there too, and quick, as he craned his neck aloft and saw that more gear was ready to fall at any moment. He hauled himself up and staggered along to the fo'c's'le head where the crew had already started to make their escape.

A rope had been suspended from the bowsprit and men were taking it in turns to make a running jump from the end of the bows out to the rope and slide down to the rocks below. The rope was new and the wet had made it greasy with the result that when it came to Lightoller's turn to jump for it he did not quite get a firm enough grip with both hands, and fell unchecked almost all the way down. The drop was some twenty feet. He was lucky to come through it with his neck, and could have at least expected to break a leg or an ankle, but apart from a nasty tingle that shot through the soles of his feet when he landed, once again he had proved indestructible.

But there was more to come. He landed on the rocks just as a huge wave came in and washed right over him, almost drowning him there and then. But despite the shock of his rapid descent he had still kept a hand on the line. It was just as well, because he would now be in trouble from the rush of water flooding back into the sea which could easily take him with it. He twisted the line round his wrist and gripped with all his strength and waited for it. The power in that backwash when it came was immense. He closed his eyes and squeezed but he could still feel the rope inching through his fingers as the sea thundered against him. And then it relented . . . at least for a moment. He felt the rope start to twitch. Someone else was coming down, so he let go and rolled clear. The other man, an able seaman, landed and the two of them scrambled quickly over the rocks to get as far away as possible from the next big wave coming in, but only to find their way obstructed by a tall rocky overhang which was impossible for the boy to climb without help. Through the pitch darkness and the roaring elements the sea could be heard powering in again.

'Quick youngster, give me your foot!' said the man to the boy and in one swift movement he was hoisted up just high enough to lever himself onto the ledge. When he turned to reach for his helper the man had managed to pull himself up unaided.

Lightoller was getting his bearings and concentrating on the next stage of the climb when another great wave came rushing up unexpectedly over the top of the rock and instantly swept him off his feet. He was in trouble again, only this time there was no rope or friendly helping hand to aid him. As the sea began surging back down the rocks in a torrent, a bitter struggle for life developed. He swam and he clawed against it like a madman, frantically trying to stop himself being taken back over the edge of the rock he had just climbed. If he let that happen he was finished, swallowed up in the tossing foam and gone forever. Down and down he was steadily sliding, all the time thrashing violently against the pull of the water, desperate to get a grip on something to halt his slide, but there was nothing to grip.

The battle looked lost as his legs went over the edge. He grabbed at one last chance to save himself, clamping his fingers to the corner of the precipice. Now, if he could just cling on long enough for the deluge to subside he might beat it yet, except that he was now taking the full force of the water in his face. It looked as though he was going to drown anyway. And then mercifully the onslaught that seemed as though it would never end died away, leaving him in a state of shock and semi-drowning, but still dangling there, clinging stubbornly to his precarious perch. But the sea would be back for him. He must get away from it. If all his breath and strength was gone he still had his will as he slowly and painfully heaved himself back up onto that ledge again . . . but this time he did not linger as he had done before. The thoughts of that sea coming back for him did instant wonders for his recovery from that terrifying ordeal as he made off blindly over the rocks tripping and stumbling as he went. He just picked himself up each time and kept running with the one thought in his mind, to get clear of the breakers. Another giant roller came roaring in, crashing up over the rocks to get him and it did—but only with a gentle caressing touch as he felt the cold water swirling tamely about his feet. The scales of fate had, in the end, tipped in his favour, but there was no doubt they had wavered for a while.

After all he had gone through on that perilous assault course Lightoller wondered if anybody else could possibly have survived it. He was surprised to learn that only one man had perished, but even more surprised, and saddened to discover that it was Mr. Williams, the Chief Mate, who had gone. The last one surely, Lightoller thought, who would have been beaten by it. Apparently Mr. Williams encountered the same problem as Lightoller but the Mate had not been quite so lucky in trying to save himself and the sea took him. Poor old Mr. Williams. A strict disciplinarian, yes, but a kind and likable fellow. He always had a considerate thought for 'the boys' who had come to look upon him almost as a father figure.

It was a long, cold, wet night. The boy managed to find some shelter under a boulder but it did not keep much of the wind and rain out. While he lay there wet and shivering in the cold, totally exhausted and yet unable to sleep he could hear above the howling gale the sound of the ship breaking up on the rocks below. There would not be much left of her by morning. At last he drifted into sleep.

When daylight came the storm had moderated. The boy awoke,

momentarily confused by his surroundings. He had never spent the night under a boulder before and it took a few seconds to remember how he had got there. He crawled out of his crude shelter and surveyed the scene. There was little to bring comfort to his cold, wet body in what he saw. Between him and the grey empty ocean lay a barren expanse of jagged, hostile rocks falling away towards the ocean's edge . . . the rocks he had scaled the night before like a terrified rabbit in blind desperation to save himself.

And then he saw her. She was lying directly below him, the tragic sight of the *Holt Hill* . . . or what was left of her. All that survived in memory of that once fine sailing ship were a few hundred tons of scrap metal which he made out to be her bows. They had broken off and been tossed up by the sea high onto the rocks. As for the rest of her there was nothing to be seen. The sea had done its work well. It was a lot for the boy to take in, seeing the pathetic remnants of his ship sprawled across the rocks below him . . . the battered shell of her bows lying there like the severed head of some giant fish, discarded, while the rest had been eaten up—his precious banjo included.

But at least he was alive, and for that he had to be grateful. He had been even more fortunate than he realised. It was to become apparent that if the *Holt Hill* had been just a few hundred yards to the north or south of the point where she finally struck, nobody would have had a chance. To the north lay sheer cliffs, an insurmountable wall of rock into which she would have crashed with no hope for anyone to leap from the ship and climb to safety.

In contrast to the south the sea was littered with outlying rocks which she would have run foul of half a mile out, with consequences equally disastrous. It had been close, very close. It was time to go and root out his shipmates and do some exploring.

6

Latitude 38 degrees 43 south, longitude 77 degrees 31 east: with precision accuracy they had run their easting down to St. Paul, an island of just four and a half square miles in that great expanse of ocean, and run right into it.

The sun was coming up and the boy was grateful to feel some warmth on his back as the crew, having slept the night scattered among the rocks, mustered and began the climb to the summit of the rocky shoreline. It was a hazardous exercise not only because of the steepness of the climb, but so much of the rock was loose. A climber might reach for what appeared to be a perfectly secure fingerhold only for it to come away in his hands. The same could easily happen under foot. In the end the threat of being hit by tumbling rocks and boulders from above became infinitely greater than the risk of a straightforward fall.

At last they reached smooth ground and for the boy it was a treat to just lie down on some warm dry grass and feel the heat of the sun seeping into his body. After his experiences in the sea followed by that cold, cruel night spent in wet clothing under precious little shelter, it was as well that he had a solid constitution.

As they set out to reconnoitre the island, they soon realised the chances of its being inhabited were slim, at least by human life. There was a large population of rabbits hopping in and out of their burrows. Occasionally the castaways surprised a family of them and they would go scurrying off in a zig-zag dash to escape these strange intruders. There were also goats on St. Paul. Occasionally the party caught sight of a horned head popping up over a rise in the distance but it would disappear as soon as they got within range. They could have done with a gun. Even if they could not get close enough to take a pot shot at a goat they could have soon bagged a meal out of the rabbits.

Lightoller wondered how the wildlife on this part of the island survived because there was precious little of anything growing, just a very sparse covering of parched and weathered grass barely long enough to get hold of between the fingers let alone provide sufficient nourishment for a creature to live on.

On and on they trudged, all the time climbing higher and higher. They were trying to get to a vantage point from where they could gain a reasonable panorama of their new domain and weigh up just what kind of a place this was and what, if anything, it had to offer them in the way of survival.

Now that they were castaways, there was no telling how long they would be here. The sun, which had been so welcome at the start of the day, was becoming less of a friend as the heat made their upward hike more arduous. The dampness of seawater about the boy's body had gone but perspiration was now taking its place as he became increasingly fed up with this endless trek that seemed to have gone on for hours. He was exhausted, he was thirsty, and as usual he was hungry. He had even lost interest in the curious great gaps in the ground which they encountered every so often along the way, belching out their strange mixture of smoke and steam that seemed to have a strong sulphurous odour. Somewhere many miles below the ground the volcano that gave birth to St. Paul was still breathing. He wondered when it might awake from its slumber and erupt again. He hoped it would not be too soon.

Lightoller, who had been gazing vacantly at the plodding feet of the man in front of him, was instantly shaken from his trance. The walking had stopped. As he looked up he thought at first that they were on the edge of some giant crater, and then he saw stretched out hundreds of feet below him the impressive panorama of a lagoon exactly of the kind he had seen in pictures of desert islands. In fact his earlier conclusion was not so far wrong because where once a gigantic volcanic eruption had taken place there was now a bay completely encircled by cliffs, and from each corner two shingle spits jutting out into the sea and round in a curving arc, their tips almost meeting, but for a narrow gap between. Here the sea came in to complete this perfect natural harbour of millpond smoothness. This island, which at first, seemed so bleak and desolate, was beginning to show some promise. Lightoller had read plenty about desert islands but never in his wildest dreams thought that one day he would actually be shipwrecked on one himself. Everyone stood still and gazed down in complete silence at this scene that lay before them. Then someone said he was sure he could see a hut of some kind. Nobody else could spot it but the only way to find out was to get down there and take a good look round.

There was one problem facing them—the sheer cliffs that surrounded the lagoon. They eventually found a point where the overhang was broken, but the drop was still dangerously steep. Very long, thick strong grass was growing all the way down the cliff-face and they found that a good handful was strong enough to take the weight of a man without being pulled from its roots. They began their descent with a mixture of bumping, sliding and swinging about in a manner that reminded Lightoller of monkeys at the zoo. On the way they discovered that the cliffs were honeycombed with caves and every so often Lightoller would find himself dangling over a yawning opening wondering what mysteries and surprises might be hidden away through the darkness within. He thought of pirates' treasure and the more he pondered on the idea the more convinced he became that the caves were abounding with priceless jewels and pieces of eight and other such pirates' plunder that by tradition, he remembered, they never lived long enough to enjoy. But he was in no position to start searching now. When they eventually reached the shingle they discovered that the man who had seen a hut had not imagined it. There were in fact a number of them and they obviously had not been used in years

Now they knew for certain that St. Paul was uninhabited. They were definitely on a desert island. But to their great relief they had at least found water, not in a river or pool, but bubbling away merrily in boiling springs around the rocks close to the water's edge. By then Lightoller had become too preoccupied with the excitement of it all to remember he was thirsty. He would have a drink in a little while, after he had taken a closer look around the huts. One of them was a barn-like structure so spacious that the whole crew could congregate down one end and still leave three quarters of the place to spare. It was obviously some kind of a boathouse which, along with the rest of the oddly assorted cluster of wooden huts, dated back to the days when a fishing community was based on St. Paul. But they found evidence of numerous visits at various different times in the past as they examined the ancient rotting boats, rusty anchors and other odd bits and pieces of gear left lying about on the shingle. Some of it must have been upwards of a hundred years old. Then they spotted the most recent evidence of human presence on the island . . . the wreckage of a ship sticking out of the water at the entrance to the lagoon. Somebody recalled the story of an early steamship called the *Megaera* bound from East Africa to Australia with three hundred and fifty passengers and crew aboard. She was an old ship and unseaworthy. In the first heavy seas she encountered she sprung a bad leak. The engineers discovered that the plates were so rusted and thin that to attempt to carry out repairs at sea would have finished the ship altogether. With every pump working flat out and every member of the crew, officers included, helping to bail out, the *Megaera*'s best chance was to make for St. Paul where she arrived after many anxious days and was run aground by the skipper . . . the only decision he could take.

Although there were many more of them on the *Megaera*, they were far better off than the castaways of the *Holt Hill*. Her people had substantial provisions salvaged from the ship to live on and also the ship's boats to use for fishing.

'So how long was it before they were rescued?'

'Four months.'

It was hardly encouraging considering the only thing the crew of the *Holt Hill* possessed among the entire lot of them of any survival value were the few matches which Braithwaite the cook by good fortune happened to find in his pocket. They would be used to light the fire to be kept going constantly while they were on the island.

But at least there was water, the boy thought to himself as the memory of his thirst suddenly returned to him with a vengeance. He went back round the lagoon and made for the springs on the rocks and took a drink from the first one he came to.

To his amazement it was salt water. He went on to the next one. That too was seawater, and the next and the next. He could not understand it. One of the crew had sampled the water earlier and said it was drinkable but there was no mistake; all the springs were full of seawater.

Now they really were in a fix. Somebody said he remembered seeing some kind of pool or well while they were on top of the island. In that case there was only one thing to do. They would have to climb back up the cliffs again with every receptacle they could find and try to relocate it.

But night was drawing on again and they would have to wait until morning. At daybreak a party of volunteers was gathered together to form the water expedition. Lightoller joined. He decided it would be far better if he took an active part in helping to solve the water problem rather than sit around with nothing to do but think of his growing thirst, counting the hours waiting for the water carriers to return—assuming they had found water to carry. The leader of the 'water detachment' was an A.B. who never failed to impress Lightoller both in his unfailing ability as a seaman, and his marvellous sounding name, Bartle McIntyre. They discovered a section of the cliffs less steep and with better provision for footholds than the route they had taken to come down, and so, armed with seaboots, oilskins and anything else that would hold water, they began their ascent. It was a climb the boy would never forget. Bartle was a merciless taskmaster whose ability as a seaman was obviously equalled by his strength and fitness. He rarely allowed them any breaks for rest during that climb and by the time they eventually reached the top Lightoller felt in no condition to go on. He had now gone almost two days without water and the gruelling climb in the heat had aggravated his thirst. He was desperate for a drink and starting to dehydrate.

Progress however would be easier now as he summoned the energy to pick himself up and press on with the group. But he found they were becoming more and more hazy and blurred, and seemed to be receding further and further into the distance. He tried to call but nothing came out. His tongue felt like sandpaper, and his lips were badly split. After a while he became aware of a figure coming towards him. The oilskin trousers tied at the bottom he had been carrying to fill up with water were taken from him. And then he was alone, but he must keep going. He continued on for a time and then suddenly he halted. Through the mist clouding his vision he was convinced he was looking at a mirage. There before him was an inviting pool of smooth, clear water. He searched his delirious mind for what he could remember about mirages, because this must surely be one. Then he thought he could see men lying face down around the pool actually drinking from it. 'Did that happen in mirages too?' he asked himself. But surely Bartle McIntyre was no mirage because he could see Bartle quite plainly drinking the water. He arrived at the edge of the 'pool' still not believing his eyes as he knelt down and touched the water to see if it was real. It was. He remembered he was carrying a quart bottle in his pocket. He brought it out and filled it, put it to his cracked swollen lips and drank the lot in one long gulp. It was heaven. Twice more he filled it and drank, without any heed to the dangers of drinking heavily after a long spell without water. But then he did seem to have a rather unusual constituion that could withstand any amount of rough treatment. The only physical effect of any kind he became aware of was thorough exhaustion as he flopped on his back and fell asleep.

There had been no sign of the skipper since they had left the scene of the wreck. He was the last to abandon ship and had made it to safety behind the rest but then refused to join the crew when they set off to explore the island. Despite some earnest, almost physical persuasion he insisted on staying behind. In the end they had no choice but to leave him there staring dolefully down at the sorry remains of his ship, tormenting himself for what he had done. He had killed his ship and his best friend all in one tragic act of carelessness. How could he have been such a reckless fool? He would never forgive himself for it. Jock's brain was turning it over again and again, the same bitter regret. 'The most daring cracker-on out of Liverpool' had become a broken man overnight. He would never allow himself to command another ship.

The water party took a diversion on their return journey to the lagoon by way of the spot where Jock had last been seen. So heavily did his anguish and remorse appear to weigh on him that it was even possible he might have been driven to doing something drastic. The cliffs on St. Paul were all a man needed who had come to the conclusion that life was no longer worth living. The men of the *Holt Hill* had been through their moments of bitter conflict with Jock which on occasions verged on plain mutiny, but they had always stopped short of that final confrontation, perhaps because they thought more of their skipper than they realised themselves. In the end their doubts in his judgment proved justified. But the damage was done and now they could feel only compassion for the 'Old Man'.

Then they found him slumped on the grass at the top of the cliff. Lack of water had made him delirious. He had collapsed and was just lying there letting the life drain out of him. As they heaved him up his incoherent mumblings were abruptly stifled by the neck of a bottle thrust to his lips in an effort to make him drink, which he did. And then part carried, part walking, Jock was at last persuaded to give up his vigil and come away from that morbid spot overlooking the last remains of his ship.

They expected on arrival back at the lagoon to be overrun by a demented horde of thirst-crazed madmen desperately rushing for the water, so they planned in advance that the apprentices would carry the water, surrounded by a strong bodyguard. But to their surprise the greeting was one of almost casual indifference. When it was suggested that perhaps somebody just might fancy a little sip of water the reply was a shrug. They had had a drink from the springs, thank you. But surely they were full of salt water? Then it dawned on the water-party: the salt water had gone from the springs which were yielding fresh water again. How stupid they had been! Obviously the springs would have filled up with salt water when the high tide washed over them, but when the tide went out they returned to their normal state. The desperate life-saving mission to find water had been a totally pointless exercise. But at least they had found Jock.

7

Lightoller found that his desert island was turning out to be a sad disappointment after all compared with the one he knew in fiction. It was certainly deserted, and it certainly had the essential lagoon, but there the similarity ended.

On this desert island the soil, apart from an assorted yield of parched grass, was almost devoid of any vegetation, much less an abundance of gently swaying palm trees rustling in the faint breeze, with a plentiful supply of tropical fruits to feast on; and definitely no wild boar either to be hunted down for roasting on the spit, even if they had possessed the means to take a shot at one, and then they would only too happily have settled for a rabbit or a goat.

As for the water in the springs, even when the tide was out and the seawater had boiled away, it was barely drinkable. It tasted to Lightoller like a mixture of rotten eggs and classroom chalk. After taking a drink the flavour lingered on in the mouth for a long time afterwards. But it was water and they had to be thankful it existed at all. Next came the food situation which was much less straight-forward. It came as a surprise to find penguins in residence. They first tried their eggs, only to find the contents were well on the way to hatching. Nobody was that hungry yet. As for the penguins them-selves, they were not difficult to catch and succumbed easily to the knife, but Lightoller soon decided he had sampled considerably more palatable fare even aboard ship, which did not say a great deal for penguin. The taste of their oily dark flesh seemed to combine the worst qualities of bird and fish. In the end it was decided the best use for penguin would be for bait as they turned to the sea as their surest hope for food.

The handful of dilapidated boats at their disposal were in such an advanced state of rot that none could have stood up to the sea even in its tamest mood, but one of them was found at least to float. And so with a pair of oars that still had enough left in them to take some strain they succeeded in getting themselves waterborne, if only within the confines of the lagoon. Here it was discovered the waters were well stocked with crayfish. But they had to be caught. An expedition back to the scene of the wreck had in the meantime been made, and although nothing much of any great use was found they did manage to salvage a length of rope which was split up and converted into lines. There was no such luxury as a hook, but they devised a way round that problem. They would tie a piece of penguin entrails to the end of the line, cast it out from the boat in the direction of their prey, and then draw the bait gently in, luring the crayfish after it. As soon as it came within arm's length a hand would reach out and make a grab for it and that would be one more crayfish for supper—but taking great care not to lose any fingers in the act, as the crayfish could inflict a lot of damage with the serrated edges of its tail.

There was however one major drawback with the crayfish enterprise. They could only be caught on an incoming tide as that was the only time when they seemed to come anywhere near the surface. Maximum advantage had to be taken of the limited time available to catch them. The haul would vary from one tide to the next but no matter how good the yield on any one occasion it was still never enough to satisfy the hunger of thirty-odd starving men getting weaker by the day. Some of them had begun vomiting blood. But at least they had the basic means at their disposal just to stay alive; the foul-tasting water from the springs and their meagre ration of crayfish from the lagoon.

As the days went by further visits were made to the scene of the wreck in hopes that perhaps something more just might have been given up by the sea to improve their chances of survival; if not food perhaps an odd blanket or sheet of canvas to help keep a few of them warm on the bitterly cold nights.

On one occasion the wreck expedition had been away for some hours when suddenly those who had stayed behind, Lightoller among them, were alerted by one of the men from the wreck party running along the beach towards them gesticulating frantically in the direction of the cliffs. They must come quickly and arm themselves with as many knives, clubs and sticks as they could lay hand to.

Their shipmates were in trouble.

They dashed off in the direction of the trouble spot which was at the break in the cliffs at the north end of the lagoon. Here the expedition had been negotiating the climb down on their return from the wreck when their attackers pounced.

When Lightoller reached the scene he was confronted with the sight of a pitched battle in progress between the men of the *Holt Hill* and a vicious flock of albatrosses that were trying to get their beaks on some food which the party had been carrying with them . . . a twelve-pound hunk of pork that had been found tossed up onto the rocks and three rabbits caught en route . . . but a route which happened to take the bearers past a heavily populated albatross rookery.

As soon as the birds got scent of the food they swarmed down.

Before the reinforcements arrived with weapons, the victims of the attack had nothing but their bare arms and hands to defend themselves against the wicked, hooked beaks of the albatrosses. All they could do was to back up against the cliff face with their precious pork and rabbits at their heels, protecting it and themselves as best they could against this mass winged assault, and hope that help would not be long in coming. Once Lightoller and the rest arrived, and sticks and knives were hastily shared round, the odds became more even, but there was no doubt that to the birds this was a fight to the death. Lightoller thrust himself into the thick of it and soon found these great birds, with wings that spanned ten feet and more, had no fear as they dived down aiming their lethal beaks at his head and face . . . beaks that had been known to kill a man with one quick swooping thrust into his skull.

A stunning blow was not enough to settle it. The albatross would soon recover and be back in the fight again. Lightoller saw that the only way to finish off an attacker for sure was to deliver it a sharp crack across the head with his stave and then, as the bird went down, quickly follow up with a powerful lunge of the knife between its shoulders.

It became a bloody battleground of flailing knives and sticks amidst wildly flapping wings and flying feathers. Heads got badly gashed as diving beaks hit home, and in reply the toll of slaughtered albatrosses rose. Throughout it all the air was filled with incessant squawking.

As birds perished, more reinforcements would descend from the rookery to attack ever more savagely as though the incentive for food had become of almost secondary importance to avenging the deaths of their brethren.

A good quarter of an hour the hostilities went on and then slowly but surely the albatrosses began to show signs of conceding defeat.

They had sensed they were getting the worst of it, and instinctively realising the wisdom of cutting their losses, started to retreat back to the rookery.

During the whole terrifying confrontation not one of the birds had been allowed to get near enough to the food to so much as take a peck at it. The same could not be said for the valiant warriors, who despite chalking up a healthy score at the expense of the opposition did not come through it quite so unscathed as the pork and rabbits they had so bravely defended. Quite a few nasty head wounds were being nursed at the end of that fierce combat.

The fire which was used for cooking their scanty fare was kept going day and night to alert any ship that might come by the island. By now they had become only too aware that they could remain trapped there until a ship running her easting down might come close enough to see them—and it was not every skipper who ran his easting down via St. Paul as closely as Jock Sutherland.

It was in the early morning of their eighth day on the island that the first man to emerge from the hut saw it. He had to blink a few times to reassure himself that he was not still dreaming, but sure enough it was there . . . a ship with all its sails set and lying becalmed close to the shore.

To the man's excited cries of 'Sail Ho!' everyone leapt from their slumber and came rushing out. Immediately they started shouting at the tops of their voices and waving their shirts in the air to attract the attention of the ship whose crew could be seen plainly moving about the decks. There did not appear to be any response to their cries, which was mystifying.

Meanwhile the old boat which was used for catching crayfish was right over on the other side of the lagoon with Mowatt, the Second Mate. He and his crew had been at work since first light catching the day's supply of food on the early tide and from where they were positioned under the cliff, they had not seen the ship. But surely the castaways would have already been sighted by now. The fire was burning well and sending up a clearly visible column of smoke. That alone was enough to tell anyone that souls were in trouble on the island. It must surely be a matter of time before their plight was recognised. Yet still there was no sign that she had seen them. It was equally frustrating trying to catch the attention of Mowatt's fishing party, but eventually after minutes of agonising delay Mowatt and his men caught sight of the ship and straightaway headed out of the lagoon towards it as fast as they could row.

They had got about halfway between the shore and the becalmed ship and would have been up alongside her within minutes. But all of a sudden a breeze sprang up, and now with wind in her sails the ship promptly swung stern on to the island and, to the dismay of the desperate watchers on the beach, started to sail away.

Try as they might in that old boat to catch her—the oarsmen pulling away furiously while Mowatt waved and shouted frantically at the bow—it was no use.

She was gone.

It was heartbreaking. Nobody could believe that it was really happening. The very first ship that had been sighted since they had been there and so close. To be any nearer to them she would have had to come inside the lagoon.

How had she failed to see them? Or had she? Even more strange, she carried no name on her stern. Not that it would have done them much good at that moment, but it would certainly have been noted for future reference. Was it possible they imagined the ship? After all, everyone was starving. But then no matter what state of health they were in, all thirty-two men could not have imagined the same thing. No, they had seen a ship all right, and the men on that ship could not have failed to see them, but for some reason had chosen to sail away and leave them. The only genuine reason for ignoring them was that perhaps it was not realised they were actually shipwrecked. They could have been inhabiting the island by choice as people had done before. But one thing was certain, they would guard against the possibility of the same thing happening again. From then on there would be a twenty-four hour look-out posted on the hilltop overlooking the lagoon where there was an unobstructed view to the north and west of the island. Also on the hill they would have a fire made up and ready to light as soon as a ship hove into sight. The 'fishing boat', which had so admirably stood up to that desperate dash out to sea to try and catch the mysterious ship, was under no circumstances in future to go beyond hailing distance.

And so with both spirits and energy at a pitifully low ebb they could do no more than try to put that depressing setback out of their minds and wait as hopefully as they could for another ship. One thing they did know, while they had survived on that island eight days, there was little chance of them all living through another eight.

'Sail Ho!' . . . To their great joy and surprise that very same day in the afternoon another ship came into sight. As the cry came from the look-out, the hilltop fire was immediately lit and a piece of canvas, the only other item salvaged from the wreck, apart from the pork and rope, was instantly run up the flagstaff that had only just been rigged.

The boat was immediately manned and set off out of the lagoon.

Lightoller forgot all about his waning strength as he clambered up to the top of the hill to see for himself. When he reached the summit there she was, a small barque rounding the point at the western end of the island. To him at that moment she was the most beautiful ship he had ever seen.

The burning question now was, would she see them? The wait was agonising. This time their signals could not fail to be noticed. The little ship sailed on. Meanwhile Mowatt and his crew, repeating their efforts of earlier that day, rowed with all their last reserves of strength to intercept the vessel.

And then they saw her sails being taken in. She had seen them and was stopping. Mowatt pulled alongside and went aboard.

Now followed an anxious wait.

After about ten minutes the boat was seen to push off from the side of the ship and head back for the shore. And then to their dismay they realised the barque was getting under way.

But their fears were shortlived. She was merely manoeuvring closer to the entrance to the lagoon so as to shorten the distance as much as possible between ship and shore.

When the boat returned to the beach, it was being manned not by Mowatt and his men, but by four of the crew from the ship.

The plan was they should all get into the one other boat on the island which had previously been found just about capable of floating and at a pinch could accommodate everyone, and then pray it would hold together long enough for them to make the half mile or so out to the ship. The boat was optimistically launched, and all of them clambered in.

Using what makeshift paddles and oars they could find they got under way across the lagoon as fast as they could, but no sooner had they got outside the entrance and hit a slight swell than the rotten old hull split wide open at the seams and water began pouring in. Those who were not paddling or rowing started baling with everything they had, in most cases just their hands. But it was impossible to keep pace with it. The boat was filling up fast. Shirts were stripped off and stuffed into the gaping split to try and stem the flood and keep themselves afloat that little bit longer, before they would finally have to abandon ship and swim for it. The situation, if it had not been so desperate, presented an almost comical picture viewed from the ship;

this dilapidated old boat sinking lower and lower in the water under its heavy cargo of occupants working feverishly to stay afloat, while oars and various other crude means of propulsion splashed frantically and without co-ordination at the sea which would surely welcome them all at any moment.

Many of them, though, were by now far too weak from malnutrition to have coped with having to swim for it, and there were a number who could not swim at all.

Yet somehow that old tub would not submit to the sea. She refused to go under even when half full of water. Finally and against all sensible odds she did reach the barque—but only just. As they got up alongside never was a sinking boat deserted with such alacrity as that one. As for old Jock, who was still not himself, he insisted even with the water rising up above his knees that as skipper he should be the last to leave her. He had just got both feet on the ladder when that ancient 'galliot', brought out of its decades of retirement for one last crucial voyage, made her final bow and promptly went to the bottom like a stone.

For Lightoller it was a fine sensation to feel the deck of a solid ship beneath his feet again. He was aboard the British barque *Coorong* under the command of Captain Hayward. She was a small ship of less than four hundred tons with an eleven-man crew, and it was only thanks to the pleas of Mowatt, when he had first gone aboard, that the Captain finally agreed to take them all off. At first, after he had recovered from the shock of learning how many of them were marooned on the island, he was only prepared to take half of them. He just had not got room for any more and he was already running low on provisions for his own crew. But when Mowatt insisted that any left behind would die within a few days for certain, Captain Hayward threw caution to the winds and consented to take them all.

So far so good, but even though the Captain seemed a good old fellow Mowatt was not going to take chances, particularly with the bitter memory of the first ship still in his mind.

He played it shrewdly. He told Captain Hayward that his boat crew were totally exhausted and far too weak to cope with the pull back to the beach. The problem could easily be solved if they stayed aboard while the skipper sent four of his own crew in the boat back to the island to pass on the word. Mowatt realised that such an arrangement would cut out any chance of the earlier misfortune being repeated. It was not exactly a worthy thought to have of their rescuer, who was almost certainly a man of high principle and integrity, but Mowatt was intent on offering nothing to chance, particularly his judgment of character.

Yes, that seemed like a perfectly sensible idea to Captain Hayward, who was totally unaware of Mowatt's motives. Lightoller now realised why it was that four of the *Coorong*'s crew came back to the island with the tidings and not their own men.

As St. Paul slowly diminished astern Lightoller, joyously happy though he was to have been rescued, could not help but think that one day he must return there.

Mean and forbidding as the island was, he was convinced it had much to offer. It was those caves in the cliffside that stuck in his mind. Yes, there was no doubt they were a perfect hiding place for pirates to store their thievish treasure and they were almost certainly full of it; untold riches lying there to be taken for just the simple job of exploring the caves one by one and finding them.

Although the castaways were now safe aboard ship their survival problems were not altogether over. There was the problem of how to feed thirty-odd extra men on a ship which had already become short of provisions for her own small complement. Captain Hayward broke out all the meat, biscuits and butter he had in order to give this pathetic crew of castaways at least one square meal, but what could they survive on after that? There was one answer only: sugar, tons and tons of raw cane sugar that made up part of the *Coorong*'s cargo. Unless they were fortunate enough to run across another ship in mid ocean and beg some provisions, that is all there would be to live on for the next three weeks until the *Coorong* made Adelaide, her port of destination.

At first Lightoller was highly enthusiastic about the idea of eating nothing else but sugar. It would be like one long sweet eating feast, but as the days went by with nothing but sugar to eat for breakfast, lunch and tea he changed his mind. He would never again so much as look at another sweet thing in his life, he decided. And contrary to its reputation sugar did not do much to put back any of those lost pounds on the boy's now-puny frame.

There were sincere prayers of thanks said as they sailed by Kangaroo Island into St. Vincent Gulf and at last entered the Port River to see up ahead, nestling snugly at the foot of the great Mount Lofty, the wonderful city of Adelaide.

When the *Coorong* came into Port Adelaide on that December day in mid summer the quayside was thronging with people. Lightoller wondered what it was all about. Little did he realise that the semaphores had been busily at work passing on the signal made from the *Coorong* further down the coast that she was bringing in ship-wreck survivors. This was a major event that everyone must turn out to see . . . and what a spectacle of freaks clustered on the deck of the *Coorong* they all must have appeared, Lightoller thought to himself; in nautical terms, a real bunch of 'ringbolt chasers'. So skinny and emaciated that every man jack of them could have threaded them-selves through any ringbolt on the deck without touching the sides. But the generous Australian hospitality he was about to experience would cure that and before long he would be restored to something of his normal healthy self. As the *Coorong* tied up there were cheers all round; cheers from the crowd on the quay, cheers from the eternally grateful *Holt Hill* survivors for their rescuers, and cheers from the rescuers for the *Holt Hill*.

But behind this grim shipwreck saga that was ending on such a happy note on an Australian quayside, there was a strange underlying twist, for the story might well have ended very differently if not for a strong intuition that came over their rescuing skipper.

Captain Hayward at the time was bound for Adelaide from Mauritius on a passage that should not have brought him within a thousand miles of St. Paul. But for some reason the place kept coming into his mind until it became an obsession.

Try as he might to rid his thoughts of it, the vision of that island would not leave him, as though something was telling him to go there.

He tried to forget the ridiculous idea by going below for a sleep, but it was hopeless. Hayward just lay awake on his bunk tormented by this strange force that seemed to be urging him to change course and head for St. Paul.

Eventually this fight with his inner conscience became far too much for him and, against all logical reason, he returned on deck to order a change of course southwards for the island. That done, he went below again and slept soundly, but on waking wondered at the folly of his actions. Here he was wasting a good Westerly wind by diverting to the south when they were already without sufficient provisions in the ship to see them through the normal course of their passage. He instantly put the *Coorong* back on her original heading, due east.

But that night St. Paul came back to haunt him again. Hayward wondered if he might be losing his reason as he paced back and forth in his cabin battling with this crazy notion that was willing him ever more strongly to go to St. Paul. There were people in distress on the island, it was telling him, and he must go there. In the end he realised his mind would get no peace until he made the decision to make for that 'damned island' and settle the matter once and for all.

So the *Coorong*, with her crew by now beginning to have doubts about the sanity of the 'Old Man', once again turned south, but this time there would be no change of mind. After enduring almost a week of nagging self doubt and plenty of grousing from his crew, Hayward finally came within sight of St. Paul and saw the column of smoke rising from the hilltop.

When it turned out to be the distress signal from the *Holt Hill* castaways, their great relief to be plucked to safety was in a quiet way shared by Hayward. His decision, based on that strange and powerful piece of intuition, had not been so irrational after all. However he would never subsequently be able to give a logical explanation why it was that once, in his many years of competent and sober command at sea, he decided to sail some two thousand miles out of his way to rescue from an island shipwreck survivors whom he had no earthly way of knowing were there. As for the mystery ship which sailed away, her identity never was discovered. Lightoller, however, would encounter that same situation again in his life, but the next time with truly tragic consequences.

Lightoller fell in love almost immediately with Australia and its people. He was overwhelmed by kindness wherever he went from these happy-go-lucky carefree folk who seemed to have a soft spot for sailors and did not seem able to do enough for these shipwreck survivors. As was the custom, the crew's pay immediately stopped when the ship was wrecked. After a meeting at the town hall a relief fund was set up for them and all possible would be done to help them in their hardship. Lightoller found himself being welcomed into homes and treated as one of the family.

He found their custom of going for picnics at the weekend a particularly enjoyable pastime. This was a place where he would definitely have to make a special effort to behave himself and keep out of trouble.

Although Christmas under baking sunshine in a temperature of a hundred degrees did seem just a little strange, for Lightoller that Christmas of 1889 went down as the best he had ever had. The knowledge that he might well not have been around to enjoy it at all helped him appreciate it so much more. That 'great to be alive' feeling was indeed the most precious Christmas gift he had ever received.

He made up his mind to stay in this wonderful country and make the best of it for as long as he could. It became a grand routine popping down to G. Wills & Co. the shipping agent every Saturday with Archer his chum for their pocket money and then straightaway to head off and enjoy a good lunch of steak, eggs, bread and butter and as much tea or coffee as he could drink for sixpence. This was a livestock town where they knew how to serve up big fresh steaks to hungry men and already the miserable crayfish and foul-tasting water of St. Paul were a distant memory.

Lightoller found this capital city of South Australia, tucked beneath the tawny shadow of the Mount Lofty range, with its carefully planned layout of straight tree-lined streets, a place brimming with charm and character. In certain respects Adelaide did not seem like Australia at all as he promenaded his way about the main thoroughfares of Rundle Street and King William Street flanked on either side by handsome well constructed buildings, and then Torrens Park, the city's main recreation area laid out with lakes, meadows and woodland sloping down to the water's edge.

It was all very different again from Frisco or Rio.

He also found there were plenty of people his own age about who were easy to befriend.

They appeared to take to this young nautical English lad of great self-confidence; and being a survivor of a shipwreck he was, after all, something of a celebrity in their midst.

Lightoller was developing a keen eye for the young ladies and he soon found himself bowled over by all the pretty bronzed Australian lasses who seemed to have a lot more about them, he thought, than their English counterparts. Yes, he decided, one day he might well get around to marrying one of these Australian beauties.

As time went by he got to venturing out of town to sample life in the outback where the welcome was equally big and where new opportunities opened up to earn a bit of extra cash. He might muck in for a few days on a sheep station and then move on to find himself helping to round up the herd on a cattle spread. Wherever he went he was always sure of a handsome welcome, which might even stretch to the loan of a horse to resume his journey.

Lightoller was glad that from childhood he had learnt to ride horses, which meant he was able to experience life to the full in the bush. It was all such a welcome change and no better way could there be to convalesce from his shipwreck ordeal. Above all it suited his independent nature. This aspect of Australia was just as he had visualised it; kangaroos, koalas, iguanas, and dingos all inhabiting their barren world of dust and desert, broken only by the occasional waterhole where you might by chance happen to run across a swagman boiling his billy.

This was tough, hard territory all right, baked by a sun that gave him no mercy at the peak of the day, but then more than made up for it at sunset. When the sun went down on this country it cast a generous spread of orange-ochre across the landscape which could not be improved, he was sure, anywhere else in the world, even in the tropics.

For one Captain George Sutherland life was not taking on such a rosy hue just now. He had the prospect of going before the Court of Marine Inquiry at the Supreme Court House in Adelaide, to answer charges relating to the loss of his ship. Jock was still in a pretty bad state and was really not physically or mentally up to giving the best account of himself at the hearing.

The four specific charges against him were that he carried a heavy press of sail (whereby the vessel was not under proper command in case of emergency) the night being dirty and the ship known to be in the vicinity of land; he did not post a sufficient look-out, having sent no-one aloft before dark; he kept an imperfect dead reckoning through the irregular use of the log; and he did not take all available precautions for certifying his position.

As Jock faced the Honourable Mr. Justice Bundey, a judge of the Supreme Court who was presiding over the case, he found the whole thing was being conducted more on the lines of criminal proceedings than the marine inquiry it was meant to be. In fact at times he wondered if he was not really on trial for manslaughter or some other serious charge of a criminal nature as opposed to accidentally wrecking his ship.

The court heard how the *Holt Hill* left Rio de Janeiro in ballast on October 14th 1889 under the command of Captain Sutherland who had held a master's certificate for twenty-three years and up to that time had experienced no casualty with any other vessel under his charge. He was also a sober man who worked well with his officers and crew.

The court was told that up to the time of the collision the passage had gone without incident except that the vessel steered badly and griped considerably. The judge decided this was irrelevant and skipped over it. The earlier break-up which had caused the poor handling never came out otherwise it might well have added more weight to the evidence against Jock which was already heavy.

When the facts came out as to how the *Holt Hill* came to collide with St. Paul they were heard with incredulity. It seemed impossible that a ship could run into such a tiny landmass which, apart from another equally insignificant island nearby called Amsterdam, was the only obstruction in many thousands of square miles of sea between the Cape of Good Hope and Australia.

Still more remarkable was how the Captain at the critical moment decided to put his vessel onto the obstruction stem-on instead of attempting to steer clear of it.

In his summing up Mr. Justice Bundey in fact praised Jock for his courage in driving the ship straight at the island. The judge realised at the outset it was the only sensible decision the skipper could take in the situation. It had undoubtedly resulted in all but one of the crew being saved. But the judge quickly added that the court had to deal with the evidence before them and they could not allow their sympathy for a brave man in misfortune to interfere with the discharge of their duty.

The evidence had shown that at sundown the vessel was between nine and ten miles from land and travelling at about thirteen knots which meant there would only be five minutes to take avoiding action once land was sighted. In this instance that was insufficient time to save the ship. 'Captain Sutherland was carrying a highly improper spread of canvas when he knew he was in the vicinity of land and is therefore guilty of reckless navigation. He is also guilty of not keeping a proper look-out. He had too much confidence that all would be right and so allowed the vessel to go on. A fine ship has been destroyed and a valuable life lost.' The judge ordered that Jock's certificate be suspended but because he had already been deprived of it for two months and therefore of the means of livelihood—and considering there was no charge of misconduct against him—justice would be met by ordering a suspension of the certificate for three further months.

Never was there a word spoken in the court of the other ship sighted shortly before the disaster which had undoubtedly contributed to the end result. 'I'll never let another ship pass me while any of my sails are furled!'

Once again, if Mr. Justice Bundey had got to hear that part of it, Jock's penalty would undoubtedly have been much stiffer. But whatever the findings of the court, Jock had already made up his mind back on the cliffs overlooking the remains of his wrecked ship on St. Paul, he would never, never take another command again.

It was odd in a way that Lightoller's first voyage under the command of the 'great cracker-on' should turn out to be the one that was Jock's final undoing—considering that up to then the proud Master of the *Holt Hill* had enjoyed such a long and healthy accident-free record. But then there were those who had said time and again that Jock Sutherland's luck would run out one day.

8

Not as soon as his employers would have liked, but far too soon for young Lightoller, who found Australia and its inhabitants (the female ones especially) very much to his taste, he signed on aboard a homeward-bounder, a famous old clipper, the *Duke of Abercorn*.

When he stepped ashore onto the quay at London's East India Dock, almost another year had gone by since Lightoller had last been in England. Apart from their annoyance at his total disregard of their orders to return, there were certain other outstanding matters for which William Price and Company required an explanation. The passage of time had, alas, not been sufficient to erase from the record certain disturbing reports that had filtered back of 'incidents' in Rio de Janeiro. That kind of behaviour just would not do. William Price apprentices who indulged in thieving and brawling their way round the ports of the world were hardly good for the reputation of the Line. When all was said and done, so much depended on the good will, friendly relations and trust which had taken years for William Price's to build up with both clients and authorities in these places.

They were intent on finding a ringleader and they had decided Lightoller was the culprit. The boy thought their attitude pretty unreasonable. It was almost as though he was being blamed for every single bad deed ever chalked up by the *Holt Hill* crowd all round the globe and he had only been one voyage in the ship and not even a complete one at that. However, as his record at sea was surprisingly good and he had, after all, been through a difficult time during the foundering of the ship, his indentures would be allowed to remain intact and there would be no further action against him. There was an inward sigh of relief.

For his next voyage Lightoller found himself back on the *Primrose Hill* amongst a crowd of new faces in the half-deck. Great pains had apparently been taken to split up the *Holt Hill* boys as much as possible by scattering them around other ships of the Line. Many a ship could boast a half-deck of dubious reputation, as police records in ports around the world could reveal, but for sheer devilry there were few who could have bettered the achievements of those 'hard bargains' that had served under Jock Sutherland. The company had opted for the policy of 'divide and conquer' in hopes that this would solve the problem once and for all.

The *Primrose Hill* was bound for Calcutta, which meant for Lightoller a return to familiar waters, as she would be 'running her easting down' via St. Paul.

When the island hove in sight it was eerie to see that forbidding place again which had so nearly claimed his life. But it also brought back to him the vision of all those chests overflowing with pirates' treasure that he was still convinced were hidden away in the caves in the cliff-side and which one day he would go back and find.

This time they passed the island without incident, but as the *Primrose Hill* turned northwards for Calcutta a different sort of menace loomed.

They were in the Bay of Bengal when they had their first inkling that trouble was imminent. First the barometer fell dramatically and then, away to the south-east, the sky could be seen getting duller and thicker. Captain Wilson knew what was coming and the call went up for all hands on deck to take in sail.

It was the height of the cyclone season and they were about to meet one.

Lightoller watched it develop. He was to discover that the cyclone was the most terrifying kind of storm to get caught up in at sea. Its behaviour was strange, too, as the seas got more and more restless and confused for all that there was virtually no wind. He learnt that when shortening canvas in anticipation of a cyclone extra care had to be taken to snug the sails down as tightly as possible. The kind of winds they were going to experience could quite easily rip even a furled sail from its yard. All sails being taken in were to be double-gasketted.

Not an area of canvas so much as the size of a pocket handkerchief must be exposed to the wind, he was told. Captain Wilson had decided to ride it out on lower topsails which meant the *Primrose Hill* was shortened down to about a third of her total available canvas.

The skies got darker and darker until it became as black as night while the sea boiled about the ship with ever increasing ferocity. The skipper's prime objective was to try and avoid the centre of the circular storm otherwise there was every chance the *Primrose Hill* would not survive it. In such a situation the ship could be swallowed up by the sea with all hands in a matter of minutes.

And then suddenly it was upon them, a storm of such spite Lightoller never thought could be possible, even after experiencing the seas round Cape Horn. This time nobody would have stood a chance on deck, let alone aloft, as the crew scurried for the nearest protection in the ship. Some made for the galley, others for the fo'c's'le and the rest for the whaleback at the stern, and then prayed for the terror to pass and for their lives to be spared.

The seas rose up and burst all over the ship from all angles; over bows and stern, from starboard and port. Then came the lightning, fierce and violent, flashing all around them, making holes in the water big enough to drop in a small boat. The sound was deafening so that a man might yell at the top of his voice right next to you and he would not be heard.

Lightoller had been amazed how the *Primrose Hill* survived the winter seas of the Horn but now she was surely being driven beyond her limit as the sea plummeted on top of the ship filling her up 'rail on rail'. It was a case of willing her to lift to it before the next sea came crashing down on top of her, trying to force her further under.

The storm continued to blast at them harder and then above the banshee scream of the wind came a crack like the sound of a cannon firing. Lightoller looked aloft to see one of the topsails being carried away leaving behind just a few tattered shreds on the yard. Then there was another crack as another sail went, and then another and another.

The seas began leaping frantically straight up in the air. The *Primrose Hill* leapt with them. It was a sign that their worst fears had materialised. The ship was right in the centre of the cyclone. They were in dire trouble and there was now only one chance of saving themselves, and that was for the yards carrying what canvas remained to be hauled round on the opposite tack to meet the imminent change in the direction of this treacherous, revolving wind.

Despite the terrible dangers of being on deck at the height of such a storm no one needed second bidding to follow the cry to man the halliards and get the ship on a new tack before she was caught 'aback'. There might have been a heavy risk of being washed overboard but it would be the end for all of them anyway if they did not quickly get those yards hauled round.

In those vital minutes both men and boys found a strength and purpose they never thought they possessed. The job was completed in time and as the wind returned once again in full force, but now blowing in the reverse direction, the *Primrose Hill* was prepared. It came with a vengeance as though trying to make up for having failed to drown the ship at the first attempt. But the *Primrose Hill* could take everything which that crazy sea threw at her.

And then it was passed and gone, and the ship was left tossing dizzily around in the heavy gale that followed in the wake of the cyclone. They were clear of the worst of it. The skipper and many of the hands who had experienced the sea in its most brutal moods had never been in anything quite like it. The *Primrose Hill* had performed miracles in the way she had survived. Few other ships, they all agreed, could have taken such punishment and survived.

But now came the job of putting the damage to rights as Lightoller found himself back in that situation of working non-stop aloft hour after hour clearing up the wreckage, replacing the remnants of ripped sails with fresh canvas and disentangling the hundreds of feet of rope that had got twisted around the masts and spars and knotted up with shreds of sail. Even though the worst of the danger had passed, the sea continued to thunder aboard and no man could afford to relax as the threat was always there of being caught unawares by a sudden torrent of water over the rail and being tossed overboard.

On reflection Lightoller decided that he would settle for a full blown gale round Cape Horn any time sooner than face a cyclone again. At least you knew where you stood with the heavy seas of the Horn, while the cyclone seemed so treacherous and deceitful. But once again he had weathered a crisis which could so easily have been the end of him. Men as well as the ship had taken a battering. No one had come through it without at least a few bruises. Lightoller had got off comparatively lightly. Some of the crew were smarting over broken ribs and one had a broken arm. But mercifully they were still alive and afloat. The other blessing was that all the masts and yards had remained intact so there would be no extra difficulties to cope with in getting the ship back to its full state of seaworthiness. That was a relief to Lightoller who was now familiar with the problems of getting repairs done in foreign ports after a dismasting.

Eventually the storm havoc had been put to rights, the ship squared away for Calcutta. In Calcutta another test awaited the apprentice seaman: he was now 'out of his time' and the moment had arrived when he had to sit his first Board of Trade examination—for his Second Mate's certificate.

Manuals on seamanship and navigation which had lain neglected somewhere in the bottom of sea-chests were being rooted out and avidly pored over as Lightoller and three other apprentices due to 'go up for their ticket' began a fierce programme of swatting up in preparation for the examinations that lay ahead of them. Todd and Whall's *Seamanship* was the textbook then regarded as 'the Bible' containing all that the would-be Mate needed to know on nautical astronomy, mathematics, seamanship and 'the Rule of the Road'.

The cover of Todd and Whall bore a picture of the White Star liner, SS *Celtic* a fine twin-funnelled four-master which Lightoller came to regard as the symbol of all that one day he hoped to achieve.

The sight of that magnificent vessel beating her way westward across the Atlantic would catch his eye every time he picked up the book and spur him on in his efforts to understand and memorise the pages. His old headmaster back at Chorley Grammar School would undoubtedly have been impressed.

When Austin, Dale, Whitney and Lightoller entered the examination room it was in the knowledge that only one of them was likely to pass, for Captain Jenny, the Board of Trade chief examiner, had boasted to them with great pride beforehand that it was his policy to fail three out of every four that came up for their ticket.

Lightoller was not feeling at all hopeful. If they had been taking bets on the ship as to who was least likely to get through he would undoubtedly have been the favourite. He just was not the academic type whereas Austin, for instance, worked out the ship's position every day.

And so the torture commenced.

'Oh this won't do,' Lightoller heard Captain Jenny say as he looked over some of the papers.

He was prepared to pack it all in that instant, and yet it turned out to be Austin, the one they all thought most likely to succeed, who was the first to be failed. There were no such formalities as papers being marked and the entrant informed at a later date whether or not he had passed. He was told on the spot in the middle of the exam if he was getting it wrong, and had to suffer the humiliation of removing himself from the room there and then. Austin was soon followed by Dale, leaving just Lightoller and Whitney surviving to face Day Two.

He was amazing himself with what he had managed to master about such things as winds, tides and currents, the points of the compass, how to read a chart, how to use the chronometer, the sextant and the stars to work out the ship's position, how to heave the log to calculate the ship's speed, the use of a lead-line to ascertain the depth of the water, the meaning of all the different buoys, the rules applying to avoid collision when two sailing ships were approaching one another, the rules when a sailing ship was approaching a steamship, the different principles applied to loading different types of cargo, not to mention the working of sailing ships themselves and how to handle them in different conditions and situations. The right answers, knowledge and practical application seemed always to be there. Whitney got his marching orders and Lightoller found himself alone and incredulous—and it took some time for his shipmates to believe it too when he arrived back at the *Primrose Hill* striding along with an exaggerated 'deep-sea roll', waving that coveted piece of blue paper which said he was now a Board of Trade certified Second Mate.

As the *Primrose Hill* sailed out of Calcutta the sea took on a new meaning for Lightoller. He felt that he now had some standing in the eyes of his harsh mistress and she would have to treat him with a little more respect from then on. He could look her straight in the face and truly call himself a seaman—and soon to be an officer at that. If he was openly proud of it who would begrudge him the pleasure? He had, after all, earned his certificate in one of the toughest schools of apprenticeship there could be for any job. Now it all seemed worth it; the deprivation, the hunger, the hardships that at times defied all description, those dangerous hours aloft in the worst kinds of weather and those times when even he might not have realised how close the end had been.

While experience taught him a healthy respect for the sea, he also grew to love it more and more. His sister was the one who did all the worrying. He had once reassured her, 'Don't you bother, the sea isn't wet enough to drown me. *I'll never* be drowned.' He had certainly come close enough to it and would again.

The cyclone season was over in the Indian Ocean. Now the sky was clear and blue and the water like glass, except for just the gentlest swell generated by the warm friendly breeze that let you know the sea was still breathing. The sea could kill, the sea could lull—Lightoller found her an unpredictable mistress.

9

Steamships were here to stay and rapidly growing in size and numbers. It was only a matter of time before they would have complete mastery of the seas.

Steam however had not been an instant success when it took to the sea, and it would take many decades before the machine-driven vessel could begin to match the windjammer for capacity, speed and economy.

For a long time they shared the seas amicably, the steamships with their greater comfort, but less cargo space operating the passenger and mail services while the sailing ships with their bigger holds and cheaper running costs continued to dominate the freight routes. During the 1880s and early '90s sail even enjoyed a new lease of life, and it was a revival which spread to the shipyards, where hundreds of new barques were built in Britain and the United States to cater for the renewed demand. Sailing ships were now being constructed of steel and of a much bigger, stronger and more streamlined design than their wooden predecessors, which made them ideal for carrying such bulk cargoes as guano and nitrate from South America, grain from San Francisco, timber from Puget Sound and Sweden, railway lines and coal from Britain, jute from Calcutta and wool from Australia.

But it was not to last as new breakthroughs in steam technology made steamships more efficient, faster and cheaper to run, and by the mid-1890s sail was losing more and more to its engine-powered competitor. The China tea route was a prime example.

There was one territory however which remained exclusive to sailing ships long after steam had invaded all the other avenues of trade and that was the west coast of South America—'The Nitrate Coast'. Sailing ships were heading down that way in their hundreds during the 1890s bringing back round the Horn cargoes of nitrate to Britain, Europe and the east coast of North America.

Among ships regularly employed in this trade was a big four-masted barque called the *Knight of St. Michael*, the largest steel sailing ship to be built on the Clyde and owned by the Liverpool-based Greenshields, Cowie and Company of 'Knight' line fame. They themselves had almost completed the transition from square sail to steam and the *Knight of St. Michael* was one of the last remaining windjammers of the line.

Lightoller was her Third Mate. Unlike most apprentices now who, once qualified, could not wait to get out of sail and into steam with its better prospects and more comfortable existence, not so Lightoller. That sailing ship man's contempt for those 'smoke-stacks' had infected him. He had started in sail and he was determined to stay in it.

He was now well on the way to earning the tag 'hard case', having developed into a sturdy, iron-hard young man thoroughly conditioned to life under sail. As Third Mate he was not yet ready to take full charge of his own watch in the ship, but he was in authority and had to show it—even if at times that required going in with both fists to prove that being young and new in the job did not necessarily mean he was soft. The crew would soon take advantage if they thought that here was an officer who could not handle himself. A Third Mate who was worth his salt would not be long in making Second, and he was keen to show himself fit for that next rung of the ladder. There could be no grumbling and growling now as the call went up for all hands aloft to shorten sail when a blow was coming on. He had to make it his business to be there first.

Occasionally the Chief Mate would hand over his watch to Lightoller at night to let him get the feel of having charge of the ship, a sure sign of confidence in the ability of the Third Mate to look after things. This gave Lightoller valuable experience in readiness for the day when he would take up the position of a watch-keeping officer.

The *Knight of St. Michael* was bound for Iquique, the principal nitrate port on the coast of Chile. She carried an outward cargo of coal which was common practice for ships heading that way. Coal out and nitrate back had become the normal run of things these days. She set sail from Liverpool at the tail end of a winter that was to go down as one of the worst in history for shipping around British shores and out on the Western Ocean. The losses reached record proportions with some dozen vessels going to their last account in one single month in the English Channel alone.

The *Knight of St. Michael* took her share of the punishment as she battled her way out into the South Atlantic through seas to match those of Cape Horn. Bulwarks were stove in, canvas torn asunder and all the lifeboats smashed or carried away. For Lightoller being tossed around by stormy seas was by now part and parcel of the life. After all, he generally seemed to come through, and this situation was apparently going to be no different as the *Knight of St. Michael*, with damage repaired and the violent gales behind her, found her way into the Trades and picked up her first escort of flying fish. As a steady, warm tropical breeze carried her sweetly on southwards through sun-sparkled seas the last concern of anybody on board was that the ship no longer carried any lifeboats. But that was an attitude about to change. The heavy weather, unbeknown to them all, had left behind another legacy and one which took some weeks to discover.

Then they smelt it . . . faint at first but getting stronger. It was the smell of burning and they knew in an instant where it was coming from.

Their cargo of coal was on fire.

For days the fire had been smouldering away quietly in the hold beneath them, having been started by the heat of constant friction as the ship tossed about in the storms.

The risk of fire at sea had become a growing occupational hazard for men in sailing ships where coal was now one of the main sources of cargo revenue. In consequence Lloyd's insurance premiums on ships carrying coal had been steadily rising. Too many coal ships had been lost because of fire, or gone missing, leaving the assumption that fire had been the cause.

Fire at sea would always be high on the list of things a seaman dreaded most, but to be caught on fire in a ship which had no lifeboats put a fine edge on anxiety.

For the men of the *Knight of St. Michael* such a nightmare had become a reality. There was just one boat left, the ship's pinnace which could take a dozen of them at the most, but only if the sea was calm.

Meanwhile the decks grew hotter and the smell of smoke and coal gas got stronger. There was little hope of tackling the fire effectively as the heat and gas was too much to allow any man to get near when the hatch was open. The fire also appeared to be a deep seated one, tucked away in the depths of the hold and difficult to get at in any circumstances.

It was decided that the hatches would be best kept closed to allow as little air as possible to feed the flames. But that in itself produced a new threat because gas steadily building up in the hold and, trapped there, could easily ignite and blow them all sky high. Whichever way they looked at it, the situation was grim.

Captain Dodd's priority now was to get the ship up to the nearest land as quickly as possible. He took the only course open to him and that was to turn the ship due west and head for the east coast of South America. But here again he was up against it. She was beating into a headwind—a 'dead muzzler'—which could severely cut down progress while the crew went through the arduous exercise of 'tack and tack' to work the ship against the wind. Land at that stage was well over a thousand miles off.

To add yet more to the skipper's problems, the only chart he possessed for those latitudes was of the South Atlantic. He had none containing any detail of the South American coast, so that when he aimed his ship at a dot on the Argentinian coast bearing the name Bahia Blanca, he realised that he could find himself reaching land anywhere up to a hundred miles either side of the target—assuming the ship made land at all.

As the days went by the strain on the crew became intolerable. To Lightoller this was strain of a new kind, totally different to that which a man might experience in heavy seas. In a storm, while he could sense fear, there was always the relief of coming off watch so that he could go below to rest his tired body. In these circumstances nobody could relax enough to rest, much less go below, where the fierce heat from the burning hold had turned the ship into a floating oven. The tropical climate exaggerated it all the more. It was impossible for any man to remain below for more than a few minutes, and knowing that the ship could erupt at any time was no incentive for the crew to go there anyway. In the end they spent their days and nights, on watch or off, on the deck, and unless manning the running gear they would be clustered round the stern to be as far away as possible from the danger zone. As the pitch boiled up through the seams of the deck over the fire, the surface became too hot for bare feet to stand, and it was almost comical to watch men dancing an involuntary jig on the hot deck while they worked the halliards for a change of tack. But Lightoller had seldom seen the whole crew of a ship go to work with such urgency and purpose. Nobody cared any more whether it was his watch or not when the order came to haul round the yards. Men almost fought one another to get to the ropes and winches.

The days went by and the ship laboured on, beating her way into the unrelenting headwind, making little more than one or two knots.

They built a raft from surplus spars and the remains of one of the lifeboats that had been smashed during the storm. It was a makeshift affair which would not have offered much guarantee to men whose lives might depend on it. But at least it gave the crew something to work on to take their minds off the furnace blazing away below, and raise their morale with the knowledge that at least they were doing something to assist their flimsy chances if the worst should happen. There were those less cheerful ones among them who came to the conclusion that if the ship went up altogether, it might be far better to go up with it. At least the end when it came would be quick instead of being cast to the mercies of the sea on some rickety raft which would either fall apart and leave its occupants to the sharks, or, if not, preserve them to die of thirst anyway. At one stage they tried singing sea shanties to forget their troubles, but even in song they couldn't forget them completely . . .

Now all ye jolly sailormen that sail the Western Sea,
An' all ye jolly 'prentice lads a warning take from me,
Steer clear o' lofty fire ships, for me they left well spent.
For one burnt all me money up an' left me broke and bent . . .

Then someone would get up and walk away from the group and put his hand on the hatch cover over the fire to test the temperature. Inevitably the singing would die away as all waited anxiously to know the verdict. Was it any hotter? The answer would nearly always be the same. 'Aye, just a bit.'

That is how it was for the next two long weeks while nerves became more and more frayed and tempers shorter. At times Lightoller wondered if the atmosphere on deck was not often more heated than it was below as arguments ensued over the pettiest of things. But no sooner did the wind make the slightest variation than all differences would be instantly forgotten as everyone jumped together to man the braces and trim the yards, all to help urge the ship on just that fraction faster towards land and safety.

All the while the apprentices were stationed permanently aloft on the fore skysail yard keeping their eyes glued rigidly ahead looking out for land. To hear the cry of 'land ho' was all that everyone prayed for now — that, and a good breeze to carry them there more quickly. But of land there was no sign. Even at their present crawl they would have expected after two weeks to sight something. But there was nothing but empty horizon.

However, throughout the whole crisis there was one way in which their luck had held. Despite the terrific heat that had spread throughout the ship, which had even started to peel the paint off the hull, the fire had remained confined to the hold. Not only that, there had been no explosion. Certain other coal ships they knew of which had got into the same fix, if they were not blown apart completely by one gigantic blast, had suffered a series of damaging explosions as gas built up and ignited. But fingers crossed, fate in that respect was, so far, smiling on them.

And then it decided to smile on them some more. Suddenly from the south-east a good healthy breeze sprang up and there was no need of any prompting from the skipper as all hands dashed forward to bring the yards round and get the ship squared away to this wonderful gift in answer to their prayers. The big question now was would the wind hold long enough to bring them up to land, or would it veer round and become a 'dead muzzler' again. Meanwhile the ship, responding well to the healthy breeze, was cutting through the water at a good ten knots. The hours went by, night came and the wind held, but still no sign of land. The smell of the fire was much stronger now and for the first time smoke was seen belching out from under the hatch covers. It started blowing in the men's faces, making them cough and their eyes water. As they sat huddled at the poop they could feel the ship getting hotter and hotter beneath them. No one managed a wink of sleep that night. At the first glimmer of daylight the horizon remained stubbornly clear and uninterrupted. The boys shinned aloft and everyone waited for the good news, but from the lofty perch of the fore skysail yard there was still no sign of land.

The wind held throughout the day and then as evening again approached and the men began to wonder if the Captain might have made some miscalculation, the hum of the wind and the swish of the sea was broken by the sudden cry from aloft . . . 'Land ho!'

In that moment the decks of the *Knight of St. Michael* became a scene of great revelry and rejoicing as a huge cheer went up, and men for once ignored the hot decks beneath their feet and danced around hugging one another in untold joy and relief. After all those days of constant nerve-racking tension, knowing that a potential volcano was rumbling beneath them that could erupt at any time, they were at last within sight of safety.

All they needed now was for the fire to keep at bay for just a few more hours and they would all be out of danger.

Meanwhile for Captain Dodd the next major concern was to establish where they were. He had aimed for Bahia Blanca, but as the ship got nearer to the coast no sign of any life at all could be seen, let alone a town. It was getting darker as he shortened sail and gently conned the ship closer in to the shore. He would need to exercise extreme care in these strange waters . . .

'By the mark 7! . . . deep 6! . . . by the mark 5! . . . And a half 4! . . .' Soundings on the lead-line were beginning to indicate that the sea-bed was shoaling up and the depth decreasing rapidly. The *Knight of St. Michael* dropped her anchor and the sails were clewed up. The ship was within a few hundred yards of the shore and everyone knew that if they had to abandon ship now those who were not lucky enough to get a place on the raft or the pinnace could swim ashore. Lightoller confidently reassured those who might have been a little nervous about the local shark population that the water was far too cold for them. Not everyone was convinced. However they were now through the worst of the crisis and the atmosphere on board had undergone a remarkable transformation during the last few hours.

Captain Dodd decided to wait until morning and then he and Lightoller would go ashore in the pinnace to try and find out exactly where they were. He realised it meant taking the only boat, but there was no other choice and as the ship was now close enough to land everyone would have an almost certain chance of getting ashore if the fire should take a turn for the worse and they had to jump for it. However nobody was quite ready to share Lightoller's amusement at the great fun they could all have trying out the raft in the surf.

When morning came and the Captain and his Third Mate made off towards the empty beach, the Chief Mate and the rest of the crew set about removing the hatch covers to begin tackling the fire. Although it was a job that had been judged far too difficult and risky to attempt while the ship was still at sea, now they could go to it in the comforting knowledge that land was close at hand—and as Mr. Lightoller had said, what fun they could all have on the raft!

As the hatch covers were lifted thick smoke came billowing out, but no leaping flames. So far so good. But they still had to cope with the smoke problem. Smoke masks were improvised out of oilskin and sailcloth and found to be effective enough to allow a man to work in the hold for up to ten minutes at a time before be would have to give up and allow another to take over. The first thing they had to do was burrow down deep through tons of coal to get to the source of the trouble.

After endless hours of much heavy digging in terrible heat and smoke they eventually got through to it. All the ship's hoses which, by another piece of improvisation, had been fitted up with iron nozzles, were driven down into the roaring glow and then the pumping began.

Slowly but surely they got to grips with it but fire in a ship's hold could be a deceiving animal and they could never be sure it was completely out until the hold was emptied.

In time, though, they were satisfied that it was well enough under control to be kept in check—provided that the Old Man and Mr. Lightoller were not too long in coming back, having found a port where they could dump their rogue cargo once and for all.

However the Old Man and Mr. Lightoller were not making too much progress in that direction. Having reached the shore through the surf and beached the boat, they had set off optimistically in search of some sign of life. But it soon became apparent to both of them that this was going to be more difficult than at first assumed as they found themselves trekking over remote, unfriendly terrain that seemed to be one endless succession of steep sandy precipices. No sooner had they worn themselves out conquering one towering obstruction than another one was waiting ahead.

Eventually, totally exhausted, they came upon their first sign of life—a small herd of horses browsing quietly in a clearing. They both came immediately to the same conclusion. Whether they were to be shot as horse thieves or not, they were going to ride and keep on riding until they found someone. They picked themselves out a couple of likely mounts and approached them cautiously. To the Captain this was all too easy, while Lightoller from his own past experience with horses was just a little bit more wary.

With plenty of sweet talking and tongue clicking and a few pats on the head Captain Dodd was thoroughly confident he had won over his beast. When he thought the moment was right he leapt aboard. But seemingly the moment was not right. No sooner had the skipper planted his gangling frame firmly on the back of the animal than it tossed its hind legs in the air and its would-be rider went flying in a beautiful curving arc to land on the ground with a resounding thump.

That was all too much for his Third Mate who, try as he might, just could not hold back roars of laughter. As for the Captain, a man fortunately blessed with a sense of humour, he slowly picked himself up, apparently not too much the worse for his spectacular display of aerobatics, and suggested with a wink and a smile, it might be better after all if they walked.

After another hour of trudging and climbing they came upon a small hut. Their troubles were over at last, they hoped. Once inside, however, Lightoller found himself confronted by the most menacing-looking band of cut-throats he had ever clapped eyes on. As he felt their piercing steely eyes behind the shadow of their sombreros weighing the pair of them up, he resigned himself to the prospect of a quick end and being robbed of all he possessed, even if it was just the clothes on his back. Captain Dodd, to his surprise, seemed perfectly unperturbed as he attempted to communicate with what little Spanish he knew. To him these men were merely some kind of farmers or gauchos or whatever it was people did for a living in these parts. His young mate, though, was horrified when he saw the Captain take out his purse, which was heavy with gold sovereigns, and start handing round a few. Now, thought Lightoller, they were really for it. He waited to be knifed. Perhaps it was just the imposing figure of the skipper standing there in the splendour of his very official looking shipmaster's uniform that was making them hesitate. Meanwhile the halting banter went on between Captain Dodd and their hosts, as he kept trying to make himself understood and grasp what was being said in reply.

It seemed they were a long way from Bahia, some thirty miles south, with nothing but rough country in between. Even if fortunate enough to walk out of this place with their lives, they would stand little chance of making it to the port that they were counting on to provide a berth for the *Knight of St. Michael* to dispose of her problem cargo, and also a tow to get her back into deep water again so that she could sail there.

And then to Lightoller's great surprise their new-found acquaintances offered to help solve their dilemma — that is, for a few more pieces of the Captain's gold. They would provide horses and escort them to their destination. Captain Dodd decided the best plan was for himself only to go on to Bahia and for Lightoller to return to the ship and let them know the situation.

The 'horses', it turned out, were hardly worthy of the description. Never had Lightoller set eyes on such a pair of old sawbones in his life. Added to that, he was not relishing the prospect of riding on such a nobbly skeleton without a saddle. But he had to admit that this would still be better than walking, if only just, and certainly the mounts looked docile enough which, after the skipper's earlier misfortune, was just as well.

It was just as Lightoller and Captain Dodd were all set to depart on their respective journeys that the gruesome act of bloody butchery commenced . . .

When the Third Mate arrived back at the ship in the pinnace without the Captain and covered all over with blood, the crew jumped to the immediate conclusion that something disastrous must have befallen the pair. However the first thing that became apparent as he hauled himself back aboard was that his wounds were not as bad as they looked. In fact it seemed he was not hurt at all. So what about the Old Man, where was he? They anxiously wanted to know. Lightoller explained the full situation reassuring them that all was well, that the 'bandits' they had met had actually turned out to be most friendly and helpful and he was quite confident that the Captain would make it to Bahia successfully and unharmed. So what about all the blood on his clothes then, they enquired, assuming that if it was not the Captain's or Lightoller's it must be someone's. That, Lightoller informed them was the result of a most gracious act of generosity on the part of their hosts, who insisted on bestowing on him a very special parting gift to bring back for all the crew.

'Gift? And where is this gift?'

With that, Lightoller hopped back down into the pinnace and drew back a tarpaulin to reveal one half sheep, complete with head, still bleeding profusely.

When the skipper arrived back the following day aboard a jaunty little tugboat tooting its way merrily down the coast he was still recovering from his 'horse' ride to Bahia Blanca. His long hot journey on that unsaddled old walking skeleton had taken such a toll of him that on his arrival at the outskirts of the town he had lapsed into total unconsciousness and fallen off.

Eventually the tug towed them clear of the bay and they set sail down the coast to Bahia Blanca, where at last they could rid themselves for good of that terrible curse in the hold.

So ended the saga of the fire at sea on the *Knight of St. Michael*.

Before they left Bahia Blanca, Herbert Lightoller was promoted. The Second Mate, who had long suffered a drink problem, had hit town and gone on a binge which finally snapped the patience of

Captain Dodd. The man was discharged there and then, and the Third Mate, Captain Dodd decided, was more than capable of taking his place. So Lightoller was now a fully-fledged officer of a ship—and a four-masted barque and three-skysail-yarder at that!

10

The *Knight of St. Michael* sailed out of Bahia Blanca with the remainder of her cargo of coal and turned south to continue her passage down to the Horn and then up to Iquique.

As Lightoller took his place on the poop for his first watch as Second Mate it was a fine sensation to be in charge of such a proud ship with all her billowing pyramids of canvas reaching high up into the sky above him. She had done well to survive the rigours of the fire and apart from the paint that had been baked off her hull she had apparently suffered no other ill effects. It was undoubtedly her steel hull which saved her; if she had been a wooden vessel the story would have ended very differently.

On arrival at Iquique, Lightoller's first impression was of the large number of sailing ships of many nationalities strung out across the wide, circular bay, tier on tier of them, gently rising and falling at their anchors in the Pacific swell. Between the ships and the shore was a constant traffic of small lighters, usually sculled by a two-man crew, some heading inwards deeply laden with coal that had just been discharged, while others headed out weighed down with nitrate ready for loading up.

Beyond the bay, overlooking the whole scene were the Andes, sloping steeply down almost to the edge of this barren coastline of rock and sand and treeless hills, where the sun beat constantly down and no rain ever fell. This, along with the flies, the smell, the dust, the crude mortar shacks that lined the narrow twisting streets—and the inevitable bars selling fire-water under such names as *anisado*, *aguardiente* and *pisco*, was Iquique, the chief port on the nitrate coast.

Having survived earthquake, fire and tidal waves in its time, Iquique now thrived more than ever on the nitrate that came through the port to be shipped off all round the world for use in the making of explosives and fertiliser.

This was territory which seamen looked upon with mixed feelings. To some it was nothing but a dreary, God-forsaken place to be cursed for its heat, drought and hard work, while for others it held a great romance with memories of good drink, good women and many happy times. There were some sailors who upon arriving at Iquique never left, settling down as drink vendors, boarding-house landlords or even keepers of 'fandango halls'. Some just deserted their ships and opted out completely, lapsing into an existence of beachcombing and drunkenness—or else in final despair ended up in the Chilean navy which could soon mend a man's errant ways, it being one of the last navies of the world to abolish flogging.

It was not many days before Lightoller had exhausted all that Iquique had to offer him, and he joined his shipmates in the sport of fishing. 'John Shark' was hunted ruthlessly, for he was regarded with the greatest hostility by sailors, who would never be more satisfied than when they had pulled the brute out of the water and nailed his tail to the mast. In Iquique however, he discovered, there were more ways to fish than with just hook and line: he found how effective a good stick of dynamite tossed into the water could be. Dynamite could be bought in unlimited quantities at any ship's chandler's or grocer's store in the port. This was after all the *Nitrate Coast* that produced the most essential ingredient for explosives. Lightoller's idea of enjoying his Sunday rest was to load up the pinnace with a good supply of dynamite and a big net and go in search of rock cod and herring, the best fish to catch by this method. Sometimes he found that the herrings came into the bay in shoals so thick that the ones swimming on top were actually being pushed above the surface. All he needed to do then was scoop them up with a bucket. But if they were running deep then the dynamite was brought into play.

He would prepare his charge by first of all pushing a hole down through the centre of the stick with a pencil. Then, taking a detonator, he inserted the end of the fuse carefully into it, nipping them together with his teeth—being mindful that if the detonator went off, his head would go with it. The fuse and detonator, once prepared, were inserted into the hole in the dynamite and all was then ready to receive the lighted match.

The deeper the fish were swimming the longer the fuse he would set. If he wanted to be sure of getting the best results a good method, he found, was to tie the explosive to a length of twine equivalent to the depth of the fish, light the fuse, then drop it down suspended on the end of a stick. If his judgement was correct the subsequent blast would bring enough fish to the surface to feed the crew for the next couple of days.

This way, however, could have its drawbacks as the Mate of the ship moored next door to the *Knight of St. Michael* discovered. After setting up his dynamite and seeing the fish, he lit the fuse and threw the charge over the side of the ship. But he had kept one foot on the twine, and the charge, still fizzling away, came bouncing back on board. He hastily grabbed the dynamite and threw it back again, but this time, even worse, he managed to get the twine wrapped round his ankle, with the result that the explosive dropped onto the deck just a few feet in front of him. By the time he had unravelled himself the fuse was nearly burnt through and there was no time to do anything but dive for the nearest cover behind one of the ship's skylights. In the mighty blast that followed he was unhurt but the ship did not fair so well. It was the steward who had most to say about it when he returned later to find a giant hole in the deck right above his pantry where every article of glass and crockery had been smashed . . . had he been in there at the time, he would have become part of the mess!

But Lightoller was to witness a spectacular incident on the coast that demonstrated the havoc that could be wreaked by nitrate even in its raw state. It happened in an American 'Down Easter' called the *Frederick Billings* where the crew, having tired of a life under constant ill treatment at the hands of the bully mates decided to desert her. But they made up their minds to leave her in style. After preparing the boats for a quick escape, the last of the deserters threw a paraffin lamp into a hold full of nitrate.

Lightoller had once seen how just one 2-cwt bag of nitrate set alight on the local beach during a gala night had illuminated the whole bay and given off a scorching heat. In the *Frederick Billings* almost fully loaded there were thousands of bags. The ship flared up like a great firework and within a quarter of an hour had burnt to a shell and sunk, but not before considerable damage had been caused to the ships close by her, destroying all their running gear and burning off every coat of paint down to their bare hulls. It was surprising no one was hurt. As for the culprits responsible, they never did have time to take to the boats and had to jump for it and swim ashore: to be turned over to the authorities, they had decided, was infinitely preferable to enduring any more of the tyranny in a Yankee 'blood ship'.

That incident was an indication to Lightoller of the highly dangerous nature of the commodity they were dealing with. The cargo of coal that had caught fire in the hold had given them a chance, but there could be no second chances with nitrate. The *Frederick Billings* fire was deliberate but in Iquique a number of ships had been destroyed by fire accidentally. As Second Mate and now responsible for the loading and stowage of cargo, precaution against fire was the very first priority. The only way nitrate could be put out once it caught light was to douse it at once with water in which nitrate had been soaked. This 'nitrate water' was kept at the ready in barrels around the hatches whilst the cargo was being stowed. To Lightoller the whole business of nitrate was grim and depressing—from the moment it left the mines of the salt desert of Tarapaca on the raw backs of the overloaded, water-deprived mules till it reached the ship where crews laboured ceaselessly from six in the morning to six at night for weeks on end in the simmering heat, getting it aboard and down into the holds.

At Iquique all the loading and unloading was done while the ships lay at anchor offshore. Before the nitrate could be brought out to the *Knight of St. Michael* the first three to four weeks had been spent discharging the coal, an arduous enough task in itself under the hot sun for men with nothing but shovels and baskets to work with, while constantly plagued by a thick, suffocating cloud of black dust. Then the nitrate in its 2-cwt bags was brought out to the ship in the lighters to be hoisted aboard by winch. Some ships had a steam winch, then it was easier. The *Knight of St. Michael* did not possess such a luxury. Hers was a dolly winch manned by six men, and never did the crew earn their pay more than when they were working on it.

Once aboard, every sack of nitrate was stowed by one man, a local Chilean. Working with the aid of a special platform constructed in the hold to suit his height, he took each sack on his back—all 2 cwt of it—and dumped it into position. Lightoller had never seen a man with a back like it. The years spent in this gruelling labour had turned what was once flesh into a patch of hard, rough leather. It seemed that life had not changed much for the natives here since the Spaniards first came and enslaved them.

The weight of nitrate was not only hard on men, but ships too. As the bags were stowed in their customary pyramid piles in each hold, the ship's hull began to buckle inwards. But it was considered quite normal, and merely required regular adjustment on the rigging each time the ropes began to sag.

Two months later, the moment arrived for the last sack to be loaded. It was time for the ceremony to begin, the 'Cheering of the Homeward Bounder', a tradition born of the days when a ship leaving some distant port for home was always an occasion to be celebrated. For the crew of a ship departing from the Nitrate Coast that was always a moment for great celebration.

And so with a good quantity of *pisco*, a very fiery, cheap local spirit, supplied by the skipper for the occasion, the *Knight of St. Michael* was ready to begin the ritual. As the last bag came aboard the youngest and smallest apprentice of the crew jumped onto it and, wildly waving the red ensign to signify the nationality of his ship, was raised high enough for all the others to see him. Then at the top of his voice he shouted 'Three cheers for the captain, officers and crew of the *Knight of St. Michael*!' In response a great cheer went up from the crews of all the ships around the bay. After that he was raised and lowered three times, and as he and the sack of nitrate were brought down towards the hold for the third and last time he cried 'Three cheers for all the ships in the harbour!' and once again a great cheer went up. But this was only the beginning of the ceremony.

At eight o'clock that night the bell on the *Knight of St. Michael* rang out, followed by other ships joining in until the bay and the valleys and hills around Iquique echoed to the scores of ship's bells all ringing wildly together. It persisted for close on a quarter of an hour.

While all this was going on, a wooden frame decked out with lights in the shape of the Southern Cross constellation was hoisted aloft on the *Knight of St. Michael* and lit up, while the crew lined up on deck each holding a lighted torch of saltpetre. Now it was time for the full cheering ceremony to begin as the ship's loudest and deepest voice cried out . . . 'Three cheers for the *Knight of the Thistle*!' another Greenshields Cowie barque anchored next to them. The crew of the *Knight of St. Michael* instantly gave three cheers. Then the crew of the *Thistle* replied . . . 'Three cheers for the homeward bounder!' and cheering erupted again. However with fifty or sixty ships in port at the time this ritual had to be gone through with every one. Any ship which the *Knight of St. Michael* overlooked and failed to cheer would regard herself as gravely insulted. In turn any ship that failed to reply, even though she might be anchored up to a mile away and might not have heard her name, would be looked upon with utter contempt and be groaned at by all the other ships around.

Hours later, with all the ships cheered, throats swollen and sore, and many a man by now well under the effects of the *pisco*, the Southern Cross, which throughout had blazed aloft on the *Knight of St. Michael*, was slowly lowered. And then with what was left of their voices everybody aboard her lapsed into the strains of that time honoured shanty that Lightoller's banjo had come to render somehow better than any other:

'The billows roll, the breezes blow,
Goodbye, fare ye well, goodbye fare ye well:
To us they're calling sheet home and go,
Hurrah! My boys, we're homeward bound . . .'

But this time the words 'Goodbye, fare ye well' took on an extra significance for Lightoller, because when the *Knight of St. Michael* broke her moorings the next morning and sailed away from that harsh sunbaked coast of barren cliffs and naked hills, the Nitrate Coast was not all he would be saying goodbye to.

PART TWO
BRIDGE WATCH

Lord thou hast made this world below a shadow of a dream,
An' taught by time, I tak' it so—exceptin' always steam,
From coupler-flange to spindle guide I see thy hand, Oh God—
Predestination in the stride o' yon connectin' rod.

Rudyard Kipling, *McAndrew's Hymn*

11

'Full ahead, Mr. Lightoller.' The skipper's command was followed by a series of rings on the bridge telegraph as the Third Officer gave the handle two firm swivels forward and back bringing it to rest in the section that said 'Full Ahead'.

There was a pause for a few seconds and then the telegraph rang again as acknowledgement came from somewhere down in the depths of the ship. The instruction had been received and understood and was being duly carried out. And that was all there was to it, apart from an increase in vibration rising through the bulkheads as the machinery below gathered momentum, a mushrooming plume of black oily smoke that began belching from the tall funnel—and a brief toot as a warning to nearby shipping.

'Full ahead, she is, sir,' answered the Third Officer. From then on all it seemed he had to do was stand on the bridge completely sheltered from the elements and keep a sharp look-out ahead, glancing occasionally at the compass to make sure course was being maintained by the helmsman, while the bows of the ship plunged resolutely on from one sea to the next, and the engines that were making it all possible never faltered in their monotonous 'thud, thud, thud . . .'

This was a completely new world to Lightoller and it was taking some getting used to, but he had realised that unless he was prepared to settle for nothing else but voyages to the 'Nitrate Coast', which seemed to be the only place left for sailing ships to go these days, then he would need to change his outlook.

The passage home from Iquique in the *Knight of St. Michael* had been a long and gruelling one. It was not Cape Horn that had given them most of their troubles, but the doldrums where they had spent six long weeks enduring endless hours of pulley-hauley, day after day, night after night, pulling the yards round one way then the other in the struggle to cross the line and pick up the Trades again. When the sun was not cooking them alive they were being bombarded by tropical downpours so heavy that the oil was washed off their oilskins. They might edge their way over the equator with hopes raised that soon they would be picking up the wind, but only to drift back south when the wind never came. That happened to them five times. The complete passage from Iquique to Liverpool took them 165 days, almost double the average time for the run. By the end of it Lightoller was totally exhausted and came to the reluctant conclusion that, no matter how much he had been in love with sailing ships—and that took into account all the hard times as well as the good—steamships perhaps had something going for them after all. He could not put it off any longer, he realised. He went up for his Mate's ticket, sailed through with ease, and decided that Elder Dempster was the company offering the best prospects for a young man going into steam. Things were looking up these days on the West African Coast which was Elder Dempster's main trading territory. The British Government had recently pumped a lot of aid into their colonies down that way with a corresponding upsurge in trade, and Elder Dempster were reaping the full benefit of it. More ships were headed there and, with the extra ships, more men were needed to crew them.

The Marine Superintendent of Elder Dempster's African Royal Mail Service was Captain John Rattray, who rejoiced in the dubious sobriquet 'Three Fingered Jack' having had two of his fingers bitten off by a negro in some lurid incident down the West Coast. He liked the look of this young 'hard case' he was interviewing who reeled off his experience—and experiences—with such a nonchalant air that even a hardened old salt the likes of Rattray had to be impressed.

And so at the age of 21 and already a veteran of one shipwreck, a fire at sea, a cyclone, and numerous other adventures, Charles Herbert Lightoller bade a sad farewell to his old friends the windjammers and went into steam. The feel of the deck of a sailing ship as she heeled under a fresh North-Easter, the sound of the wind in the rigging, he would miss it all, yes, but there was no denying the advantages of steam: much greater comfort, better and more varied food, and, not least, higher pay. Also the voyages were shorter: instead of being away at sea for months that could add up to a year and more, his trips now lasted a matter of weeks, which kept him more in touch with the world.

He found that West Africa offered him yet another novel experience. In this trade most of the loading and unloading—passengers and cargo alike—was done by surf boats while the ship lay at anchor offshore. When working along the coast a ship carried two crews. The white crew worked the ship while a black crew worked the cargo with their special training in the loading and discharging techniques peculiar to the surf ports. The first stop would be made usually at Freetown, Sierra Leone, to pick up the 'Kroo' labour which consisted of about sixty boys led by a headman and his deputy. The ship would then set off on her voyage down the coast to her scheduled ports of call—such places as Grand Bassam on the Ivory Coast, Takoradi, Winneba, Cape Coast and Accra on the Gold Coast, and various stops along the Nigerian Coast such as Lagos, Opobo and Old Calabar.

In most cases the 'port' was little more than an open roadstead. On arrival the ship would anchor two to three miles out beyond the surf and then first thing in the morning a great armada of boats, perhaps fifty or sixty of them, would begin making their way out to the ship, their crews paddling furiously through the surf. The boats which were owned either by the shipping company or a local merchant were manned by boys recruited from one local village. A contract would be entered into between the local shipping agent and the village headman on terms of payment according to how many trips were to be made. To Lightoller's surprise it was a contract in which full payment was made before the work was begun.

When it came to the loading and unloading, everybody in the ship, officers included and often the Captain, mucked in on the stevedoring work, loading and stowing and manning the winches to hoist and lower the freight between the ship and the boats. The surf boats, which were heavily built and specially designed for the job, could carry anything up to two tons. Once each boat had completed its contracted number of trips a brightly coloured flag would be flown from its bow and with that the crew would return to their village for 'de rest'.

Since going to sea Lightoller had developed a great love for messing about in small boats but for him there was little to beat the thrill of riding in a surf boat with five boys either side of him paddling for all their worth whilst the coxswain, standing up at the stern with his curious rudder—a four-foot pole with three prongs on the end——skilfully steered them through the mountainous green swell.

These were conditions that could be extremely dangerous and demanded very special skills in seamanship, and not just in the boat but on shore where the surf man was stationed. The surf man would stand on the beach holding a long bamboo staff with a flag on the end which he kept in a dipped position until he saw the right moment for the surf boat to make its final run for the shore. Half a mile or so out on the edge of the breakers the surf boat crew would wait for the signal, back paddling to keep the boat in position while the coxswain held them stern on to the seas as they soared to the top of the swell one moment then down into a trough the next.

Ten, twenty minutes, half an hour might go by before they would get the signal that the moment was right to go but they must be patient, the greatest incentive being that their lives depended on it. The man from his position on shore could see what the men in their boat on the edge of the surf could not.

Then at last up would go the surf man's staff while he raced back and forth along the beach wildly waving his flag to make sure that it could be seen from the boat. And now having put all their trust in his judgement the boat crew, shouting their native cries, would dig their paddles into the water and drive like mad for the shore. Suddenly the boat would be picked up on the back of a mountainous comber and hurled towards the beach. But the control and judgement of the surf-boat men have to be precise. They must keep the bow of their boat just ahead of the crest, but not too far ahead, otherwise the boat would be pushed further and further up at the stern and do a somersault into the sea with everyone almost certainly being drowned. But similarly they must not let themselves fall too far behind the crest, to become stranded helplessly by the drag in the path of the next breaker which would crash down on top of them with equally disastrous results.

So expert were the surf-boat crews and their signalmen that accidents were rare but Lightoller was to learn just how dangerous the West African surf could be when not treated with the proper respect.

Not all the ports of call were on the coast. Sometimes the ship would move up river to places like Warri, Sapele, and Benin in total contrast to the surf ports of Cape Coast and Accra. Getting to these humid inland destinations meant navigating up miles of winding rivers and creeks through jungle and mangrove swamps. It could be a tricky job with a five-thousand-ton ship. At some places the bend in the river would be so sharp that the bows had to be driven up into the jungle while the tide swung the stern round to allow the vessel to negotiate the turn. It was easy to get lost in such territory with so many creeks and inlets looking exactly the same. Many a ship had found itself 'up the wrong creek', sometimes getting stuck and unable to get out for days.

Occasionally they took on a local pilot, but usually it was all left to the local knowledge of the skipper built on years of experience on the West Africa run, who knew the landmarks and the makeshift signposts that marked the way. It might be that a sign carved on a tree meant 'Take the right fork for Warri,' or a white mark on a stump, 'Turn left for Benin.'

Every so often the ship would pass a clearing to reveal a native village with all the inhabitants standing spellbound watching this great iron monster belching its black cloud, go rumbling by almost at arm's length.

He was having a good time in the African Royal Mail, never being far from port, having so many new sights to see and interesting people to meet. Banquets that were sometimes given aboard ship could be entertaining affairs and not without incident particularly when the hospitality was being extended to local native chiefs.

Lightoller never ceased to marvel at the sight of a native chief decked out in all his full tribal regalia heading out to the ship in his magnificent war canoe, twenty men paddling either side making a good ten knots. Waiting at the gangway to meet the guest as he arrived alongside, he found that often, instead of being addressed by some obscure tribal utterance, a hand would be graciously proffered with a very refined greeting of 'Good Evening' delivered in perfect English. Lightoller would find it even more surprising to learn that the man had not only been educated in England, but graduated at Oxford or Cambridge with a first class degree in Law. It would always be a source of fascination to him how they could then simply return home and go back to their old native ways and customs again.

But there would be the times at these functions when he discovered that, no matter how much a man had been educated in the ways of the civilised world, the old tribal instincts of aggression could soon come out if one chief upset another or a gaffe should unwittingly be committed. Sometimes they might be entertaining fifty chiefs or more where old scores between some of them were still far from settled. One chief's canoe ramming his rival in the race to get alongside could be enough for a full-scale battle to erupt. Then it would take all the tact and calming influence of the skipper to settle things down.

Sometimes the meal would be progressing happily, with everyone having a pleasant time, until all was upset by a trifle—almost literally in one case: Elder Dempster had been fitting out their ships with refrigeration, and apart from the obvious benefits to the food supply in those climes, it also meant that ice cream could be carried on the menu. To most ordinary thinking white men there could be few things more harmless and enjoyable than a scoop or two of ice cream for dessert—but in one particular instance the palates of the guests did not react in the same way. When the ice cream arrived and the first few guests took a spoonful they instantly shot up from their seats, eyes blazing and looking for the nearest implement with which to inflict the most damage on the man responsible for this outrage. The skipper looked worried. It did not at once occur to him that they had quite simply never eaten ice cream before and the cold shock of it entering their mouths had driven them into a frenzy. Ice cream to them was eqivalent to something piping hot to a white man and they were convinced that a trick had been played on them. To an African chief this was a serious insult. It was an anxious moment, and only the hasty intervention of those among the guests better acquainted with the mysteries of English desserts, and the calm way the skipper and his officers carried on eating it induced the chief to take a happier view of the ice cream. Ice cream was never served again in such circumstances.

If Lightoller's life at sea over the next couple of years was better than it had ever been, it was all about to change with his appointment to the African Royal Mail Steam Ship *Niagara*, an aging rustbound vessel that had undoubtedly seen better days. But the ship did not bother Lightoller so much as her skipper, one Captain William Waters—better known about the Port of Liverpool as 'Bully' Waters.

He was a notorious tyrant hated by all who had ever been under his command. So hated was Waters that he could not walk the streets of Liverpool in safety. Everywhere he went he took a cab for fear he might be set upon by one of the many who held a bitter grudge against him. Waters loved to boast that he had killed two men. That was almost true. They had in fact committed suicide, driven to it by his constant brow-beating and bullying. For Lightoller, life under Waters' command would be no different. He was determined, however, to stand up to this portly little martinet with the hysterical high-pitched whine and the puffed up crimson face with matching nose that glistened persistently under the heat of the West African sun.

It was a mystery to Lightoller why nobody had put paid to Waters once and for all, and even more mystifying how he had kept his command. But then he was an old sparring partner of 'Three Fingered Jack' having been Rattray's Mate once upon a time and they were old pals. Rattray must surely have been the only friend Waters had left in the world. He was obviously a loyal one because so well known was Waters' lurid reputation around Liverpool that no one else would have entertained for a moment giving him command of a ship.

So far in his sea career Lightoller had been fortunate in the skippers he had served with—even 'Jock' Sutherland who, for all his reckless ways, was at least a likable man. But the only emotion Waters ever seemed able to stir up in people was loathing. He also drank and the more he drank, the worse he got, particularly first thing in the morning when the ship was loading and discharging cargo. He would emerge hung-over from his cabin, lurching about the deck, touring the hatches, continually mopping the beads of sweat from his livid red face, shouting, swearing and complaining about the slow progress of the work. He argued and quarrelled with his officers, tormenting them to the limit of their endurance. Waters was unbearable enough under normal conditions but add to it the heat, the hard work, and constant thirst, it was hardly surprising he drove many a man to the brink—and one or two beyond it.

Lightoller would just stand there and shout back at him but always managed to control himself until Waters would go to another hatch and try bullying somebody else. Lightoller noticed that Waters had the knack of stopping short at the moment when the man he was confronting looked on the point of erupting. Like all bullies, he realised, particularly small ones, he was a coward. Eventually Lightoller hit upon a very good way of dealing with Waters.

One morning early, while cargo was loading, Waters happened along as usual with his criticisms and complaints about the progress of the work and the way it was being done. 'Stop everything, stop!' Lightoller commanded. All work stopped and Lightoller stood there, arms folded, glaring at Waters with the clear message that the Captain was going to get everyone's undivided attention to all he had to say. Not until Waters had finished his grumbling would work start again. Waters was, for once, lost for words. He just muttered something incoherent about 'the slowness' and stalked off back to his cabin, mopping his face more vigorously than ever, had another drink of gin and went back to sleep. But Waters was not finished with Lightoller yet—he did not intend to let his subordinate get the better of *him*.

The *Niagara* had arrived off Grand Bassam on the Ivory Coast to take
on a cargo of mahogany logs. But there had been a storm out in the
Atlantic and as a result the sea had banked up along the coast and the
surf was too high for boats to work in. Waters had to make up his
mind whether to wait for the weather to moderate or forget the cargo
and head for home, this being the last call of the voyage. He ordered
the Chief Officer to take the ship's surf boat, go in as far as possible
and try to make contact with the beach to see if they intended to send
out any logs. The Chief took a crew of boys and set off towards the
shore. Once he had got as close in as he dared he anchored the boat
and started trying to signal the beach. The surf was terrifying and
there was little chance of any work being done that day; but Waters
was not satisfied. He got more and more impatient, complaining that
if the man got nearer in he might stand a better chance of attracting
some attention. Then he called for Lightoller to come to the bridge.
'Why the hell can't the Chief get in touch with the beach? He's too far
out!' he snapped. Lightoller suggested that it was difficult to tell from
the ship but agreed that it did look as though he might get a little
nearer in.

Lightoller had fallen for it. Waters leered at him through his
narrow little eyes. 'I don't know what the blazes you fellows are *afraid*
of,' he sneered. It was a perfectly calculated bait for Lightoller and he
fell for it: nobody ever accused him of being afraid. Waters jeered at
Lightoller, 'In that case, take the gig and see what *you* can do.'

The whole idea was madness. The conditions were risky enough
for a surf boat that was double ended and designed for the job, but for
a rowing boat with a square stern it could not have been more
dangerous. Lightoller, however, was too intent on picking up
Waters' gauntlet to consider the risks involved. As he stormed off
the bridge to organise the boat and a crew Waters called after him
'And while you're at it, take a lead-line and see how far I can bring
the ship in!' That meant he would need to take a Quartermaster
along.

Lightoller with three boys and a rather apprehensive Quartermaster rowed away in the boat to take soundings with the lead-line first of
all, as ordered by Waters, and then to head on further in to make
contact with the other boat. When they reached it Lightoller realised
that the Chief Officer could not possibly have been any closer to the

beach. As the two boats came together they were rising and falling like stones in the heaving swell right on the edge of the breakers. Still no contact with the shore had been made.

Lightoller decided to move a little further up the coast to see if he might have better luck. It took all his skill and concentration at the tiller to steer the boat through the surging swell. One moment the boys would be rowing for all their worth up to the top of one curler, then careering down into a deep valley the next with the boat all the time perilously close to the edge of the surf. With much energetic flag waving Lightoller and the Quartermaster tried as best they could to attract attention on the shore but it was hopeless in that kind of sea. Being out of sight half the time when the boat became hidden in a trough did not help their efforts. Lightoller was getting angry and frustrated. He was determined not to give Waters the pleasure of gloating over his failure.

And then it happened. Whether it was because they had been paying too much attention to the shore instead of handling the boat, or that one sea had decided to break further out than the rest, or simply that the officer at the tiller was too preoccupied in trying to prove something to his skipper, Lightoller would never be sure. He turned his head towards the sea and there it was—a great overhanging wall of green water higher than all the rest, with the sun filtering through, about to crash down on top of them. Lightoller gave the order to row straight at it, but although he managed to get the bow of the boat round in time the situation was already hopeless. The great wave came tumbling down on top of them driving them under. Lightoller felt the keel of the boat hit the sand and then, remarkably, the boat returned to the surface with everybody still sitting in their places. But another huge curler was coming in and this time there would be no second chance. They were now beyond the edge of the surf and beyond the point of no return. Lightoller shouted and yelled at the boys to keep rowing into it in a last desperate hope that they might still be able to pull clear, but they just cowered over their oars at the sight of the massive sea thundering towards them. When it came crashing down on the gig and its five occupants, the boat was instantly overturned.

As Lightoller was thrown out and went under he realised that the lead-line they had been using to take soundings was wrapped round his feet. Now followed a desperate underwater struggle to untangle himself. While he fought with the line he was being rolled over and over by the force of the water. After much frantic tugging he managed to get free of it. When he came gasping to the surface the boat was upside down and there was no sign of anyone. Then he saw the Quartermaster's hands waving limply above the water. He was drowning. He grabbed him by the wrist and pulled him towards the upturned boat, getting the man's hand onto the keel. He was still conscious enough to try and pull himself up onto it, but just as he was about to succeed another wave broke over them and washed him off. Lightoller tried again to hoist the Quartermaster up but when he had almost got him there another wave came and again threw him off. By now Lightoller was in trouble himself. He did all he could for the other man, grabbing some gratings and oars that were floating about in the surf and shoved them under his arms. That was the last he saw of the Quartermaster, as instinct told him he must now try and swim for the shore.

He discarded his jacket and tried to remove his trousers but they kept catching round his ankles. His attempts to make swimming easier had only put him in greater difficulty. As each comber rose up and broke, it came smashing down on top of him, tons of water, forcing him under and bowling him along the seabed. No sooner would he find himself back on the surface, lungs bursting, and panting for air than the sea would come again to beat him mercilessly under once more.

He was drowning and was beginning to submit to it and then into his mind came his sister Janie and what he had once told her—'Don't you bother, the sea is not wet enough to drown me, I'll *never* be drowned . . . I'll *never* be drowned . . . I'll *never* be drowned . . .' It kept going through his mind again and again and making him more and more angry. After all those reassurances he had given her here he was really drowning. He cursed the sea, hating it for what it was trying to do to him. Damn the sea, he would not let it beat him. He must not surrender to it. From somewhere he summoned a last reserve of breath and strength. He was determined to live. Then something told him, don't run away from it swim into it.

He turned and faced the sea. If the sea really wanted him then she would have to fight for him. He threw himself head on at the next breaker roaring in. In that instant he was whisked upwards and hurled along as though he had mounted the back of some winged steed that had galloped mercifully in to the rescue and plucked him to safety. If there were really such things as miracles then this felt like one as he found himself being thrown down onto the sand and swept up the beach—but he was not out of trouble yet.

The beach was steep and he had nothing left in him to claw those last few crucial yards. His lungs were full of water and he was only half conscious. The sea could still claim him as he was dragged in again by the backwash. Then with the next comber that came he was swept back up the sands.

Now she was toying with him.

He could see some figures running along the beach towards him, joining hands in a human chain. He felt a hand grab his wrist, and then he passed out.

When he came round he was lying there alone, his trousers still round his ankles. His lungs felt as though they were on fire and weighed down by lead weights. He frantically gasped and hunted for breath and went into a fit of coughing and choking. As more seawater came up, the breathing got easier. He was recovering. But the negroes who had hauled him out evidently had not thought he would. Having got him up the beach they came to the conclusion that he was dead, and it being their taboo not to touch a dead white man, they dashed off to tell the authorities. But there would be no sign of a body when they arrived. Instead it had hitched up its trousers, found its way to a nearby sawmill and was occupied in knocking back a few stiff whiskies. Lightoller had certainly earned them, having just succeeded in being the first white man ever to swim through the surf at Grand Bassam—and live.

But the Quartermaster and three boys had not lived and 'Bully' Waters for once in his life was sorry. He realised he had been wrong to goad Lightoller into going on that suicide mission—even if Lightoller himself had been over-impulsive in rising to the challenge. Waters had been taught a lesson but at a tragic cost and there would be hell to pay when he got back to Liverpool and Rattray learnt the news.

As for Lightoller he had kept his word after all to his sister Janie in what was yet another remarkable escape from the clutches of the sea.

But while he was deciding whether he had finally had enough of 'Bully' Waters and West Africa, his trials, it seemed, were not yet over. On the passage home he caught a heavy dose of malaria. His temperature soared to over 106°F and once again it looked as though his life was hanging in the balance. However in one last kill-or-cure effort his fellow officers rolled him up tightly like a mummy with hot bottles and blankets, loaded him with quinine and succeeded in breaking the fever, and he eventually recovered.

After that he was left in no doubt at all that he had definitely had enough of the West African Coast—in fact he was beginning to wonder if he had not had enough of the sea.

12

Lightoller had arrived at the crossroads. He was undecided about his future. After spending some weeks in convalescence at his lodgings in Liverpool he was now more or less fully recovered from his heavy bout of malaria—and his experiences with 'Bully' Waters and the surf at Grand Bassam. But somehow for once the prospect of going back to sea did not appeal to him. There were a number of alternatives he had considered—which all required capital and therefore could not be pursued. Lightoller's constant dream was to find his pot of gold at the end of the rainbow: he would be a rich man and his own master. Of one thing he was certain—the sea would never make him a rich man, so why waste his time on her anymore? That was the mood of disillusionment Lightoller was in when he picked up the newspaper and saw the headlines:

THE WORLD'S NEW GOLDFIELDS! FABULOUS RICHES TO BE FOUND IN THE NEW ELDORADO! WONDERFUL YIELD IN THE KLONDIKE!

That was it! He was off to the Yukon. He had not seen the other headlines which told of 'Terrible Mortality! Two Thousand Deaths In Three Years! More Famine and Heavy Mortality Inevitable! Warnings to Emigrants!' Even if he had seen the warnings and taken notice it would have made no difference. He was determined to go. He sold almost all he had; his sextant, telescope, binoculars, even his officer's uniforms. There was one thing however he did not sell—his banjo. That was coming with him.

He took a ship to Montreal—this time as a passenger at the cheapest fare he could find—and then a long slow train journey thousands of miles across country via Winnipeg to Edmonton. On his travels he met another seaman called Bill, headed the same way with the same ambitions, so they teamed up. It was a tedious journey and Lightoller was glad he'd brought the old banjo. It helped to pass many a boring hour not just for himself and Bill who happened to be a useful singer and dancer, but for their fellow travellers also headed for the gold trail . . . even if sea shanties were getting just a little inappropriate by the time they reached their destination.

Edmonton was thriving on the gold rush, having benefited very profitably from some heavy promotion by the town's Board of Trade who had advertised it as the 'perfect route' to the goldfields. 'The Back Door to the Yukon' they declared; 'the trail was good all Winter,' and 'the Klondike could be reached with horses in ninety days.' In fact of the four main routes to the Yukon the Edmonton route was by far the most impractical. It involved either a 2500-mile trip along the Mackenzie River almost to the Arctic Circle, or the 'short' 1700-mile journey via the Peace River. The routes were not just impractical—they were killers.

Before Edmonton put itself on the gold-rush map it was a small village of seven hundred people with one main street, one hotel and one bank. When Lightoller arrived there early in 1898, four thousand men and four thousand animals were jamming the streets. The whole area for miles around was white with tents. Lightoller would not see a wider cross section of people anywhere than among these thousands that had swallowed the advertisement and converged on Edmonton to take the 'perfect route' to the goldfields. They included frontiersmen, Texas cowboys, Chinese and Indians, doctors, dentists, lawyers, a large complement of sailors, a D'Oyly Carte Opera singer who never stopped singing, and even an English lord who came with a party of fifteen friends, an army of servants and more than four tons of supplies, which included seventy-five cases of the best vintage champagne.

The conveyances he saw were as varied as the people. There was a device with wheels made of wine barrels which its owner christened 'The Duck' to which swamp, snow, river and mountain would present no obstacle. The whole thing fell apart within a few miles. Then there was the steam sledge called 'I Will' propelled by a huge spiked drum complete with trailers tacked on behind for carrying equipment and supplies, and of course for bringing back the gold. A huge crowd gathered as it prepared to set off for the Klondike in a flurry of smoke and steam. It merely succeeded in bedding itself deeper and deeper into the earth, flinging up a great shower of snow and clods of frozen mud into the faces of the spectators. So much for 'I Will'. The most amusing sight to Lightoller was the man who set off on a bicycle with jars of Bovril fastened on the back.

Not so humorous was the temperature. Lightoller thought he would never be any colder than the time he found himself on the edge of the Antarctic with the *Primrose Hill*, but he was wrong. He discovered that at times the temperature in Edmonton could be as low as 40 degrees F below freezing, and with only a tent for shelter, it took some getting used to, even for a 'hard case' such as he. But there was always the thought of that grand cache of glittering gold he would be bringing back from the Klondike to convince him that it was all worthwhile. As he got himself set up for the trail with horse, stores, rifle and the very essential gold pan, he and his partner decided not to weigh themselves and their horses down too heavily with a lot of unnecessary food supplies. They would rely on being able to shoot what they required along the way. In the meantime their staple diet would be beans and bacon.

And so after joining forces with two other hopeful young prospectors from the Black Hills off they set on a heading of WNW for the Klondike and their fortune. Lightoller could not help wondering what his shipmates would have thought of him had they seen him then. It was certainly all very far removed from the *Niagara*, 'Bully' Waters and the West African Coast, and there would be little chance of being troubled by malaria out here.

It was still winter and conditions were atrocious but Lightoller was undaunted. He had been told by an experienced prospector that the trail would not bother a sailor like him, and he was determined to prove it so. No tenderfoot was he. The going was painfully slow, little more than a mile an hour through forests of spruce—acre on acre of trees which had fallen down and barred the way. Then there were the swamps where the horses would go in up to their bellies and have to be unloaded of their 250-pound packs, piece by piece, before they could be hauled out. When the horses were not nearly breaking their legs getting through the fallen timber or plunging headlong into swamps they were battling to get through the blizzards with the snow sometimes five foot deep.

And then came the rivers, rivers the like of which Lightoller had never encountered before. It was fine while they were still frozen, but when winter ended they were faced with the prospect of crossing through a swirling torrent of water that careered down from the snow melting on the mountains. And that was not the only difficulty that confronted them. With the rushing water came great blocks of ice, bumping and grinding along together, that would easily flatten a man on his horse that happened to get in the way.

Lightoller now realised what the man meant about the advantages of being a sailor. He was always the one to venture across first with the line, locating a suitable spot beforehand on the opposite bank further down stream to allow for the push of the water against the rope and his horse. Then off he would go on his diagonal course through the ice-cold water that would swirl around his legs as he went.

He had to get his calculations just right because if he missed his spot at the first attempt he would have to return to his starting point on the bank and begin all over again. Once he reached the other side with the line, the shuttle service with the raft would begin, back and forth, back and forth, until all the equipment and supplies were across. The ferrying job had become more prolonged as another three had now joined the group, making the number up to seven.

They had been very proud of crossing the Pembina River, until they came upon the Athabasca. When Lightoller saw it his heart sank. It looked at least two miles across. Their two original companions from the Western States who up to then had kept repeatedly saying 'We're from the Black Hills, we ain't no tenderfeet' immediately had second thoughts about even attempting to cross this great barrier of racing, tumbling water that lay before them. As for Lightoller, his spirits did not stay down for long. They were going to cross and what was more they were going to cross it there and then. Merely because evening was coming on there would be no question of 'Let's make camp now and wait until daybreak.' Better to have dry clothes and the river behind them in the morning, rather than wake up with the job still facing them. By nightfall they had compromised by getting the job half done, having found a fording place and arrived at an island in the middle. But as they prepared to bed down for the night they became aware of a new menace threatening them from the river. It was rising rapidly and before long the whole island would be submerged. There was evidence that water regularly covered it.

At first light with the river still rising and the island getting noticeably smaller Lightoller set about trying to find a fording spot. Their next target was not yet going to be the opposite bank of the river but another island that lay adjacent about a hundred yards away. It looked much more substantial than the one they were on and would, they hoped, be the last stepping stone before they reached the other side. Lightoller could find no place to ford, so he would have to swim his horse across. So far the animal had done all that had been asked of him. Lightoller was sure he would have climbed the roof of a house if he had asked him—which inspired him to call the horse Rufus. He had picked him out of a corral of fifty or sixty. He did not look much with his unkempt shaggy coat and slight stiffness of movement, but there was nevertheless something about the old fellow that attracted Lightoller. He looked like a horse that would stick with a man and not easily let him down. But if Rufus had so far lived up to all expectations and much more, gamely tackling every mountain, river and swamp that had confronted him, he most certainly did not like the looks of the racing white flood of the Athabasca. Just the sight of it made the horse excited and upset, but he would have to try. Lightoller with lariat attached mounted Rufus and, with much urging and kicking, persuaded the horse to enter the raging torrent. As the horse went in, snorting heavily in protest, the freezing water foamed about his legs. Step by step they got deeper and deeper and then, sensing that he was losing touch with solid ground, the horse took fright and tried to swing round and go back the way he had come. Lightoller was aware of the dangers of trying to force a frightened horse to go where it did not want to but in this situation he had no choice. He landed the horse a heavy smack on the nose which was enough to do the trick. Suddenly Rufus pricked up his ears, stretched himself out and was away through the water swimming as though he had been born to nothing else. Before the rider knew it they were mounting the opposite bank, Rufus jumping and trembling all over and going wild with excitement.

But now came the job of getting the others across, starting with Bill who, being a sailor like Lightoller, was confident enough about facing the water, but unlike Lightoller was no horseman. He immediately got into difficulty. As soon as he entered the deep water his horse went over and they were swept down towards the rapids. They looked doomed but Lightoller realised there was one chance to save his friend. Coiling up the lariat he galloped off downstream to the lower end of the island. When he got there he drove his horse on as deep into the water as he dare while still being sure of a firm footing. Here he waited for Bill as he was swept past. He realised his judgement would have to be near perfect. He would only get one throw. He must make it land somewhere near so that he could easily swim to it—or if he was really lucky get it near enough for the man to grab onto the rope and still keep hold of his horse. Bill and his horse came sweeping by. Lightoller judged his moment then cast the rope. It could not have been better. It landed right alongside him. Lightoller in the meantime had got his end of the lariat round his waist and, yelling to his companion to keep hold of his horse, took the strain. It was a heavy struggle; Bill hung on to the rope with one hand and to the halter of his horse with the other, while Lightoller wrestled with the rope, concentrating on not being pulled into the water himself. But gradually by easing his horse backwards Lightoller managed to swing them round and pull them into shallower water and safety. It had been a close thing. If they had been swept on down to the rapids neither man nor horse would have stood a chance of surviving.

As for the others who were still marooned they just could not face it. They ended up waiting until the following day when Lightoller, who had managed to ford the rest of the way to the far bank, came back in an Indian canoe which he 'borrowed', and ferried them across, towing their horses behind. By then the island was almost under water and they were preparing to take to the trees. For all that they had kept saying 'We ain't no tenderfeet' they seemed to be relying on Lightoller a great deal. But there remained the problem of the party's equipment and supplies which were still on the rapidly shrinking island. Lightoller had to start a very hasty shuttle service with the canoe to get all their things off before it disappeared completely.

Once again he was in his element. Handling one of these canoes in fast water took a lot of skill and practice but he seemed to take to it as naturally as the Indians that used them all the time. After he had towed the canoe with its load to an eddy of calm water he would pick a similar spot on the opposite bank down river to aim for. Then with a good firm push of the canoe, in he leapt, landing expertly on his knees and feet together to begin paddling as hard as he could for the shore. The canoe would tear across the river with water foaming all around it. As soon as he got near the eddy he was making for he did not fall into the trap of slowing up but kept going for it flat out so that when the bows of the canoe entered the dead water, the river sweeping down swung the stern round, bringing the boat to rest alongside the bank in one neat movement. Much as Lightoller enjoyed his fun in the canoe he was exhausted at the end of the day with the constant ferrying to and fro. By the time he had got the very last of their packs and equipment to the mainland the island had disappeared, trees and all. They had crossed the Athabasca—and largely thanks to a master mariner's horsemanship!

The one item which had miraculously survived it all so far was the banjo. It seemed capable of coming through all the worst kinds of ill treatment that a musical instrument could be subjected to. Even after a prolonged ducking in the water it came up sounding as sweet as ever. Not only did it give them some entertainment at the end of the day round the camp fire but it helped relax the tensions that had built up after a hard day's battle against the terrain and the elements —times when Lightoller had to exercise all his powers of self control not to launch into a full-scale argument with anyone who came near him.

The gold prospectors were not the only ones who enjoyed the music. When Lightoller struck up on the banjo the local Indians would emerge from out of the darkness and surround them listening intently to the music, their granite faces registering no expression at all. And then as soon as he had put the banjo down they would gather round peering into it trying to work out where the sound came from. Those Indians were friendly but not all of them were. Indians still reigned supreme in this country and had resented the invasion of the gold stampede.

After one group of Klondikers had destroyed Indian bear traps in which their horses had got caught, the Indians retaliated by attacking their camp, wrecking the wagons and equipment and stampeding the horses. Lightoller however never encountered any problems with Indians, and eventually he and his companions did not even bother to keep watch at night.

On and on they trekked, sometimes plodding through a forest for days without seeing the light of day and then suddenly emerging into a great wide open space with nothing but endless snow-covered prairie before them. It was bleak, monotonous country, desolate and rolling, where they were forever getting caught up in snowstorms and were always wet through. Above all the cold was intense. But none of these discomforts bothered Lightoller. The resistance and toughness of his constitution had been proven a dozen times over before now. All he thought about was finding gold. He was bitten by the bug and as far as he was concerned daylight could not come soon enough so that he could be on his way again and be yet one day nearer to finding his dream.

Everything in this country seemed so much nearer than it really was. He would aim for a gap in the mountains that looked no more than a day away and find it took three days to get there. Looking up at the Rocky Mountains towering thousands of feet above him, he would think to himself he could be tobogganing down them within an hour if he wanted. Just the foothills were fifty miles away. He was struck by the eerie silence. In the thin, rarefied atmosphere the bough of a tree breaking four miles distant would echo round the hills like a gun going off a few yards away. When the snow came down it was like concentrated powdery dust, so thick that at times he wondered if it might suffocate him. Then they would lose the trail—what there was of it. In fact the so called Peace River trail was virtually non-existent, just a part of the advertising put out by Edmonton's Board of Trade to profit from the gold stampede. It had been a highly successful public-relations exercise but many of those who had been taken in by it would pay with their lives.

'Gold!' It happened while they were prospecting in a creek along the way. Whenever they met water they would always pan on the off-chance that something might show up. On this occasion something did. When the usual pan swirling ritual had been performed and the mercury added to the residue of black sand, there it was—gold gleaming up at them bright and clear. There only remained one last test, the test of hydrochloric acid which would make it shine all the brighter if it was gold. It so happened that the member of the expedition who had got the hydrochloric acid in his pack was away trying to shoot their supper, but they had some acetic acid so they decided in the meantime to try that. Sure enough it gleamed all the brighter. They had done it, they had struck gold! More panning was done and more gold appeared. Everyone was beside themselves with excitement as they began planning the layout of their camp, the setting up of the sluice boxes and all the other engineering works essential to the perfect gold mine. Yes, they were all rich at last.

Just then their companion arrived back in camp with the usual bad news that he had bagged no game, to be greeted with the good news that they had struck gold. As a formality he got out the hydrochloric to put their find to the test, just to confirm what they already knew. They gathered round to watch it being poured on and see their gold gleam even more brightly . . . with the result that as soon as the acid made contact, the shining gold went black and disappeared. It was iron pyrites—fool's gold—and their morale was shattered. But Lightoller did not stay depressed for long. He was looking at the bright side and wanting to be back on the trail again. Why, for all they knew the real thing could be waiting for them over the next hill. But all the gold in the world was not going to solve a new problem that was beginning to loom. They had become desperately short of food. Despite heavy rationing in the more recent days their supply of bacon and beans had almost reached its limit. The original idea to shoot what food they required had been a dismal failure. Their total tally

had been one bull moose, a partridge and a porcupine. Lightoller shot
the porcupine which they boiled three times a day for seven days
before they could get their teeth into it . . . teeth that were getting
gradually looser from malnutrition. But they were not the only ones
having a hard time. So cruel was the winter that even the Indians
were starving and had started burning out whole areas of forest for
game. If the Indians in their natural habitat were having such trouble
surviving off the land, outsiders were going to find it virtually
impossible, and there were those in Lightoller's company who were
beginning to realise that, but to him at that stage it would have been
inconceivable to give up. In the end he was forced to.

The moment of decision came when he and Bill, who had been away
from the camp prospecting, returned to discover that the rest had
gone. They had finally decided to turn back. That did not bother
Lightoller so much as the paltry share of the food they had been left.
But once he and his partner had simmered down and set about
reviewing their whole situation they realised if they were to go on,
their survival depended on much more than just a few extra days'
food. There was only one thing for it. They would have to kill one of
the horses, smoke the meat and hope it would keep them in food long
enough to reach their next target, Peace River Landing. It was a
drastic decision to take, but it would have to be done. A coin could be
tossed to decide whose horse was for the slaughter. It was all so
callous. Was there no other way? To put a bullet through the brain of
the beast that had been a loyal and faithful friend through thick and
thin along the trail seemed so ruthless and inhumane. For Lightoller
the thought of murdering his dear old pal Rufus was bad enough, but
then to sit down and eat him was just too much to contemplate.

He took one look at the horse and began loading him up for the
long trail back. He felt a dismal failure and was racked with disappointment, but he knew there could be no alternative. He also came
to realise that even if they had brought themselves to shooting one of
the horses, their chances of making it across the many hundreds of
gruelling miles that still lay before them to the North-West, where
the real gold was to be found, were slim. The whole expedition,
and the way he had gone about it, had been hopeless right from the
start.

From that moment the search for gold was replaced by a new priority—survival. Estimating that they had three days' food left between them, they set out on the return trail keeping one thought firmly in their minds: 'Don't lose heart in the mountains,' the maxim of all men experienced in the ways of that rugged, unforgiving country. Amongst that lonely expanse of prairie, precipice and endless rolling mountains, Lightoller realised how easy it would be just to lie down and die. But again, his upbringing with the sea would come into its own to combat that dangerous feeling of hopelessness and futility which could be felt so strongly in those remote parts, even in the company of another.

They caught the others up at the Athabasca. As Lightoller and his partner happened upon them sitting at the water's edge dismally surveying that great stretch of forbidding flood it became obvious what their ploy had been; leave a quantity of food small enough to make Lightoller think twice about going on, but just enough for him to get back to the Athabasca and help them with the return crossing. Right then Lightoller felt like leaving them all there to rot, but shrewdness got the better of his anger as he set about the task of organising the crossing. When he had got two of them to the other side, while the rest, plus the all important provisions were still to cross, he decided the time was right to strike his bargain. He informed them that because they had behaved so selfishly over the food he did not feel in the mood to be ferryman any longer so from then on they could take the canoe and get on with it themselves. Lightoller felt mean in taking such a cruel advantage but in this case he thought it justified and it did achieve his purpose. He and Bill got their fair share of the provisions and in return Lightoller completed the job of ferrying everyone, horses, packs and all back across the treacherous flood. He got them across the Pembina River too. If by then the boys from the Black Hills had conveniently forgotten how to say 'We ain't no tenderfeet' Lightoller took sadistic delight in reminding them at every possible opportunity. With an estimated week's hike still ahead of them, their food supply finally ran out and they resorted to living off the inner bark of pine trees. The effect of the resin from the bark on the considerable beards they had developed made Lightoller wonder if he might sell his as a doormat when he got back. He would certainly need to raise something from somewhere because when he and Bill eventually did stagger back into Edmonton half dead from starvation, all they had between them was three cents. But they realised by then that they could count themselves lucky just to be alive.

Bitter disappointment though it was, it was perhaps just as well that circumstances forced Lightoller to turn back when they did. Of the two thousand and more who set out on the so-called Edmonton route in that late winter of 1897/98 an estimated five hundred perished. As one of them wrote before committing suicide in despair, 'Hell can't be worse than this trail. I'll chance it.'

Many like Lightoller had relied on being able to shoot game along the way only to find that because of the severe winter there was none to be had. There were those who somehow did manage to make it those hundreds and hundreds of miles over mountains and down river to Dawson City, the capital of the Gold Rush but not until late 1899—some eighteen months to two years after they had set out, and by then it was all over. Nobody who started for the Klondike from Edmonton found gold. Lightoller was not alone in his failure. Of the estimated 100,000 total who set out on all the gold trails to the Klondike, about a third managed to get there and a few hundred found gold in large enough quantities to call themselves 'rich'. History shows that a mere handful of those succeeded in hanging on to their wealth.

As for a young sailor and the horse he had not the heart to kill, they had cut their losses and headed for the Prairie where they were to be found on a new trail—this time with another kind of herd. The sailor had now become a cowboy.

Tearing about the Canadian prairie trying to keep a few thousand head of cattle moving in a straight line could not have been a better antidote for his depressed spirits. Not only had his dreams been shattered but he felt ashamed of his failure and that in its own particular way was even harder to take. The miserable few dollars he got for selling his tent, gun and other trappings from the 'Trail' rubbed it in all the more, but being half-dead from hunger there was no choice. At least it had been enough to buy a few square meals and keep him going for a day or two until the cow-punching job came up. Gold in this country he may have found none, but cattle there was aplenty, and with spring by now well advanced things were on the move across the prairie and men were needed to join the drives. That was not Bill's kind of work so they had parted and within a week Lightoller and Rufus—and the banjo still with them, still in one piece and playing as sweetly as ever—were experiencing a completely new way of life that had distinct advantages over labouring uphill and down dale through endless snowstorms and freezing floods. No need to bother about blizzards and the cold now as he lay contentedly down on the prairie at the end of each day to fall fast asleep under the stars. He found it a happy, carefree, well fed life even if it could be tough and hazardous at times, particularly when the steers were not behaving themselves and took it into their heads to stampede. Then it would be a matter of trying to head them off without getting trampled to death or ripped to shreds by those long lethal horns. But he was a proven horseman and despite his inexperience with cattle he seemed to cope quite well.

As the weeks went by Lightoller had plenty of time to weigh up his whole situation. Eventually he got around to thinking that while things could have been worse they could also have been considerably better. This cowboy's life was all very well but he could see that for him there was no future in it—and certainly not for his pocket. The work had provided him with a lifeline at a time when he desperately needed it but now he had to beware of getting into the habit of just aimlessly drifting along, going nowhere in particular and losing all purpose in life—and from his life at that moment he could not help feeling that something was definitely missing.

In the back of his mind was a pact he had made with himself before setting out for Canada and the great North-West. If he failed he would return home. He could not deny that he had failed and therefore he must be true to his promise. It was one night as he sat contemplating his pipe and gazing into the flickering flames of the camp fire that he finally made up his mind. He must go home and go now . . . home? . . . what home? Deep down inside he knew only too well where that was.

But first he had to get the hard part over with. He would dearly have loved to take old Rufus with him but it could not be. And what was more, he was going to need every penny he could lay hands on to get out of the country and back home. What he got in the end for Rufus fell far short of matching that and amounted to nothing more than a gross insult to the beast that would have carried him across the ocean himself if it were remotely possible. But then who could blame the man at the stables if all he could see was a rather shabby, ungainly looking animal getting on in years whose worth in terms of horse flesh quite frankly was not much—and certainly much less than its owner paid. Again it was a case of take it or leave it and so with tears in his eyes and a sinking feeling in the pit of his stomach Lightoller said goodbye to the best pal he had ever had. He would never forget Rufus.

He boarded a train to begin his two-thousand-mile journey to Montreal and a ship that would take him back to England. But for him there was no comfortable seat in a saloon. He was riding the rods which was the way he discovered the 'hobos' did it. Hobo was a new word he had come across in this part of the world, and it now applied to him. It did not exactly mean he was a tramp in the English sense—more a traveller without the means to pay for his travel. Riding the suspension rods was hazardous and involved an endless battle of wits with the 'brakies' of the Canadian Pacific Railroad. He soon became acquainted with their favourite trick for ejecting non-paying passengers. If it was suspected that a hobo was riding the rods the 'brakie' would suspend a heavy linchpin on the end of a long rope so that it would bounce viciously up and down along the track beneath the train repeatedly hitting anyone who happened to be roosting there. The biggest danger was of being knocked out and falling off under the wheels; otherwise it was a case of sheer determination to hang on while trying to dodge the bruising blows and hoping the sadistic 'brakie' soon got bored with his little game. That is how it was for Lightoller over the next thousand miles and a dozen or so unpleasant train rides until he eventually reached Winnipeg, halfway to Montreal and with another one thousand miles still to go. He discovered that he could not have arrived in Winnipeg at a better time as a big international festival and exhibition was getting under way. It was a perfect chance to earn some money. Within a day he had got himself fixed up with a job helping to erect and paint the stands being set out for this big event. His training in British sailing ships could not have been a better qualification for the work. He stuck with it for three weeks and then decided he had earned enough to move on. He had made up his mind from the start of his return journey that not one penny would be spent on drink until he had got together sufficient funds to see him back to England. He made for the railroad again but this time it would be as a fare-paying passenger.

When his train pulled into Montreal, Lightoller's troubles were over and he was as good as home. He was now in familiar surroundings, back amongst the docks and shipping. From now on it would be easy. To him crossing thousands of miles of ocean presented far less of a problem than crossing a few hundred miles of land. He found a ship bound for Liverpool and when she sailed he was on it. But it was not as a passenger, or an officer, or even as an ordinary seaman, but as a cattleman. However, once he had got accustomed to the vile stench of their excrement and seasickness, their wild tantrums as they tried to break out of their stalls in panic when the ship rolled badly, and their constant lowing, it was not so bad. The main thing was he was on his way back to Liverpool where he would soon be picking up the old threads again of the career he had left behind. It did not seem to matter anymore that he was coming back broke and a failure. He felt no regrets. He realised now that the whole venture of going out to join the gold rush had been a crazy one and stood no chance of success from the start. But he had had the guts to do it. It had been an educating experience and one that had taught him a good few lessons and not just about himself but about people in general. As he looked at the pathetic cattle in their pens on the ship he could not help but compare them in many ways with those human herds he had encountered on the gold trail. At least he had managed to find a way to get back. When he left Edmonton there were thousands still stranded there with not the remotest idea of how they were going to get home, if they indeed had one left to go to.

And so it was, just a little over twelve months after sailing out of Liverpool bound for certain fame and fortune, that a rather evil-smelling young man strangely clad in buckskins and ten-gallon hat, clutching the only thing he had left in the world — a banjo — stepped off a ship back at the port where he started and crept quietly away in the darkness to the seaman's mission for a much needed bath and a long sleep, followed by a long serious think.

13

It was a reformed Herbert Lightoller spurred on by new resolve and fresh ambition (and a number of outstanding debts to pay off) that strode purposefully down Castle Street, Liverpool, to the offices of Greenshields, Cowie and Company, looking for a ship.

Now the proud holder of a Master's Certificate (No. 029, 706) which he had just acquired, he had decided that if the sea was where his future lay, from then on he must dedicate himself to making a proper career out of it. Never again should he allow anything to distract him from his loyalty to his mistress, however harsh the treatment she could at times mete out to him. It seemed to him that theirs had become the typical love-hate relationship, but then was not that the kind that was the most durable?

With the necessary sea-time under his belt he had passed for Master at the first attempt and now he thought that it would be a good idea to gain experience on the North Atlantic. The Managing Director of Greenshields, Cowie, remembered him well from the *Knight of St. Michael*. After two more fires at sea they had finally sold the vessel to a French shipping company, who had renamed her *Pacifique*, and Greenshields' had completely finished with sail. The man recalled what a fine, promising young mate Lightoller had been in the company's last sailing ship, and found him a berth there and then in their newest, biggest and best liner, the *Knight Bachelor*.

Yes, that would do very nicely, thought Lightoller, expecting to be offered the position of First Mate, or at the very least Second. But here there was to be some disappointment: he would be Third Mate. (In a more prestigious ship he would be called Third Officer—but would still rank one below Third Mate on a sailing ship.) However, he received reassurances that in view of the good service he had given the company in the past, and as he would undoubtedly prove himself a highly capable Third Mate, he could expect quick promotion. Lightoller was not too happy about it, but the *Knight Bachelor* was a fine ship, he would be out on the Western Ocean—and he did need the job pretty badly. He would just have to make sure that no time was wasted in getting the step up. She was lying at Tilbury dock and he was to join her right away.

During the train journey down to London Lightoller began to feel unwell. At first he thought he had caught some kind of chill which he knew was unusual for him; however, as the journey went on and the fever and perspiration got worse, he realised this was no chill and remembered the last time he had felt this bad was down the West African Coast in the *Niagara*. His malaria had come back. By the time he reached Tilbury all he wanted to do was find his ship and a bunk to collapse on and forget the world. He asked the porter at the station where the *Knight Bachelor* was lying and was told she was just over the bridge. Seeing what a bad way the young ship's officer was in, the porter suggested putting his luggage on a trolley and running it over for him to the ship. Splendid fellow, thought Lightoller. It would not be long before he was lying between the smooth sheets in a nice airy cabin with a steward attending to his every need and a doctor to see him to a speedy recovery.

He staggered over the bridge and along the quay in the wake of his kindly porter, getting weaker with every step. Presently the porter stopped and Lightoller who had been trudging dolefully along behind with his head bowed, conscious of nothing but his worsening fever and the man's feet in front, raised his bleary eyes and there before him lay the rustiest, filthiest, most decrepit old tub he had ever seen. He was mystified: this was not the *Knight Bachelor*, so why had they stopped? 'Oh, but the *Knight Bachelor* sailed last week,' the porter informed him. 'This is the *Knight Companion*.' Lightoller sank into despair. Even in his advanced state of fever, he cottoned on instantly to what had happened. There had never been the slightest intention to see him in the *Knight Bachelor*. He had been shanghaied! *Knight Companion* indeed! Could there ever have been a greater misnomer, he thought. She was no companion of his, but it was too late now and he was far too ill to turn round and go home. All that mattered was finding a place, any place, to get his head down and die quietly.

As he approached the gangway the smell was the first thing that hit him—a smell he knew of old and reminded him of a certain ship he had come back from Montreal in. She was a cattle boat. As he walked up the gangway he could see how her rusty sides had become streaked with their disgusting overflow. Once on board he found himself surrounded by a litter of old cattle pens that were lying about the deck amongst the ashes, coal and other muck, including the kind that was particularly unpleasant to walk in.

Just then a scruffy looking unshaven man in a collarless shirt, more reminiscent of a cowhand than a seaman, approached Lightoller and asked him what he wanted. He told him he wanted the Chief Mate; the man replied he was the Chief Mate. Lightoller looked the man up and down and drily informed him that he was in no mood for playing games and would he mind telling him where the Mate was. At this the man with a plainly injured look on his face straightened himself up, stuck out his chest and, glaring at Lightoller, informed him very firmly that he *was* the Mate.

Lightoller this time believed him, apologised and introduced himself. When the Mate asked him when he was going to 'turn to' Lightoller simply replied he was going to 'turn in' and please could he tell him where the steward was who could show him to his cabin. In this ship, Lightoller was told, a man found his own cabin. After clambering over a pile of coal and ashes and other unmentionables he eventually found it, and so much for the nice airy cabin and clean white sheets that he had earlier anticipated. He had never been in a cabin so filthy in all his life, not even in the half-deck of a sailing ship. Before it could even be washed out it would have needed scraping out, but by then he was past caring as he slumped on to the lumpy mattress of his bunk, pulled a couple of musty old blankets over himself and went out for the count.

When the Mate realised just how ill Lightoller was he became quite concerned and set about doing all he could to help. But Lightoller knew that if he was to get rid of the fever once and for all there was only one sure way: 'The West Coast Cure', a drastic but simple 'hard-case' remedy for malaria. There were just two items required, a tin of quinine powder and a packet of cigarette papers. Take a cigarette paper, put as much quinine into it as it will hold, roll it up, seal it and swallow it. One dose might have been enough for most people but Lightoller was determined to do the job properly so he swallowed a few. From that moment on the brass bands started to play in his head and kept it up for two solid days until finally there was one whole-hearted eruption of the fever, which he was convinced was to be the end of him for sure. But instead it was the end of his malaria and he never suffered from it again. This happened round about the Nore lightship in the Thames estuary as the *Knight Companion* was outward bound and by then it was too late to walk off. The shanghai had been successfully completed, and there was nothing else for it but to rest and get his strength back as soon as he could and be fit enough to 'turn to'.

As it happened his voyage in that rusty, smelly old tramp, turned out for a while to be almost enjoyable. It was new territory again for him, this time the Caribbean and the Gulf of Mexico. The people of the West Indies attracted him, and he loved their music, with that very distinct kind of easy lilting rhythm and harmony which brought him out in goose-pimples and made him wish he had his banjo with him.

Perhaps the *Knight Companion* was not so bad after all—or so he thought until they arrived in New Orleans and loaded up with their cargo for home; grain in the holds and on the deck—cattle! From then on the good times were over and the ordeal was to commence as the ship, suffering a distinct list, wallowed and lurched her way out into the Atlantic. Lightoller thought he had seen the last of cattle when he stepped off the ship at the end of his voyage home from Montreal, but it seemed he was destined never to escape them. Oh, their smell, their seasickness and their fear at being in such an unnatural habitat which made them constantly threaten to break out of their pens and go stampeding across the deck! And their incessant mooing and bellowing, would it never end?

Then they ran into the storm.

The trouble with the *Knight Companion* was that she had not been built to withstand the rigours of the Western Ocean, having spent most of her working life in the Indian Ocean and China Seas to which she was more suited. Her owners knew that too, and this was to be her last voyage under the Greenshields, Cowie flag before she was sold to an Italian shipping company to ply the more docile waters of the Mediterranean. But as she hit that wall-sided sea crossing the Grand Banks off Newfoundland the big question that loomed in Lightoller's mind was would she survive long enough even to change hands? The heavy seas that could build up in the shallower waters of the Banks were a particular threat to small- and medium-sized ships and even more so if they happened to be as deeply loaded as the *Knight Companion* was on that passage. Lightoller came to realise that not only was the ship unsuited to it but so was her skipper, who had little experience of conditions in the Western Ocean. The correct thing to do in those circumstances was to heave to and ride it out; this is what Lightoller tentatively suggested to Captain Finnis, who scoffed: surely his Third Mate was not afraid of a bit of bad weather. Lightoller said nothing and went below to get some sleep—except that the ship was heaving and wallowing around so badly by now that when he tried he was repeatedly thrown out of his bunk.

Quite unperturbed, he proceeded to make up his bed on the grimy floor of his cabin in a position where he could wedge himself in and not be tossed around by the violent movement of the ship. As he lay there trying to forget the storm and go to sleep he could feel the pounding of the seas getting heavier and the ship rolling and pitching more and more dangerously. He thought about the cattle and what they must be going through out on the open deck. Thankfully the roar of the wind and the sea was drowning their pitiful, terrified lowing as they were thrown about their stalls and deluged by the sea continuously crashing over them. Still the skipper refused to heave to. What kind of a damn fool was this man, thought Lightoller, cursing the day he ever allowed himself to be shanghaied into this wretched old bucket. Who said that coffin ships were a thing of the past?

The *Knight Companion* was running before a following sea and Lightoller could tell as she struggled along that she was having increasing difficulty rising to the Atlantic waves that were banking up behind her.

He knew what was coming and was dreading it. Then it happened: a great wave broke over the back of the ship tearing along her decks and swamping her from stern to stem. She was pooped and now they really were in trouble. As a torrent of water came gushing into his cabin he decided there was no point in rushing out on deck and being washed overboard. If the ship was going down he might just as well go down with her where he was. The water in his cabin was washing around his knees as he began to feel the ship heel over. He could tell she was now beam on to the sea and being pushed over more and more on her side. She could not possibly recover now he thought as he leaned against a bulkhead that was normally perpendicular and found himself going over into an almost horizontal position. Now came one of those agonising delays while the ship made up her mind: would she right herself or—would she roll right over?

Slowly but surely, and to his mind miraculously, she began to right herself. Up and up she came, having been brought round more by the grace of God than by good seamanship to face into the wind and earn herself a merciful reprieve. He waded through the water sloshing about his cabin and went out on deck, and was horrified by what he saw. The sea had wreaked havoc among the cattle, washing many overboard which he could see struggling in the foaming seas, while others lay badly injured and dying all about the decks. The worst part was yet to come and that was to release those that could not be put back on their feet and get rid of them over the side. Lightoller had been in a few nasty situations in his time at sea but this was one he had never bargained for: wrestling with terrified cattle, many of them badly maimed, while heavy seas continued to crash across the rolling, pitching decks. It was one thing to stop himself being washed overboard, but it would be another matter if he got caught up in a mid-ocean stampede of fear-crazed cattle over the side. Yet somehow order of sorts was restored on deck and the remaining cattle that had survived uninjured were secured in their pens. The *Knight Companion* had shipped a lot of sea during her ordeal and the pumps were now hard at work trying to get rid of it. She had been low enough in the water as it was but now she was wallowing in it even more heavily, with her decks constantly awash as the sea continued to attack her. Captain Finnis had got the fright of his life, and he needed no prompting from Lightoller now to appreciate the wisdom of heaving to until the gale blew out. Lightoller could not help thinking to himself that it would be a long time before this skipper joked again about a 'bit of bad weather' in the North Atlantic.

By good fortune not all the ship's boilers had been doused by the sudden inrush of sea and she could still raise sufficient steam to give her engines the power to hold her head on into the gale. In that position she leapt and tossed about for the next couple of days until at last the weather gave up and allowed the *Knight Companion* to resume her easterly heading and continue her journey to Liverpool with her cattle, what was left of them, still crying mournfully in their pens.

There was nobody more relieved than the *Knight Companion*'s Third Mate when the 'Brazil' buoy came in sight and she finally lumbered into the Mersey estuary at the end of that harrowing passage. By then Lightoller had firmly made up his mind that a farmer was a farmer, a sailor a sailor, and was in no doubt which he intended to be from now on. No more cattle boats for him. As for the 'promise' the man made that he would be promoted to Second Mate in no time at all, he could not help but feel a certain mistrust of the promises made by that particular employer. It might be a good idea, he thought, to sacrifice his prospects with Greenshields, Cowie— —whose name even carried a strong odour of their trade—and go in search of something that held out a more assured future.

His avowed intention had been to start carving out a proper career for himself at sea, and now that he had his Master's Certificate nothing should stand in his way. He was now twenty-five, an age when most career-minded young people were already on their way up the ladder and, having had more than ten years in his own chosen profession, he was certainly not lacking the experience or the qualifications. So what was he waiting for? If he really wanted to make his mark now was surely the time to go ahead and do something positive about it: a new year and a new century were on the way in.

It was in that newly determined frame of mind that one day in early January, 1900, Herbert Lightoller once again found himself walking down a Liverpool street seeking an appointment to a ship. This time it was James Street, to No. 30, the head offices of the prestigious White Star Line.

14

At the turn of the century the ships of the White Star Line were the élite of the British Mercantile Marine. With the addition to its transatlantic mail-boat fleet of the *Oceanic*, undisputedly the finest and most luxurious vessel afloat, the White Star had drawn ahead of its nearest rival, Cunard.

In keeping with the reputation of its ships, the White Star Line had the pick of the best captains, officers and men to run them. They too were looked upon as the cream of the merchant service. For a young ship's officer there could be no higher mark of approval than to be selected from among the hundreds of applicants to serve in one of the Royal Mail steamers of the White Star Line. The basic requirements of an applicant were that he should have had a full training in sail, hold a Master's certificate and, on joining the company, be prepared also to join the Royal Naval Reserve. None of that presented any problem to Lightoller, but these were just the initial qualifications. What really counted in the end was the overall impression given by the man himself. Apart from an unquestionable competence as a seaman, certain qualities of character and personality were also looked for. These included soundness, reliability, alertness, confidence, common sense and initiative, allied with a degree of toughness and determination; these are what made the kind of seaman who one day would be up to taking a command of one of these 'queens of the sea'.

After being told by the White Star Marine Superintendent Captain Joseph 'Daddy' Hewitt that he would be given an appointment just as soon as there was a ship, Lightoller received his first posting within a week of interview—clearly he had made a good impression. While the business of the company up to this time had been devoted almost exclusively to its crack Liverpool–New York service, Lightoller was bound in the opposite direction as Fourth Officer of the *Medic*, the first of five twelve-thousand-ton passenger-cargo liners inaugurating a new White Star service to Australia via South Africa. The company could not have timed better the opening of this service. South Africa was in the grips of the Boer War and the *Medic* was working almost exclusively as a troop carrier, and not just for the thousands of soldiers from Britain, but also from Australia, where the patriotism and keenness to fight for the Empire cause was even more fervent than in the Mother Country.

On board the *Medic* everything was done by the book—the White Star Book. Under her skipper Captain Ranson everything had to be meticulous, with navigation more thorough and precise than Lightoller had ever known it, the ship always spotlessly clean, and discipline of the strictest in the interests of a well-run ship.

As the *Medic* steamed through the mile-wide opening of 'The Heads' and into the smoky blue waters of Sydney Harbour on Lightoller's first voyage, he could see why this great natural land-locked harbour was considered the most beautiful in the world. There could be no comparison with Frisco or even Rio. Beyond the sun-bleached strips of Sydney's white beaches he could see the great expanse of green that was Sydney's main park, The Domain, with Government House nestling in the middle of it; next door the colourful Botanic Gardens with their umbrella-shaped fig trees spreading themselves out over the steep slopes dipping down to the harbour's edge. Away to the north were the fruit-growing hills where stood the fine homes of the Sydney rich amidst the orchards of oranges and the peach farms; and still further beyond and surveying it all, the Blue Mountains of the Great Dividing Range.

Apart from the heavy shipping traffic in this, one of the Empire's chief ports, the harbour was busy with small vessels, some purely for pleasure and others of a more commercial nature like the variety of passenger ferries, some reminiscent of Mississippi riverboats, scurrying about the harbour which boasted some 150 miles of bays and points around its perimeter.

When the *Medic* tied up in Circular Quay, a little blue bay ringed with wharves, warehouses and wool stores where all the important ships docked at Sydney there was a great crowd on the quayside to greet her. To the Australians any ship arriving from Britain was a great event, but the *Medic* was something special. She was the biggest and finest ship ever to come into Sydney Harbour and not only that, she had come to carry Australia's soldiers off to fight a war against a force hostile to the British Empire of which Australia was such a loyal part. As an officer in the *Medic* Lightoller found himself treated almost with deference. He had not forgotten the kindness of the Australians after his shipwreck ordeal all those years ago in the *Holt Hill*. Once again he was invited to their homes to be treated like a lord and enjoy the most cordial hospitality. There seemed no end to the picnics and parties that were forever being given in honour of the men from the *Medic*.

Lightoller, whose great joy was messing about in small craft, rigged up one of the ship's boats with a keel and a sail and enjoyed many happy hours pottering about the harbour. It was while he was on one of these jaunts with a couple of midshipmen from the *Medic* that they hit upon an idea for a prank that threatened to cut short his promising future with the White Star Line. Despite all the resolutions and promises he had made to himself that he was going to keep his nose clean, Lightoller still could not resist a bit of good clean mischief.

Lightoller and his young shipmates had one day been across the harbour to Rushcutter Bay to collect sand for holystoning the ship's decks. As they were returning they passed beneath the walls of Fort Denison, a big stone fort built on a small rocky island in the middle of Sydney Harbour. The idea of the fort was conceived when a squadron of American warships sailed into the bay unannounced in 1839, but by the time it was completed some twenty years later, its main value was seen as a protection for the harbour against invasion by the Russians. The big muzzle-loading guns that lined the battlements of Fort Denison were never fired in anger and the fort these days was simply a place of historic interest; but the guns had remained in place, including an especially large one that projected from the battlements of a tall circular turret at one end of the fortress. As they sailed by under the lee of the tower they looked up and caught sight of the muzzle of this big gun trained across the harbour. It was then that someone in the boat happened to suggest what a lark it would be to fire it off one night. They all looked at one another, glanced up again at the gun and no more words were needed. They were going to do it, by God! But it would need careful and detailed planning and all to be done under complete and absolute secrecy. The *Medic* had not long been in port, and as she usually remained there for a month to six weeks there would be plenty of time to carry out this stunt.

First of all they would need to find out more about the gun and whether it could definitely be fired. That called for a preliminary visit to the fort to examine it. But the next problem was getting out to the island. Their pleasure craft from the ship obviously could not be used as they would soon be rumbled if they tried to lower it in the middle of the night. However they remembered there was a little old rowing boat used for cleaning out the swimming pools that lay off The Domain and decided to commandeer it. And so at midnight a day or two later they crept stealthily off the ship and made for The Domain, located the boat and pushed off towards the island.

They soon realised that their chosen mode of conveyance was barely up to the task. The old tub that was normally used by one man around the sheltered confines of the pools was not quite the same vessel with three aboard out on the less docile waters of the harbour—a harbour which they were only too well aware, was infested with sharks. They had to be careful not to row too quickly or the water came over the bows, while at the same time maintain a steady baling to keep pace with the water seeping in through the numerous holes and tired seams. But somehow they got there and, after tying the boat up securely among the rocks beneath the 'martello' tower where their gun stood, they set about finding a way of climbing up to it. As far as they knew the fort was uninhabited apart from an old caretaker, but they would still need to be very quiet. If they were discovered that would be an end to their ploy and probably a lot more besides. Eventually they discovered the perfect means of access to the top, a lightning conductor which ran all the way up the side of the tower. They began shinning up it. The climb was about fifty feet, but that would present no problem to these acrobats of sail training.

On reaching the top of the turret and climbing over the battlements Lightoller found the interior to be a spacious circular well around which the gun, mounted on a large carriage, was meant to revolve. He reckoned the whole set up weighed about twenty tons.

So now came the moment of truth. Would it fire? The business end, the bore, was clear. Now to examine the vent where the fuse would be inserted. Yes, that too was clear. Their luck was in and what was more, there was even a ramrod provided for pressing home the charge. It could definitely be done. What could not be done was to train the gun on a target: they wistfully eyed a Russian warship anchored out in the harbour. However, an alternative idea appealed to them even more: on firing the gun they would hoist the enemy flag—the flag of the Boers. That would really set them hopping in Sydney, they thought, where hatred for the Boers was more bitter than anywhere else in the Empire.

During the weeks to come all their spare moments were spent in preparation for the night of the 'One Gun Salute' as they came to call it, with everything done under a strict code of secrecy. They pooled their limited funds and found that there was just enough to cover their shopping list. To do the job properly Lightoller calculated that fourteen pounds of blasting powder would fill the bill very nicely, plus an equal amount of slower burning 'fine grain' powder to go at the rear of the main charge to give it the necessary ignition. To pack the charge down the muzzle of the gun he would need three good-sized wads of cotton waste, and then to be sure and give themselves plenty of time to get away, once the lighted match had been applied, fifty feet of fusewire.

For the flag, bunting from the ship would have been ideal except for the one drawback that it just might be traced back to the source. Bed linen, however, would not be so easily traced. A few days later a bed sheet that happened to disappear unnoticed from the linen cupboard of the doctor's surgery while he was not in attendance was proudly bearing the green, red, white and blue stripes of the *Vierkleur*—the Boer flag, great care having first been taken to cut off the tab on the corner displaying the tell-tale words 'White Star Line'.

And then came the night when all was ready. As darkness fell across Sydney Harbour they met in Lightoller's cabin and shared out the load; Lightoller carried the heavy bags of powder slung across his shoulders and under his armpits with the fusewire wrapped around his waist, all concealed under his coat, while the other two shared between them the great wads of cotton to press home the charge, and the rope for hauling it all up the ramparts of the fort.

As midnight approached one last check was made to be sure that nothing had been forgotten and then they slipped quietly off the ship and into the night. As luck would have it they stole into The Domain and found their boat without being challenged. Also on their side was the weather. A fine drizzle was falling across Sydney Harbour cutting down visibility nicely as they once again launched the leaky old craft and rowed precariously out to the island.

On arrival at the fort Lightoller took the rope and clambered up the lightning conductor to the top of the tower to begin hauling up the ammunition as it was being tied on by his accomplices below, who then followed on up. The arrangement was that they would look after the hoisting of the flag on the mast that stood in the centre of the tower while Lightoller got on with the business of loading and preparing the gun. It would not be easy. Because the muzzle was projecting out beyond the battlements the only way he could get at it was to lie back underneath the gun with the upper half of his body suspended over the precipice of the tower. Working from that position was not only difficult, it was dangerous. He found that he could just reach out far enough if the other two held firmly onto his legs.

He inserted the flannel bag containing the finer grain powder, driving it right down the gun with the ramrod as far as it would go, followed by the main charge of blasting powder and then the wads of cotton waste, the third and last one having been soaked in water to make sure that all would be good and firmly packed in position. Lightoller was intent on being absolutely sure as he pounded away at it with the ramrod until the loud thumping threatened to wake up the caretaker. That part of it done to his satisfaction he slid back inside the walls to begin setting up the fuse for firing.

The first job at this end of the operation was to drive the pricker —in this case a steel knitting needle—down the vent to puncture the flannel bag containing the fine grain powder and then pour down the same hole more of the powder. Into that he inserted one end of the fifty-foot coil of fuse.

After giving the fuse a few turns round the breach of the gun he unwound it the full length across the well of the tower to the point where he would be making his getaway down the lightning conductor. His shipmates had already slid back down and were standing by at the boat. They had done their part as Lightoller could see as he glanced up and made out the silhouette of a flag fluttering gaily against the night sky where there had not been a flag before.

So now it was time for the final act, the simplest, yet most significant one of the whole plot. When Lightoller struck the match and put it to the fuse it spluttered into life, crackling and fizzling violently as it began burning its way rapidly—too rapidly for his liking—towards its destination. He did not stop to watch it for long as he leapt for the escape route and scrambled down the wall like a demented spider. But when he reached the boat it was to be greeted with news of disaster. The wash from a passing ship had driven the boat against the rocks and holed it, and despite frantic baling efforts by the other two in a bid to stem the flood it was by now half full of water. They were well and truly caught, unless . . . Lightoller ordered them into the boat and told them to row as they had never rowed before. Jumping in after them he ripped off his shirt and stuffed it into the hole, lodging it there with his feet while he baled like fury.

They would have to forget about returning the boat to where it belonged. It was now a case of aiming for the nearest point in the harbour and hoping they got there before she finally went from under them. Lightoller was grateful that his oarsmen were Conway-trained and knew how to put their backs into it. If any pair could make it, he thought, it would be these two. They did not let him down. But it was a close run thing as they ground up onto the beach with water swilling round their legs. They had very nearly been supper for the sharks. The boat was yanked out of the water and left for someone else to find. All was still quiet out at the fort. Had he done everything? they asked as they dashed through The Domain, over the tall spiked gates of Government House and through the grounds, tumbling into the rose beds as they went. Had he lit the fuse? Yes the fuse had been lit. They climbed the gates at the far side. Had he got the fuse properly into the hole? Yes, he was sure he had. Silence still reigned on the island.

When they finally arrived, panting heavily, back at Circular Quay they had resigned themselves to the bitter disappointment of failure. 'The One Gun Salute' had been a non-event. Lightoller could only assume that he had not sufficiently punctured the canvas bag containing the fine powder to allow the charge to ignite. Oh well, at least they would have the consolation of knowing that in the morning the sight of the Boer flag would take everyone by surprise and give them plenty to talk about.

Then all of a sudden the night sky over Sydney was lit up with a tremendous flash. At first the trio thought it was a flash of lightning and waited for the thunder, but when it came it was no thunder. It was an enormous explosion that seemed to rock the ground beneath them. The blast was staggering as they felt the concussion from it hit them.

THEY'D DONE IT! They whooped and cheered with delight tossing their caps in the air, dancing round together, madly shaking hands. Then they remembered that they had better calm down or else they might attract attention to themselves. It was hard stifling the chuckles as they crept back on board and tip-toed to their cabins in the early hours of that morning with no-one aware that anyone had even left the ship.

The next morning, as the hundreds of passengers going to work on the ferries passed by Fort Denison and saw the flag of the hated enemy flying proudly from the flagstaff, the whole of Sydney could only gape in dismay. In fact the affair was a major talking point throughout the city for days as the people speculated on what it all could mean, the firing of the gun that had woken everybody up in their beds with a start and then the mystery of the 'darn Boer flag' that had been raised right under their noses. It was all most disturbing. There was even a question asked in the Australian Parliament on what provision the Government had made to defend the country in the event of a Boer invasion. The newspapers were full of it.

Meanwhile three mischievous young officers aboard a ship in the harbour could hardly contain their glee at having caused such a stir. 'The One Gun Salute' had caused all the fuss they had hoped for. As the speculation persisted, it gradually dawned that somebody had played a prank but who were the pranksters? The military blamed the navy, but the navy denied all responsibility, insisting that the fort was an army establishment and nothing to do with them. Then the fingers of accusation started pointing at those various characters of Sydney renowned for enjoying a practical joke, but no obvious culprits emerged. The guessing game went on. It was still going on as the Royal Mail Steamship *Medic* sailed out one fine day loaded with yet more troops going off to fight the war against the hated Boer and, departing with them, the secret of a magnificent practical joke that Sydney would remember for a long time.

Lightoller decided to write out his resignation in preference to being fired, and he was in no doubt whatsoever that fired he was going to be as he stood before the imposing white-bearded figure of the Marine Superintendent of the White Star Line, Captain Hewitt. The secret had somehow leaked out in the ship on the way home and now Lightoller must prepare himself to reap the consequences of his foolishness and pay the full price. Hewitt sat there glaring at Lightoller with the resignation letter laid out on the desk in front of him, and then launched into his attack. What a damn stupid thing to have done! He was a disgrace to the White Star uniform! What did he think he was playing at!? He was old enough to know better than to pull off such a stupid, harebrained stunt!

Lightoller agreed with him totally as he wondered whether he might perhaps go back to the great North-West again and have another crack at the Klondike. It was, after all, a big country, and there surely had to be some gold left there . . . And not only had he endangered the lives of the midshipmen, Hewitt went on, but he had done something which many would interpret as an act of treason—and everybody knew the punishment for that! . . .

Hewitt calmed down. For the record he would need to know in full detail the facts of the incident. Lightoller had nothing to lose. He might as well tell it all and get it over with. He embarked on his story; how they had seen this big gun out at the fort and thought what a great idea it would be to have a go at firing it one night, how they had gone out there to examine it and make sure it could be fired and then planned everything in total secrecy, getting together all they needed to pull it off, the blasting powder, the wads of cotton waste, the fuse and even the flag made out of linen stolen from the doctor's surgery; and then the night when they had gone out and actually done the deed, only to find that their boat had been holed on the rocks resulting in the panic of trying to get back ashore before it sank . . .

Hewitt's hand hid his mouth, giving the impression that he was rubbing his beard, and Lightoller just for a moment thought he perceived a flicker of amusement. But that could not be possible as he went on to describe how they had finally made it back to The Domain and run for their lives, tumbling among the rose beds of Government House in the process, before finally arriving back at Circular Quay, the night still silent and convinced they had failed in their mission, but then that unforgettable moment when the great flash came followed by the tremendous blast . . .

Captain Hewitt could not hold himself back any longer as he erupted into a fit of laughter. As the tears rolled down Hewitt's red cheeks and into his beard Lightoller shifted his feet about the carpet uneasily not quite knowing whether to laugh with him, smile or just retain the deadpan expression that he had held throughout the recounting of his tale. When 'Daddy' Hewitt finally brought himself under control, which took some minutes, he sat there smiling at Lightoller, wiping his eyes, shook his head sagely and then very slowly, very deliberately picked up the resignation, ostentatiously tore it up into as many pieces as he could, tossed it in the basket and then in a booming voice as loud as his laughter, roared at Lightoller, 'Get out and get back to your ship!' As a rather bemused Lightoller closed the door behind him he heard Hewitt suddenly burst out laughing again and he could still hear the laughter as he went out through the front door of the White Star head offices into James Street.

As it turned out, Lightoller did not sail on the next voyage of the

Medic, as it was thought wise for him not to go back to Sydney for a while. He was taken out of the Australian service and transferred to the Atlantic. However, following a promotion some time later, he did return to the *Medic* for a short spell and it was then that he forged a lifelong link with his beloved Australia. True to his word of those years back, he wed one of its daughters. Sylvia Hawley-Wilson was the most beautiful woman he had ever set eyes on and he fell in love with her at first sight. A Sydney girl, petite as a little doll, she had been over to England staying with her aunt, combining music studies and finishing school with watching cricket. The Australian touring team were over that year and they had adopted her as a mascot. As she could not walk easily owing to a foot deformity from childhood, and the motion of the ship taking her home to Australia constantly threatened to send her headlong, 'Lights' stepped forward and literally swept her off her feet to carry her up and down the companion ways.

On the return passage to England, she travelled with him as his bride.

15

The newly-weds settled down in Crosby, a pleasant coastal suburb of Liverpool, and started a family. Meanwhile Lightoller, now back permanently in the New York service, concentrated on improving his prospects with the line which already regarded him as one of their most promising younger officers. The first thing he did was to gain his Extra Master's certificate, the highest qualification that a seaman could have.

His early years on the Atlantic run were spent mostly in the *Majestic* under the command of Captain Edward J. Smith, a typical Western Ocean mailboat commander. When Lightoller first encountered this tall, broad-shouldered figure with the full white beard, he expected him to be the bluff and hearty type with a loud deep voice to match, but was surprised to discover that 'E.J.', with his characteristic easy smile was in fact a rather soft-spoken man —until he boomed out an order. Captain E. J. Smith was destined to play a more significant part in Lightoller's sea career than any other skipper he ever sailed with.

Lightoller's introduction to the Atlantic mailboats was a nerve-racking one. The *Majestic* would be pushed for all she was worth through all kinds of weather. Everything was devoted to making the six day passage on time. There was far too much competition from Cunard and the crack Continental liners to risk falling behind schedule. That applied just as much in the depths of winter when the old *Majestic* would be driven flat out through the worst Atlantic seas with little regard for damage. More than once she docked with life-boats smashed or carried away and the look-out cage flattened against the mast where a particularly big sea had crashed on top of her. Everything in the ship would be battened down tight with all the passengers shut in and kept off the decks. Getting them (and the mails) there on time was far more important than any discomfort, seasickness, and alarm the terrible buffeting might cause.

Fog made no difference. Only in the very worst visibility would the skipper consider sacrificing so much as a knot. The mailboats were blamed for the loss of many a fishing schooner or dory on the Grand Banks off Newfoundland when the fog came down, but the blame was seldom proved. A ship like the *Majestic* cutting through the water at eighteen or nineteen knots would barely register a jolt as she smashed through a flimsy wooden boat, scattering it as so much matchwood while she continued on her way with no-one on board any the wiser, not even the Officer of the Watch—or if he was, he might neglect to mention it.

If it was known there was ice in the vicinity of the Grand Banks a more southerly—but barely more southerly—course would be taken to avoid it. Meanwhile another couple of boilers would be fired up to make sure delay was restricted to the absolute minimum. Only in the gravest emergency would the Officer of the Watch touch the telegraphs without the authority of the Master. It seemed the all-important maxim to follow in the mailboats was 'Get On or Get Out!' There were those officers who did get out because they could not stand the strain of working in conditions where the golden rules of the sea were continuously tossed aside, often to the point of recklessness.

Lightoller developed into the model Western Ocean mailboat officer, cool, relaxed, impeccably self-assured, and promotion came his way. From the *Majestic* he was transferred to the *Oceanic* and promoted to Third Officer.

The *Oceanic*, known as 'Queen of the Seas', was a magnificent ship, the pride of the line. It had been the practice for the White Star Line to build its mailboats in pairs, for instance the sister ships *Majestic* and *Teutonic*, or the *Cedric* and *Celtic*. Cunard followed the same policy with the *Ivernia* and *Saxonia*, the *Umbria* and *Etruria*. But the 17,000-ton *Oceanic* was in a class of her own, a liner unsurpassed till then in size, luxury, and design. A sleek 700-foot ship, she could carry a maximum of two thousand people, over four hundred in First Class, three hundred in Second, and in Third Class—or steerage —there was accommodation for a thousand. The crew numbered nearly four hundred.

The influential, rich and famous of both sides of the Atlantic paid anything up to £150 (a year's wages to many workers) per single trip for the privilege of being installed in one of her twenty most luxurious suites with their marble baths and lavatories, their walls panelled in silk. Soon after the *Oceanic*'s maiden voyage the journal *Marine Engineer* enthused that the First-Class saloon had as many seats as First-Class berths so that everyone could dine at the same time. 'The room is remarkable for its decoration,' the writer declared. 'It is panelled in oak washed with gold, while its saloon dome (designed by a Royal Academician) decorated with impressive figures representing

Great Britain and the United States and Liverpool and New York is very beautiful and striking.' The light fittings in the smoking room were gold-plated, on the walls hung valuable paintings depicting the life of Christopher Columbus, and in niches set into the corners were beautifully carved Italian figures. It was luxury up to then unparalleled at sea.

In contrast to all this, way down below in the stokehold it was a very different picture. Here, worlds apart from all the wealth, finery and ostentation of the upper decks, shifts of forty-five sweat-soaked stokers toiled ceaselessly to feed the hungry furnaces with seven hundred tons of coal each day, the quantity devoured by the liner at her top speed of twenty knots under the power of two triple-expansion steam engines, the largest of their type ever built.

Lightoller felt deep compassion at times for the miserable lot of the 'Black Gang' in their terrible sweated labour in heat that seemed beyond the bounds of ordinary human endurance. Steaming through the Gulf Stream at the height of summer it was no uncommon sight to see two, three or perhaps four men hoisted up the ash shoot with a chain slung roughly under their arms to be dumped unconscious on the deck. Once a few buckets of water had been tossed over them they were left where they lay to recover, but they would not be able to take too long about it, otherwise the leading fireman would soon appear and launch in with boot and fist to beat them back below again where they belonged, in the heat and hell of the stokehold.

Their task was to 'keep that arrow up' and woe betide those loafers who let it drop. They were a mean, hostile crowd and whenever there was trouble below it could usually be traced to the stokehold. Fights were not unusual where lethal shovels would be used as weapons. A man might go missing after such an incident and never be seen again. It could only be assumed that he had gone overboard, but there were those who secretly knew where he had really gone. However by the time it came to raking out the furnaces there would be nothing left to prove it.

Lightoller was promoted from Third Officer of the *Oceanic* to Second; as an Officer of the Watch, he took charge of the ship when it was his turn for duty on the bridge. It should not be long now before he got his own command, although he realised it would not be easy to emulate the likes of Captain John G. Cameron, Master of the *Oceanic*. A tall, imposing figure with darting blue eyes and full ginger beard, Cameron was a brilliant seaman who ruled his ship with an iron fist and often terrified his crew with his tough, dictatorial ways, but never to the point of losing their respect. When on watch, the officers could not afford to relax for a moment because Cameron would arrive on the bridge and immediately fire off a volley of questions to which the answers would have to be delivered without a second's hesitation. Lightoller soon got to know what the most likely questions would be and was always ready for them . . . 'Evening Mr. Lightoller, what's our position?' 'What's our speed?' 'How's the wind?'

Lightoller was rarely caught out. However there was one embarrassing moment when Cameron did catch him out, but not with one of his notorious quizzes. The bridge of the *Oceanic* was rather special in that the flooring from end to end was laid in a stylish covering of white rubber, very attractive but not too practical. For one thing it needed constant scrubbing to be kept clean, but its greatest inconvenience was that it became very slippery when wet, particularly after a heavy squall. For Lightoller, however, this was a splendid opportunity to relieve the monotony and enjoy a little sport. As the ship rolled he would delight in sliding from one end of the bridge to the other, the ultimate achievement being to pass straight through the wheelhouse, negotiating the tricky curve around its bow front, and reach the far side without touching anything. On one such occasion he was totally immersed in this manoeuvre when the skipper just happened to appear on the bridge; Lightoller was unable to stop himself and careered right into him. Cameron went a bright red to match his beard and boomed: 'What the hell do you think *you're* playing at sir?' To which Lightoller replied meekly that he 'slipped, sir'. Cameron, who always addressed his man as 'Sir' when he was angry, was sharp and to the point: 'Slipped did you? I wish you had broken your damn neck, sir, because you damn nearly broke mine!' From that moment on Lightoller ceased his little sliding games. It did not do for any man with an eye on promotion to get on a collision course with Captain John G. Cameron.

As the years passed, the North Atlantic run became a familiar routine. On the outward run down the Mersey from Prince's Landing Stage they would swing south round the North Wales coast, down channel to Queenstown on the south east corner of Ireland, there to anchor off Roche's Point and pick up the final batch of mails and passengers, mostly Irish emigrants brought out in the company's own tenders. Then away again at full speed, the liner's tall funnels belching out an oily trail of thick black smoke as she rounded the rocky, undulating southern Irish shores past the lighthouse perched on the high precipitous cliffs of the Old Head of Kinsale, followed by another fifty miles or so of bays, inlets, promontories and islands that marked the way out into the Atlantic, landmarks he came in time to know so well; the wide, rich green beach-skirted expanses of Court-macsherry Bay and Clonakilty Bay, then, in contrast, the probing, rocky extremities of Galley Head and Toe Head, the sea foaming and swirling hungrily around them. On WSW past the lofty shores of Cape Clear Island and then the last landmark of all, the tall, slim, conical lighthouse perched on Fastnet Rock where the final bearings were taken as the liner forged on out into the North Atlantic to commence her 2,800-mile Great-Circle passage across open ocean to New York. All being well, in a little over five days they would sight the Nantucket Light, signalling the last 200-mile lap to Sandy Hook, the 'winning post' for the Atlantic greyhounds as they prepared to enter New York harbour. From Sandy Hook light they would swing due north up the Main Channel of the Lower Bay, through the mile-wide Narrows between Staten Island to port and Brooklyn to starboard and into the Upper Bay.

But first under the watchful, inscrutable gaze of the guardian Statue of Liberty, the liner had to anchor offshore for the immigration and medical authorities to come aboard and examine the passengers and crew while the mails were sent away in tenders. Then presently they were under way again, heading straight into the Hudson River and the White Star piers No. 59 or 60 in New York's Chelsea district.

Lightoller found New York a fast, noisy, restless city which he grew to know well. It was the last place where he would have expected to discover in himself an interest in religion. However, Christian Science came into his life in the way that such things can happen to many people; a leaflet thrust into his hand in a New York street that was stuffed indifferently into a pocket, then glanced at in an idle moment sometime later when off watch aboard ship; then the spark of curiosity leading to a keen desire to find out more about this faith in which sickness and death played no part and where there was no such thing as sin and evil and all things material from the kitchen sink at home to the ship he was sailing in were unreal and purely illusory. In Mary Baker Eddy's book *Science and Health with Key to the Scriptures* he read that the Christian Science cure for sickness was to help a person understand that he was not really sick, that his pain was imaginary and that this 'imagined ailment' was only the result of a 'false belief'. The true Christian Scientist, it seemed therefore, should have no need of doctors and the surgeon's knife.

Lightoller was convinced by the Christian Science doctrines outlined in the writings of Mrs. Eddy. He had for some time harboured the feeling, if only subconsciously, that someone, somewhere was watching over him. On more than one occasion he had found himself close to death where his survival in the end had been due purely to the strength and will he had summoned from somewhere to conquer it, and now he could relate it to this, the faith he had happened upon called Christian Science. He became converted and so did Sylvia.

In 1907 the decision was taken by the White Star Line to open up a new route to New York from Southampton to be more conveniently placed for London, the South-East and the continental ports. This would become the principal New York service and be operated by the company's best and fastest vessels. The route included calls at Cherbourg and Queenstown.

The change of base for the *Oceanic* meant a move for Lightoller, as the family, which now included a three-year-old son Roger and a second child on the way, packed its trunks and moved south to Netley Abbey, a quiet village overlooking Southampton Water. Their new double fronted, detached home, Nikko Lodge on Station Road, was a much larger and more prestigious residence than their previous terraced home on Cambridge Avenue, Crosby. This ten-room house complete with its own bakery, servants' quarters, stables and large back garden with tennis court would do very nicely for the growing Lightoller family, for regular promotion was bringing it a steadily improved standard of living. The house was also conveniently placed for Lightoller to pursue his greatest delight when he was not sailing in big boats and that was messing about in small ones. He bought a small sailing boat which he kept moored nearby at a pier built out into Southampton Water from the grounds of Netley's Royal Victoria Hospital.

From Second Officer of the *Oceanic* Lightoller was moved up to First of the *Majestic*. He was pleased with the promotion but missed the *Oceanic*. However it would not be long before he was back once more serving under Captain Cameron in the 'Queen of the Seas' retaining his rank as First Officer, which amounted to a further promotion.

Meanwhile, far removed from Lightoller's world on the bridge of the *Oceanic*, one evening in 1907 the Managing Director and Chairman of the White Star Line, J. Bruce Ismay and his wife came to dine at the London Belgravia home of Lord Pirrie, the head of the Belfast shipbuilders Harland and Wolff. When the meal was over the two men retired to the study and over their port and cigars got down to drawing up plans for the building of three new sister ships for the White Star Line. They would be bigger and better than anything seen before in the 'Atlantic Ferry' business.

Harland and Wolff and the White Star Line had enjoyed a harmonious and successful business relationship for some decades during which the agreement had always been that Harland and Wolff would never build a ship for any competitor of the White Star Line and in turn the shipping line reciprocated by not entering into any contract with rivals of Harland and Wolff.

As Pirrie and Ismay mulled over their ideas that night and drew up rough plans of the 'Wonder Ships' that were going to take over the cream of the transatlantic passenger routes, they came to the conclusion it would be pointless to try and compete on speed with the big new Cunarder which had recently arrived on the scene. The *Lusitania*, with her sister-ship the *Mauretania* soon to join her, was bigger and faster than anything the White Star Line had to offer at this time. The *Oceanic*'s crown as 'Queen of the Seas' was starting to lose some of its glitter. The much larger 31,000 ton *Lusitania* with her top speed of 26 knots had established herself as the fastest ship on the run between Liverpool and New York and was the present holder of the 'Blue Riband'. But speed ate up coal and reduced profits. Better to leave the speed records to others, Ismay and Pirrie decided, and put all the emphasis on size and luxury with ships half as big again as the rival Cunard liners which could reliably guarantee a regular week's crossing at a standard of comfort and opulence never before offered and that no-one else could possibly match. However these big ships would still be capable of well over 20 knots.

No time was wasted in putting the plans into effect as an army of designers and draughtsmen went to work at Harland and Wolff. Keels were to be laid down for twin ships, with a third to follow later. Side by side the two great leviathans began to take shape. Each would have a gross tonnage exceeding 45,000, measure almost 900 feet in length, and their height from keel to bridge would be 104 feet. The first of the two giant liners, the *Olympic*, was launched in 1909 and on June 14th 1911 she embarked on her maiden voyage from South-ampton to New York.

'The *Olympic* is a marvel!' proclaimed Ismay in a cable back from New York to Lord Pirrie, her builder.

The liner became so popular with the rich, particularly the American rich, that there was not sufficient First-Class accommodation to meet the demand. The White Star Line had achieved their objective and beaten everything else out of sight in the North Atlantic arena.

It was on the very same day that the *Olympic* nosed her way out of Harland and Wolff and had headed down Belfast Lough on her sea trials that the second of the big sisters slid down slipway No. 3 and was made ready for fitting out. She was named the *Titanic*.

As the months went by and completion day neared the world's press and the various shipping journals enthused over the heady statistics and outstanding engineering and accommodation features of this new 'Wonder Ship' the world was about to see. Her gross tonnage was over a thousand tons more than that of the *Olympic*. Her exact gross weight was 46,328 tons, all held together by some 3 million rivets alone weighing 1,200 tons. Her four gigantic funnels, each weighing 60 tons, were large enough for two railway locomotives to pass through side by side. Her 100-ton rudder was as high as a large house. Her main anchor weighing 15 tons had required a team of strong horses to haul it on a special platform to the ship for fitting. The machinery to drive her huge triple screws amounted to the equivalent of more than 50,000 horses, and to generate the steam to drive the machinery there were 29 coal-fired boilers through each of which could pass a double-decker tramcar. Apart from giving the ship a potential top speed of 23 knots, the power plant supplied electricity for 8 cargo cranes, 4 passenger lifts, a telephone switch-board connected up to 50 extensions throughout the ship, a Marconi wireless station, several hundred heaters, and numerous galleys and pantries which boasted all the most up-to-date gadgetry available to the contemporary caterer in the way of electric slicing, peeling, mincing and whisking machines. From these kitchens working round the clock would come the necessary food to satisfy the daily require-ments of more than 3,300 passengers and crew which the ship was designed to carry.

Getting the best of everything would be the 735 passengers travel-ling in First Class. Because the demand for First-Class berths in the

Olympic had far exceeded availability Ismay decided to increase the First-Class accommodation of the *Titanic* by a hundred. He also instigated numerous other modifications and refinements that would bring the *Titanic* up to the highest attainable standards of comfort and luxury. The pièce de résistance were the two 'Millionaire Suites' which cost a staggering £870 for a single crossing—between four and five times the annual salary of a senior officer with the Line. Those élite fortunate enough to afford such a vast sum for a sea voyage would bask in surroundings that were the ultimate in gracious living. 'There is complete habitation with bedrooms, sitting room, bathroom and service room complete. Twin bedsteads, perfect examples of Empire or Louis Seize, symbolise the romance to which the most extravagant luxury in the world is but a minister,' said one contemporary writer of these extraordinary First-Class suites where the pampered inhabitant could indulge in 'the privilege of being quite alone, cut off from the common herd who are only paying perhaps five-and-twenty pounds a day and with the privilege, if he chooses, of seeing nothing at all that has to do with a ship or even the sea.' No ship afloat, not even the *Oceanic*, could match the *Titanic*'s First-Class à la carte restaurant for sheer elegance, with its walnut panelling, thick pile carpet and the large bay windows at which hung full-length curtains of silk. Adjoining the restaurant outside beneath a glass verandah was the Café Parisien decorated with trellises entwined with climbing creeper plants reproducing superbly the effect of a French boulevard with pavement café. Only a gentle rolling from side to side might suggest it was on a ship and not the Champs Elysée. This would appeal particularly to the younger set. Thought had even been given to the fact that the rich often liked to have their servants travel with them so there was a special lounge set aside purely for the butlers and maids of the First-Class passengers, not forgetting the quarters for First-Class dogs. To ensure that the top-notch clientèle would never get bored on their six-day passage, various leisure facilities to suit all preferences were provided. There was a gymnasium, a full-size squash court, a swimming pool, a Turkish Bath lit by valuable Moorish lamps, a dark room for keen photographers to develop their own pictures at sea and an extensive library with books to suit all interests and tastes. The Second Class had a library too, because even for the lesser mortals of Second Class the *Titanic* offered a level of comfort far better than many other ships could provide in their First Class. As for the 'common herd' of a thousand-odd which the *Titanic* could accommodate in her Third Class, or steerage section, many of them would find the standard of comfort and food far better than they had ever experienced in their day-to-day lives back home.

To man and run the great liner and cater for all the needs and desires of its potential 2,400 passengers there would be a total of more than 900 people employed over a wide range of duties. Apart from those involved in the actual handling and running of the ship, such as the seamen, engineers and stokers, there were the chefs, butchers, bakers, waiters, barmen, stewards, chambermaids, pursers, clerks, accountants, barbers, musicians, masseurs in the Turkish Bath, a coach in the squash court and a professional gymnast in the gymnasium.

There was, however, one other feature possessed by the liner which made her even more special. She had a system of electrically operated watertight doors which at the flick of a switch on the bridge could be lowered and closed in an emergency, for instance in the event of the hull being holed below the waterline. This meant she could still float with any two of her watertight compartments flooded. The *Titanic* was unsinkable.

The man taking command of this ocean-going phenomenon on her maiden voyage scheduled for April 1912 was Captain Edward J. Smith, who was by this time the Commodore of the White Star Line. He was perhaps the most highly regarded and certainly the most highly paid skipper in the British merchant service, earning £1,250 per year, more than double the salary of Cunard's top commanders.

'E.J.', however, was due to retire and would probably take command of the *Titanic* for only this one voyage. To back him up in the navigation and running of the ship he had seven officers, comprising three senior watch-keeping officers, the Chief, First and Second and four junior officers, the Third, Fourth, Fifth and Sixth.

Appointed First Officer of the *Titanic* was Charles Herbert Lightoller.

PART THREE
RMS *TITANIC*

'I cannot imagine any condition that would cause a ship
to founder . . . Modern shipbuilding has gone beyond that.'

Captain Edward J. Smith, Commander of RMS *Titanic*

16

When Lightoller first laid eyes on the *Titanic* her size completely overwhelmed him. She looked enormous sitting there in her fitting-out berth at Harland and Wolff, her sides rising up like cliffs, while still higher, some 70 feet higher, rose her four great funnels standing up like mighty sentinels towering above the Belfast skyline. Beside her, the *Oceanic* looked like a steam yacht.

During the last few months much overtime had been put in at the shipbuilders to meet the deadline for the *Titanic*'s maiden voyage. When Lightoller stepped aboard, the main construction work had been completed and she was swarming with joiners, decorators, electricians, carpet-layers, soft furnishers and numerous other contractors, craftsmen and tradesmen beavering away amongst her labyrinth of decks putting the final touches to the liner. At this stage Ismay himself had made a number of recommendations. He wanted firmer mattresses: a person did not sleep so well, he had perceived, on a mattress that was too soft. He wanted cigar holders in the First-Class bathrooms. That had been an oversight in the *Olympic* but there would be no such deficiencies in the *Titanic*. To keep pace with the food requirements of the crew he ordered an electric potato-peeler to be installed in their galley.

With just two weeks to go before her maiden voyage, Lightoller found the job of preparing this mammoth new ship for sea strenuous work. Finding his way about her several miles of decks, passages and stairways was a full-time job in itself apart from all the organising that needed to be done; allocating the various duties to seamen here and there, receiving and signing for the tons of stores, provisions and equipment being taken on board and testing all the various apparatus installed in the ship, some of which was totally new to him, such as the *Titanic*'s system of electrically operated watertight doors, the highly advanced electric cargo cranes and the new type of Welin davits for the lifeboats. These worked differently to systems he had previously been familiar with and also made it possible for up to four lifeboats to be carried between one set of davits. However the *Titanic*'s davits each carried only one boat. Any more, it was decided, would have created too much of a restriction on deck space. She still provided the necessary lifeboat accommodation to satisfy Board of

Trade requirements, which ruled that any ship of 10,000 tons and over must carry 16 lifeboats of a laid-down minimum capacity. The *Titanic* carried that number plus four extra rafts with collapsible canvas sides. It seemed she was complying with the rules and more—if only a little more.

As he explored the ship the one thing that crossed Lightoller's mind was the considerable distance between steerage and the boat deck and the problems that might be encountered by the Third-Class passengers finding their way to the boats, and the time it would take them to get there in the event of an emergency. There were those of course who considered the lifeboats in the *Titanic* rather pointless anyway, the ship being unsinkable.

One of Lightoller's most important responsibilities before the ship sailed was ensuring that she was fully equipped with all the necessary navigational instruments and aids and that those with working parts functioned properly; for instance the chronometers had to be synchronised and checked for accuracy, and the chartroom supplied with all necessary dividers, compasses and parallel rulers, nautical almanacs and inspection tables for use in computing and charting the ship's position, and of course the charts themselves which must be complete and fully up to date, in particular Chart No. 2058, the North Atlantic Track Chart.

During her trials in Belfast Lough the *Titanic* behaved impeccably. As she was put through her various manoeuvres, turning circles at various speeds, running on a set course to see that she steered straight and true, and the 'full speed astern test' to time how long it would take for the ship to come from full speed ahead, to stop, no fault could be found. The 'full speed astern test' was timed at more than three minutes, covering a distance of just over half a mile. A long time for a ship to stop, but then it had to be agreed, this was to be expected for a liner of such size and power. Harland and Wolff had done their work well. During the trial runs Lightoller as First Officer was at his appointed station aft paying attention mostly to the Cherub patent log, the bell in its register ringing every sixth of a mile as it recorded distance travelled enabling the speed to be calculated. The highest speed reached during trials was 18 knots but everyone knew the *Titanic* would be capable of much more, perhaps 23 or 24 knots, once her engines were fully run in.

Her trials successfully completed, the *Titanic* headed down the Irish Sea for Southampton where at midnight on April 3rd, 1912, she loomed into the Ocean Dock and tied up. It was here in due course that Lightoller was to find himself experiencing another kind of trial, this time under the eagle eye of Captain Maurice Clarke, the Board of Trade marine surveyor. His job was to inspect all the lifesaving gear and make sure everything came up to Board of Trade safety standards, and there was no-one who did this job more thoroughly than Clarke. He was totally unimpressed by all the charisma that surrounded the 'biggest and finest ship in the world'—much less that she was 'unsinkable'. He was determined to inspect everything thoughout the length and breadth of the ship. Even when it came to the smallest detail an officer's word was not good enough for Clarke. He must see and check everything for himself: that the ship was fully supplied with lifebelts sufficient for every passenger on board, that the required number of lifebuoys were placed at regular intervals around the decks, that she was carrying all the necessary rockets, flares and other fireworks for setting off in distress and, most important of all, that the 16 lifeboats and their lowering mechanisms functioned efficiently. In this department Clarke's inspection was especially rigorous. By the time Lightoller had finished raising and lowering lifeboats 70 feet up and down to the water, sometimes having to repeat the operation with the same lifeboat if Clarke was not quite satisfied, he had not felt such frustration and anger inside him since his days with 'Bully' Waters. Now he knew why the dreaded Captain Clarke had built a reputation for being the most exasperating Board of Trade Surveyor that had ever set foot on a ship.

There were deep sighs of relief when he finally bade his farewell and was gone, having at last put that hard-earned signature to the certificate of approval which now declared the *Titanic* safe to carry passengers at sea.

As sailing day got nearer, however, there was to be a disappointing setback for Lightoller. He was demoted, although it was no reflection on him, and it would be only for the one voyage. Captain Smith decided to draft in as Chief Officer Henry T. Wilde, who had been his Chief in the *Olympic*, thinking it would be a good idea to have Wilde along with his experience of the sister ship. Although it might have seemed in some respects like a good idea at the time, it also created considerable confusion. Wilde himself, who was soon to take command of his own ship, was not entirely happy about the switch which meant the *Titanic*'s originally appointed Chief Officer, W. M. Murdoch, taking a step down to First to assume Lightoller's duties while Lightoller in turn stepped down to Second to take over from his good friend David Blair who, having joined the ship as Second Officer in Belfast, was now to his bitter disappointment forced to drop out. The four junior officers, Pitman 3rd, Boxhall 4th, Lowe 5th and Moody 6th remained as they were.

Lightoller had at first been severely put out at his demotion but he had no choice but to accept it. It was just one of those things and it would only be for the one trip and after all this was the *Titanic* and there was no skipper he liked and admired more than old 'E.J.', a skipper any man in his opinion ought to be prepared to 'give his ears' to sail under. In fact Smith was popular with crew and passengers alike. Many of the western world's richest and most celebrated people would often plan their trips specially just so they could sail with Smith and enjoy his genial personality and after-dinner good humour, which never interfered with his air of authority and tact, even when chatting with children for whom he invariably had plenty of time.

The great thrill that always stood out for Lightoller when Smith was in command was the way he would take the *Majestic* into New York harbour at full speed, not even slowing down for a particularly tight corner known as the South-West Spit which he would round with the liner heeling over to the helm, leaving only feet to spare between each end of the ship and the mud-banks. It never failed to make Lightoller's hair rise every time 'E.J.' executed that dashing manoeuvre.

After a couple of days Lightoller and Murdoch got themselves reorganised and settled in their new relegated positions in the *Titanic* but there was one oustanding matter resulting from the reshuffle that was never sorted out, and the problem would not fully come to Lightoller's notice until after the ship had sailed. By then it would be too late . . .

'I herewith report this ship loaded and ready for sea. The engines and boilers are in good order for the voyage and all charts and sailing directions up to date. Your obedient servant, Edward J. Smith.'

The Master's report made out to the company and duly signed, the *Titanic* was at last ready to embark on her maiden voyage. Due to a coal strike, fuel had been taken in from other White Star liners in the harbour including the *Oceanic* and *Adriatic* whose trips were cancelled and their passengers transferred to the *Titanic*. Coal had even been bought from the holds of ships belonging to other companies to make up the 6,000 tons needed to feed the *Titanic*'s 159 furnaces during her voyage.

As noon departure time approached on that morning of Wednesday April 10th 1912, the busiest man in the *Titanic* now was her Chief Purser Hugh McElroy, second only to Captain Smith in the White Star Line popularity poll.

'Good morning Mr. Stead, good to have you with us again . . . C89 sir . . . your steward will be along any moment to take you there . . . Yes madame . . . ah yes down the passage and then to the right, there will be a steward on hand to help you from there . . . Yes sir, your luggage should be on its way to your cabin at this moment . . . let me know if you have any problems . . .'

The *Titanic* would not be full for her first voyage. The First-Class was booked to less than half its capacity but the total wealth of the First-Class passengers still amounted to hundreds of millions, most of it in American dollars. There were such names as Benjamin Guggenheim, whose millions had been made in minerals and smelting, Isador Straus who had risen from a penniless young emigrant to build the name of Macy's department store into an American national institution, the colourful Molly Brown of Denver, wife (although they were at present separated) of James Joseph Brown whose wealth was in goldmines, John B. Thayer, President of the Pennsylvania Railroad, Charles M. Hays, also a Railroad President, Major Archibald Butt, military aide to the American President, George Widener, son and right-hand man to Philadelphia Street Car Magnate P. A. B. Widener, Arthur Ryerson another steel magnate who had been visiting Europe with his wife, three children, a maid, a governess and sixteen trunks, all now aboard the *Titanic*. And then there was the richest of them all, John Jacob Astor, said to be worth 150 million dollars and once described as the world's greatest monument to unearned income. Astor was at the centre of much gossip and publicity these days, not least in the American press following his divorce and subsequent remarriage to an eighteen-year-old girl younger than his son. She was with him in the *Titanic* after spending winter abroad with her new husband away from the disapproving eyes of New York society. These, then, were the people that epitomised the so called 'Gilded Age' for whom the *Titanic* had been created. J. Bruce Ismay, who was making the maiden voyage with them, had every right just now to be feeling pleased with himself.

Galaxies apart from all the wealth and splendour of the *Titanic*'s

First Class, stationed out on the fo'c's'le head as the clock neared noon was Second Officer Lightoller. He was standing by with Chief Officer Wilde and 'Big Neck' Nichols the Bosun and his gang preparing to see to the forward moorings and the tugboat hawsers just as soon as the orders started coming from the bridge.

Then the *Titanic* spoke. As her three deep-throated sirens, the largest and loudest ever made, boomed out a sequence of blasts that reverberated round the whole of Southampton, those not sailing bade their last farewells and hastened ashore. By now a great throng of people had crammed the quayside of the Ocean Dock to watch the departure. Somewhere in among them was a proud wife and two young sons aged 8 and 4 craning up in hopes of catching just a glimpse of the Second Officer going about his important work on the fo'c's'le. At this moment Lightoller was standing by the telephone waiting for the commands that would now start coming down from the bridge. Then through the earpiece came the unmistakable Welsh twang of Fifth Officer Lowe who was manning the bridge telephones, 'Make fast the tugs!' Lowe sang out, relaying the order from the pilot, 'Uncle' George Bowyer. Lightoller passed on the order to Chief Officer Wilde who in turn commenced to issue a string of directions to 'Big Neck' Nichols and his men, while the powerful winches began to rattle and belch out steam and heavy ropes zipped and sang round the drumheads. All just then was a flurry of waving and cheering both on the quayside and way up on the packed lofty decks of the ship as, barely perceptibly at first, she began to part from the edge of the quay in response to the straining, snorting tugs that were gradually pulling her off. 'Let go the head rope!' came the voice of Lowe. Lightoller passed it on at the same time helping Wilde direct Nichols and his helpers who scurried about the deck casting off the score and more of ropes, springs and hawsers that had held the *Titanic* fast to her berth. There were just as many moorings aft to see to where the same procedure was at this moment being carried out under the direction of First Officer Murdoch.

'Let go forward tug!' called Lowe down the phone to Lightoller again. The steel hawser splashed into the water as the forward tug was let go coinciding with the distant jangle of telegraph bells up on the bridge, followed almost immediately by the faintest hint of vibration beneath the deck. The *Titanic*'s engines had begun to stir. Her two 38-ton wing propellors were turning in response to the command telegraphed from the bridge, 'Slow Ahead!'

The great liner began creeping forward, easing her way gently towards the entrance to the dock. As she did, many of the spectators ran along the quay keeping pace with her, eager to get in a final wave to friends and relatives on board. Now came an incident which made Lightoller realise just how much power there was in the engines and propellers of this gigantic ship. As the *Titanic* went by a much smaller liner, the *New York*, the suction of the passing leviathan began drawing her out from her berth. Then came a number of loud cracks echoing across the harbour like rifle shots as the *New York*'s steel moorings snapped like cotton, whipping up into the air and sending screaming onlookers scattering in panic. Looking aft, Lightoller could see the stern of the *New York*, its gangway having crashed into the water, being drawn out towards the *Titanic*. As he watched helplessly a collision looked imminent. On board the *New York* there was much frenzied activity as seamen dashed about lowering mats over the side to try and deaden the almost certain crash. Yet somehow disaster was averted as the *Titanic* glided by, missing the *New York* by what seemed inches. The tugs that had towed the *Titanic* off her berth and were following her out of the dock immediately diverted to the *New York* and pushed her back alongside the quay. Lightoller later learnt that Captain Smith had reacted instantly to the situation by ordering a touch ahead on the *Titanic*'s port engine which actually washed the *New York* away from her until the tugs took over. It had been a near thing and there were those in the *Titanic* who looked upon it as a bad omen. As for Lightoller, he simply felt relief that a disaster had been averted which would have put paid to the *Titanic*'s maiden voyage before she had even got out of the harbour. In his and everybody else's mind was the incident the previous summer when her sister ship the *Olympic* had collided with the cruiser HMS *Hawke*, having sucked the warship right off her course. There was obviously still much to learn about the handling of these giants in confined waters.

At this moment everyone's trust was in the pilot 'Uncle' George Bowyer and there was no-one more capable and experienced than he to manoeuvre a ship of such huge proportions as the *Titanic* through the tricky twists and turns and tides of Southampton Water and the Solent as she forged her way out into the open sea. Bowyer guided her round the awkward turn to starboard past Calshot spit; through the narrow shallows of the Thorn Channel, followed by another ticklish right-angle turn this time to port round the West Bramble buoy; past

Cowes roads on the Isle of Wight to starboard where crowds were lining the front to watch the magnificent liner go by; past the naval anchorage at Spithead to port and then on to the Nab lightship where she slowed right down to drop the pilot. With good wishes and handshakes all round 'Uncle George' took his leave and climbed down into the waiting Trinity House pilot cutter, quite taking it for granted that in a fortnight or so he would be reboarding the *Titanic* at the Nab and guiding her back up into Southampton harbour on her triumphant return home.

After a few minutes' wait until the pilot cutter was well clear, the telegraphs on the bridge were rung to 'Full Speed Ahead' and the *Titanic* was away on the first leg of her journey to Cherbourg.

'What is it, Symons?' Lightoller recognised the voice outside his cabin as that of one of the look-outs and came out to inquire what he wanted.

'We have no glasses in the crow's nest,' came the anxious reply.

'All right,' acknowledged Lightoller and went along to Murdoch, the First Officer to see if he could sort it out. Murdoch told Lightoller that he knew all about it and would see to it.

The glasses still did not materialise and the *Titanic*'s team of six look-outs became more and more agitated about it. Why, they were unable to understand, were the glasses that had always been supplied to them in the *Oceanic* being denied them now? Equally mystifying there had been a pair in the crow's nest during the trip from Belfast to Southampton which had in the meantime unaccountably gone. Sometime later two other look-outs, Hogg and Evans, came to ask Lightoller again where the glasses were.

He never did manage to sort the problem out, but he was not entirely to blame. The root of it lay in the confusion caused by the reshufffle of senior officers back in Southampton. Glasses had been supplied for the look-outs in Belfast by the original Second Officer Blair who had dropped out, but unbeknown to Lightoller, on leaving the ship in Southampton he ordered them to be taken from the crow's nest and locked up in his cabin. The glasses were never located and neither were any to replace them. It seemed the ship that was the last word in everything and wanted for nothing—even down to cigar holders in the First-Class bathrooms—could not provide a pair of glasses for the look-outs. Short of the officers' sharing their own glasses with the crow's nest, which would have been considered not only impractical but highly abnormal, there was no choice but for the look-outs to do without them. They would have to rely on the naked eye for just this one trip.

By the evening of Thursday April 11th the *Titanic* was skirting the south coast of Ireland and heading out into the Atlantic, having made her two brief interim stops at Cherbourg and Queenstown to complete her final tally of 1,300 passengers and nearly 3,500 bags of mail. Also on board was a varied assortment of baggage and freight, amongst it a valuable consignment of diamonds from Amsterdam, hundreds of cases of the best French wines, an abundant selection of the finest Calais lace, a number of automobiles and the latest spring creations from Paris eagerly awaited by the fashion houses of New York. There was also a rumour that she was carrying a large consignment of gold bullion and that somewhere securely locked away in one of her many safes was a priceless jewel-encrusted edition of the *Rubaiyat of Omar Khayyam*. The personal jewellery carried by the élite of her passengers was itself worth a few king's ransoms, worlds away from that of the 700-odd passengers in steerage, most of them emigrants representing most nationalities of Europe venturing out to the New World full of heady dreams of the fortune they too might one day amass in the new life awaiting them.

Over the next couple of days Lightoller settled down to his duties in his new ship. As he was warming up to his work so too was the *Titanic*. She had been originally designed as a twin-screw vessel to do a maximum speed of 21 knots, but while she was in the building it was decided to add a third centre screw driven by a steam turbine, the latest marine-engine development which had been tried and successfully proven in smaller ships. This additional power now meant the *Titanic* was theoretically capable of much more than 21 knots and as day followed day and more boilers were fired up that theory was being put into practice. Yet despite that awesome power plant that was driving the *Titanic* at an ever increasing speed across the Atlantic Lightoller noticed there was an almost total absence of noise and vibration which he had become so accustomed to in the *Majestic* and to a lesser extent in the *Oceanic*. As the weather continued fine and clear the passengers revelling in all the comforts and luxuries of this remarkable floating palace, found it hard to believe they were at sea at all—even if it was just a little too cold to spend any length of time out on deck. While for many of them this was all very akin to a holiday cruise, for Lightoller up forward on the bridge it was very much work, and work where he rarely got the chance to enjoy more than a few hours' sleep at a time.

His 24-hour day consisted of 4 hours on watch and 8 off, which in his own case as Second Officer was 6 till 10 in the morning and the corresponding watch in the evening. But once relieved on the bridge by the next Officer of the Watch, he had to make his rounds which, in a ship the size of the *Titanic*, even when he more or less knew his way about her miles of decks and passages, could take another hour or more. Then he might be called upon to relieve other watch-keeping officers during meal times, and he would always have to be there at the daily muster of officers on the bridge at noon to 'take the sun'. Along with the others, Lightoller would level his sextant to his eye and follow the sun as it rose and, when it reached its zenith, measure its altitude from the horizon. The ship's latitude determined from the noon sight, when related back to the observation taken at dawn, gave them their midday position which, on Sunday April 14th, showed that in the last 24 hours the *Titanic* had steamed 546 miles, 27 miles further than the previous day.

Captain Smith was confident that the next 24 hours would see an even better performance and had suggested to some passengers that if the fine weather held they might well arrive in New York on Tuesday evening, a good few hours ahead of the originally scheduled arrival time of 5 a.m. Wednesday. Meanwhile down below in the stokehold more boilers were lit.

At 12.30, soon after the noon sight had been taken, Lightoller relieved First Officer Murdoch for his lunch. It was a beautiful clear day with just a faint breeze which slightly disturbed the calm sea as it glinted and sparkled in the spring sunshine. Compared to the kind of conditions Lightoller was generally used to on the Atlantic at this time of year the weather was being unusually kind.

Presently he was joined on the bridge by 'E.J.' who showed him a wireless message that had lately come in from the Cunard mail steamer *Caronia*. 'Captain *Titanic*—West bound steamers report bergs, growlers and field ice in 42°N from 49° to 51°W.' According to this message ice lay 250 miles ahead of the *Titanic*'s present position. It did not appear to be of any undue concern to Captain Smith as he stood next to his Second Officer staring ahead from the bridge before leaving him to go down to his table in the dining room for lunch.

When Murdoch returned at 1.00 Lightoller mentioned the ice message to him. It was the first Murdoch had heard of it.

After handing over the course and speed ('Everything the same') Lightoller went below for his own lunch and then to grab a few hours' sleep. He was due back on the bridge for his next 4-hour stint at 6 p.m.

17

'Captain *Titanic*.—Have had moderate variable winds and clear fine weather since leaving. Greek steamer *Athenai* reports passing icebergs and large quantities of field ice today in Latitude 41°51′N, Longitude 49°51′W. Wish you and *Titanic* all success, Commander.'

The *Baltic*'s message was one of a number of further ice reports that reached the *Titanic*'s wireless room during the second half of Sunday April 14th in amongst all the other traffic being dealt with by the overworked, underpaid Marconi operators Phillips and Bride. The major part of their work was taken up with passengers' messages and receiving the latest world news for the *Titanic*'s newspaper the *Atlantic Daily Bulletin* including, most important of all, the latest prices on Wall Street and the London and Paris Stock Exchanges. The *Baltic* message had spent the afternoon in the pocket of J. Bruce Ismay after the Captain had formally acknowledged it and handed it to him at lunchtime when it came in. 'E.J.' liked to keep his Managing Director informed of what was going on. Sometimes they were important matters, sometimes trivial. It did not come to the attention of the officers until the evening when Smith asked Ismay if he could have it back so that he could put it up in the officer's chartroom for their information. In the meantime more ice warnings had been intercepted . . . '*Amerika* passed two large icebergs in 41°27′N, 50°8′W' . . . 'To Captain *Antillian* 6.30 p.m. apparent ship's time, Latitude 42°3′N, Longitude 49°9′W. Three large icebergs to the southward of us.' . . .

It was nearly dusk when Wilde handed over his watch to Lightoller and, after informing the new man of the ship's course and speed, left him to it. The engines were turning over at 75 revolutions per minute which told Lightoller that the *Titanic* was now easily exceeding 21 knots, her fastest speed so far.

Shortly before he came on watch she had 'turned the corner'. This was the point about 300 miles south east of Newfoundland where all Atlantic mailboats following the so called 'Great Circle' route across the Grand Banks needed to make a significant alteration in course to starboard to bring them back on a more direct line with their destination. The *Titanic* was following the ice-track, the correct course laid down for the time of year, a more southerly and longer one than the lanes taken during autumn and winter specifically to steer clear of the ice that always drifted south from the Arctic in spring. There were those mailboat commanders who did not take the precaution and would continue to use the more northerly route whatever the time of year at great risk to their ships and passengers purely in the interests of making a smart passage.

It had earlier been noted by one of the junior officers, Boxhall, while working out the *Titanic*'s latest position, that 'E.J.', in his written order for the time of course change and the new heading, had instructed it to be carried out some three quarters of an hour later than it would ordinarily have been done. It could only be assumed that the Captain, having in mind the reports of ice, had opted to remain on the more southerly course for longer to lessen the chances of encountering it. It seemed he was heeding the warnings and playing safe. Such reports of ice were commonplace at this time of the year except that this time, because it had been an abnormally mild Arctic winter, more ice than usual seemed to be drifting down the Labrador Current.

Between 7 o'clock and 7.30 that Sunday evening Lightoller was relieved temporarily by Murdoch while he went down for his evening meal. When he returned to the bridge the temperature in that short space of time had dropped sharply, some 4 degrees, Murdoch informed him, as the Second Officer resumed his watch.

It was now almost dark and the cloudless sky had become a mass of stars. Looking out from the bridge Lightoller could see them setting down all the way to the horizon. It was time to take the evening fix and the conditions could not have been better. He took up his sextant and called out to Pitman, the Third Officer to stand by the chronometer, the precision-accurate ship's clock slung on gimbals in its special mahogany box for timing celestial observations. Lightoller peered through his sextant at the heavens . . . Polaris . . . Sirius . . . Arcturus . . . Cappella . . . Alpha . . . Altair . . . They were all there bright and clear as he made his selection of stars for latitude and longitude. Each time he took a sight Lightoller called out 'Stop!' and with each call the junior officer noted down the star and its precise time on the chronometer.

His work with the sextant finished, Lightoller went back to concentrating on the sea ahead while Pitman got down to work in the chartroom armed with the logarithm tables and nautical almanac from which he could compute the ship's position from Lightoller's sights. Before Pitman had got properly into the job Eight Bells were struck for 8 o'clock and time for the junior officers to change watches. It was with some relief that Pitman handed his work over to Boxhall. 'Here's a bunch of sights for you, Old Man. Go Ahead!' As Boxhall, something of an enthusiast in the art of navigation, went to work where his colleague had left off he was highly impressed. A better set of stellar sights he could not have for working out a fix. If ever there were beautiful observations, he reflected, Lightoller had got them on this night.

Unbeknown then to Boxhall much was going to depend on the accuracy of the *Titanic*'s position he calculated from those stars.

Lightoller continued to peer forward from the bridge, his eyes glued to the horizon, in his mind a footnote from the Captain in the night order book to keep a sharp look-out for ice. Meanwhile the temperature continued to fall. When he noticed it had dropped to 1° above freezing he told Hitchens the standby Quartermaster, to give his compliments to the carpenter and advise him to look to his water as it was about to freeze, at the same time sending word to the engine room warning them to take the necessary similar precautions with the steam winches. Lightoller saw no significance in the rapidly falling temperature. He would claim he had known it to drop to freezing in the North Atlantic even in mid-summer.

It was around 9 o'clock when Captain Smith decided it was time to take his leave of the cheery dinner party being given in honour of the retiring commander by a select group of millionaire American passengers. It was a token of their gratitude to this popular English mailboat captain who had always looked after them so well. This, his latest and last command, was the crowning glory of an illustrious career in which he had commanded no less than seventeen ships of the White Star Line. Now he was to bury the anchor and settle down at last with his pension to the peace and quiet of his neat little home on the edge of the New Forest with his devoted wife and young daughter. Taking command of the *Titanic* on her maiden voyage could not have been a better climax to it all, and with a bit of luck, if the weather remained kind, well they would be unlikely to smash any records this trip, but they could still make the smart passage which everyone, not least Mr. Ismay, the Managing Director, was quite rightly expecting on this, the maiden voyage of 'the finest ship in the world'.

As 'E.J.' stubbed out his second cigar under the chandeliers of the First-Class restaurant, made the appropriate excuses to his rich

American friends, the ladies in their fabulous minks and sparkling jewellery and headed for the bridge, all just then could not have been better with the world.

The first thing he remarked on was the cold as he picked out Mr. Lightoller, his Second Officer, in the darkness of the bridge and made his way over to him. Lightoller readily agreed, informing his commander he had already advised the engine room of the sharp drop in temperature and seen to it that the necessary precautions had been taken with the ship's water supply.

They progressed onto the subject of the freak weather conditions generally; the total absence of wind and the apparently flat calm sea. From what Lightoller knew of warnings received so far by the *Titanic*, ice did not appear to pose a serious threat to the liner on her present course, but Captain Smith nevertheless seemed concerned about the difficulties there might be of spotting ice in these exceptional circumstances. Lightoller was equally aware of it, remarking to his commander what a pity it was that the breeze had not kept up while they were passing through the ice region. His experience of ice in the North Atlantic had taught him the signs to watch for. Even the slightest breeze would create waves breaking round the base of a berg which produced a phosphorescent glow visible for miles. And all icebergs he knew had a crystallised side from exposure to air that displayed a certain amount of 'ice blink', the reflected light from a berg which could quite often be seen even before the ice came over the horizon. However 'ice blink' was at its most visible when there was a moon, and on this night there was no moon, another factor adding to this unusual combination of sea conditions.

In fact in all the years Lightoller had been crossing the Western Ocean he had never known a night quite like it; hardly a breath of wind and the sea as flat as a table top. But then appearances could be deceptive way up on the lofty bridge of a ship like the *Titanic*. On this ocean there was bound to be some degree of swell even if it was not perceptible from 70 feet above the surface.

'It's quite clear, though,' said the Captain to him as he began to get his night vision. Lightoller agreed, adding there was sure to be a certain amount of reflected light from a berg. 'E.J.' had no doubts about that, suggesting that even if the 'blue side' was towards them —the side of a berg recently broken off from a main body of ice—they would still see the white outline in plenty of time. The Captain was obviously awake to the possibility, if in his own mind only remote, that they might come across ice, which he underlined as he departed from the bridge to his room with instructions to Lightoller that if it became at all doubtful to let him know. Any sign of haze and he would have to slow down.

Meanwhile the bridge telegraphs remained on 'Full Speed Ahead' and Lightoller saw no reason to question this. In all the years he had been crossing the Atlantic in the White Star mailboats he had never yet known speed to be reduced in clear weather, day or night, even when it was definitely known that the ship was in the vicinity of ice that lay directly in her path. All the rival lines followed the same practice. An iceberg coming into view 1½ to 2 miles off could always be avoided by a turn of the wheel.

Although the policy of 'cracking on' at full speed in all kinds of weather and adverse conditions had been one that Lightoller found difficult to come to terms with in his early days with the line, he had long since accepted it as the normal way of things on the North Atlantic mailboat run. And there was no doubt that he could not recall any incident worth speaking of to suggest that perhaps a more prudent approach towards speed might be adopted. The days were long past when as a mate in a sailing ship such as the *Knight of St. Michael* he had spent his watch vigilantly pacing the poop, carefully monitoring the behaviour of every sail and yard, constantly on the alert to every vagary of the wind and sea and any dangers that might lie ahead. Somehow that unwavering respect for his 'harsh mistress' that had been so rigorously instilled into him in those early adventurous years of sail training did not seem to apply these days to quite the same degree. In a ship like the *Titanic* it could apply even less.

However on this night his seaman's sense of danger was telling him of the need to be more vigilant than usual. Soon after the Captain had gone to his room Lightoller decided to make sure that Jewel and Symons in the crow's nest were on their toes. He called to Moody, the tall willowy young Sixth Officer and told him to phone up and tell them to keep a sharp look-out for ice, particularly small ice and growlers (ice almost submerged). Moody picked up the phone, twizzled the bell handle and when one of the pair answered from their perch high up on the foremast Moody, following Lightoller's directive, told him to keep a sharp look-out for ice, especially small ice and put the receiver down. Lightoller was not satisfied. Moody had forgotten to mention growlers. He picked up the phone again this time repeating the message in full.

1 *Primrose Hill*, a steel-built four-masted barque of William Price & Co.,
Liverpool. (*National Maritime Museum, London*)

2 The crater, the island of St. Paul, Indian Ocean, where the *Holt Hill* was
wrecked in 1889. This sketch appeared in the *Illustrated London News* of 19
August, 1871. (*The Illustrated London News Picture Library*)

3 Lightoller as a young merchant-marine officer of about twenty, c. 1894.

4 The *Knight of St. Michael* after she was sold and renamed the *Pacifique*. Lightoller was Third Mate, then Second Mate in this vessel which experienced a fire at sea. (*National Maritime Museum, London*)

5 Lightoller as First Officer aboard the *Oceanic*, c. 1910.

6 (above) The *Medic* in Sydney harbour. This was his first White Star appointment. It was on this liner that Lightoller brought his Australian bride back to England. (*National Maritime Museum, London*)

7 (right) The White Star liner *Oceanic*, fated to run onto a reef in Scottish waters while under joint Royal Navy/Merchant Marine command in 1914. (*Harland & Wolff*)

8 (right) RMS *Titanic*. (*National Maritime Museum, London*)

9 Second Officer Lightoller of the *Titanic* (center) chats with Captain Rostron (right) and another officer of the rescue ship *Carpathia* on the trip back to New York. (*Courtesy of Walter Lord*)

10 On this upturned lifeboat, found drifting in mid-Atlantic some time after the sinking of the *Titanic*, Lightoller and thirty other survivors clung for the night until rescued by the *Carpathia*.

11 Lightoller (second from left) with Sylvia during an interval at the Board of Trade inquiry into the sinking of the *Titanic*. (*Syndication International*)

12 The only known picture of the *Titanic*'s four surviving officers photographed together. Left to right: 2nd Officer Lightoller, 3rd Officer Pitman, 4th Officer Boxhall, and seated below, 5th Officer Lowe. (*Courtesy of Walter Lord*)

13 The torpedo boat-destroyer HMS *Falcon* on the Dover Patrol under the command of Lieutenant Lightoller, RNR. She later sank beneath him after a collision in the North Sea. (*The Trustees of the Imperial War Museum*)

14 The destroyer *HMS Garry* which rammed and sank *UB 110* in the summer of 1918. (*National Maritime Museum, London*)

15 The yacht *Sundowner*, a converted Royal Navy pinnace, at Ostend.

16 'Lights' in command of a sailing vessel of the Admiralty Small Vessels Pool.

17 (above) Lightoller with his eldest son Roger, soon after Dunkirk. Roger was killed in France in the last month of the war. (*Syndication International*)

18 (below) 'Granny Lights': Sylvia Lightoller at 80 years of age bound for Dunkirk in *Sundowner* on the 25th anniversary of the evacuation. (*Sunday Times*)

Lightoller wanted to be absolutely sure in his own mind that if any ice could be drifting into their track it would be seen in plenty of time. From the ice information he was aware of he was alert to the possibility of seeing it but he was not expecting it. He could not recall sighting an iceberg for the last three years on the run despite the usual warnings that came every spring. But because it did appear that this time the ice was reaching further south and in greater quantities, there was just a possibility that the smaller ice which generally formed the ice limit might have drifted into the latitudes they would be passing through.

Despite the intense cold he decided to walk out almost to the end of the exposed wing of the bridge and station himself in a position clear of the mast, stays, backstays and so on, to have an unobstructed view right ahead. To him fog and haze were the most ominous of all danger signs on the Grand Banks that icebergs were about, but there was as yet no sign of visibility reducing. The night remained absolutely clear with the stars out in their multitudes.

The liner's bows, 190 feet before him, were now cutting through the smooth Atlantic Ocean at an easy 22½ knots as her speed continued to increase. In his cold ears the gentle hum of the air in the rigging played along with the swish of her wash spreading out on either side of the ship in jumping, tumbling breakers of foam, glinting under the glow of the bright lights that stretched way back along the 900 foot length of the liner as she drove on through the night. Standing their lonely vigil high up in the crow's nest, the isolated figures of Jewel and Symons kept their eyes fixed on the sea ahead, mindful of that instruction from the bridge to keep a special look-out for small ice and growlers. Two hours on, four off, they knew only too well on this wickedly cold night they were earning their extra five shillings per voyage look-out pay. Each half hour the peace would be suddenly broken by a sequence of clanging as the bell struck on the bridge was answered by the bell in the crow's nest with the look-out man's cry of 'All's well and lights burning brightly!'

In the shadow of the wheelhouse Quartermaster Olliver bathed in a faint glow from the binnacle, gripped the spokes of the helm, his task to keep the liner on her steering compass heading of N 71 W, course S 86° W true, as chalked on the course board hanging nearby illuminated by a dim hooded light, just enough for it to be read without affecting the night vision of the officer on watch.

Keeping Olliver company was his opposite number Hitchens, due to take over the wheel from him at 10 o'clock, but in the meantime standing by to run messages for the officer of the watch and keep an eye on such things as the compass lamps, the readings on the thermometer and barometer. At the rear of the wheelhouse was the door leading to the chartroom where, on a long mahogany chest in the centre, was spread out a large sheet, the North Atlantic Track Chart with the *Titanic*'s course clearly marked upon it. Meanwhile up on the wall the Master Clock, which controlled all the clocks in the ship ticked the *Titanic*'s minutes by with unfaltering accuracy. It was 9.30 p.m. and aft of the chartroom in the officers' quarters it would not be long before First Officer Murdoch was being knocked up by Hitchens for his next watch, while Chief Officer Wilde and juniors Pitman and Lowe continued to enjoy their well earned rest in the few hours still to go before they were next due on. Behind them, next door in the Marconi wireless room, Phillips, the Chief Operator toiled on, wishing right now that he too could be slipping off to sleep in his bunk, but there was too much work to do. The transmitter had broken down the day before and, having spent most of the following night diagnosing and rectifying the fault with Bride, his junior, he was faced with an immense backlog of work. Pale-faced and exhausted, Phillips battled away, bent over his Morse key . . . 'da. .dit. .dit . .da. .dit. .dit . . .' It seemed he would never get through the pile of passengers' business that had to be dealt with. He was in the midst of coping with all this private traffic when a message suddenly broke through from another ship: 'From *Mesaba* to *Titanic* . . . In Lat. 42°N to 41°25'N, Long. 49°W to 50°30'W, saw much heavy pack ice and great number of large icebergs. Also field ice. Weather good, clear.' Phillips hastily scribbled the message down and acknowledged it, 'Received thanks', and put it under a paperweight at his elbow. He would take it to the bridge just as soon as he got through with the rest of his work. However once the business on the wireless was finished there were still the accounts to be written up. The message lay there forgotten.

Lightoller was coming to the end of his watch. He was perishing cold and beginning to think longingly of his warm bunk, but he remained stationed out in the open, in the position along the bridge he had chosen to get the best unobstructed view forward, every so often raising his glasses to his eyes and scanning the horizon carefully. He could see that visibility was still crystal clear with no sign of ice. He did not know that a message had just come in to the wireless room which would have told him instantly that a great mass of ice, including many large bergs, was sitting in the *Titanic*'s path and little more than 40 miles away.

'Lights' could not have been in a happier frame of mind. A happily married family man of 38 with a future that could hardly have looked more rosy. Another year or so and he would be promoted to Chief, if not in the *Titanic* perhaps the *Olympic*, or in the third of the big sisters still in the building, and then after another couple of years, perhaps three, his own command! A smaller ship of the line, no doubt, but she would be his. That would be a proud day for sure, not least for Sylvia, who was just as keen if not more so, for her husband to get on in his career as he was himself.

It was chilly on the bridge-wing, though. His mind went back to those horrendous seas of the Horn where, as a fourteen-year-old, he had found himself fighting his first life-and-death battle against the elements as he endured those endless, gruelling hours hanging on aloft. And then came that dark, moonless night when the storm just died away and the sea became an oily calm as the wind dropped with not so much as a breath of air to disturb the sails slatting idly at the yards. They were in amongst ice and in the worst conditions for seeing it; no wind, not even the slightest breeze, the sea as smooth as glass, and no moon—and never had the boy felt such cold . . .

'It's pretty cold!' said Murdoch as he arrived on the bridge, wrapped up in scarf and thick overcoat and flapping his arms about his body. Lightoller hardly needed reminding as he informed Murdoch the temperature had now fallen to freezing point. He had been rarely more grateful for the welcome sound of Four Bells and the end of his watch on that cold bridge.

The two of them stood together yarning for a spell gazing ahead while Murdoch got his night vision. Murdoch and Lightoller were old shipmates by now, having sailed together many times in the White Star mailboats. A little older than the Second Officer, Murdoch, from a Scots seafaring family, was hoping for his own command soon and had also been slightly taken aback by his own temporary demotion from Chief Officer to First. They talked about the ship and how no fault could seemingly be found with her; her steadiness, the absence of vibration and how comfortably she slipped along. She was in a different class altogether from the *Oceanic*, and even her sister ship the *Olympic* from which Murdoch had come. She had shown herself capable of a good turn of speed so far but both were agreed she would eventually do even better.

They got on to more immediate matters, the ice reports and the weather conditions. The biting cold, apart from the discomfort it caused was equally insignificant to Murdoch who, like Lightoller, knew the temperature could fall to freezing at any time of the year in these waters, summer, winter or spring.

Lightoller mentioned the commander's earlier visit to the bridge and his discussion with him about the chances of encountering ice, but how he had seemed quite satisfied that visibility was clear enough to see it in plenty of time. There had been no apparent deterioration since, though the horizon did not seem to have quite the same marked definition that it had shown earlier.

The *Titanic* had now reached the general zone where from their own past experience Lightoller and Murdoch would be on their guard for ice, but there was still nothing in the warnings they knew of to suggest to either of them, on the liner's present course that the risks of encountering it were that much greater on this April passage than in any past year. There was more ice about this time, they did know, but as far as the pair were concerned the *Titanic* ought to be passing to the south of it. However Lightoller let Murdoch know he had already detailed the crow's nest to be on special look-out just in case. In the event Lightoller was well aware there was nobody more capable than his senior to handle a tricky situation should it arise.

He had proved that one foggy night some years earlier in another White Star liner. Murdoch was Second Officer at the time and had just come on duty on the bridge when there was a sudden cry from the look-out: 'Light on the port side!' It was a large sailing ship which was almost on top of them. 'Hard a-port!*' yelled the First Officer who was still on the bridge, but before the man at the helm had a chance to turn the wheel Murdoch had jumped across and shoved him aside and grabbed onto the spokes himself, holding the ship firmly on her original course, while everyone else on the bridge looked on in horror. 'Hard a-port for God's sake!' screamed the First Officer again but Murdoch stood rigidly still, ice-cool, not moving the wheel an inch as a three-thousand-ton four-masted barque bore down on them from out of the fog. Would she hit? She must surely do as everyone on the bridge ducked expecting the yards of the sailing ship

---

*The helm order to 'port' in those days meant turning the ship to starboard.

to come crashing through the wheelhouse at any moment. But miraculously she missed, only just, perhaps by mere inches, but she went free.

Murdoch fearing a confusion of orders had acted swiftly and decisively on his own initiative and held the ship on her course. A change of direction either way could have ended in collision. No, there was no doubt about it, as Lightoller knew, few could handle themselves better in an emergency than Bill Murdoch.

Meanwhile the ice warning from the *Mesaba* remained under the paperweight in the wireless room as Phillips continued to plug away at his transmitter.

While a grateful Jewel and Symons were being relieved by Fleet and Lee in the crow's nest and passing on the order to keep a sharp look-out for small ice and growlers, on the bridge Lightoller went through the final formalities of handing on the ship's course, speed and revolutions to Murdoch, wished him well for his next four freezing hours and set off on his rounds. It would mean covering a mile or more of decks as well as a few hundred feet of ladders and staircases.

The Sunday night revelry in the *Titanic* was drawing to a close. It was a night that many were agreed they would remember for a long time as they laughed and chatted their way to bed on the Grand Staircase under the gaze of the magnificent showpiece clock flanked by its two bronze figures symbolising 'Honour and Glory Crowning Time'. In the Palm Court the ship's versatile eight-piece orchestra under the leadership of Wallace Hartley was rounding off its concert with a selection from *The Tales of Hoffmann*, which many of the audience had seen and enjoyed at one of the celebrated opera houses of Europe during their travels. Hartley always knew just how to please the customers; whatever the mood, his little orchestra expertly catered for it. From Ragtime to Beethoven, it was always played to absolute perfection. There was a ripple of applause, Hartley bowed obligingly, Lightoller pressed on.

In the male-dominated smoking-room there were still a few scattered groups sitting around, some playing bridge, some just reading and others, over a final brandy and cigar, immersed in conversations ranging from amusing personal experiences to more weighty matters on the economic and political front. The coal strike, Lloyd George's budget and the Stock Exchange boom were the main talking points just now among the English passengers, while for the Americans the big sensation was Roosevelt's victory over Taft in the Pennsylvania primaries.

As Lightoller got on with his extensive tour, working his way down through the decks, the other public rooms and bars were emptying. The First-Class lounge on A Deck, the Second-Class smoking-room and bar on B Deck and the Third-Class common room and smoking room on C Deck, where the appearance of a rat that evening had provided an hilarious diversion. The various dining rooms and restaurants about the ship had long since closed but the rattle and clatter of crockery and cutlery was still much in evidence as waiters, chefs and general kitchen staff busied themselves preparing for tomorrow's breakfast. More than 500 people were engaged all round the clock in the work of keeping everyone in the *Titanic* fed and looked after, almost eight times the number of actual seamen thought necessary to navigate and work the ship.

Descending further on down, Lightoller made his way briskly along a wide working passageway running almost the whole length of the ship, known to some of the crew as 'Park Lane' and to others as 'Scotland Road', then deeper still to find himself in amongst the lowest form of life, in every sense, in contrast to the palatial surroundings many decks above. Down here in the heat, noise, grime, sweat, curses and crudities of the engine room and stokehold, the 'Black Gang' toiled to satisfy the demands of 150 furnaces; the taut muscles of their bare arms and backs glistened with perspiration in the heat as ton after ton of coal was cast into the roaring glow. 'Clang, scrape, clang', went the shovels while the trimmers with their barrows scurried to and fro along the narrow dark passageways that led from the bunkers to the furnaces . . . filling, trundling, tipping and then back again for more to be sure and maintain the constant supply needed to 'keep that arrow up' on the steam gauges. On this night the gauges were hovering at 210lbs per square inch, just 5lbs off the maximum working pressure, but by this time tomorrow it was expected that the needles would be registering on the limit, when the *Titanic* was due to make her fastest run. Further aft in the cavernous engine room amidst the deafening roar of throbbing, rumbling, whining machinery, the engineers under the supervision of Bell the 'Chief' were preparing for it. They had been hard at work for most of the day tuning up every moving part of the three massive steam engines for the turn of speed that would be asked of them the next day.

As Lightoller eventually surfaced on deck at the after end of the ship it would have been impossible for the men enduring that thick roasting atmosphere 60 feet below to believe how bitterly cold it was out in the open. Here on the poop he checked round to see that Quartermaster Rowe and his men were at their stations, and then with his rounds complete, hurriedly made his way back forward along the length of the liner to the officers' quarters behind the bridge and the warmth of his tiny cabin. He was never more thankful to roll himself up in the blankets and close his eyes at last.

It was just as he was nodding off in the quiet calm of his little room that suddenly he felt an ominous shudder run through the ship.

18

The smoothness and steadiness of the *Titanic*'s progress up to then had made this sudden grinding vibration of just a few seconds all the more pronounced to Lightoller as he instantly leapt from his bunk and, still in pyjamas, nipped out on deck and peered over the port rail. He looked fore and aft along the side of the ship, and could see nothing in the darkness. He glanced towards the bridge and saw Murdoch from behind standing there looking straight ahead in his normal watch-keeping position apparently unperturbed. He scampered over to the starboard side, once again scanning the length of the ship but still saw nothing. He noticed that she had slowed right down. The wash of the ship was not frothing and foaming in its usual way, and he estimated her speed had reduced to around 5 or 6 knots. He turned towards the bridge again and saw Captain Smith silhouetted in the same position as Murdoch had been on the other side, standing very still, looking ahead.

Just then he came across Third Officer Pitman, who had also been brought out of his bunk by this abnormal disturbance in the ship's movement. 'We must have hit something,' said Pitman. 'Evidently!' replied Lightoller grumpily, feeling the cold cutting through him like a knife as he stood there in his night clothes. His first instinct was to go up to the bridge and find out what was wrong, but there did not appear to be any undue alarm, and what with the freezing cold and knowing that an officer off watch would not be welcome there—especially in pyjamas—opted to return to his cabin and wait. If they wanted him, better to be where they could find him. He lay back down on his bunk wondering what it was they had struck. There had been no real sense of collision, more a kind of shiver that ran through the ship. He was pretty sure it was ice but he had seen nothing when he looked over the side. Perhaps one of the propellors had struck, sheering a couple of blades off.

He would not wonder for long. Barely ten minutes had gone by when Fourth Officer Boxhall opened Lightoller's door and poked his head round. 'You know we've struck an iceberg.' 'I know you've struck something,' Lightoller answered, feeling rather irritated at this distraction from his precious sleep. 'The water's up to F deck in the Mail Room,' added Boxhall quietly. He needed to say no more.

As the Fourth Officer went out Lightoller was up and, pulling on a pair of trousers, pullover and bridge coat over his pyjamas, went out on deck. The first thing that hit him was the awful din. The *Titanic* was now stopped and because she had been running under a full head of steam, every safety valve was lifted and the steam was roaring off at all exhausts. It was deafening and impossible for anyone to be heard.

Meanwhile Captain Smith, who had come out of his quarters and onto the bridge the moment he felt the slight jar, was sizing up the situation.

Fleet, sharing the look-out with Lee up in the crow's nest, had been the first to pick out the dark shape looming up at them from out of the night. Realising within seconds what it was he gave three sharp clangs on the crow's nest bell and then instantly rang up the bridge. 'Iceberg right ahead!' 'Hard a-starboard!' ordered Murdoch, and then 'Full speed astern!' But it was already too late—even for Murdoch. The ship turned but not enough. After an agonising wait of 37 seconds she struck the berg which tore a three-hundred-foot gash along the starboard side starting just forward of the foremast, while tons of ice cascaded down across the foredeck. The time on the Master Clock was 11.40 p.m.

The watertight doors had been closed and 'E.J.' was now looking at the inclinometer, the device to indicate how much the ship was listing. 'Oh, My God!' he muttered into his beard. He saw that the ship was already listing 5 degrees to starboard. An inspection of the damage by the Captain with Thomas Andrews, the Harland and Wolff Managing Director, who had come on the trip to iron out teething problems, would reveal that the *Titanic* had been holed 20 feet below the waterline in six compartments. With two flooded she could have floated easily, with three of her first four holed she would have been all right, even with four of her first five compartments flooded she might just have had a chance, but with six laid open to the sea which was now gushing in at hundreds of tons a minute she had no hope.

Captain Smith gave the order to Chief Officer Wilde for the lifeboats to be uncovered and, in response to Nichols the Bosun's pipe for 'all hands', the *Titanic*'s seamen began tumbling out on deck. By now alarm bells were jangling in the crew's quarters all over the ship. Lightoller took charge of the even-numbered boats on the port side starting up forward, but the terrific roar of steam blowing off overhead was still making it impossible to be heard. For a time confusion reigned amid the noise while seamen, still strange to the ship, were sparsely distributed about the boats and assigned by mime to their duties. There seemed so few of them. Lightoller found that a wave of the hand and a tap on the shoulder was enough to convey the message to his men, who hurriedly set about stripping off the boat covers, fitting in the cranks to the davits, hauling tight the boat falls, and coiling them down on deck to make ready for swinging out and lowering. There had never been a boat drill aboard the *Titanic*, not even a boat muster, and Lightoller was thankful just then that the men of the British Merchant Service were showing some initiative in the difficult circumstances. He was convinced by now that the situation was serious—mailbags floating about in the mailroom was obviously serious—but at this stage he did not think for one moment that the ship was actually going to founder.

Passengers were beginning to appear on the boat deck in an assortment of garb; some fully dressed, a few still in evening wear, some in their night clothes and others in an odd mixture. Most of them were wearing lifebelts that had been hastily helped on to them by stewards, who had been going round the cabins and staterooms knocking up their passengers and ushering them up on deck. Many had come reluctantly. There was hardly any joy being herded out onto the deck of a ship in mid Atlantic on that freezing cold night. As they stood there looking anxious and bemused, things were not helped any by the wild thunder of steam blasting off above.

Lightoller was getting impatient. His boats were uncovered and he was ready to swing them out. He rooted out Chief Officer Wilde, whom he found coming across the boat deck between the funnels, cupped his hands to his ears and yelled 'Shall we turn the boats out?' 'Wait!' said Wilde. The Chief Officer seemed reluctant to get on with it. Lightoller returned to the port side feeling slightly frustrated as his men hopped about in the bitter cold trying to keep themselves warm. Just then he saw the Captain coming out of the wireless room, went up to him and, funnelling his hands to his ears as he had done with Wilde, asked again whether he should swing the boats out. 'Yes, swing them out!' shouted back 'E.J.' Lightoller got his men to work again. 'Easily now . . . easily . . .' Even if this was just a precaution that would amount to nothing more than a rather ill timed boat drill they might as well see the job through and have it done efficiently. What he did not know just then was that the Captain's visit to the wireless room had been to instruct Phillips and Bride to send out the international distress call. The whole idea had seemed ridiculous to the pair as Phillips started up the transmitter . . . 'CQD . . . CQD . . . CQD . . . CQD . . . CQD . . . CQD . . .' and then the *Titanic*'s call sign 'MGY . . . Have struck an iceberg. We are badly damaged. *Titanic*. Position 41°44′N, 50°24′W.'

CQD up to then had been the recognised international distress call but at the suggestion of Bride, Phillips changed it to the new one, SOS. 'It may be your last chance to send it!' Bride jested to his partner. Captain Smith was there at the time and they all laughed. A few moments later the *Titanic* became the first ever passenger ship to send out an SOS.

Lightoller was starting to get impatient again. His boats were now swung out and ready. He sought out the tall hefty figure of Wilde and asked whether they should start putting women and children into them. Wilde was still in no mood to rush things. 'No, wait!' Lightoller was not satisfied. He strode up to the bridge, found Captain Smith and once again shouted into his ear above the din. 'Shall I get the women and children away, sir?' The Captain just nodded. Lightoller returned to his lifeboats on the port side and motioned the order for No. 4 boat to be lowered to the level of A deck, the next one down. He judged that it would be easier and safer for people to get into it from there. A strong hawser running the length of the ship level with A deck, ordinarily used for coaling could be utilised for fastening the boats to while passengers got in. At the top of his voice he ordered that women and children be sent down to get into No. 4 when it arrived. However when it did, it was discovered that the windows of the enclosed forward end of A deck were locked, preventing the would-be embarkers from climbing through. He sent orders for the windows to be unlocked and opened at once and in the meantime for all the people sent down to be brought back up again. They were not taking too kindly to being messed about. Boat No. 4 would have to wait and he moved aft to the next one, No. 6. For the first time Lightoller noticed that the ship was distinctly down at the head. So far nobody had told him of the true gravity of the situation and he had not had time to ask. He had worked it out in his own mind that the *Titanic* had more than likely hit the iceberg a glancing blow with her bow which had holed her in one, or at the most two forward watertight compartments and it was water flooding into these that was causing her to settle at the bow. In that event he expected that when they had filled to capacity the ship would trim down until she balanced her buoyancy and remain afloat—at a very uncomfortable angle—but still floating.

'CQD . . . CQD . . . SOS . . . SOS . . . CQD . . . SOS . . . Come at once. We have struck a berg. CQD OM . . . Position 41°46′N, 50°14′W, CQD SOS . . .' Phillips beavered away at his set. He was now transmitting a new position. Initially he had been given one hastily worked out from dead reckoning, but E.J. ordered Boxhall to calculate a more accurate position based on the stellar fix from earlier that evening. Many lives were now going to depend on those observations taken by Lightoller through his sextant a few hours before . . . 'MGY CQD . . . Position 41°46′N, 50°14′W. Require immediate assistance. We have collided with iceberg. Sinking. Can hear nothing for noise of steam.'

Just then the earsplitting row of the steam blowing off stopped leaving in contrast a deathly silence as passengers milled about the boat-deck, filled more with curiosity than alarm at all the activity around the lifeboats. Many had noticed the tremor running through the ship earlier and most now knew from the talk that had gone around that the *Titanic* had struck an iceberg. Some passengers had even been out to the foredeck to grab lumps of ice to show off to others, but no-one was yet near contemplating that the ship was going down. She was unsinkable wasn't she?

At last Lightoller could make himself heard, and was quite startled at first by the sound of his own powerful voice. As he was preparing No. 6 he ordered half a dozen seamen to go below to open the lower deck gangway doors on the port side. He would part fill the boats from the boatdeck and then have them loaded up to their maximum capacity by rope ladder from the gangway doors when waterborne. It would save women and children the terrors of climbing into a small boat at such a dizzy height from the water—some 70 feet—but more important, too many people occupying a lifeboat as it hung at the davits, as every seaman knew, could put dangerous strain on the boat and the lowering gear. In fact just as he was ignorant of how serious was the plight of the *Titanic* at this time, he was also unaware that the lifeboats had been designed and fully tested to be loaded up at the davits and lowered with their full complement of 65 people—something else he had not been told. Placing one foot on the deck and one in the boat he started to call for women and children. The response was not enthusiastic, but steadily in ones and twos they came forward, often persuaded by their husbands . . . 'You get into the boat dear . . . it's all right . . . nothing to worry about . . . I'll get a later one . . .' Many women were reluctant to leave their men and, once in a boat, sometimes demanded to be put off again. As all this was going on people were repeatedly asking Lightoller why they were putting the boats out and why were they putting women and children in them. He cheerfully reassured them that it was all merely a precaution and that by daylight everyone would be back on board again, or at worst they'd be taken on board the ship which everyone could see some miles off. All her lights were clearly visible off the *Titanic*'s port bow, yet so far she had failed to respond to any of their wireless calls or signals with the Morse lamp, even though other vessels all around the Atlantic had by now heard the SOS and were making for the scene. Lightoller continued to call for women and children for his boats. 'Any more women?' 'Any more women?' The thought of leaving the warmth and safety of the *Titanic* to go through the perils of being lowered all that way down to the cold, dark waters of the Atlantic still did not appeal. His confidence that the ship was not going to sink was seemingly conveying itself to others more than he bargained for.

Suddenly there was a brilliant glow of light cast over the decks that distracted everyone's attention from the boats towards the sky. 'A rocket!' came the gasp as they watched the cascade of white stars bursting with a muffled explosion over the sea. Everyone knew why ships fired rockets and those who might have had any doubts up to then about the seriousness of the situation were beginning to think again. Another burst of stars lit up the sky, then another and another.

Lightoller had managed to persuade about 25 to get into No. 6 when he decided it was time to lower away, but there had been no sign of the men he had sent down to open up the forward gangway doors to pass more people through into the boats. They were never seen again. It was later assumed that in carrying out the order they had been trapped and drowned by a sudden inrush of water. The *Titanic* was indeed in bigger trouble than Lightoller realised. The loss of half a dozen men now presented him with serious manpower problems. It had already been apparent that the number of seamen to work the boats was precious few, without any going missing at this stage. He found he had not even enough seamen to lower a boat. 'Someone for that after fall!' he called out as No. 6 was ready to go down, but there was no-one at the after fall. 'Aye, aye sir, all ready!' replied Seaman Hemming an old shipmate, who unbeknown to Lightoller had instantly jumped out of the boat to which he had been assigned, to answer the officer's call. No. 6 began creeking and jerking its way down. When it had got about halfway to the water the cry came up, 'We have only one seaman in this boat!' Lightoller called out for a seaman. There was no response. Then from the back of the crowd looking on, a man came forward. 'I am not a seaman, but I am a yachtsman. If I can be of any use to you.' He was Major Arthur Peuchen, a Canadian. Lightoller looked him up and down and then simply said 'If you're sailor enough to get out on those falls and get down into the boat, go ahead.' Major Peuchen stood poised for a moment in some trepidation at the prospect of making the perilous 10 foot leap out to the falls, but he plucked up the courage and jumped. He made it and slid all the way down into the boat. It was a brave stunt to attempt yet he would be criticised unfairly for it later. Lightoller would stand by him. He had given the man an order and Major Peuchen was the only male passenger he was to allow into a lifeboat that night. Among the women that Lightoller helped into No. 6 was Mrs. J. J. Brown, who was later to make a legendary name for herself as the 'Unsinkable Molly' Brown.

Lightoller moved on to the next boats. The shortage of seamen had made his work more arduous. He could hear the orchestra playing now above the murmur of the crowd. They had come out on deck complete with lifejackets and were entertaining the throng to a medley of ragtime. To one who had specialised in sea shanties on the banjo such numbers as 'Oh you Great Big Beautiful Doll' and 'Alexander's Ragtime Band' weren't exactly to his taste but it seemed to help. Despite the lack of assistance Lightoller had got the situation fairly well organised and under control on the port side, where his strong, resounding voice could be heard ringing out across the deck above everything else.

On the starboard side things were not being handled quite so well. Lightoller had insisted right from the start on having the people kept back so that he could have a clear channel to work in. On the other side things were going less smoothly for Murdoch and Wilde. People were getting in the way of the seamen trying to work the boats, tripping over the falls coiled on the deck, getting their feet entangled in them, and there was considerably less discrimination between men and women being loaded up. Lightoller was following the rule of women and children first to the letter, insisting that the 'Law of Human Nature' be rigidly enforced—when he could find and persuade the women actually to go. At this stage those offering to get into the boats were considered more brave than those preferring to remain on the *Titanic*'s solid decks. One boat on the starboard side was to go away with just 12 aboard, only two of them women, the celebrated Lady Duff Gordon, of London society fame, and her secretary. The rest comprised Sir Cosmo Duff Gordon, two other male passengers, plus crew. The Duff Gordons would find themselves having a lot to answer for later.

Lightoller continued to tout for business. 'Any more women?' 'Any more women and children?' Still there was hesitation. Boat No. 8 went away with 24 women, a seaman, two stewards and a cook with orders from Captain Smith to row towards the lights of the ship still clearly visible to everyone but still not responding. It looked so close that the Captain was prompted to call through his megaphone to Jones the seaman in charge of 8 to come back once he'd dropped his people off. Certain boats had been ordered to remain round the ship when waterborne but the instruction apparently was not being heeded.

Lightoller could now feel that the ship had gone down considerably further by the head. He discovered that a good yardstick to go by was the rate at which water was rising up a long emergency staircase leading from the boatdeck down to E deck. In between helping passengers into the boats he would nip over to the entrance, look down and count the number of steps it had climbed. Each time he looked, the water had advanced a few more steps, the lights still shining below the surface with a weird, ghostly effect. Although the engines were finished with and the boilers shut down, Bell and his engineers, all 35 of them, had remained below at their station to keep the pumps and emergency dynamos going. But for them the *Titanic* would have been going down much more rapidly and the lights would not still be shining brightly on the boat-deck, and Phillips would not have had the power at his fingertips to keep tapping out the most important wireless message of his young life . . . 'MGY CQD SOS We are in collision with a berg. Sinking. Head down. 41°46'N, 50°14'W. Come as soon as possible . . . MGY . . . CQD . . . SOS . . . *Titanic* to all ships. Engine room now full up to the boilers . . .' The firemen were now released but Bell and his men stayed. They would do their duty to the end.

It was now becoming more apparent to the passengers that the ship was in serious difficulty, yet there was still a reluctance to leave her.

After one of his trips to check on the progress of the water coming up the staircase, Lightoller passed the elderly Mr. and Mrs. Isador Straus leaning up against a deckhouse chatting together quite cheerfully. 'Can I take you along to the boats?' he asked Mrs. Straus. 'Why don't you go along with him, dear?' said her husband. 'No, not yet' she replied. 'Where you go, I go . . .' Then he came upon a young couple whom he guessed were from the Western States and obviously not long married. He asked the girl if he could put her in one of the boats. 'Not on your life!' she replied with a determined smile. 'We started together and if need be we'll finish together.' Lightoller walked away wondering just how near the finish was. He would never be really sure when the truth fully dawned on him that the ship was going to founder, except that he began to work with ever growing urgency and piling more and more women and children into his boats along the port side which were now going away with increasing frequency. Lightoller now knew there was no longer any hope of filling the boats up from the lower-deck gangway doors. They were now well under water. Boat No. 12 went away at 1.25 loaded with 40 women and children, with orders from Lightoller to stay close to the ship. No. 14 went down the falls at 1.30 under the command of Fifth Officer Lowe with 50 women in his charge. Lowe had earlier told J. Bruce Ismay 'to get the hell out of it!' not recognising this interfering passenger who was ordering him in a frenzy to 'lower away! lower away! lower away!' Five minutes after No. 14 departed, Boat No. 16 began its downward journey packed with women from Second Class and Steerage. For a time steerage passengers had been kept back but now the women were being brought up to the boat-deck in controlled numbers to take their turn, but there were still hundreds waiting.

Lightoller sensed there was no time to lose, and thought it a waste of precious time when Wilde came over from the starboard side and asked him where the firearms were. It had been one of Lightoller's responsibilities originally as First Officer to see that the ship was equipped with them. At the time they seemed like irrelevant ornaments to have in a ship like the *Titanic*. Now he was being asked for them on her maiden voyage. He had thrown them in a locker in the First Officer's cabin which had since been taken over by Murdoch. With the Captain, Chief Officer, and First Officer looking on Lightoller hauled them out; Webley revolvers, brand new, still wrapped in their paper and tacky with grease.

'Here you are, you may need it,' said Wilde as he handed one of the guns and some rounds of ammunition to Lightoller. Although he felt all this was an unnecessary distraction from his work at the boats at the time, later he would be thankful it happened, but not for the gun. He was about to return to the boats when he heard Wilde say he was going to put on his lifebelt. At the same moment he just happened to glance in through the open door of his cabin and see his own lifebelt sitting on top of the wardrobe. He fetched it down and put it on. He would never have thought of it otherwise. He resumed his work at the boats. The ship's lights were still functioning but getting dimmer, although still bright enough to work in. Lightoller had been puzzled for a time by a strange dazzling light waving about on the deck, giving him spots before the eyes. He then discovered it was installed in the head of a lady's walking stick and she had taken it into her mind to start directing operations with it. He instantly told someone to have her switch it off otherwise he would 'personally throw the damn thing overboard!'

There now remained just one of the full-size lifeboats to be lowered on the port side, No. 4 which was still hanging level with A deck after the earlier setback with the locked windows. They had eventually been opened and it was time to get it loaded up and away. His earlier shortage of seamen had been eased slightly by one or two sent over from the starboard side. A number of stewards and even the Captain were now helping to work the davits. A few passengers were also giving him a hand, one of them a gentlemanly and courageous U.S. Army officer called Colonel Archibald Gracie. He and a companion had been helping to round up women and children and assisting Lightoller generally around the boats. Colonel Gracie found himself impressed by the efficient and commanding way 'that splendid officer Lightoller' went about his work at the lifeboats almost as though it was an everyday occurrence. Gracie would later declare: 'Lightoller's strong and steady voice rang out his orders in clear firm tones, inspiring confidence and obedience.' However Lightoller's confidence that the mystery ship whose lights were still plain to all aboard the *Titanic* would soon come to their aid was beginning to ebb. She could not have been much more than 5 miles off yet she had remained thoroughly indifferent to the rockets, wireless calls and signals from the Morse lamp. 'She cannot help but see our signals, and must soon steam over and pick everyone up,' he had repeatedly assured passengers. How he could have done with that big gun out in Sydney harbour now, to wake them up . . .

As Lightoller was loading up No. 4, one of the passengers he helped to her seat was the pregnant teenage wife of the *Titanic*'s richest passenger, J. J. Astor. She had not been well and while Lightoller was helping her aboard Astor leaned over the rail and asked if he could join his wife as she was 'in a delicate condition'. 'No sir,' he replied. 'No men are allowed in these boats until the women are loaded first.' Astor then asked Lightoller which boat it was. 'No. 4' —growled the officer thinking the man, whom he did not know, intended to make a complaint. It had not occurred to him that his main reason for asking was to help him find his wife later.

Then Lightoller saw a thirteen-year-old boy being put into the boat among the women. 'That boy can't go!' he called. The boy's father, steel magnate, Arthur Ryerson strode up. 'Of course that boy goes with his mother, he is only thirteen.' Lightoller let him pass, muttering, 'No more boys'. Boys not much older than this one were being exposed every day to all the perils of full grown men in the world that he knew. Lightoller skipped back up to the boat deck to check his gauge. The water seemed to be coming up faster now, the lights still shining with that ghastly green glow below the surface, while the *Titanic*'s bow continued to settle lower and lower in the water. Just then someone pointed out to him that a group of men had got into Boat No. 2, one of the smaller emergency boats up forward. He went over, jumped into the boat and flourishing his gun at the men who appeared to be foreigners of some kind yelled 'Get out, you damn cowards! I'd like to see you all overboard!' They hopped out smartly, not knowing what Lightoller knew: The gun was not loaded. 'Any more women and children?' he called out for the boat he had just so effectively emptied of men. It was still a job to find takers, but eventually they were brought along in ones and twos and it began to fill up. 'Hello, Lights, are you warm?' It was Simpson, the ship's junior surgeon, renowned for being a wag. Lightoller had long since discarded his coat and was still perspiring freely in the Arctic conditions in just sweater and trousers over his pyjamas. Simpson was standing on the boat deck with his senior, Dr. O'Laughlin, and Purser McElroy who, with his two assistant pursers Barker and Denison, was watching over the ship's bags and papers. They all insisted on shaking Lightoller's hand and saying goodbye. He was too busy to be in the mood for jokes and pleasantries just then but he could not help feeling, as he hurried back to No. 4, that 'goodbye' was beginning to take on a rather poignant significance.

19

The *Titanic* did not have much longer to live and Lightoller knew it. No more did he need to look down the emergency stairway to see how fast she was going. He could tell only too well by her steadily increasing forward tilt, with her foredeck by now well under water. There was no time to waste if they were to avoid the unforgiveable disgrace of going down with lifeboats still hanging at the davits.

Considering that there had been no previous boat drill and that none of the ship's limited complement of seamen was familiar with the new type of Welvin davits, the lowering operation had been carried off with remarkable efficiency, without any major hitches or embarrassing disasters. There had at times been delay but much of it was caused by the problem of finding women and children available and willing to go away in the boats. It was largely due to the sterling efforts of Colonel Gracie and his friend Clinch Smith that 36 women and children were eventually found and rounded up to be loaded into No. 4. When Lightoller finally gave the order for it to be lowered away at 1.55 a.m., with instructions to Quartermaster Perkis in charge to lie off as close as he could, the lifeboat only needed to travel 15 feet to the water. In normal circumstances the distance would have been nearer 60 feet. This was the last of the *Titanic*'s main lifeboats to be got away. Her total of 14 full-size boats plus the 2 smaller emergency cutters Nos. 1 and 2, were now gone. Many men were still standing around on the boat-deck having made no forceful attempt to get into any of them. They could not have stood more quietly if they had been in church, Lightoller reflected. On his port side there now remained just 2 collapsible Engelhardt-type boats with canvas sides, one lashed upside down on the boat deck just abaft the bridge and the other close by on top of the officers' quarters. The more accessible one on deck was hastily lifted up and righted and hooked into the tackles where Emergency Boat No. 2 had been. Fearing that it might be rushed, Lightoller organised a ring of crewmen to lock arms round it through which only women and children were to be allowed to pass. 'Women and children! Any women and children!' he called out poised in his usual stance of one foot in the boat and one on the deck.

He had got about 15 women into it when the cry came 'There are no more women!' The boat could take 47. Men began climbing in and

Lightoller did not stop them. There were no more women and they were entitled to their place. Then someone shouted, 'There are more women!' The men without prompting immediately stepped out and made way for them, including a pair that were hurriedly escorted there by Colonel Gracie, two of the five 'unprotected ladies' he had offered his services to at the start of the voyage. Lightoller was standing in the boat helping the women in and getting them seated when Chief Officer Wilde came across and said to him, 'You go with her, Lightoller.' 'Not damn likely!' came the instant retort as he stepped back on deck. It was not any feeling of martyrdom that made him do it, just a kind of impulse. He was nevertheless starting to feel fear but was determined to conquer it. He began to turn his mind more and more to the sanctuary of his spiritual beliefs. He must not feel fear. He must cling to the 'Truth'. 'Life is Real, Death is the Illusion'.

'Lower away!' he called, manning one of the davits himself. As the canvas boat went down the falls he saw two men leap into it from A deck immediately below which was beginning to flood. 'Best of luck to them,' muttered Lightoller. As far as he knew they were the only two male passengers apart from Major Peuchen the yachtsman who went away from the *Titanic*'s port side in a lifeboat that night.

Captain Smith was now freeing Bride and Phillips from their post at the wireless. 'Men, you have done your full duty. You can do no more. Abandon your cabin. It's every man for himself.' Phillips, almost zombie-like, went on working, hunched up over his Morse key. He had long since forgotten how near he had been to the limit of his exhaustion even before all this happened. The Captain tried to persuade him again. 'You look out for yourselves now. I release you,' then adding quietly after a slight pause, 'That's the way it is at this kind of time.'

Some dozen ships at varying distances from the *Titanic* all round the North Atlantic had responded to the distress calls and were racing to the scene. The nearest to answer was the Cunarder *Carpathia* which was about 60 miles away when her wireless operator first picked up the signals. She could be up with the *Titanic*'s radioed position in about 3½ to 4 hours.

Meanwhile the ship which might have been the best rescue hope, the one that had been clearly visible throughout it all, continued to remain totally oblivious of the great sea drama building up a few miles away. Lightoller was almost beside himself with rage at this dozing bystander who surely could not have failed to at least see the distress signals which had been sent up and yet for some reason had just ignored them—but then, if he could remember, this was a situation not entirely new to him . . .

The water was now starting to swirl around the boat-deck and people were throwing deck chairs, barrels and anything else overboard that might conceivably float and support life in the sea when the time came to pluck up courage and jump—and that was not many minutes away. The deck lights were still on, but burning now with an ominous red glow.

Lightoller had just one more boat on his port side to get off, the second of the two collapsible canvas Engelhardts, the one stowed upside down on top of the officers' quarters. As the water began washing about his legs he leapt up onto the roof, stripped off the covers and with a penknife borrowed from Colonel Gracie, began furiously cutting away the ropes. There was no point now in getting it to the davits, the water was covering the boat-deck anyway. It would just have to be floated off. He called out for seamen to help him heave the boat down to the rapidly flooding deck. The *Titanic* seemed to be moving forward almost as though she had actually got under way. Indeed she had—on the last lap of her maiden voyage that was about to take her two miles down to the bottom of the Atlantic.

'All ready sir!' It was Hemming again, the man Lightoller thought he had sent away in an earlier boat. 'Why haven't you gone?' Lightoller asked him as they worked feverishly together to launch the boat. 'Oh plenty of time yet, sir!' he cheerfully replied. Lightoller would not forget Hemming. It was a difficult job getting the Engelhardt down to the deck with the rising slant of the ship, making it literally an uphill struggle, but somehow with much heaving and straining they managed to send it bumping and bouncing down to the deck where it landed with a splash upside down. Perhaps a few people might be able to scramble on to it as it floated off. Lightoller's work was done on the port side. All his boats were now away. He and Hemming ran round the top of the officers' quarters to the starboard side to see if there was anything further they could do there. He saw Murdoch and Moody bundling people into the very last starboard collapsible boat and preparing to float it off the ship.

There was no more for him to do. Every single boat had gone and Captain Smith, the man who had once said he could not conceive any condition which would cause a ship to founder, was going round issuing his last command, 'Every man for himself!' Hartley and his band were still playing, not ragtime anymore but smoother less lively music than earlier. Some recognised the strains of 'Autumn', others thought they heard the hymn 'Nearer My God To Thee'.

Just then the *Titanic* took a great plunge forward and the sea came rolling up in a huge wave over the top of the bridge where Lightoller was standing. He turned and looked aft and was horrified to see masses of screaming, wailing people, many women among them, running up the ever increasing gradient towards the stern away from the advancing deluge. Many lost the race and were drowned there and then. For a moment he watched feeling helpless to do anything for this great mass of humanity which had seemed to come from nowhere, all huddled together, some of them down on their knees praying as the decks continued to lift higher and higher beneath them.

Lightoller realised it would be pointless to become part of them as they hung desperately on to what was surely now a lost cause. It was only prolonging the inevitable. He might as well get it over with. He turned around to face the sea and dived in. Having worked up a considerable sweat during his exertions over the previous couple of hours the effect of hitting the icy water was excruciating. It felt as though a thousand daggers had been driven into his body. The shock of it for a moment caused him to completely lose his grip and he began to strike out blindly for the crow's nest which was normally a hundred feet above the sea but was now almost level with it. As he came to his senses he realised the stupidity of holding on to anything remotely connected with the ship. He turned and started to swim away. Despite his lifejacket he was finding it difficult to keep afloat. For a while it puzzled him and then he realised it was the big Webley revolver that was still in his pocket pulling him under. He hastily disposed of it and continued to swim clear as fast as he could saying to himself, 'Now I'll see how much I have learnt from Christian Science.' Then he noticed his progress being impeded by a force that seemed to be drawing him back to the ship. The next moment he found himself driven bodily up against a grating at the mouth of a large ventilator at the base of the forward funnel leading straight down into the stokehold. The tremendous inrush of water cascading down the shaft was pinning him there rigid and immovably. He went under struggling and kicking for all his worth to get free but it was no good. Sooner or later the flimsy grating must surely give way and down he would plummet, a hundred feet to his certain end in the depths of the stricken liner. But even if the grating held his chances were looking slim. The *Titanic* was now going down fast and she was taking him down with her. Kick and fight against it as he might he was powerless to escape. Further under he was taken, quicker and quicker, 5 feet, 10 feet, 20 feet, he could not tell how far he had gone except that now he realised he was drowning, but determined not to have fear, concentrating his mind on the belief that if he was not going to survive in this world he would in the next. The surf at Grand Bassam was child's play to this but whereas then he had remembered a boast that he would 'never be drowned', into his mind now came words of the 91st Psalm, 'He shall give his angels charge over thee' . . . Suddenly there was a great hot blast against his back, a kind of explosion possibly caused by the tons of freezing water coming into contact with the still hot boilers below. The force of it blew him clear and he found himself gasping for life back on the surface in amongst hordes of people being washed past him by the water viciously swirling about the sinking ship. Then he was sucked under again, this time against the grating of another shaft where water was gushing down.

How he managed to get clear of this he would never know because by then he had begun to lose consciousness. When he arrived back on the surface for the second time he was alongside an upturned boat. As he fought to collect himself it occured to him it was the one which he and Hemming had thrown down from the top of the officers' quarters. It had been washed over from the other side of the ship to the starboard side where he now was. He found a length of rope attached to it and desperately clung on, making no attempt to get aboard, all the time surrounded by a mass of souls struggling for their lives in the whirlpools of water, gasping, choking and crying for help. In the grip of the ice-cold sea he watched the front end of the *Titanic* sinking more and more quickly, her stern by now reaching almost clear of the water. Then a rending, cracking sound broke through the mayhem as the forward funnel carried away from its guys and mountings and started to topple his way. It must surely land right on top of him but as the giant funnel, all 60 tons of it, through which two railway locomotives could pass side by side, came crashing down upon the sea in a shower of sparks it missed him by what seemed inches, the great wash it created throwing him and the boat he was grasping further away from the ship. Others were less fortunate.

Among the scores of people it fell on was J. J. Astor whose charred and crushed body would later be identified by his large diamond ring set in platinum and the 4,000 dollar roll in his pocket.

Men started to scramble up onto the upturned boat and Lightoller followed, just in time to see the end of the *Titanic*. As he watched he found himself almost mesmerised by the sight of her, standing out black and massive, silhouetted against the starlit sky, her lights continuing to shine from her portholes and from the portion of her decks still above the surface where hundreds of people, both men and women, could be seen clustered together on what remained visible, panic-stricken and helpless to save themselves. The second funnel had just gone under when suddenly all her lights went out, flashing on again for just a second or two, and then going out for good to leave the foundering liner looking like a great black finger pointing up at the heavens. People were now plummeting into the water from the stern in ones and twos and scattered groups, some jumping, others falling. Then above the screams and cries of despair there came a great rumbling roar which Lightoller took to be the engines and boilers leaving their beds and crashing down through the bulkheads. The end was near. He watched her stern rear up higher and still higher, her dripping rudder and propellers clearly visible against the stars as they hung there suspended in mid-air, climbing on up until the hull reached a totally perpendicular angle to the sea, seemingly to tower right over him. It was in that incredible upright position she remained for about half a minute and then quite quietly, slowly at first but going quicker and quicker the ship which 'God Himself could not sink' slipped majestically beneath the smooth, dark surface of the Atlantic Ocean. As her stern finally disappeared from sight there followed a slight gulp that left a gentle whirl of water fussing around the spot where she had been swallowed up and hanging above it a thin, grey vaporous cloud. 'She's gone!' came the gasp from the growing crowd of men that had begun to seek refuge with Lightoller on the upturned boat.

Then across the water through the clear night air came the horrendous strains more emphasised than ever of a desperate, hopeless struggle for life to bring home the full reality of the holocaust taking place. By chance one of those who had managed to get up onto the overturned Engelhardt was Colonel Gracie, who had helped Lightoller at the boats to the very end. He too had been sucked down with the ship before somehow getting clear. The dreadful pathos of it all drove him to utter distraction. 'The agonising cries of death from over a thousand throats, the wails and groans of the suffering, the shrieks of the terror stricken and the awful gaspings for breath of those in the last throes of drowning, none of us will ever forget to our dying day. "Help! Help! Boat ahoy! Boat ahoy!" and "My God, My God!" were the heart-rending cries and shrieks of men which floated to us over the surface of the dark waters continuously for the next hour' . . .

Lightoller determined to close his ears to it. There was little he could do to help them now. He had done all that anyone could ever have asked of him and then taken his chances with the rest and taken them to the utter limit, to the point of going down with the ship, accepting at that moment if must be his end—at least in this life. But by some decree of fate he had found himself still in the world of the living. Once more he had cheated death at the hands of his mistress. Was it just luck or was it something else? He resolved to cling to 'The Truth' and he must cling to it more firmly than ever because he had not by any means beaten death yet on this night.

Lightoller stood in hushed silence at the bow of the upturned boat which had by now turned itself around to point away from the horror of the wreck. Because of the crowd that had clambered up behind him he had been obstructed to a large extent in getting a full picture of the last harrowing scenes immediately after the *Titanic* went down. There were now well over 30 men packed from stem to stern on the slippery wooden surface of this precarious floating platform, that sank deeper with every additional person squeezing on to it. It was hopelessly overloaded and in the end one or two men who tried to climb up at the stern had to be discouraged. 'Hold on to what you have, old boy! One more aboard would sink us all!' came the repeated cry from someone amongst the group. Lightoller remained silent. He could not see and he had not heard, he did not want to hear as Colonel Gracie behind him did not want to hear either for fear he might be forced to refuse some poor struggling wretch in the water begging to be helped on. Bar jumping off and swimming away into the night which would quite likely have upset the boat and everyone on it anyway there was nothing else Lightoller could do but stay put and give thanks for this seemingly miraculous new lease of life he had been granted.

Eventually a seaman somewhere further back spoke up and said 'Don't you think we ought to pray?' There was unanimous heartfelt agreement all round and in unison everyone standing on the upturned boat launched into the one prayer they all knew best. In all the time

Lightoller had known the Lord's Prayer, and heard it recited over himself since childhood, he would never be among a gathering who put such conviction and feeling into it as his companions did just then. Everyone with him was now only too aware that if they were to live through this night they were going to need all the help they could get from wherever it came. There was no sign of any of the other lifeboats. They had just rowed away and disappeared into the blackness. All was now quiet, the cries of those struggling in the water had died away. They were quite alone with nothing but an overturned boat between 30 of them and the cold, grey, unfathomable depths of the Atlantic.

In company with Lightoller, apart from Colonel Gracie, were two other First-Class passengers, the two Marconi operators Phillips and Bride and the rest all crew, mainly firemen. Because of the way everyone was huddled together in the darkness it was some time before any real identities were established. It was soon obvious that a large complement of the 'Black Gang' were aboard by some of the strong language coming from further back which took Colonel Gracie quite some time to get used to. When Lightoller's voice was eventually recognised hopes were immediately buoyed. Colonel Gracie was particularly encouraged. Having observed Lightoller's performance getting the boats away, he felt that here was one officer who would surely see them through to safety if there was any chance at all. 'We will obey what the officer orders!' cried out one of the more outspoken crew members back at the stern who sounded distinctly under the influence. At that moment there was little in the way of useful orders that Lightoller could give to anyone. Some men began repeatedly shouting 'Boat ahoy! Boat ahoy!' more to keep up their spirits than in hopes that their cries might be answered.

Lightoller eventually told them to be quiet and save their strength. When he realised the Marconi operators were aboard he enquired what ships were coming to the rescue. From the various names and positions recalled it looked as though their best hope lay in the *Carpathia* which Lightoller calculated would be up with them at about daylight. It was then he learnt of the ice warning from the *Mesaba* which never came to him on his last watch. Well, it was too late now.

Lightoller concentrated his mind on conquering the tormenting cold which was driving everyone to the limit of endurance as they stood, sat or knelt on the slippery planks of the Engelhardt's bottom while the freezing water lapped around them. It might not have been quite so bad had they been able to shift about a little to help keep some circulation going, but it was patently obvious that the slightest untoward movement would upset the lot of them into the sea. However while the severe overloading was a big disadvantage in one respect there was small but thankful blessing in the tiny degree of body heat radiating amongst the closely huddled group which was undoubtedly helping to reduce the effects of exposure.

But there were those who still would not make it.

Three men were to die as the night went on, one of them Phillips the senior wireless operator. Naturally frail and already at the end of his tether before the ship went down, the cold and the strain in the end was just too much for him as he lost consciousness and slipped overboard. There was nothing any man could do to help him. Anyone who collapsed and fell off was gone for good as it was impossible for those balancing on that unsteady perch to lean over and pull him back. Somebody offered Lightoller a swig out of a bottle that smelt of peppermint. It was some kind of alcohol. He rejected it. Somehow the thought of consuming anything just then repelled him. He was determined to rely on the powers of his own being to pull him through. He was holding fast to 'The Truth'. For him that was the key to survival if ever he was going to get out of this.

He could feel the icy water creeping slowly up his legs. The underwater air pockets in the canvas that would normally have formed the sides of the upturned boat were evidently flooding and taking it further under. The chances of it lasting the night seemed remote. Occasionally hopes were raised by green lights that appeared at intervals in the distance. It was difficult to tell whether they were from a steamer or lifeboats but they were too far away to hail and they certainly did not seem to be getting any nearer, turning hope into even deeper despair.

Two hours, three hours, four hours went by and then the first shafts of daylight began to appear on the edge of the horizon and with it the glorious sight of a ship approaching, a medium-sized passenger liner with one funnel. It must be the *Carpathia*. She was weaving her way in and out of the icebergs which in the dawn light had begun to loom up out of the ocean, great islands of ice dotted here and there as far as the eye could see, some gigantic, as big as cathedrals reaching as high as 200 feet. This was the ice that had sent the *Titanic* to the bottom.

The *Carpathia* looked so hopelessly far away as they saw her heave to and a lifeboat being taken on board. Then she moved off and other lifeboats could be seen rowing towards her. She was still 3 to 4 miles off. Would she see them? The suspense was agonising. But by now the men on the upturned boat had a more immediate problem to contend with. A breeze was coming up and the sea was beginning to rise, making their half submerged craft rock about violently. If they were not all to be pitched into the Atlantic and drowned there and then some concerted action was called for without delay.

Lightoller immediately ordered everyone to stand up who could and form two columns facing the front either side of the keel. Every time the boat lurched to the sea he ordered 'Lean to the right,' or 'Lean to the left,' and then 'Stand upright'—whichever movement was appropriate to keep the boat as steady as they could in the rising sea. It would have been taxing work in any circumstances but for men by now drained of all their reserves of strength it was more than their weak legs could stand, but Lightoller was insistent 'Lean to the left' . . . 'Lean to the right,' he persisted.

Meanwhile the *Carpathia* continued to steam around getting no nearer as the Engelhardt sank lower and lower in the water. Then Lightoller spied a group of lifeboats strung together about a quarter of a mile off. They were too far away to hear their shouts but he remembered his officer's whistle. He fetched it from his pocket, put it to his cold lips and blew one long, shrill blast. To the unbounded relief of all on the upturned boat the sound was heard. 'Come over and take us off!' Lightoller yelled. 'Aye aye, sir!' came the welcome reply in recognition of the symbol of authority. Two of the boats broke away and began rowing towards them, but the going seemed painfully slow. Would they get up to them in time? As the boats got gradually closer the reason for the snail-like progress became all too apparent. Much of the rowing was being done by women.

At last they got alongside. One of the lifeboats was already nearly full so all but a few would have to pile into the other. As Lightoller organised the transfer he told the men not to scramble and each to take his turn patiently. He waited to the last and then picking up a lifeless body and heaving it into the boat climbed in himself and took charge. It was Boat No. 12 and he soon realised his work would be cut out keeping this one afloat for any length of time. At a quick count he roughly estimated there were 75 in the 65-capacity boat. She was loaded down to the gunwales and as he detailed men to the oars and took the tiller it was all he could do to keep her head up to the rising waves which might swamp her at any moment. He tried redistributing the weight by bringing more people towards the stern to lift the bows but it hardly helped. She was grossly overloaded and virtually impossible to row. The *Carpathia* went on cruising around picking up survivors from the other lifeboats scattered about the sea ignoring Lightoller's. She must surely spot them soon and come over. The situation was getting critical. Meanwhile a kindly lady taking pity on Lightoller standing up at the tiller wet through and stiff with cold (in the same pullover and trousers over his pyjamas) insisted he have her cape. As she draped it round his shoulders and pulled the monk's hood over his head he felt not a little odd. But it did not matter. That little bit of warmth it gave was heartily welcome just then. Colonel Gracie tried to revive the man that Lightoller had hauled in with them, but it was too late. He was dead. Lightoller had thought for a while that it was Phillips but it turned out to be another member of the crew.

Then the *Carpathia* turned her nose towards them. If their wallowing boat could now just stay afloat long enough to get alongside. She could not last many more minutes. The sea was getting choppier as he steered her under the *Carpathia*'s bows. A wave came tumbling in and then another even bigger one. The next one she just managed to ride and then at last they were in smooth water under the *Carpathia*'s lee. Her gangway doors were open with rope ladders dangling down while bosun's chairs were lowered for those less able to climb. Lightoller did not stand on ceremony as he bundled women regardless of age and size—and terrified screams—into the chairs to be hoisted up. Then with everyone out of the lifeboat and safely aboard, including the corpse, he heaved his cold tired body to the rope ladder and thankfully hauled himself aboard. Boat No. 12 was the last of the boats to be picked up and Lightoller was the very last *Titanic* survivor to be taken on board the *Carpathia*. 'Hello "Lights", what on earth are you doing here?' The Cunard First Officer at the gangway doors was Dean, an old friend. It was 8.30 a.m., just over 6 hours since the *Titanic* had gone down. 'What a splendid position you gave us!' Captain Arthur Rostron of the *Carpathia* remarked to Boxhall, who recalled Lightoller's stellar observations. If they had but known it, hundreds of souls had much to thank for them, but alas in the end it was still nothing like enough. As the *Carpathia* turned away from Lat. 41°46′N, Long. 50°14′W, Lightoller was to learn the full appalling statistics of the disaster. A little over 700 survivors had been taken on board the rescue ship, which meant that some 1,500 had been lost. Apart from all the men, women and children among the passengers who had perished, every engineer to a man, all 36 of them, including Bell the Chief, had gone down with the ship having done their duty to the last, as had all the musicians who had played on bravely to the end. As for his own department, Captain Smith, Chief Officer Wilde, and First Officer Murdoch, they had gone too, leaving Lightoller the only senior officer of the *Titanic* to survive.

20

'What is your name?'
'Charles Herbert Lightoller.'
'Mr. Lightoller, where do you reside?'
'Netley Abbey, Hampshire.'
'England?'
'England.'
'How old are you?'
'Thirty-eight.'
'What is your business?'
'Seaman.'

Lightoller's luck was out. Instead of being on his way home to England, to the bosom of the loved ones he had never expected to see again, he was trapped beneath the crystal chandeliers of the East Room in the Waldorf Astoria Hotel, New York, feeling thoroughly resentful towards this vigorous, self-important gentleman of diminutive stature who was asking him searching questions. To Lightoller it was the height of impertinence that the Americans should take it upon themselves to open their own inquiry into the loss of a British ship, a loss that had not even occurred inside their territorial waters. But he had no choice. No sooner had the *Carpathia* made her sensational arrival in New York before a crowd on the dockside of some 40,000 people plus an excited mob of jostling reporters than the subpoenas were slapped on them. Chairman Bruce Ismay, Officers Lightoller, Pitman, Boxhall and Lowe, and all the rest of the crew who survived were to be detained until the American authorities were satisfied that their investigations were complete.

As the true facts of the tragedy began to emerge from out of the earlier jumble of wild and inaccurate reports in the American press, it was revealed that among the 1,500 who had gone to their last account were some of the nation's wealthiest and most prominent sons; Astor, Straus, Guggenheim, Hays, Ryerson, Thayer, Widener, Harris, Butt—the loss of Major Butt, one of President Taft's closest associates, played no small part in the Senate decision to hold its own inquiry but then there were the hundreds of emigrants on their way to America to start new lives who had also been lost to the country before ever having the opportunity to set foot on its shores.

In both Britain and the United States reaction to the news had progressed from disbelief to shock building up into a wave of grief that was sweeping both nations on a scale that neither had known before. In one place the loss was being felt particularly badly, the port of Southampton. The city was stricken. Six hundred homes had been hit by the catastrophe and at one school there were more than a hundred children dependent on parents or relations who had sailed on the liner.

Lightoller himself was also trying to adjust to the shock of losing many of his own good friends and shipmates: dear old 'E.J.', Henry Wilde, Bill Murdoch, young Moody; McElroy, Denison and Barker from the Purser's department and then Bell the Chief and all his clan, many of whom he had known intimately. Lightoller just then was feeling a very lonely man, without even the consolation of having his wife and family near him.

To add to the pressure, reaction to the disaster in the United States had begun to stir up other emotions—anger and outrage, with one man in particular at the centre of it, J. Bruce Ismay. The Managing Director and Chairman of the White Star Line had got away in one of the last lifeboats to leave the starboard side and the American public were demanding to know why his life should have been spared when so many others had perished. One senator demanded that Ismay be held responsible for the whole tragedy and face a criminal prosecution. The Press pilloried him mercilessly. He was accused of interfering with the navigation of the vessel, that he wanted to break the record for an Atlantic crossing, of jumping into the first lifeboat and even that he dressed up in women's clothes. The most savage attack of all came in the form of a cruel full-page cartoon in the *New York American* which portrayed Ismay cowering in a lifeboat while the *Titanic* sank in the background with the caption 'Laurels of Infamy for J. BRUTE Ismay' and then the inscription underneath, 'It is respectfully suggested that the emblem of the White Star be changed to a White Liver.'

This, then, was the mood of public outcry in the United States that hung over the inquiry which the Senate had taken the initiative to launch. Its self-appointed Chairman was Senator William Alden Smith, a man of legal background who made up for a lack of inches by his thrusting dynamism—if not his knowledge of the sea, as Lightoller was to discover.

When Smith realised that the Second Officer was the most senior member of the crew to survive, he set about grilling him with a will. Lightoller in turn resolved to make his answers as terse as possible. He must give nothing away to this man that would allow the finger of blame to point at any one connected with the ship or the line, himself included. But there was much to answer for; why the ship had continued to drive across the Atlantic at full speed despite warnings of ice; why so many lifeboats left the ship only partly loaded; why there were not enough lifeboats in the first place; why there were so few men to man the boats, and why such a large proportion of the survivors were made up of crew and men from the First Class, when so many women and children from steerage had been lost.

If his Managing Director was bearing the brunt of a ruthless hate campaign, on the lone shoulders of a mere Second Officer had fallen the whole burden of protecting everyone from attack, not just J. Bruce Ismay, but the Commander, Chief Officer Wilde, the unfortunate Murdoch, in fact the policy of the whole company towards the safe navigation of its ships. And then there was the big question-mark hanging over the British Board of Trade whose out-dated regulations on the number of lifeboats in relation to tonnage of ships had now well and truly come home to roost. Even if all the *Titanic*'s lifeboats had been loaded to capacity there would still only have been room for 1,170 people, and that in a ship which when full could carry more than 3,300 passengers and crew.

All these questions and many more would undoubtedly be thrashed out at the inquiry waiting for him back home. That was going to be the important one, but first he had somehow to get over this awkward hurdle and take care not to prejudice the English proceedings to follow. Senator Smith got down to business:

'When did you go aboard the *Titanic*?'

'March 19, or 20.'

'Did you make the so-called trial trips?'

'Yes, sir.'

'Of what did they consist?'

'Turning circles and adjusting compasses.'

'In what waters?'

'Belfast Lough.'

Smith's early cross-examination of Lightoller covered the initial trials of the ship, the testing of the lifesaving equipment, whether there were enough lifebelts to go round and how they actually worked. Lightoller endeavoured to describe a lifebelt to the Senator with the aid of a sketch: 'It consists of a series of pieces of cork—allow me to show you by illustration—a hole is cut in there for the head to go through and this falls over front and back, and there are tapes from the back then tied around the front. It is a new idea and very effective, because no-one can make a mistake putting it on.'

'Have you ever had one of these on?' enquired Senator Smith.

'Yes, sir.'

'Have you ever been into the sea with one of them?'

'Yes, sir.'

'Where?'

'From the *Titanic*.'

'In this recent collision?'

'Yes, sir.'

'How long were you in the sea with a lifebelt?'

'Between half an hour and an hour.'

'What time did you leave the ship?'

'I didn't leave it.'

'Did the ship leave you?' (titters)

'Yes, sir,' came Lightoller's stern and perfectly truthful reply.

Chairs creaked around the room packed with spectators and reporters as everyone craned forward to listen in awe as this 'strong and powerfully built' mailboat officer of medium height with 'the virile sea-worn face' recounted his dramatic escape from the wreck. Lightoller was to thank his good sense a thousand times over that he disobeyed Wilde's order to get into a boat. As he spoke he impressed those around him with his clear, unhurried style of speech in a voice deep and resonant, with a slight West Country burr. His temperament suggested coolness and competence and courage as he talked quietly about his close encounter with death. But Senator Smith became less impressed as he realised that his man could also be very tricky and evasive, particularly over the matter of ice warnings. There was one that the Senator seemed especially interested in, the ice warning from the *Amerika* which had been relayed by the *Titanic* herself and picked up by the wireless station in Washington.

'Did you know of the wireless message from the *Amerika* to the *Titanic*?'

'I cannot say I saw that individual message.'

'Did you hear of it?'

'I could not say, sir.'

'Would you have heard of it?'

'Most probably, sir.'

'If that had been the case?'

'Most probably, sir.'

'In fact it would have been the duty of the person receiving this message to communicate it to you, for you were in charge of the ship?'

'Under the Commander's orders, sir.'

'But you received no communication of that kind?'

'I do not know whether I received the *Amerika*'s. I knew that a communication had come from some ship. I cannot say that it was the *Amerika*.'

Lightoller had in his mind the message from the *Caronia* which the Commander had shown him earlier in the day, although he could not recall the name of the actual ship it had come from. That warning had particularly registered itself in his mind because it was the most easterly ice reported and therefore the nearest, and by his mental calculations they would be up with the longitude given in this message when he was back on the bridge for his evening watch. He refused to concede that he had seen any other. The warning from the *Amerika* had been among those received by the *Titanic*'s wireless room during the afternoon he had been off watch. He had been aware of them all right but he had not specifically noted them as he did not consider they directly concerned him. The one that did, the later really vital warning from the *Mesaba* received towards the end of his watch he had neither seen *nor* heard of until afterwards when it was too late. He must not breathe a word about that one if he could avoid it, and certainly nobody would be asking Phillips, the operator who received it. Just so long as he answered the questions 'truthfully' he need do no more. He must try not to lie. That was his strictest rule, the very top of his own personal code of principles.

As Senator Smith continued his cross-examination of Lightoller his manner of questioning at times seemed strange and unco-ordinated, often going over the same ground again and again, some of it of doubtful relevance, and it appeared that he did not always take in the answers Lightoller gave him.

The Senator decided he would like to know what the captain was doing during the evening leading up to the collision.

'From 6 until 10 o'clock was the captain on the bridge at all?'

'Yes, sir.'

'When did he arrive?'

'5 minutes to 9.'

'5 minutes to 9?'

'Yes, sir.'

'But he was not there from 6 o'clock until 5 minutes to 9?'

'I did not see him, sir.'

'You would have seen him had he been there, would you not?'

'If he had actually been on the bridge, yes, I should have seen him.'

'You did not see him?'

'I did not see him.'

'And you were there during all that time?'

'During all that time.'

'When he came to the bridge at 5 minutes to 9 what did he say to you or what did you say to him? Who spoke first?'

'I could not say, sir. Probably one of us said "Good Evening." '

'But you do not know who?'

'No.'

'Was anything else said?'

At this point Lightoller decided to relieve the monotony and volunteer the conversation he had had with Captain Smith about the weather, the calmness of the sea, the clearness of the visibility and how they were 'freshening up' their minds to recognise ice if it should appear and how Captain Smith had remarked that if it was in the slightest degree hazy they would have to slow up.

'Did you slow up?' the Senator asked.

'That I do not know, sir.'

'You would have known if it had been done, would you not, during your watch?'

'Not necessarily so, sir.'

'Who would give the command?'

'The Commander would send orders down to the Chief Engineer to reduce her by so many revolutions.'

'Through a megaphone?'

As Lightoller patiently explained that the Captain would not ask for speed to be reduced through a megaphone or for that matter down a speaking tube it became obvious that Senator Smith had much to learn about ships. In fact his knowledge of the sea seemed to fall well below the simple facts that even a schoolboy would know, such as that a ship going down by the head and going down by the bow was one and the same thing. When Lightoller told him about the forward funnel crashing down on swimmers in the water Smith asked him 'Did it hurt anyone?' Lightoller resigned to the man's apparent ignorance simply replied that he did not know. He would ask another officer what icebergs were made of. 'Ice I suppose,' he was told. But Senator Smith was to excel himself even further when he asked Lightoller whether it was at all possible that any of the crew or passengers might have sought refuge in the *Titanic*'s watertight compartments 'as a final last resort, as a place to die?'

'I am quite unable to say, sir,' was Lightoller's tactful reply.

'Is that at all likely?' the Senator persisted.

'No, sir, very unlikely,' answered the witness thinking it better if he committed himself a little more on that one. From that time on Senator Smith won himself a new title being gleefully acclaimed 'Watertight Smith' by a large section of the press back home in Britain. However, despite the fact that Lightoller had a great advantage over his adversary in matters of seamanship, the Senator was still more than capable of putting him on the spot, particularly when he realised that the officer had charge of loading and lowering the lifeboats on the port side. The unfortunate failure of Lightoller's initial plan to have the boats loaded to their full capacity from the gangway doors when waterborne had undoubtedly left him with egg on his face.

'You say there were about 25 in this first lifeboat?'

'About that.'

'And that it was loaded under your orders?'

'Under my orders.'

'What happened to that lifeboat, the first one loaded?'

'It was loaded and sent away from the ship.'

'Did it not return, because it was only half loaded?'

'Not to my knowledge, sir.'

'As a matter of fact it was not much more than half loaded was it?'

'You mean its floating capacity?'

'Yes.'

'Floating capacity, no.'

'How did it happen you did not put more people into that boat?'

'Because I did not consider it safe.'

'In a great emergency like that, where there were limited facilities, could you not have afforded to try to put more people into that boat?'

'I did not know it was urgent then. I had no idea it was urgent.'

'You did not know it was urgent?'

'Nothing like it.'

'Supposing you had known it was urgent, what would you have done?'

'I would have acted to the best of my judgement then.'

'Tell me what you would have thought wise—'

Lightoller interrupted, 'I would have taken more risks. I should not have considered it wise to put more in, but I might have taken risks.'

'As a matter of fact are not these lifeboats so constructed as to accommodate 40 people?'

'65 in the water, sir,' Lightoller conceded but emphasising 'in the water'.

'65 in the water and about 40 as they are being put into the water?'

'No, sir.'

'How?'

'No, sir; it all depends on your gears. If it were an old ship you would barely dare to put 25 in.'

'But this was a new one.'

'And therefore I took more chances with her afterwards.'

In fact both Lightoller and the Senator were still unaware that the lifeboats and their lowering mechanisms had been so designed that their full complement of 65 people could be safely loaded into the boats while they hung at the davits. Lightoller omitted to mention that he was lucky to find 25 women at all who were willing to get into the boat in the first place.

The Senator then moved on to the question of manning, and the evident shortage of seamen to take charge of the boats once in the water. Here Lightoller took the opportunity to explain how he had ordered Major Peuchen, the Canadian yachtsman, into a boat when there were no other seamen available. Major Peuchen had since found himself heavily criticised for his actions, but Lightoller made it plain that he had ordered him in and took full responsibility for the decision. But how, then, could Lightoller in pursuing his strict rule of women and children only explain the number of men that had evidently got away in the boats and that out of the seven hundred-odd people saved more than two hundred were crew?

'I don't know, sir. I know that a great number were taken out of the water. I made it my special business to inquire and as far as I can gather, for every six people picked out of the water five of them would be firemen or stewards.'

'From what you have said, you discriminated entirely in the

interest of the passengers—first the women and children, in filling these lifeboats?'

'Yes, sir.'

'Why did you do that? Because of the Captain's orders, or because of the rule of the sea?'

'The rule of human nature,' came the convinced reply, followed by a murmur of approval round the room. By the time Senator Smith had finished with Lightoller on that Friday afternoon it was approaching 7.30 p.m. He had been under cross-examination for over five hours. But this was only the preliminary inquiry.

There was more to come in Washington where the proceedings were to be re-opened at the Senate the following week. Here the bulk of the evidence was to be taken from all officers and crew subpoenaed to attend.

Meanwhile J. Bruce Ismay, who had been first to give evidence at the preliminaries in New York, asked for a second time if he could be released to go home. Like Lightoller and the rest of the surviving officers and crew, he had been detained in the country against his will. But despite Ismay's insistence that 'the inquiry as it is proceeding now may wreak great injustice rather than clear up points in question,' Senator Smith would have none of it. The inquiry must go on and J. Bruce Ismay must attend. To Lightoller the so-called 'inquiry' amounted to a complete farce where the rules and customs of the sea appeared to have no place, simply because the men conducting the proceedings displayed no knowledge of them. Lightoller was thoroughly fed up with it and just as anxious to get home as everyone else, but instead found himself pushed off to Washington to be herded with the rest of the crew into a so-called 'hotel' that appeared to him nothing better than a doss house and in his opinion distinctly unworthy of the men that formed the crew of the *Titanic*. The whole affair he found degrading. Many of the crew refused to have anything more to do with the inquiry. They felt beholden to nobody. Their pay, according to their articles of agreement, ceased the moment the ship went down. They had families at home to think of. Lightoller complained bitterly and after the intervention of the British Ambassador peace, albeit an uneasy one, was brought into the camp, and treatment improved. But it still did not solve the problem of the battalions of pressmen that hounded them wherever they went, even to the point of looking over the crewmen's shoulders when they signed the hotel register. 'Where I come from, I say a man should get a punch in the nose if he attempted to look over the guest book!' declared the fiery Welshman, Lowe, to inquisitive reporters . It seemed there was no limit to the lengths the American newsmen would go to get the very last ounce out of this sensational story. As the hearing got under way at the Senate building in Washington on the Monday, the proceedings were immediately thrown into disruption by the explosions and flashes of pressmen's cameras. Senator Smith had all the photographers instantly ejected including the man turning over a cine camera.

It so happened it was because of one particularly loaded report that had appeared in the press among the numerous others, that Lightoller was prompted to come out of his shell and make a statement before the committee. It concerned a number of telegrams which had been despatched from the *Carpathia* by J. Bruce Ismay to the company's New York Office asking that the departure of the White Star liner *Cedric* be held back so that he and the surviving officers and crew could get home in her when the *Carpathia* made port. This had leaked out and been fastened on to with eager delight by the newspapers, with accusations of an attempt by Ismay to run away from an investigation. Lightoller wanted to make out that there was no such motive and that the plan was all in the interests of keeping the crew together to get them back for the inquiry waiting at home:

'Otherwise you understand, once the men get in New York, naturally these men are not going to hang around New York or hang around anywhere else. They want to get to sea to earn money to keep their wives and families and they would ship off . . . and we would have lost a number of them, probably some very important witnesses . . .'

Lightoller then told the committee that it had been principally on his strong advice that the telegrams were sent by Ismay to request the holding of the *Cedric*, adding that at that time Ismay did not seem to be in a mental condition to decide anything for himself:

'I tried my utmost to rouse Mr. Ismay, for he was obsessed with the idea and kept repeating that he ought to have gone down with the ship because he found that women had gone down. I told him there was no such reason . . . I tried to get that idea out of his head but he was taken with it and I know the doctor tried too but we had difficulty in arousing Mr. Ismay purely owing to that, wholly and solely, that women had gone down in the boat and he had not. You can call the doctor of the *Carpathia* to verify that statement.'

Certain observers would see in this a man currying favour with the boss. However those who knew Lightoller better would argue that, when the chips were down, no-one would stand by you more loyally if he considered the cause was right. The overwrought Ismay had taken a dreadful pounding all round which Lightoller himself resented bitterly and thought it was time to try and lift some of the pressure off him. In the end it was a rather ineffectual attempt but it was the only card he could play in a bid to restore some of the poor man's lost dignity and credibility. In short he simply felt sorry for him. 'But then "Lights" always was one of those curious creatures that followed a natural instinct to go to the aid of the underdog,' an old friend would declare and certainly there was no dog more under just then than the Chairman and Managing Director of the White Star Line.

Lightoller would go on to tell the hearing that in fact Ismay did not get into a lifeboat of his own accord but was forcibly thrown in by Chief Officer Wilde. It was a collapsible and the second last boat to go away from the starboard side. When asked by Senator Smith to state what he knew of Ismay's escape Lightoller testified:

'It is that Chief Officer Wilde was at the starboard collapsible boat in which Mr. Ismay went away and that he told Mr. Ismay "There are no more women on board the ship." Wilde was a pretty big, powerful chap, and he was a man that would not argue very long. Mr. Ismay was right there. Naturally he was there close to the boat because he was working at the collapsible boat and that is why he was there, and Mr Wilde who was near him simply bundled him in.'

Lightoller never claimed that he had seen the incident and could not recall where he had learnt of it, but any suspicions that Ismay himself might have put him up to saying it were later dispelled when the man himself testified that he had after all got into the boat of his own accord. Lightoller's testimony on Ismay's departure from the ship led to one of the most comical of all question-and-answer sequences to be heard at the whole inquiry. The Senator had already thrashed out with Lightoller earlier how well he knew Ismay and whether he had spoken with him on the night of the wreck, seemingly in an effort to establish whether Lightoller had been party to helping Ismay from the sinking ship. But once again it appeared that Smith had either not taken it in, did not believe him, or had simply forgotten what Lightoller told him the first time. Again he insisted on going over it as he subjected the witness to another rapid volley.

'You did not speak to him that night?'

'I did.'

'You told me that you looked at one another and said nothing.'

'I might have spoken and I might have said "Good evening".'

'I mean after the collision—'

'After the collision. No.' Now Lightoller was confused.

'One moment. After the collision you said you saw Mr. Ismay standing on the deck?'

'Yes.'

'Looking out at sea?'

'I do not know what he was looking at.'

'You were standing out on deck about 20 feet from him?'

'No, sir.'

'You say now that you did not say that?'

'No, sir.'

'Would that not be true?'

'I do not think so. I was walking along that side of the deck.'

'How far from Mr. Ismay?'

'I walked past him within a couple of feet of him.'

'And he said nothing to you and you said nothing to him?'

'I might have said "Good evening". Beyond that I said nothing. I had work on hand; something else to do.'

'Did he say anything else to you?'

'Not that I know of. He may have said "Good evening." Perhaps I said that, perhaps I did not. I do not remember.'

'In a great peril like that, passing the managing director of the company that owned the ship, you passed him on the ship and said "Good evening"?'

'I would as I would to any passenger that I knew.'

'And he passed you and said "Good evening"?'

'I could not say. I say I may have said "Good evening" and may not, and he may have said it and he may not.'

'I only want to know as well as you can recollect.'

'I cannot say for certain.'

'My recollection of the testimony is that you said you did not speak to him.'

'I am not certain. If I did speak, it was purely to say "Good evening," and nothing more and nothing less.'

'How long was that after the collision?'

'I think you will find that in the testimony.'

198

And so it went on with a flagging, brow-beaten Lightoller getting more and more confused as to what exactly Senator Smith was trying to prove, other than that he had been lying and that Bruce Ismay was 'guilty'.

However it was one of Senator Smith's colleagues, Senator Fletcher, who would get the most profound of all answers from Lightoller, who by then had taken just about as much as he could stand. Certainly no-one could say that Senator Fletcher had not given a good deal of thought to his highly complex and involved question:

'I will get you to state, not only from your actual knowledge of the immediate effect, but also from your experience as a navigator and seaman, what the effect of that collision was on the ship, beginning with the first effect, the immediate effect; how it listed the ship, if it did; what effect it had then, and what in your opinion was the effect on the ship that resulted from that collision.'

'The result was she sank.'

21

There could scarcely have been a happier woman in London on that beautiful May morning in 1912, than Sylvia Lightoller, resplendent in brand new hat, walking arm in arm with her husband towards the imposing entrance of the Scottish Hall in Buckingham Gate. She had got her man back—a good stone and a half less of him, perhaps, and looking distinctly drawn about the face—but he was alive and at her side and that was what mattered. Sylvia was now going to make it her business to give him all the moral support she could through the next ordeal awaiting him.

The British Inquiry into the *Titanic* disaster had already started when the *Adriatic* tied up in Liverpool's Prince's Dock some days earlier, bringing home Ismay, Lightoller and the rest of the surviving officers after their eventual release from the clutches of Senator Smith.

However, despite the Senator's apparent shortcomings during his inquiry which had prompted the British journal *Syren and Shipping* to question his sanity and gave rise to a rumour that he was to be offered an engagement at the London Hippodrome, his closing speech did on certain points come all too close to the truth. He was obviously a man of much greater perception than his conduct had often suggested:

'We shall leave to the honest judgement of England its painstaking chastisement of the British Board of Trade, to whose laxity the world is largely indebted for this awful fatality. Of contributing causes there were very many. In the face of warning signals, speed was increased and messages of danger seemed to stimulate her to action rather than to persuade her to fear. Captain Smith knew the sea and his clear eye and steady hand had often guided his ship through dangerous paths; for forty years the "Storm King" had sought in vain to vex him and menace his craft; not once before in all his honourable career was pride humbled or his vessel maimed . . .

'The mystery of his indifference to danger, when other and less pretentious vessels doubled their look-out or stopped their engines, finds no reasonable hypothesis in conjecture or speculation; science on shipbuilding was supposed to have attained perfection and to have spoken her last word; mastery of the ocean had at last been achieved; but over confidence seems to have dulled the faculties usually so alert.'

In the end Senator Smith spared J. Bruce Ismay any further pain by not singling him out as a major culprit for the disaster or suggesting that he was guilty of knowingly saving his own skin at the expense of others. But there was one man who did find himself on the receiving end of a heavy rap for his actions—or lack of them. He was Captain Stanley Lord of a 6,000-ton cargo vessel called the *Californian*, bound from Liverpool to Boston, which had stopped her engines for the night in the same icefield where the *Titanic* went down (Smith had actually asked whether she anchored there!) The *Californian*, it was summarily decided, was the ship which had been seen from the *Titanic* and had failed to respond to her distress signals. She had come to light after one of her crew, on the ship's arrival in Boston, made a statement to an American newspaper (for which he was handsomely paid), telling how he had come out on deck that night and seen rockets being fired from 'a very large steamer about ten miles away'. Officers on the *Californian* had seen them too but when Captain Lord, resting at the time on the chartroom settee, was informed of them he asked, 'Are they company signals?' to which he was told they appeared to be white rockets. The fact that white was the internationally known colour for rockets of distress was not sufficient to stir Captain Lord who advised his man to 'go on Morsing' with the Morse lamp. The *Californian*'s one and only wireless operator was off watch at the time and therefore did not hear the *Titanic*'s distress calls. Eventually the big ship, which had assumed a posture that looked distinctly 'queer' to Stone, the officer of the watch and Gibson the apprentice on the bridge with him, slowly disappeared. Lord was informed that she had gone and had fired a total of eight rockets.

'Were they all white rockets?' he enquired. When he was told they were, he asked the time. It was 2.05 a.m. The skipper of the *Californian* did nothing and went back to sleep. The circumstantial evidence against him was damning and he barely helped his cause when he came under cross examination at the British Inquiry. The subject of the *Californian* was dealt with some days before Lightoller was called to the stand and Lord's sorry performance in the face of some very pertinent questions put to him by counsel condemned him all the more:

'What did you think it was firing rockets for?'

'When? I did not know anything about these rockets until 7 o'clock the next morning.'

'But you saw one fired?'

'I heard of one rocket. I did not see it fired.'

'You heard of one?'

'Yes.'

'That was *before* you went to the chartroom?'

'No, at a quarter to one.' Lord had only just then said he knew nothing of the rockets until 7 o'clock the next morning.

'Was it then you told him to Morse her and find out what ship it was?'

'Yes.'

'After the white rocket had been sent up?'

'After the white rocket had been sent up.'

'And did you tell him to send Gibson, the apprentice down to let you know his reply?'

'Yes.'

'You did?'

'I did.'

'Then, so far as you were concerned, you did not know at all what the rocket was for?'

'No.'

'And you remained in the chartroom?'

'Yes, I remained in the chartroom.'

'And you did nothing further?'

'I did nothing further myself.'

'If it was not a company's signal, must it not have been a distress signal?'

'If it had been a distress signal the officer on watch would have told me.'

'But you had been told he did not know?'

'He said he did not know.'

'Very well, that did not satisfy you?'

'It did not satisfy me.'

'Then if it was not that, it might have been a distress signal?'

'It might have been.'

'And you remained in the chartroom?'

'I remained in the chartroom.'

Captain Lord seemed totally unable to give a satisfactory explanation as to why he had failed to rouse himself from the chartroom settee to go and see for himself or at least have the wireless operator woken up to make contact with the vessel firing the rockets. Sylvia Lightoller made a point of spending a great deal of time talking with the officers of the *Californian* during the inquiry and reported back to her husband how they had openly admitted to her that several attempts had been made to rouse Captain Lord and tell him of the rockets but that he seemed unconcerned. She also got the impression that his officers were nervous of him and dared not do anything that might incur his annoyance. She would later recall an incident when her husband endeavoured to introduce her to Captain Lord during an interval at the inquiry and she indignantly refused to shake his hand. 'Come on now, Sylvia,' Lightoller said earnestly, putting his arm round her. 'Don't kick a man when he's down'. Strangely Captain Lord would claim never to have met Lightoller or his wife. However he would write to Lightoller seeking support to clear his name after the British Inquiry severely censured him for ignoring rockets which were concluded to have been those from the *Titanic*. Lightoller was sympathetic in his letters back to Lord but there was little he could say or really do to help. He had seen merely the lights of a ship 5 or 6 miles off that night. There was nothing else in the way of concrete evidence he could offer to assist Captain Lord's case. Lord would fight to the end of his life to try and clear his name, claiming, on the strength of positions, timings and types of rockets seen, that his ship was not the one sighted from the *Titanic*.

But then there would always be the argument against him that even if the signals seen from the *Californian* were not from the *Titanic*, they were from some ship and more should have been done by Captain Lord to find out who was firing them and why. No other vessel ever did come to light that was firing rockets or distress signals of any kind in the vicinity that night.

Eventually Lightoller, who had determined to keep an open mind on it, could not help but be convinced himself that the 'stand by' ship was the *Californian*. The arguments, however, still go on to this day.

Monday, May 20th 1912 was to be an important day at the Scottish Hall. On this the eleventh day of the inquiry the most important witness was due to take the stand, Charles Herbert Lightoller, but first there was the matter of the Duff Gordons to be dealt with. Lady Duff Gordon and her husband Sir Cosmo had been among just 12 people sent away in a boat from the starboard side by Murdoch. Lady Duff Gordon's secretary was the only other woman in the boat which rowed off from the wreck and never came back despite the clearly audible cries of people struggling in the water. There had since been much talk about a present of £5 which Sir Cosmo offered to the firemen and seamen with them in the boat to compensate for their loss of pay and kit. As a result No. 1 had become dubbed 'The Money Boat'. The Duff Gordons' reputation was indeed looking shaky.

As Sir Cosmo took the stand, the hall looked for all the world as though some top London Society occasion was in progress, with the ordinarily sombre surroundings lit up in a blaze of colour by the elegant ladies in their bright spring dresses and flowery hats, some friends, some not such good friends who had come to see through their opera glasses how the Duff Gordons got on.

Mr. Thomas Scanlan, who was to turn out to be Lightoller's most formidable adversary, tackled Sir Cosmo:

'Is it your evidence that while the cries of the drowning people were heard after the *Titanic* sank there was no conversation whatever between you and your fellow passengers and between you and the members of the crew?'

'I said that after the *Titanic* sank there was a dead silence.'

As Scanlan turned on the screws the handsome and erect Sir Cosmo began to look less and less composed:

'When the people were crying out for help were you all mute in the boat?'

'I think as soon as that occurred the men began to row at once.'

At this Lord Mersey, the Commissioner in charge of the inquiry, intervened:

'And, as I understand, to row away from the cries?'

'I presume so, my Lord. I do not know why.'

After Sir Cosmo had emphatically denied that his wife had pleaded with them not to go back for fear of being swamped Mr. Harbinson, counsel for the Third-Class passengers, took over the cross-examination. He showed particular interest in Sir Cosmo's offer to present each crewman in the boat with £5:

'Was not this rather an exceptional time, twenty minutes after the *Titanic* sank, to make suggestions in the boat about giving away £5 notes?'

'No, I think not,' insisted Sir Cosmo. 'I think it was a most natural time. Everything was quiet; the men had stopped rowing; the men were quiet, lying on their oars doing nothing for some time, and then, the ship having gone, I think it was a most natural enough remark for a man to make: "I suppose you have lost everything"?'

Harbinson was representing clients who had lost relations in the wreck, many of them poor families who had never seen a five-pound note in their lives. Like his colleague Scanlan he was an Irishman. Many of those who had perished were his own countrymen and women. He rounded on Sir Cosmo:

'Would it not have been more in harmony with the traditions of seamanship that that should have been the time you should have suggested to the sailors to have gone and tried if they could to rescue anyone?'

'I have said that I did not consider the possibility—or rather I shall put it that the possibility of being able to help anybody never occurred to me at all.'

'Would I accurately state your position if I summed it up in this way, that you considered when you were safe yourselves that all others might perish?'

'No, that is not quite the way to put it.'

After Lord Mersey cut in with an angry reprimand of the counsel for putting such an unfair question (greeted by a burst of applause all round the hall) it was Lady Duff Gordon's turn to take the stand. As Sir Rufus Isaacs, the Attorney General, took up his cross-examination of the lady she told the court that when she and her husband asked the officer at the boats if they might get in he had replied, 'Oh certainly. I will be very pleased!'

'Then somebody hitched me up from the deck and pitched me into the boat . . .'

'Did you hear anything said about suction?' asked Sir Rufus.

'Well perhaps I may have heard it but I was terribly sick and could not swear to it.'

'Did you hear a voice say, "Let us get away"?'

'Yes, I think so.'

'Did you hear it said,' continued the Attorney General: ' "It is such an enormous boat, none of us know what the suction may be if she is a goner"?'

'Yes, I heard them speaking of the enormous boat. It was the word "suction" I was not sure of. I see what you mean.'

'It is not what I mean, Lady Duff Gordon,' said Sir Rufus, determined to break through the lady's apparent attempt to fall back on timid femininity and dodge the crux of the question. 'It is what you are said to have said to your solicitor.' Somewhere along the line there had obviously been some breach of confidence. The Duff Gordon supporters looked anxious while certain others in the hall began to gloat.

'Well I may have said so . . .'

So any hopes the Duff Gordons may have had that the inquiry would clear their name of an unfortunate smear were not quite fulfilled. If anything, in choosing to give evidence on their own account, they had merely rubbed salt into their gossip-infested wounds.

The next witness called to the stand would have less trouble telling the hearing about 'suction'. He knew all about that only too well from his own horrific experience of it. Second Officer Lightoller's turn to give evidence had come and at that moment no-one was more aware than the sole surviving senior officer of the *Titanic* what perils awaited him at the hands of some of the ablest legal minds in the country. One slip and they would make a meal of him. He had in the end acquitted himself admirably at the inquiry in America but, compared to what was confronting him now, that was merely a warm-up bout. In contrast to Senator Smith, Lord Mersey, the Commissioner of Wrecks appointed to take control of the British Inquiry, could at least claim to be familiar with the basic rudiments of the sea, and he had determined to ensure that all those cross-examining the witnesses knew exactly what they were talking about, and in turn that all the evidence given was fully understood by the court.

As Lightoller took the oath before the large packed hall, at his back stood a great half model of the *Titanic* revealing a white cross marking the point below the waterline where the iceberg had struck. Next to the model was a map of the North Atlantic. The chart and the model together took up more than half one side of the hall. To his left up on the dais sat the rotund figure of Lord Mersey flanked by his team of five assessors, while down in front of them were seated the various clerks and legal assistants advising and taking notes, and then to his right at the front of the massed assembly of spectators and army of reporters were ranged the battery of lawyers who would be taking it in turns to cross-examine him. Lightoller was in no doubt there would be a few of them straining to get at the star witness. Each was after a share of his flesh; Sir Rufus Isaacs KC, MP, the Attorney General; Sir John Simon KC, MP, the Solicitor General; Mr. Butler Aspinall KC for the Board of Trade; Mr. Thomas Scanlan, counsel representing the Sailors' and Firemen's Union; Mr. Clement Edwards MP

acting for the dockers; Mr. Harbinson for the Third-Class passengers
. . . It was one of the most formidable gatherings of legal brains that
had ever been brought together under one roof, and now they all
confronted one solitary seaman, each preparing to take him to task on
the worst shipwreck in history and one where 'the case for the
defence' was all too vulnerable. But he had to keep his wits about
him. As before the Senate Committee he must remember to just
answer the questions as put, no more, no less, and somehow stick to
the truth, but without incriminating himself, Captain Smith and
those other officers who could not be here to speak for themselves,
and of course The Company. To Lightoller's way of thinking, so long
as the lessons could now be learned from the tragedy, then there
would be no useful profit in holding any one man or body to blame for
it. But he knew that would be no easy job.

However from out of this jungle of legal hostility there was one
thing that could emerge in his favour: while Senator Smith had said it
should be left 'to the honest judgement of England its painstaking
chastisement of the British Board of Trade,' what the Senator failed
to realise was that the body instigating the inquiry was that very
department. The Board of Trade would hardly therefore be searching
rigorously for reasons to have that judgement turned against itself.
The whitewash brush would be applied liberally where possible and
Lightoller was only too aware of that. The Board of Trade was relying
on him, if furtively, as much as the White Star Line was. But by the
same token if blame *was* unavoidable, the BOT would want a
scapegoat other than itself.

So in that underlying area of hidden support Lightoller the Second
Officer was still walking a very precarious tightrope which even the
most accomplished of politicians would fear to tread.

Sir John Simon, the Solicitor General, was the first to cross-
examine him. After going through the formalities of his rank, the
times of his watches and the route and schedule of the *Titanic* from
leaving Southampton to the collision, he moved straight on to the ice
messages. Lightoller stuck to the same line as he had done during the
American Inquiry, playing down the warnings by admitting specific
knowledge of only the one message shown to him by Captain Smith
when he was relieving Murdoch for his lunch earlier on that day.

'Did you learn while you had been off duty during the afternoon
whether any further information had reached the *Titanic* about
ice?'

'Not that I remember.'

'Of course in the ordinary course Mr. Wilde would pass on to you any information that was necessary to help you during your watch?'

'Yes.'

Sir John might well have tried to press the point, suggesting to Lightoller that surely he had at some stage come to know of further ice warnings and that Wilde, whom he was relieving, would have said something about them, but the Solicitor General was quite satisfied with the response. Lightoller's stern commanding way on the stand was already paying dividends. If he had known about more ice warnings at the time he could not remember them now. He was therefore telling the truth but he would also have to summon all his guile to satisfy his own conscience that he was not lying. Sir John moved on to tackle him about the drop in temperature during his watch that night:

'What did that circumstance, the serious drop in temperature, indicate to you as regards the probable presence of ice?'

'Nothing,' replied Lightoller with unhesitating conviction.

'You do not think it indicates anything?'

'Nothing whatever; you may have it any time in the year, summer and winter, going across the Atlantic. It is not quite so noticeable in winter because the air is generally cold.'

'That may be,' Lord Mersey intervened, 'but is it not the fact that when you are approaching large bodies of ice the temperature falls?'

'Never in my experience, my Lord.'

'It does not go up I suppose?' suggested Lord Mersey tongue in cheek. But Lightoller had a surprise for him as he replied:

'Well, though it may seem strange, it is quite possible for it to go up if ice happens to be floating in slightly warmer water, or if the wind were to come round from the southward . . . You will be frequently passing through a cold stream, and if the wind comes from the southward you will almost invariably look out for fog, owing to the warm wind striking the cold water. The atmosphere may be comparatively warm. The moment the wind comes back again to the northward you expect the weather to clear and it will get very much colder of course.'

Some might have disagreed with Lightoller's, assuming they could follow his explanation, but he was the seaman with the firsthand knowledge and experience, and they had little choice just then but to accept what he said.

'Then I may take it that that fact of the temperature did not make you any more cautious?'

'Oh no, not in the slightest.'

They got on to the Captain's evening visit to the bridge and Lightoller again recounted his conversation with 'E.J.' about the general weather conditions. Lord Mersey was prompted to suggest that if they had discussed the visibility in relation to seeing ice, then they must have had it in their minds that icebergs could be encountered:

'No, my Lord, not necessarily.'

'It sounds very like it, you know,' Lord Mersey persisted.

'No, not necessarily, my Lord.'

'You were both talking about what those icebergs would show you?'

Some might have found this challenge by Lord Mersey rather awkward to get round, but not Lightoller:

'We knew we were in the vicinity of ice, and though you cross the Atlantic for years and have ice reported and never see it, and other times when it is not reported and you do see it, you nevertheless do take necessary precautions, all that you can to make perfectly sure that the weather is clear and that the officers understand the indications of ice and all that sort of thing. That is a necessary precaution that is always taken.'

What more could they ask? Lightoller had once again got it his own way, but it was only a matter of time before they worked round to a certain question that might not be so easy to rebuff. When it came it was carefully framed:

'Supposing anybody's duty is to look out for ice at night what is your view as to the usefulness of glasses?'

It was the look-out man Fleet who had 'blown the gaff' at the American inquiry by admitting under pressure that there had been no glasses in the crow's nest. As Second Officer it was Lightoller's responsibility to see them provided but, as we know, in that general confusion over the officers' regrading in Southampton they had been overlooked. Lightoller would now have to answer for it.

'I have never picked up ice at night-time with glasses, so it is difficult for me to say,' was his guarded reply.

Lord Mersey interjected:

'What were you using them for on the bridge?'

'To assist me in keeping a look-out'

'Then you were using them; you were looking out for ice?'

'I was looking out for ice.'

For once Lightoller had put himself in danger of falling into a trap, having already admitted using glasses that night on the bridge. Thanks to a brief exchange which took place just then between Lord Mersey and the Solicitor General over exactly what points were being established on the use of glasses, Lightoller was able to prepare himself for the direct question when it came. Had he ever found ice with glasses?

'Never,' came his instant reply as he then went on to qualify it:

'I have never seen ice through glasses first, never in my experience. Always whenever I have seen a berg I have seen it first with my eyes and then examined it through glasses.'

Lightoller's message was simple. If he always saw icebergs first without glasses then the same ought to apply to the crow's nest. Glasses should not therefore be regarded as a vital tool of the look-out man's trade. It was accepted this time without query. But the question was to crop up again later, and the next time it would not be disposed of so quickly.

Meanwhile Sir John moved on to cross-examine him about his hand-over to Murdoch at the end of his watch, and what had passed between them regarding the Captain's earlier visit to the bridge:

'As far as you remember did you report anything about orders as to speed?'

'No orders. No orders were passed on about speed.'

Then came the most significant question put to Lightoller during his cross-examination so far:

'You have had great experience of the North Atlantic at all times of the year. Just tell me, when a liner is known to be approaching ice is it or is it not, in your experience, usual to reduce speed?'

'I have never known speed to be reduced in any ship I have ever been in on the North Atlantic in clear weather; not on account of ice.'

'Assuming that the weather is clear?'

'Clear.'

A murmur went round the hall, but it was a fact, as a procession of Atlantic mailboat commanders, not just of the White Star but of other lines, would confirm when later called to the stand.

When the hearing eventually adjourned for the day Lightoller could feel satisfied with his performance. He had done extremely well in the face of some very probing questions by the Solicitor General and points regularly picked up by the Commissioner, Lord Mersey. He answered each question carefully without hedging, never appearing ruffled or for one moment that he was speaking anything other than the absolute truth. Of course he knew he always had his one great ally to fall back on, an intimate knowledge of the sea and the North Atlantic which kept him that one vital step ahead of the opponent when things got difficult. It would be the same when the Solicitor General resumed his cross-examination the following day. The possible occurrence of haze was a crucial factor and the court was keen to establish whether or not there had been any sign of it which would explain why the iceberg was not seen sooner. Lightoller had already testified that the Captain said he wanted to know if visibility became at all doubtful:

'Did you hear after the accident in the course of that hour and a half or two hours from any of your superiors any information at all about how they did come to run into this iceberg?'

'None whatever.'

'No reference to what the weather had been after 10 o'clock?'

'No. The weather was perfectly clear when I came on deck after the accident, and the slightest degree of haze on the surface of the water would have been very noticeable.'

Lightoller then went on to qualify his opinion by suggesting that if there had been any haze present the lights of the ship which had been seen in the distance would not have been so clearly visible.

'Can you suggest at all how it can have come about that this iceberg should not have been seen at a greater distance? asked Sir John.

Lightoller could not answer that, but he put forward a theory:

'Of course we know now the extraordinary combination of circumstances that existed at that time which you would not meet again in a hundred years; that they should all have existed just on that particular night shows of course that everything was against us.'

Lord Mersey asked Lightoller to explain:

'In the first place there was no moon . . . Then there was no wind, not the slightest breath of air. And most particular of all in my estimation is the fact, a most extraordinary circumstance, that there was not any swell. Had there been the slightest degree of swell I have no doubt that berg would have been seen in plenty of time to clear it . . . The moon we knew of, the wind we knew of, but the absence of swell we did not know of.'

Although they had been aware that the sea was exceptionally calm that night, from experience looking down at it from the bridge of a big ship it might often appear dead flat when in fact there was quite a swell. Lightoller's point was that no matter how calm the sea might seem from a great height one would always expect *some* movement on the surface to produce visible waves at the base of a berg.

He went on:

'You naturally conclude that you do not meet with a sea like it was, like a table top or a floor, a most extraordinary circumstance, and I guarantee that 99 men out of 100 could never recall such an absolute smooth sea . . . The berg into which we ran in my estimation must have been a berg which had very shortly before capsized and that would leave most that was above the water practically black ice.'

'Does that in your opinion account for the man on the look-out not seeing the iceberg?'

'Yes.'

Lightoller's picturesque theory on the 'extraordinary combination of circumstances' appeared to be convincing the inquiry. After all there would never be anyone else to take the stand to disprove it. He was winning, but the battle was not over yet.

22

Thomas Scanlan was counsel acting for the National Sailors' and Firemen's Union. He was primarily concerned with protecting the look-outs from blame and proving that the *Titanic* was not carrying enough lifeboats and seamen, but he had another axe to grind. As MP in the House of Commons for North Sligo, and an Irishman like his colleague Harbinson, he had a strong commitment towards those Irish families who had lost loved ones in the wreck. He was a talented and, as Lightoller would learn, aggressive advocate. The witness had coped admirably with Sir John Simon, the Solicitor General but, there was no doubt that on certain points he had enjoyed a comfortable ride. That was now over and the real test was about to come.

After trying unsuccessfully to use Lightoller to expose that more seamen should have been available on the *Titanic* to launch and crew the lifeboats, Scanlan moved on to the question of visibility. Lightoller had already told the court that in his opinion there had been no haze that night to have made it dangerous to continue at full speed, but Scanlan was out to prove otherwise and he had already been helped by evidence previously given by the look-out men both in America and at the British Inquiry that a haze did develop:

'You did not observe any haze. Is it possible that the man in the crow's nest would have a better opportunity than you had of observing whether or not there was a haze?'

'No.'

'You say you would have as good an opportunity where you were stationed on the bridge?'

'Better.'

From high up, haze could be as deceptive to detect as swell and in Lightoller's opinion a man up in the crow's nest looking down on the sea would be less aware of a low-lying haze than the man on the bridge looking ahead from a lower angle. Scanlan brought up earlier testimony from the look-out men who claimed to have seen haze and tackled Lightoller again:

'Can you explain, if these men are truthfully giving their evidence, how it is that they could have observed a haze while you on the bridge would not have observed it?'

'No, I could not.'

Lightoller had, after all, left the bridge an hour and a half before the collision. For all he knew visibility could have deteriorated later, and if so, Murdoch should have realised it and taken the appropriate action. Lightoller was now in the position of having to defend a man who could not speak for himself, without knowing the full circumstances. The look-outs did know them, and claimed there was haze. They of course had their own interests to protect. The iceberg had not been seen until the *Titanic* was only 500 yards from it:

'If an iceberg loomed up ahead of you would the person on the bridge have as good an opportunity of observing it as the man in the crow's nest?' asked Scanlan.

'Quite.'

'Does it strike you in any way as a singular circumstance that when the iceberg did appear and was sighted, the observation of it was by the man in the crow's nest, and not by the men on the bridge?'

'Have we any conclusive evidence to that effect?' came Lightoller's guarded reply.

There was in fact no conclusive evidence to prove it, although evidence so far heard suggested strongly that the look-outs saw it first. Since the collision, Lightoller had endeavoured to establish just who had been the first to sight the iceberg, Murdoch on the bridge or Fleet in the crow's nest. He had come to the subsequent conclusion that they had both seen it at the same time. Some might have wondered how much it mattered. It seemingly mattered a lot to Scanlan, as he was about to reveal:

'Now you did state yesterday that you yourself had used binoculars for the purpose of detecting ice. Do you think it would have been . . .'

Lord Mersey immediately interrupted Scanlan:

'I do not think he said that. What he did say to my recollection was that he would much prefer his eye-sight for the purpose of detecting an iceberg.'

'That is right, my Lord,' Lightoller readily confirmed.

So Scanlan was out to take him to task over the absence of glasses in the crow's nest and it was obvious that Lightoller would not be allowed to get away with it quite so easily as he had done the day before. Yet Lord Mersey seemed to be showing an intention to try and help him over it as he continued to put Scanlan right:

'. . . having seen the iceberg with his eyes, he then would probably take the binoculars for the purpose of examining it more particularly.'

'Yes,' agreed the counsel graciously, but he was not going to be shaken off:

'Do you not think that before the look-out man stationed in the crow's nest ventured to report an iceberg he would require to satisfy himself that what he saw was really an iceberg?'

Before Lightoller had a chance to reply Mersey cut in again.

'Forgive me, he did not report an iceberg. What he reported by the three bells was something ahead.' (The Commissioner in fact was quite right. It was not until after Fleet had struck the collision-warning on the bell that he had rung up the bridge to inform them it was actually an iceberg.)

Lord Mersey was not making life easy for Scanlan to pursue his line of questioning on the use of glasses. For some time the banter went on between the Commissioner, the barrister and the witness on the role of the look-out man, when the crow's nest bell would or would not be struck, and the value of glasses for seeing icebergs. Scanlan battled on. He was determined to get to his point. He recounted evidence given by Fleet, the look-out man, in America to the effect that he could have seen the iceberg sooner with glasses — soon enough in fact for the ship to have avoided it. Scanlan took it up with the witness:

'From the evidence you gave to the court yesterday, at what distance ahead do you think you yourself in the peculiar conditions which prevailed this Sunday night could have picked out an iceberg.'

'About a mile and a half to two miles.'

'Do you mean with the naked eye?'

'Yes.'

'And with glasses could you discern it at a greater distance?'

'Most probably.'

'I do not follow you,' said Lord Mersey, interrupting again.

He was sure that was not the answer Lightoller meant to give. The witness corrected himself:

'I meant to convey that we do not have the glasses to our eyes all the time, and naturally I should see it with my eyes first. If I happened to be looking directly ahead at the moment an iceberg came in view and I had the glasses to my eyes at that particular moment it is possible I should see it, whereas I should not have seen it quite as soon with my eyes.'

Lightoller was endeavouring to explain that while glasses magnified, in doing so they also reduced the field of vision and in that way were a disadvantage unless they just happened to alight by chance on the object. Lord Mersey had some questions to put to Lightoller:

'Apparently binoculars are placed in a bag or a box in the crow's nest at times. At the time of the accident it is said there were no binoculars on the *Titanic* in the crow's nest. Is that true?'

'That there were none?'

'No, is it true that there is a place for them in the crow's nest?'

'I believe so.'

'Then presumably it is intended that they should be there?'

'Yes.'

'And they are there to be used I suppose?'

'Yes.'

Lord Mersey appeared to be swinging against Lightoller, or was he?

'When they are being used in the crow's nest are they used in the sense of being always held up by the look-out man to his eyes, or are they merely for recourse to as occasion seems to suggest?'

'That is it, your Lordship.'

'The man on the look-out is not always standing with the binoculars up to his eyes?'

'No, certainly not.'

'They are there for use when he thinks it desirable to use them?'

'Precisely.'

Lord Mersey was certainly going out of his way to assist Lightoller. He could hardly have done better for him had he been briefed as his own counsel, but Scanlan still was not to be put off.

'What you said was that you could see an iceberg with the naked eye from a mile and a half to two miles off, and I put it to you that with the glasses you could probably see it at a greater distance and you agreed?'

'I agree.'

'Of course the same thing would apply to the look-out man as to you?'

'Yes.'

'So that it is a matter of great consequence, do you agree, to have binoculars for look-out men?'

For once Lightoller started to show signs of losing his composure:

216

'Do you want me to pass an opinion as to whether look-out glasses ought to have been in that crow's nest? Is that it?'

'I do not think so,' interjected Lord Mersey: 'I will put it in the same form to you. He wants to know whether the look-out man ought to have the binoculars glued to his eyes?'

'Oh no, your Lordship, certainly not!'

Whether that was what Scanlan meant or not, it was so as far as Lord Mersey was concerned, Scanlan, however, pursued doggedly:

'Is it not very desirable to have glasses provided for the look-out men so that they can use them when necessary?'

'It is a matter of opinion for the officer on watch. Some officers may prefer the man to have glasses and another may not. It is not the general opinion.'

'I am not talking about the opinions of officers in general, but the particular opinion which you entertain as to the usefulness of glasses?'

'Yes. Now I can answer you decidedly. Certainly I uphold glasses.'

At last! Scanlan had broken through Lightoller's defence. Now to press home his advantage.

'I am glad you do. Do you know now that a complaint was made at Southampton by the look-out man that glasses were not provided in the crow's nest?'

'I know of no complaint.'

'Do you know there were not glasses in the crow's nest?'

'I do.'

Although it had already been established that there were no glasses in the crow's nest, there had been no suggestion up to this time as to who was responsible. Scanlan had known all along that it was Lightoller's job as Second Officer to see that the crow's nest was supplied with them and that he had been asked for them more than once by the look-outs, but he wanted to set Lightoller up first. Lord Mersey had come very near to thwarting his efforts but the barrier was finally broken down—at least almost. As far as Lightoller was concerned there had been no complaint as such. He did not like the word 'complaint' but he had to admit it had been reported:

'Can you explain to my Lord why, when such a report was made, glasses were not provided for the look-out men on the *Titanic*?'

'No, I cannot offer you an explanation.'

Lightoller might well have tried to explain the problems, but it would merely have complicated the issue.

'If it had been a matter of your discretion, would you have provided glasses then?'

'Had they been on the ship I might have done.'

'Were there glasses on the ship available for the look-out man?'

'That I cannot say.'

'Had you glasses on the bridge?'

'We had.'

'How many pairs?'

'A pair for each senior officer and the Commander and one pair for the bridge, commonly termed pilot glasses.'

'So that there would be from time to time during the whole course of the voyage a pair of glasses available?'

'On the bridge.'

'On the bridge that could have been handed up to the look-out man?'

Lord Mersey decided it was time to butt in again, which he did, using to great effect a point based on the earlier argument.

'It appears to me that whether those glasses were there or not made very little if any difference, because the man would not have them to his eyes, and when he did sight this thing it was too late to use glasses.'

Scanlan was for a moment foiled and Lightoller took advantage of this new opening presented by Lord Mersey to make his recovery:

'I should like to point out that when I speak favourably of glasses it is in the case of a man on whom I can rely, but if I have a man in a case like this . . . who is to put the glasses to his eyes before he reports, I most utterly condemn glasses. The man must report first and do what he likes afterwards'.

'I believe that is right, Mr. Scanlan,' observed Lord Mersey. 'It would be quite improper for a man who sees something ahead with his eyes to wait until he has used glasses before he reports.'

So Lightoller, with considerable assistance from the Commissioner, did in the end manage to squeeze through on the argument that glasses would have been no use to detect the iceberg into which the *Titanic* ran, despite Fleet's earlier evidence to the contrary. But it was curious why Lord Mersey had made such a point of helping Lightoller through in this case. If it was because there were no Board of Trade regulations regarding glasses for ships' look-outs, which might have been considered an oversight on their part, no legislation regarding binoculars was to appear in the numerous changes that would subsequently come about as a result of the disaster.

The most cynical among observers would say it was just part of Lord Mersey's efforts to keep Scanlan pegged down as much as he could, recognising that he was the one man most likely to succeed in throwing mud at the whitewash. As for Lightoller's claim that he had always seen an iceberg first with the naked eye before examining it with glasses, it would, according to contemporary maritime opinion (and certainly that of the *Titanic*'s look-outs) put him in the minority. But if that is what he had experienced personally, who could argue? Certainly no-one could prove he was lying.

After being on the stand throughout the morning session of May 21st, Lightoller was recalled to it straight after lunch and Scanlan resumed his cross-examination. He questioned Lightoller on why the *Titanic* had not slowed down in response to the ice warnings. The witness stuck doggedly to the line that year after year ice would be reported—never sighted. The exchanges between them grew heated:

'Am I to understand, even with the knowledge you have had coming through this *Titanic* disaster, that at the present moment if you were placed in the same circumstances you would still bang on at $21\frac{1}{2}$ knots an hour?' (The *Titanic* was in fact going faster.)

'I do not say I should bang on at all. I do not approve of the term banging on.'

'I mean drive ahead?'

'That looks like carelessness, you know. It looks as if we would recklessly bang on and slap her into it regardless of anything. Undoubtedly we should not do that.'

'What I want to suggest to you is that it was recklessness, utter recklessness in view of the conditions which you have described as abnormal, and in view of the knowledge you had from various sources that ice was in your immediate vicinity, to proceed at $21\frac{1}{2}$ knots?'

'Then all I can say is that recklessness applies practically to every commander and every ship crossing the Atlantic Ocean.'

'I am not disputing that with you, but can you describe it yourself as other than utter recklessness?'

'Yes.'

'Is it careful navigation in your view?'

'It is ordinary navigation, which embodies careful navigation.'

'Is this your position then, that even with the experience of the *Titanic* disaster, if you were coming within the near vicinity of a place which was reported to you to be abounding in ice, you would proceed with a ship like the *Titanic* at 21½ knots?'

'I do not say I should.'

'At night time, and at a time when the conditions were what you have described as very abnormal, surely you would not go on at 21½ knots?'

'The conditions were not apparent to us in the first place. The conditions of an absolutely flat sea were not apparent to us till afterwards. Naturally I should take precautions against such an occurrence.'

It seemed he was no longer a witness. He was on trial.

'And what precautions would you take if you would not slow up or slow down?'

'I did not say I would not slow up.'

'Cannot you say whether you would or not?'

'No, I am afraid I could not say right here what I should do. I should take every precaution, whatever appealed to me.'

'I suggest to you if you acted carefully and prudently you would slow up, and that if you did not slow up you would be acting recklessly. You know you have described the conditions of abnormality as having been apparent at the time while you were on your watch. You have told my Lord that at great length and in your conversations with the Captain did you not discuss that? You have said that you did not recognise that the sea was flat?'

Scanlan had found a contradiction in Lightoller's evidence. Having earlier told the court how he and the Captain had discussed on the bridge the 'flat calm' sea he had since said it had not been apparent to them until afterwards. Scanlan had a point. As he read back Lightoller's evidence the witness might well have explained that he did not become fully aware of just how calm the ice cold sea was until he found himself swimming in it, but he declined. When Scanlan asked him if those factors he apparently discussed with the Captain on the bridge were not sufficient to warn them of the extreme danger Lightoller simply replied, 'No.'

'I do not think anything would convince you that it was dangerous that night!'

'I have been very much convinced that it was dangerous,' replied Lightoller drily, followed by sniggers round the hall.

'I mean that the conditions that you have described were dangerous?'

'They proved to be.'

Lightoller remained steadfast. Scanlan became more frustrated.

'What I want to suggest to you is that the conditions having been so dangerous, those in charge of the vessel were negligent in proceeding at that rate of speed?'

'No.'

Scanlan was forced to give it up. After spending the next half hour going back over such questions as the number of lifeboats on the ship, how well they were equipped and, with particular relevance to his clients, the policy towards recruitment and employment of seamen and look-outs, he came to his last point of all. The inference in the question was all too obvious:

'Do you know whether or not a Captain of a first-class ship like the *Titanic* has a great many duties to perform of a social nature apart from his duties on the bridge? I mean looking after the passengers?'

'Oh no,' answered Lightoller emphatically. 'Of course the purser is responsible to him as everyone in the ship is responsible to him.'

'Has not the Captain as a matter of fact to be a great deal away from the bridge?'

'Oh dear, no, not at all. He does not need to be away from the bridge at all.'

'In practice is not the Captain a good deal away?'

'No,' Lightoller insisted. He knew full well what Scanlan was fishing for as he made a point of putting the record straight:

'Do not misunderstand me. Say it is hazy weather or anything like that, he would never be away from the bridge. You might go from New York to Southampton and the Captain be never away down amongst the passengers as far as that goes.'

Scanlan might well have anticipated a reply of that nature from Lightoller but he had at least made his point. He sat down and made way for the procession of his learned friends who would take their turn with Lightoller during the rest of the day. There was Mr. Roche, counsel for the Marine Engineers' Association who would ask him about the operation of the watertight doors and the lay-out of the engine room. All the engineers had gone down with the *Titanic* and Lightoller could give little useful information about that part of the ship or what was happening down there while it was sinking. Then there was Mr. Harbinson for the Third-Class passengers. He might well have taken Lightoller heavily to task on why so many Third-Class passengers had perished, but strangely he did not broach the subject at all, and in the very short time he took to cross-examine the witness he seemed preoccupied for some reason with lifeboat falls. Mr. Edwards for the Docker's Union could ask little about dock-workers in relation to the foundering of the *Titanic* so he asked instead about the possibility of local haze round the iceberg which Lightoller dismissed, how the Board of Trade surveys of the life-saving equipment had been carried out, which the witness remembered only too well, and why the ship had eventually taken on a marked list to port when she had been holed on the starboard side:

'Does not she usually list to the side from which the water is pouring in?' enquired Mr. Edwards.

'Not necessarily.'

'You would expect there would be a list to that side in which the water comes in would you not?'

'No.'

'Why not?'

'Why should I?' Laughter rang round the hall.

Mr. Edwards never did get his curiosity satisfied. He had been hoping to prove it had been caused by water rushing in through the port gangway doors which Lightoller had ordered to be opened.

Next came Mr. Lewis briefed by the British Seafarers' Union. Lightoller had earlier told the inquiry that all look-o*ts were required to have regular eye tests. Mr. Lewis commenced to take him up on it. He had since found something out to trip up the witness—or so he thought:

'I understand you to say that the eyesight test has been maintained by the White Star Company?'

'As far as is practicable.'

'Is that from general knowledge or your own experience?'

'Personal experience.'

'Would it surprise you to know that as a matter of fact the eyesight test has been discontinued for some considerable time at Southampton?'

'I might on the other hand say, would it be of any use to you to know that I insist on it?'

Laughter again filled the hall.

By the end of the inquiry which went on for 36 days, he had

answered 1,600 questions and rarely been caught out by any of them. His performance throughout, if at times a little shaky under the rigorous cross-examination of Mr. Scanlan, had been generally quite remarkable; so much so that when it was all over Lord Mersey was tempted to draw him aside and ask him discreetly whether he had at any time ever considered taking up the law for a career instead of the sea. As the eminent maritime historian Geoffrey Marcus observes (*The Maiden Voyage*) 'he proved as useful to the Company at the Court of Inquiry as he had on the bridge.' There can be no doubt that it was mainly due to his efforts on the witness stand that the White Star Line—and the Board of Trade—came out of it as well as they did. His theory on the 'most extraordinary circumstance', the absence of any breeze, the flat-calm sea and no moon, did much to convince the court that bad luck had played a large part in the tragedy. Predictably Mr. Scanlan in his closing address was not so convinced, blaming it on bad seamanship and negligent navigation through total disregard of the ice warnings. He also heavily criticised the Board of Trade for the lack of lifeboats and shortage of seamen to handle them. His Irish colleague Mr. Harbinson took the same line, also blaming the Board of Trade's outdated safety regulations for the inadequacy of the lifesaving equipment.

Lord Mersey, however, had other ideas. In his summing up he said that because Captain Smith had merely followed what had been the general policy for years it could not be said that there had been negligence, and therefore he should not take any blame. Lightoller himself had always known there was the ever-present possibility of such a disaster because of the practice of maintaining full speed in the vicinity of ice while putting all trust in keeping a keen look-out to avoid it. Because no accident had occurred there had been no cause to exercise greater caution. Alas, when the accident came it was with consequences far beyond anybody's wildest imagination. Having absolved Captain Smith of responsibility for the disaster, Lord Mersey concluded:

'It is, however, to be hoped that the last has been heard of the practice, and that for the future it will be abandoned for what we now know to be more prudent and wiser measures. What was a mistake in the case of the *Titanic* would without doubt be negligence in any similar case in the future.'

So the whitewashing was complete. It was a mistake and nobody, in Lord Mersey's opinion, was to blame, not Captain Smith, not the

White Star Line, not the Board of Trade, nor Charles Herbert Lightoller—even though there had been no glasses in the crow's nest. One thing, however, was certain: nobody, least of all Lightoller himself, would ever believe again in the unsinkable ship. Many preachers were inspired to use the *Titanic* as an example to all. The Bishop of Winchester, for instance, observed to a congregation in St. Mary's church, Southampton, the Sunday after the wreck:

'When has such a mighty lesson against our confidence and trust in power, machinery, and money been shot through the nation . . . The *Titanic* name and thing will stand for a monument and warning to human presumption.'

But if Lightoller presumed that the conclusion of the British Inquiry was to be an end to it, he was wrong. A small farmer from County Cork called Thomas Ryan would see to that. He had lost a son in the disaster and, refusing to accept Lord Mersey's verdict as final, and undaunted by the mighty legal guns that would undoubtedly be ranged against him, he decided to sue the White Star Line for damages. So Lightoller had to go through it all again, this time not in the almost carnival atmosphere of the Scottish Hall but in the High Court, where he would find the approach to it all very different. Instead of Lord Mersey being there to help him along when things got tough, he would find a dispassionate judge of the King's Bench in Mr. Justice Bailhache sitting without bias, shrewdly weighing up and analysing all the evidence put before him to be carefully interpreted for the jury who would deliver the final verdict. He also found he was once again up against his old adversary, Thomas Scanlan, who was appearing for the plaintiff. Lightoller's evidence did not work quite so effectively this time, in fact much of it, including his 'extraordinary circumstance', was discounted. The result was that the White Star Line lost the case after the jury found that the Captain had been negligent in respect of speed. However they found no evidence of negligence with regard to the look-out. The White Star Line took it to the Court of Appeal but the verdict was upheld. Captain Smith had been guilty of negligent navigation. The dangers facing the *Titanic* from ice should have been foreseen, but instead they were ignored. The whitewash so skilfully applied with Lightoller's help at the Inquiry had all been wiped away to present a very different picture of the facts behind the wreck.

By the finish Lightoller felt more like a legal doormat than a mailboat officer. To carry virtually the whole burden of answering for the *Titanic* disaster through two inquiries and then to the law courts had built up into an almost unbearable strain. When all was said and done, he was not the Captain. He was merely the Second Officer who had had the good fortune to survive, but the misfortune to be the only surviving officer of seniority. He was not even on the bridge when the collision occurred, although the more critical observer would say that in certain respects he had been as complacent about the dangers of ice as the others had appeared to be. But that was the 'practice' into which he had been moulded over the years and to a large extent by Captain Smith himself. As he said at the British inquiry 'if it was recklessness then recklessness would apply to every Commander in every ship crossing the North Atlantic.'

But it seemed that Lightoller had to end up being the whipping boy for them all and it dawned on him that the company never considered—or simply did not care—how much of a strain it had all been. If they had, perhaps there might have been the odd helpful word of encouragement and just someone to say thank-you at the end of it. But nothing of the sort ever came. It was almost as though they were disowning him. One man who would not be in a position to show gratitude on behalf of the company was J. Bruce Ismay. As a direct result of the disaster, the Chairman and Managing Director was manoeuvred off the board. If the White Star was to somehow recover its tattered reputation and win back the lucrative American clientèle who were now avoiding White Star ships like the plague, then the last man they wanted at the head of the firm was 'J. BRUTE Ismay'. Poor Ismay had suffered cruelly over his escape in a lifeboat but Lightoller would never need to fear similar scorn. He had bravely taken his chance in the sea and lived to tell a hair-raising tale. It was perhaps not surprising that subsequently he became even more devoted to his religious beliefs. Some months afterwards he was to write an article in the *Christian Science Journal* describing his escape from the wreck and how he believed that his determination to hold on to the 'Truth' had saved his life. It also occurred to him that the reshuffle of the *Titanic*'s officers, although doubtful in one respect, had played a part in his survival, calculating that if Wilde had not been on the ship he would never have been reminded to put his lifebelt on. However he might well have paused to consider that, were it not for the change-over, those binoculars would still have been in the crow's nest and, most significant of all, Lightoller would have retained his rank as First Officer and, by the system of watches, have been on the bridge instead of Murdoch at the critical moment when the iceberg loomed up. Lightoller could have reacted, if not more quickly, differently to Murdoch and the tragedy might never have happened at all.

In years to come much would be written about the *Titanic* disaster, and among the first of the numerous books to appear was one by Colonel Archibald Gracie, whose fortunes on the night of the wreck had so closely followed Lightoller's. His book published in 1913, entitled *The Truth About The Titanic*, was an impressive piece of detective work putting together, from his own view as a First-Class passenger, the events leading up to the wreck, the loading of the lifeboats, who got away in what boats and when, his own lucky escape and subsequent survival on the upturned boat. Lightoller supplied Colonel Gracie with much information to help him put it together. Sadly the author, who never fully recovered from his ordeal, died shortly before the book came out.

While he pulled no punches in writing of 'the heedlessness of danger' on the part of Captain Smith and the officers of the *Titanic*, for Lightoller at least he found cause for a generous tribute:

'For what he did on the ship that night whereby six or more boatloads of women and children were saved and discipline maintained aboard ship, as well as on the Engelhardt upturned boat, he is entitled to honour and the thanks of his own countrymen and of us Americans as well.'

The tennis party was in full swing at Nikko Lodge on that lazy, sweltering summer's day in 1913. 'Lights' had not felt so relaxed and at ease with the world for a long time as he walked from the court at the end of a lively and enjoyable game. But he was hot and perspiring from his exertions. He made his excuses and went into the house for a while to cool off.

After more than an hour had gone by and he had not reappeared, Sylvia went inside to find him. There was no sign of him on the ground floor so she went upstairs. Perhaps he was in the bathroom. The door was slightly ajar. She knocked and after getting no reply poked her head round and was horrified by what she saw. There, lying in the bath, was her husband in a kind of trance-like coma, his body rigid, his eyes glazed over in a look of fixed terror. He was still breathing. She cried for help and a couple of the men managed to lift him out of the bath and get him to a bed. Presently he began to come round and appeared to be recovering. It was as though he had suffered some kind of shock, the doctor was told.

He certainly had, and it would be a long time before Herbert Lightoller jumped into a cold bath to cool off: it brought back too many terrible memories.

PART FOUR
DOVER PATROL

Of destroyers we'd the 'Tribals' and the ancient 'Thirty-knotters',
We'd ships that carried kite-balloons and seaplanes for our
   spotters,
We had steamers armed for boarding to search for contraband,
And armed drifters and torpedo boats to lend a helping hand.

Anon, *The Dover Patrol*

23

After so many weeks in dusty court rooms under attack by lawyers, it was good to feel the deck of a ship under his feet again. To Lightoller the *Oceanic* had always been the finest ship that ever graced the Atlantic Ocean. Given time, the *Titanic* might have changed his view . . . but the *Titanic* sank underneath him.

Many lessons had been learned from the shock of the *Titanic* disaster. No more would ships drive at full speed across the North Atlantic ice region however clear the weather. From now on great caution would be observed at the slightest hint of ice, and there would always be plenty of warning in advance. The vessels of the newly established International Ice Patrol permanently on station in the ice region saw to that, keeping a continuous look-out for errant icebergs that might pose a threat to the shipping lanes. However the shipping lanes themselves were now moved further south as an added precaution.

The experience of the *Titanic* had also exposed other deficiencies, such as the hopelessly outdated Board of Trade regulations on the number of lifeboats that ships should carry. There now had to be enough boats for everyone on board regardless of the tonnage of the ship, and with a sufficient number of trained seamen to handle them. It had been realised that even if the *Titanic* had carried enough lifeboats to save everyone, the seamen would not have been available to launch and crew them. The *Titanic*'s sister ship, the *Olympic*, had been taken back to Harland and Wolff for modifications at a ruinous cost to the White Star Line of £250,000. Apart from tripling her number of lifeboats, her watertight bulkheads were raised so that she would now be able to remain afloat with six compartments flooded. Her hull was strengthened with a double skin, a feature which had been omitted when the two big sisters were originally built. That had been to save on cost. Had the *Titanic* been constructed with a double skin in the first place it was possible that the iceberg would not have inflicted such a serious wound and she could have stayed afloat. Lightoller would always maintain that if it had been the *Oceanic* that struck the berg, her much thicker, stronger hull would not have sustained anything approaching the damage that had been done to the *Titanic*.

Icebergs however were to be overtaken by a new threat to shipping on that warm day in early August as the *Oceanic* zig-zagged home from New York under full steam. The assassination of Austrian Crown Prince Franz Ferdinand by a Serb had precipitated a confrontation of European Powers. Now it was August 4th 1914 and the Great War had begun.

It was an anxious time as the *Oceanic*, deviating considerably from her normal course, neared the Irish coast and two columns of black smoke appeared on the horizon and drew nearer. As the two approaching vessels closed on the liner it was obvious they were warships of a large class. Whose, though? There were sighs of relief on the bridge when the White Ensign of the Royal Navy came into view, fluttering reassuringly in the Atlantic breeze to herald the arrival of two cruisers of the Grand Fleet to escort the *Oceanic* the rest of the way home.

When the *Oceanic* docked at Southampton she was immediately overrun by a horde of naval designers, draughtsmen, engineers, Government officials and naval brass. She was to be prepared for war. The ship that had once been the pride of the White Star Line was to have her White Star on the Red Burgee taken down, and her 'red duster' replaced by the White Ensign of the Royal Navy. In earlier years the White Star Line along with other shipping companies had negotiated a deal with the Admiralty whereby in return for ships being designed to allow rapid conversion to carry armaments, the Government would pay a grant towards their upkeep and maintenance. The *Oceanic* had been so built that her decks could be easily modified for guns to be mounted, although Lightoller wondered just how useful the old 4.7s being fitted to her would be in the event of encountering any opposition. But that was all there was available and they would have to suffice, and within two weeks RMS *Oceanic* had become HMS *Oceanic*, and was considered ready to sail to war classed as an armed merchant cruiser. Mr. Lightoller, First Officer of the White Star Line, now found himself transformed into Lieutenant Lightoller of His Majesty's Navy. If he felt some reluctance, it was not at the prospect of fighting for his country. He was fully ready. But Lightoller was a merchant-service man through and through, and to him the ways of the Royal Navy were worlds apart. As a member of the Royal Naval Reserve he had been obliged to spend a number of days each year on exercise in Royal Navy warships and had at times found their methods, to his way of thinking, verging on the farcical.

He had no time for all their pipes, bugles and traditional rituals. In the service where he had been brought up, if a job needed doing, men simply set about it with a minimum of fuss, quite often without having to be told, but not so in the fighting navy, as the rest of the crew were soon to discover.

They now had a new skipper, Captain William Slayter of the Royal Navy. However Captain Henry Smith (no relation to 'E.J.') who had been commander of the *Oceanic* for the last two years, was to stay on also as Captain, but in a kind of undefined advisory capacity. In effect the *Oceanic* would now have two captains, which Lightoller predicted right away would cause problems, not just for himself and the rest of the officers but between Smith and Slayter themselves, who would not find it easy coming to terms with this questionable policy of double-headed command. It was a situation that would surely lead to difficulties at the top. Naval officers and ratings also joined the ship to swell the company, adding to the overall confusion. Like Lightoller, the merchant seamen of the *Oceanic* all the way through her ranks saw themselves as a totally different breed to the men of the Royal Navy. They resented this sudden intrusion into their domain by the 'blue-jackets', which immediately created a rift between the two factions. It was a gap that would take some time to bridge.

When the day came near for the *Oceanic* to put to sea under her new flag, the ship's original crew were 'fell in'—a completely new experience in itself for these merchant servicemen—to be asked which of them wished to remain with the ship in her new role. At this stage of the war men still had a choice, and as Lightoller surveyed the somewhat dishevelled bunch that he knew so well scattered about the well-deck looking anything but 'fell in', he had no doubts what their answer would be. The *Oceanic* was their life, for many of them since she was built, so they would see little point in deserting her now, particularly if she was breaking off from the usual routine with the chance of some excitement in the offing. The rumour had already gone round that she was off to the Far East.

'Those now wishing to volunteer to remain in the ship, one pace forward, *march*!' barked the petty officer, a Royal Navy man down to the tips of his highly polished boots. Here was the first evidence of the new atmosphere that would prevail from now on in the *Oceanic*—at least for the next few weeks, because that surely was all this war was going to last. The navy man did not appear too impressed with the crew's interpretation of 'forward march', watching aghast as three hundred-odd men quietly shuffled a few steps forward. Lightoller quietly explained that this was meant to convey a positive response by all to the invitation to volunteer.

As the *Oceanic* proudly set off for the war down Southampton Water on August 25th she was not as it turned out bound for the Far East. Instead she headed north with orders to proceed to Scapa Flow, the Navy's principal anchorage on the island of Orkney off the north of Scotland. For Lightoller the next couple of weeks were to be a mixture of frustration, confusion and sheer comedy. An early example of the comedy was when the Bosun and Carpenter were each vested with the new rank of Warrant Officer which neither fully understood, but even more mystifying to this rough and ready pair was the sword they were presented with to go with their new rank. 'What the hell am I supposed to do with this damn thing?' growled Bob Collins the Carpenter to Lightoller. 'Take it round with me when I'm sounding ship?'

Then there was the occasion when an order was given to lower the gangway. Normally Jones the Bosun would muster a few hands and have it out through the doors to the quay in a matter of minutes. But now he was in the Royal Navy. Jones was a Bosun no longer but a Warrant Officer and must not bend his back to such manual labours. The hands must first of all be piped, then fallen in, then assigned to that particular detail before the job could actually start. Meanwhile Jones got more and more irritable and impatient as time went by and no-one had appeared. When they did, a mixture of naval ratings and his own men, such confusion followed in the execution of this normally routine job of seamanship that Jones could stand it no longer. Lightoller knowingly observed it all, finding it more and more difficult to stifle his amusement. In the end Jones, with a hail of blue language that could only come from the mouth of a Western Ocean mailboat bosun boomed at the ratings to 'get the hell out of it!' called on a couple of his own men, and with utter disregard for his rank and naval formalities had heaved the gangway out to the quay in the same minute or two it had taken him those hundreds of times before. It might not have mattered all that much, but that it happened in full view of a gathering of bemused civic dignitaries and their wives waiting to come aboard on the quay at Reykjavik in Iceland where the *Oceanic* was paying a courtesy call. How impressed these worthies of Iceland's capital were with this experience of Royal Navy 'courtesy' Lightoller was not sure; but for Jones's unorthodox intervention, however, they might well have been loitering about on the quayside for considerably longer that day.

Back at Scapa Flow saw the commencement of their training for war in earnest with gunnery practice the first priority. This too had its moments, with gun crews made up of men who had rarely been near a gun before, much less fired one. Lack of experience in this field was all too evident, highlighted by the occasion during one session of night firing practice when the ship towing the target politely signalled that it was the target they should be aiming at, and not her.

To crown it all, as though there was not enough confusion and disorder at this stage among the men of the *Oceanic* she was joined by a large contingent of Shetland fishermen who signed on to make up the required complement. Up to now Lightoller had found the going tough enough but with these new men, fine seamen though they were, when giving them an order he now had the added problem of trying to make himself understood first, not helped by his own difficulties understanding *them* and their strange dialect. This came home particularly during emergency drills for such things as 'Action Stations', 'Collision Stations', 'Fire Stations', and so on which none of the new recruits had ever heard of, so how could they identify the appropriate bugle call? Lightoller endeavoured to put them in the picture with a lengthy, painstaking explanation of what they all meant and where each man was to go in the event of these various alarms. Then he tried it out. The bugle was sounded for 'Fire Stations!' with the indication that the fire was in the forward magazine. Everyone dashed off except three. 'Come on!' yelled Lightoller at the forlorn trio still lingering on the deck with mystified looks on their faces. 'What the hell are you standing there for? There's a fire in the forward magazine!' There was a moment's pause and then the biggest one of the three, a giant of a man, gaped down at Lightoller, his eyes positively bulging out of their sockets and exclaimed: 'Guid God Sirr! Ye dinna say so!'

Eventually everyone began falling in with the method of things, at least as much as they ever would, and the *Oceanic*, complete with her glass domes, carved mahogany doors, silk cretonne walls, marble lavatories, Shetland fishermen, 4.7 inch guns and all, went to work with the Northern Patrol. Her job was to patrol a 150-mile stretch of water from the north of the Scottish mainland to the Faroes, in particular the area around Shetland. She was to carry out spot checks on shipping, look over their cargoes and check out people and personnel to ensure there were no Germans aboard, or any with German sympathies. This work would be done by boarding parties of the *Oceanic*'s complement of marines.

Lightoller's first experience of action came when they fired a shot across the bows of a ship that ignored their signal to stop. It turned out to be the very innocent and harmless coaster, S S *Watchful* of Wick which on that occasion had apparently not quite lived up to her name.

For the people on the island of Shetland it was the novelty of a lifetime to have a ship as big and famous as the *Oceanic* anchored offshore in full view. There were hundreds of them lining the harbour quay at the island's capital of Lerwick that day on September 6th to gaze on the spectacle of this proud giantess of the White Star Line weighing anchor and heading out to sea to resume her wartime patrol.

As the *Oceanic* steamed away from Lerwick on the eastern seaboard of the island she turned south on a zig-zag course for the tiny Fair Isle midway between Shetland and Orkney.

The crew of the *Oceanic* had become nicknamed 'The Muckle Flugga Hussars' by the Grand Fleet up at Scapa, Muckle Flugga being the most northerly point of Shetland and the British Isles; the name suggested that the *Oceanic*'s men would have been better off doing their job on horseback in this zone than in a ship. 'The Muckle Flugga Hussars' did not quite share the joke, realising that it was far closer to the uncomfortable truth than the wags of the Grand Fleet themselves might have realised, as the *Oceanic* steamed around in waters that were notoriously treacherous. It was an undeniable fact that the 17,000-ton, 700-foot liner was far too big and totally unsuited to the kind of work she had been put to in seas infested with reefs, shoals and outcrops of rock waiting at every turn to trap the unwary. Add to it a confused network of constantly changing, fast running tides, and the job of keeping the ship clear of trouble amounted to a navigator's nightmare, particularly for men more at home in the wide open spaces of the North Atlantic.

Captain Smith was thoroughly unhappy about the idea of his ship being exposed to such hazards. It seemed madness. He only really felt at ease when she was out in the open sea. He made those feelings quite plain to Slayter during some heated exchanges between the pair which Lightoller had discreetly observed. But the *Oceanic* was now a ship of His Majesty's Navy, Slayter was the Royal Navy man and therefore must be considered the officer in overall command. As a senior watchkeeping officer, it was hardly a situation in which Lightoller himself could feel relaxed, particularly when more than once he found himself faced with conflicting orders. Who was the Captain he should answer to? Now that he was in the Royal Navy, Captain Slayter was the man whose commands he must ultimately obey, but then he felt a strong loyalty to Captain Smith who had, after all, been the man that Lightoller had always recognised as the one and only master of the ship, an experienced skipper with more than forty years at sea to his credit, whom he liked and respected. Now it seemed Smith was at times reduced to little more than a glorified look-out in the ship that had once been his own.

But then there was someone else for whom life in the *Oceanic* was far from easy just then, Davy Blair, Lightoller's old shipmate since his early years with the White Star Line. Blair was the officer who had suffered the disappointment of having to stand down as Second Officer of the *Titanic* before her maiden voyage, only to thank his lucky stars afterwards—except that is for the secret grilling he got from Lightoller over a certain pair of binoculars that mysteriously disappeared from the *Titanic*'s crow's nest. But the two never fell out over it and always remained firm friends. However Blair just now was a man under pressure: his was the responsibility for navigating this huge liner through these tricky waters, a job made all the more complicated by the continuous zig-zag course being steered to evade submarine attack. Blair was a very accomplished navigator in normal circumstances, but now his skills were being stretched to the limit. Even Blair would be hard put to thread the *Oceanic* through the eye of a needle which at times was almost what he was being asked to do as he pored day and night over unfamiliar complex charts, his eyes bleary with the strain. Blair had the most unenviable job of trying to plot courses first this way and then that, as each Captain took it into his head to order a change of course when the mood took him. In fact the whole business seemed like a ready-made recipe for disaster.

It was at this stage of her patrol that the *Oceanic* was to get her first, and as it turned out, her only taste of wartime success. The day after leaving Lerwick a Norwegian barque was sighted and ordered to heave to. A search by the marines uncovered a single terrified German subject of undefined intentions who was brought back aboard in heady triumph. With their prisoner safely locked up in the brig, the *Oceanic* continued her patrol heading back north, but this time towards the tiny island of Foula, about twenty miles west of Shetland

and the remotest inhabited outpost of the British Isles. In Captain Slayter's mind this was just the kind of place where a German U-boat or spy vessel might lay in hiding to pose a threat to the warships of the Grand Fleet going about their business at Scapa Flow.

However of potentially far greater hidden menace to shipping in the vicinity of the bleak and spectacular Foula was the cluster of rocks and reefs which lay around her coast, in particular the dreaded Shaalds—otherwise known as the Hoevdi Grund—two miles to the east of the island and lying only a few feet under a fast-running tide which in calm weather gave no sign of danger, as many a vessel through the centuries had learned to its cost. If there was one area the *Oceanic* should keep clear of it was this, as Smith well knew, but despite warnings to Slayter that it would be the height of folly to go dicing with the treacherous waters around Foula, Slayter would not listen. He had made up his mind to set a course for the island and the decision would stand.

Lightoller was Officer of the Watch at dawn on September 8th. At this time no land was in sight although during his watch the previous evening Foula had come into view and he had been with Blair in the chartroom observing him plot the ship's position, accurately taking his bearings from the north and south ends of the island. During the night, while Lightoller was away from the bridge the ship had continued to zig-zag around the area, with Blair plotting the reckonings and laying off the courses as each alteration was ordered by Slayter. One arrangement which the two captains had managed to agree on was that Smith would take charge of the ship during the day while Slayter took over at night. At one point during the night, thick fog was encountered and the engines were stopped, but as dawn broke and Lightoller arrived back on the bridge to take his morning watch visibility, apart from a thin mist, had cleared and the ship was steaming in a calm sea at a cautious $8\frac{1}{2}$ knots. According to Blair's calculations the *Oceanic* was shown on the chart just now to be well south of the island and, working off this, Slayter had ordered a new change of course to take them back towards it. Before retiring to his stateroom below the bridge where he was billeted, Slayter told Lightoller to maintain the same course, keep a sharp look-out for land and let him know when it was sighted. When he had gone, Blair and Lightoller studied the chart once again. Neither officer was feeling too happy about the ship's position. Blair knew his job all right, and if there were any calculations that Lightoller would stake his life on they were Blair's, but right now the navigator was just about at the end of his tether. As though his job was not already onerous enough, to further complicate matters for him, the *Oceanic* was now working to two different times. Slayter in his wisdom had decided to have the ship's clocks put back forty minutes, his reasoning being that when the full ship's company went on General Alert at daybreak, the time when the ship was most vulnerable to submarine attack, the men of the middle watch who had been at the guns all night had to come straight back up again and join the alert having already completed a full stint. Slayter worked it out that by putting the clocks back forty minutes the middle watch would end at the same time as the General Alert and so relieve that extra pressure being put on one section of the ship's company. However the change of clocks only added up to more pressure on poor Blair, who found that in working out the ship's position with the chronometer he would always have to make an allowance for forty minutes' difference between *Oceanic* time and Greenwich Mean Time. Why on earth, he wondered, could Slayter not have simply altered the turn-out times of the watches and left the clocks as they were? It seemed an odd way of doing things and only gave him more headaches.

Blair was exhausted. He decided to go for a lie down, asking to be called in an hour and a half. Worn out though he was, that was all the time for rest he dared allow himself. When the officer was woken up and went back to the bridge, Captain Smith had by this time arrived and again the chart was scrutinised by Smith, Lightoller and Blair. Foula had not yet been sighted and they did not expect it to be, as Blair's plot showed that on their present north-easterly heading they were still about 14 miles to the south and west of it. Smith continued to fret over the chart. He was most uneasy about steering for Foula. Taking the initiative, he made up his mind to change course without consulting Slayter. He would turn the ship due west towards open sea and away from any danger round the island—or so he thought. At this stage no-one on the bridge believed the ship was in any real jeopardy though nagging doubt had prompted Blair to suggest taking soundings to be on the safe side. Smith rejected the idea. Even if the navigator was slightly out in his reckoning, visibility, despite a lingering mist, appeared to be a good four to five miles, which would give them plenty of time to see any land ahead. Meanwhile the look-outs were told to keep a special watch aft on the starboard side where the island was expected to appear as the morning brightened and the horizon cleared. Land still had not been sighted when Lightoller's watch finished and he made way for Wiles.

It was twenty minutes after he retired to his cabin to rest that a cry from the crow's nest that land was dead ahead brought sudden consternation to the bridge. It was Foula. On the bridge all was confusion as they realised that instead of seeing the island slide by astern, they were heading straight for it. Blair had obviously been miles out in his reckoning. Smith had two choices open to him. He could either put the ship astern on the principle that if they had not hit anything going ahead the same would apply in reverse, or he could turn her away from the island and hope in that way to steer clear of trouble. He estimated that the island was still at least four miles off which, therefore, by his reckoning would put him well short of the Shaalds. He opted for the latter course and turned the ship several points to starboard with the apparent intention of bringing her round to the south again in a wide sweep. As Lightoller drifted off to sleep he was unaware of the panic on the bridge, where Slayter had just then chosen the opportune moment to arrive.

Now would see the culmination of the problems that had been simmering on the ship with two Captains. After quickly sizing up the situation Slayter, realising that they were closer to the island than Smith evidently thought, countermanded Smith's order and had the helm swung hard over in a sharp turn to starboard to get right away from it, while Blair was told to quickly take a fix on the land which was looming larger by the minute. Moments later Blair came dashing out of the chartroom and yelled 'We're close to the Hoevdi Reef!' As he spoke, before there was even a chance to make a grab for the engine telegraphs, a sickening crunch reverberated through the *Oceanic* as she ground onto the wicked Shaalds and was driven further and more firmly onto them by the fast-running tide. For Lightoller the sensation of *déjà-vu* as he lay in his bunk half asleep made him think he was having nightmares from the terrible past, but as he shook himself fully awake and hurried out on deck he realised he had not been dreaming. It really was happening again.

The Shaalds had got the 'Queen of the Seas', now looking anything but a queen as she sat straddling the reef, stern on to the island of Foula, like some stranded whale, unable to move one way or the other. There was one blessing at least in that there was no immediate further threat to the ship or the lives of the men in her as the sea was relatively calm. If one of the notorious gales familiar to the area had been blowing it might have been a very different story but in the Force Two conditions prevailing there was even a chance she could be pulled off and saved. Presently the trawler *Glenogil* from Aberdeen arrived and tried to tow her clear by the stern, but the combined weight of the liner and the strong tide running soon forced her to give up. The *Oceanic* would not budge. Then onto the scene came the Royal Navy cruiser *Forward*. Using a heavy hawser, the *Forward* tried to succeed where the *Glenogil* had failed, but as the slack on the line was taken up it just snapped like a piece of cotton under the strain. It was beginning to look like a hopeless case, and soon enough those worst fears were confirmed when an inspection of the ship revealed that her double bottom, for all that thickness and strength, was badly holed and three of the forward holds were rapidly filling with water. Even if they succeeded in getting her off she would sink in no time.

For Lightoller the distress of feeling his beloved *Oceanic* breaking up beneath him on the reef was driving him almost to tears. He already had plenty of experience of being shipwrecked but the *Oceanic* had a special place in his heart: she had been the ship in which he had spent more years of his career than any other. Now she too, like the *Titanic*, looked lost. If not for the war it would never have happened, yet ironically it took no enemy shell or torpedo to put paid to her. The Shaalds had done the job. The Hun would certainly have plenty to chuckle about over this.

Later that day the order finally came to abandon ship and once again Lightoller found himself supervising the job of loading and lowering lifeboats. In this work no one could say he lacked experience but this time, thankfully there would be no loss of life. The departure from the ship of six hundred-odd men (and one German prisoner who thought it all a great joke) was carried off in efficient and orderly fashion while ships stood by to take men from the boats. Lightoller was particularly impressed with the way the Shetlanders performed that day, treating it all as though being shipwrecked was almost a daily routine.

It was as he sat at the tiller of his bobbing lifeboat some yards off the wreck waiting his turn to be picked up that Lightoller was suddenly overcome by an urge to have just one more look around his old love before leaving her. He had his men row back alongside the ship, leapt to the rope ladder and scampered back aboard. It was a haunting experience to walk about the deserted, silent decks which had once buzzed with such life and activity through almost a decade and a half of Atlantic crossings. Three consecutive passages between Liverpool and New York she had made under John G. Cameron without a minute's difference between them. Oh, if he were to see her now! So much for her beautiful staterooms more recently occupied by naval personnel who could not believe the luxury they had found. What price now the silk cretonne walls, marble toilets and gold-plated light fittings, to say nothing of the saloon panelled in oak, the beautifully carved mahogany doors and glass domes? With a lump in his throat Lightoller walked onto the bridge to stand for one last time where he had spent so many vigilant hours; hours brimming over with memories, some funny, others less funny such as in the depths of winter at the height of a raging North Atlantic gale; but then when it lifted, such a lark it was sliding on the wet rubber floor from one end of the bridge to the other, an art he developed to perfection until the day he crashed into Captain Cameron.

He was going out through the chartroom when he caught sight of it, that familiar old face he had scowled at with scorn as often as he had smiled upon lovingly. There it was still gazing down at him as ever with that customary two-faced grin, friendly but with an unmistakable hint of smugness—the ship's clock. He walked up to it, looked it squarely in the face and then, gripped by a rush of blood to the head, clutched it in both hands and wrenched it from its mountings. As he bore it away under his arm in triumph what better memento could he have of his *Oceanic* years: it would look well in the hall at Nikko Lodge or, who knows, perhaps one day it might find a place in his own proud vessel.

For three weeks the *Oceanic* remained standing in statuesque grandeur on the reef where her glorious career had come to such an inglorious end. Then one night a vicious storm blew up as only they can in those parts, and the next morning she was gone from sight, swallowed up by the sea which had now vested Lightoller with the dubious honour of three shipwrecks to his credit. But she had not finished with him yet.

24

For Lightoller losing the *Oceanic* was as though his last link with the merchant service and the White Star Line had been snapped, and now he felt like some lost orphan wondering what fate awaited him.

The stranding on the reef had been the result of sheer incompetence and bad judgement; the blame lay as much with her unstable command as with the ill-conceived decision to put her in such an unsuitable role in the first place. Yet at the courts martial which followed back at the naval headquarters in Devonport, where Lightoller this time was grateful to be a witness merely on the fringe of the proceedings, it was Blair alone who came away with a blot on his record. Captain Smith and Captain Slayter were both completely exonerated. Once again Lightoller was observing the whitewash brush being liberally applied, but sadly this time at the expense of the unlucky Blair. The court found that he had been at fault for not taking the precaution of sounding, and not advising that the ship be instantly stopped when land was sighted. For some reason it was not taken into account that he did suggest taking soundings—a suggestion which Captain Smith rejected, and secondly, as both captains were on the bridge at the critical moment, surely it was their decision to stop the ship and not his? If Lightoller had once known what it felt like to be the whipping boy for everyone, now it was Blair's turn to sample a taste of it. However his reprimand was only minor and no further action would be taken against him. Nevertheless the navigator was left a disillusioned man. Recalling how Blair, by a blessing of fate, had escaped the demise of the *Titanic* Lightoller could not resist smiling a little to himself at the irony of his colleague's subsequent misfortune.

The armies were now bogged down in the trenches on the Western Front. Lightoller's next assignment, however, was some thousand feet up—where he found himself now, feeling all too vulnerable as he sat clad in unfamiliar leather helmet and goggles in the observer's cockpit of a Short 184 seaplane, getting an unaccustomed airborne view of the ocean. The sailor had taken wing and he was not at all sure if this abrupt change was suiting him—particularly as his new mode of conveyance was proving far from reliable. There were no lifeboats, either, to give him a fighting chance should the engine cut out and the little biplane go plummeting down into the sea, assuming that he survived the impact.

What first introduced Lightoller to the perils of flight was his appointment to the *Campania*, a seaplane carrier with the Battle Fleet at Scapa Flow. She had been an aging 13,000-ton Cunard liner on the Liverpool–New York run. If she was as unsuited to her new role as the *Oceanic* had been to hers, it was not in this case the ship that was in jeopardy so much as the airmen who flew in the planes she carried. The original intention of the Admiralty had been to convert her, like the *Oceanic*, to an armed merchant cruiser, but during the conversion work at Cammell Laird in Liverpool it was decided to fit her with a large wooden flying deck forward on which to launch planes on wheeled trollies whilst the ship was under way. It was a modification that gave her a most bizarre appearance. He remembered the *Campania* as a ship with handsome lines, but now, with her weird forward deck conversion, she looked like one of Heath Robinson's less well inspired ideas. He was hard put to appreciate that the *Campania*, under her skipper Captain Oliver Schwann, a self-taught pilot who believed passionately in the crucial role of aircraft in naval strategy, was making maritime history. With her had dawned a new era in sea warfare—the advent of the aircraft carrier. However Lightoller was just a little doubtful about the privilege of being one of Captain Schwann's pioneers—particularly when it came to sacrificing the comparative safety on the bridge for the terrors of the sky, or worse, the decidedly greater terrors of trying to reach it. In Lightoller's view a seaman was a seaman and an airman an airman; the ship's officers had no choice, however, if they were called upon to act as observers when the seaplanes were ordered out on patrol—when they managed to get up.

So far no aircraft had succeeded in taking off from the *Campania*'s 'flight' deck which, it soon became evident, was not long enough for the job. A number of intrepid airmen had found this out to their cost as their planes, instead of going skywards, plummeted ungracefully off the end of the ship into the water—although the pilots suffered nothing worse than a ducking in the cold North Sea. So for the time being the planes were hoisted by derricks over the side to take off from the sea on their floats. But this compromise could still be fraught with hazards, especially when the sea was choppy. Often the fragile machines would be badly damaged during the lowering operation as they smashed against the sides of the rolling ship. Once in the water the problems were far from over. If the floats did not break up as the aircraft was preparing for take-off, they did as the take-off attempt was being made. Consequently Lightoller began to get increasingly irritated as he spent more time swimming for his life than observing from aloft, where he assumed he was supposed to be. If he found little amusement in the exercise, it was a different matter for those looking on from the rest of the Grand Fleet. They found it all a hilarious diversion from the boring routine which at this stage of their war had yet to be interrupted by an encounter with the enemy. It was not long before the Short 184 earned a new nickname for itself on the *Campania*, 'The White Coffin', which Lightoller considered perfectly appropriate. The all too regular sight of a white fuselage standing upright out of the water after yet another mishap gave him a definite impression of the ideal floating gravestone.

Then one June day in 1915 off Iceland it was time for the *Campania* and her seaplanes to prove their true worth. The entire Grand Fleet had got under way from Scapa for a major exercise in which the seaplane carrier was to play a vital part. The top brass had decided to split the Fleet in two, sending one half, the Blue Fleet, sailing off over the horizon leaving the other half, the Red Fleet, which included the *Campania*, to find and 'engage' them. The job of the seaplanes was to seek out and reconnoitre the enemy.

As zero hour neared, all twelve planes were ordered out by Captain Schwann in readiness for the Admiral's order to send them off. But alas, when it did come, of the dozen seaplanes that were intended to take to the air only one managed to get airborne—Lightoller's.

As the 184 lumbered into the sky leaving behind a circus of chaos below, she headed off towards the approximately known vicinity of the 'Blue Fleet', climbing steadily to her maximum height of 9,000 feet in her minimum time of three quarters of an hour. With the 225-HP Sunbeam engine powering them sweetly along at a steady 80 mph, Lightoller for once in his airborne career felt optimistic. Perhaps at last, he thought, sitting contentedly behind the pilot surveying the wide expanse of blue ocean beneath, the White Coffins —or one of them at least—might just prove to be of more use than their nickname had so far been suggesting. So now to hunt down the enemy!

There was quite a low cloud ceiling which was ideal for their purpose, as every so often they would drop down for a quick glimpse round the sea before climbing back up again, all to lessen the chances of the 'enemy' spotting them first.

They continued on this tack for half an hour or so with nothing to see but the ocean clear all the way to the horizon. 'Lights' had been given a rough position of the 'Blue Fleet' as there would after all be little point in the exercise if the two forces were not going to have an even chance of meeting up to do 'battle'.

Down they came again and, sure enough, there they were, looking like a large collection of miniature toy ships, each surrounded by a tell-tale plume of cotton wool, spread out below in full view. Lightoller got quite excited as he wound up the aerial and prepared to signal back on his wireless that contact had been made with the enemy. They flew around the sky darting in and out of the clouds while he carefully tapped out all the relevant information on the Morse key in the code contained in the manual on his knee; how many battleships, cruisers and destroyers there were, their position, what direction they were heading in and at what speed. Now it all seemed worthwhile. History was being made. For the first time ever a plane sent up from a fleet at sea had succeeded in locating and spying on the enemy.

Although Lightoller could transmit from the plane, wireless technology of the air had not yet progressed to the stage where an aircraft could receive a reply, so to make absolutely sure he transmitted all the data a second time before winding down the aerial, thoroughly satisfied with a job well done. Then with a tap on the pilot's head they were happily on their way home to the *Campania* and some well earned tea, and, without doubt, the personal congratulations from the Admiral of the Fleet, Sir John Jellicoe himself.

But unfortunately, when they returned to the position where the Red Fleet should have been, there was nothing but empty sea. Having succeeded in locating the opposing fleet they had now lost their own. They continued to fly around the sky while Lightoller checked and rechecked his calculations, directing the pilot to turn this way and then that in an ever more desperate bid to find their ships. As time went by with still no sign of them a new emergency began to arise: the Short 184 had almost expended its $2\frac{3}{4}$ hours of fuel. If a ship was not found soon—any ship—their mission looked destined to a watery conclusion. Yet again Lightoller tapped the anxious pilot on the head and pointed in a new direction. The plane turned; by now Lightoller had given up all hope of trying to solve the problem by orthodox navigation. His decision this time was based on pure instinct. He made up his mind they would just keep flying in that direction and let fate take its course. The fuel gauge had already taken its own course, with an anxiously gesticulating pilot pointing out to his observer that the needle was now resting firmly on 'Empty'. Lightoller began to think of their chances if the engine cut out before they found someone. They would not be too good. Even if they succeeded in gliding to a safe landing on the sea there could be little hope of finding a tiny aircraft lost somewhere between Norway, Shetland and Iceland. The wireless would be of little use to them as he did not know where they were to send out even an approximate position. The sea was calm just now but that could not be guaranteed to last indefinitely in these latitudes, and it would not take much of a sea to swamp this flimsy plane. It was ironic, after the adventures he had been through from one shipwreck to the next, that the sea was about to claim him from out of the sky.

Ships! Yes definitely they were ships all right as Lightoller managed to make out a line of silhouettes through his binoculars way over on the horizon. It did not matter what ships they were, red, blue or even the real enemy's, as they turned and headed for them with the engine stuttering ominously. By now the plane could only be surviving on fumes, but if she could last just a few minutes more they would be home and dry. Those minutes seemed to last an age to Lightoller as the little 184 spluttered, oh so slowly, towards the distant shapes that seemed to be getting no closer.

But gradually they did get closer, and enough for Lightoller with overwhelming relief to pick out the unmistakable lines of the *Campania* in amongst the warships of the Grand Fleet. Never would he be so pleased to set eyes on that ugly old mutation of the sea as he was then. With the fuel-starved engine coughing and spitting almost to a stop the pilot, working to the limit of his skills, succeeded in getting them safely down and before long they were alongside the *Campania* and swinging cheerfully on the end of her derricks being hoisted back aboard.

So what happened to them? came the question from the big brass. As Lightoller explained how they got lost it turned out that was not quite what they wanted to know. It seemed that not a thing had been heard from them since they took off. Lightoller's wireless signals never got through. The whole exercise had been a complete waste of time. So much then for any ideas he had of breaking new ground in naval strategy, much less receiving the personal congratulations of Admiral Jellicoe.

From that moment on Lightoller's sole aim in life was to get away from the *Campania*. He was fed up with her and he was fed up with her wretched seaplanes. Just to find himself in a ship, any ship, where he could keep his feet firmly on the deck and do the job he was trained to do; no more cavorting about all over the sky (but more often in the sea) in contraptions that seemed more of a threat to those riding in them than to any enemy. The last straw was being put to the doubtful task of 'training' new 'observers', presumably because he was the only one that had so far actually observed anything, regardless of whether he had managed to communicate it. Consequently there was no-one more relieved than Lightoller when word went round that the *Campania* was going back to Liverpool for a refit and to have her flight deck extended. At last, a chance to escape. He was determined that he would not still be with her when she was recommissioned and returned to the Fleet. He decided to convey his thoughts in strong terms to Captain Schwann. The skipper was disappointed. Lightoller was a useful asset to have around despite his deep-rooted merchant-navy ways, and in his view had seemed to adapt well to the unfamiliar demands of the *Campania* in her special role.

However he would see what he could do.

It was just a few days before the Christmas of 1915 that the news came through and a better Christmas present it could not have been. He was to get his own command! She did not have a name, just a number, HMTB *117*. She was a torpedo boat and he was to join her right away at Sheerness naval dockyard on the north Kent coast where she was completing a refit. HMTB *117* was attached to the Nore Defence Flotilla, a small force of destroyers, torpedo boats and minelayers whose role was to patrol the Thames estuary, guarding the river and the capital against enemy attack from sea and air.

HMTB *117* was getting on in years and lacked the more rakish compact looks of her modern counterparts but Lightoller would be proud of her. It did not matter to him that she would probably soon have been obsolete but for the instant demands of war on a navy unprepared for it. At a time when oil-fired engines were becoming standard, particularly in the smaller vessels of war, *117* was a coal burner, though she could still work up a good turn of speed, up to 25 knots if pushed, as Lightoller discovered to his great satisfaction when he first took her out of Sheerness to put her through her paces. *117*'s main sting was not in her three small Hotchkiss three-pounder guns, but in her three torpedo tubes which in theory could inflict a mortal wound on the biggest of warships afloat—assuming the target gave her a chance of an accurate shot.

It was unlikely such a situation would ever confront Lightoller and *117* with the Nore Defence Flotilla, certainly at this stage of the war. Instead he found that the work with Admiral Callaghan's overstretched little force of 10 aging destroyers and 17 torpedo boats entailed long, busy hours on routine patrol. But it was very convenient to be based at Stangate Creek, just around the corner from Sheerness. Such a contrast this was to the frustrations and hazards of life in the *Campania* imprisoned somewhere between the North Sea and the Atlantic Ocean where the winter days were dominated by long hours of darkness with very little to look forward to but the next ducking. And even better, not only was he enjoying the independence of his own little command, but he had been joined by his growing family, which now comprised two of each with yet another on the way, all happily settling down in their new home on the Isle of Sheppey.

Lightoller would prove to be a strong and able commander who soon earned the respect and, in time, the affection of his 30-man crew. While they realised that their skipper was not a man to be trifled with, he did not set himself apart from them as other skippers might do. He made a special point of getting to know them individually, as much to judge each man's strengths and weaknesses as to get every member of the crew to feel that his part in the team was no less important than the next man's. When the moment demanded, he would expect each to act on his own initiative and not have to be 'told off' via the more formal procedures of command that he had found so much the practice in the Royal Navy. In a ship, particularly of this size, that to his mind was the only way—the merchant-navy way. Having had more than twenty years' experience handling men at sea in those well tried methods he saw no cause to alter them now. If there were some who said that Lightoller displayed too much contempt for Royal Navy ways, and he should keep in step, they would never see him compromise with his attitude. Under his command *117* would turn out to be one of the smoothest and most efficiently run vessels in the Nore Defence Flotilla, and it was noticeable that the morale among her crew always seemed high in an atmosphere ever cheerful. Perhaps more significantly, Lightoller would never have to discipline a man, either in *117* or in any other ship he would go on to command in the war.

As the weeks slid by into months Lightoller settled down into the routine of the Nore Defence Flotilla (so called because the focal point of their patrol radius was the Nore lightship, situated right in the estuary). Undoubtedly there could be worse ways of spending the war than joy-riding about in a torpedo boat, not only compared with his own previous calamitous experiences of it, but with the many thousands of others who, according to disquieting reports coming back from the front, were having a much worse time. A war constantly out of sight of the enemy, though, could be monotonous.

Then came the exercises with the submarines. The Navy had been working on various ideas to try and quell the growing U-boat menace. The British trawler fleet, being such easy prey, had been coming under particularly heavy attack. One ploy the Navy came up with to try and combat this was to have, in amongst a group of vessels fishing, a decoy naval trawler towing a submerged submarine to which she was linked by telephone. As soon as the raider surfaced to attack with her deck gun the trawler would alert the submarine which then manoeuvred into position to torpedo the U-boat. It had worked a couple of times but the system was still prone to failure: either the telephone link broke down or the cable attached to the submarine refused to slip. *117* was put on towing exercises to try and perfect the system. However, after spending a few farcical weeks playing about with submarines in mock actions, getting tangled up with tow lines and telephone cables the whole idea was scrapped. Relieved, Lightoller went back to the old routine of steamer escort, carrying mails, and patrolling the mouth of the river, waiting for something to have a crack at. He would not have to wait much longer.

Towards the end of July 1916, after a break of nearly three months, German airship raids had started again over the East coast and South-East of England. So far the damage they had done with their bombs had created more alarm than actual destruction. Most of the time their bombs fell short in the sea, or in open country, at worst destroying the odd barn or glasshouse, or if she was particularly unlucky, the occasional cow. Now and again, however, the airships had proved able to hit the mark, as on the night when one arrived over London and unloaded its rack on the heart of the city, killing twenty people and doing half a million pounds' worth of damage. The Zeppelins were in fact more prone to destruction than the enemy targets they sought. Because of their immense size they were easy to shoot down and often in spectacular fashion. The highly inflammable hydrogen gas that inflated the ship would erupt into a blazing inferno as it came crashing down to earth.

It was around midnight on July 31st 1916 that the vessels of the Nore Flotilla received the 'executive signal' to go to action stations in readiness for a reported raid coming in. Lightoller took *117* out at full speed to his usual position beside the Tongue lightship a few miles downstream from the Nore midway across the river mouth. As a wartime precaution the lightships in the estuary had stopped displaying their full glare but Lightoller signalled the Tongue to ask for just a dim riding light to help him keep station, then put his engines to Stop, had the anti-aircraft gun loaded, made ready to fire and settled down to wait. The order went round for everyone to be absolutely quiet and concentrate on listening. Having responded to the executive signal on so many previous occasions without ever seeing anything, he was quite prepared for the usual disappointment and in half an hour or so to get the signal to stand down and return to base.

A thin mist hung over the river as *117* gently rose and fell in the easy swell with no sound but the water lapping round her hull and the muted hiss of steam rising from her funnels. The minutes went by and Lightoller continued to wait patiently. Soon he would be heading back up river to the creek at the conclusion of another fruitless exercise. He decided to slip down to his cabin for a while, leaving instructions with Lieutenant Hewitson, his second-in-command, to alert him the moment anything was sighted.

Not many minutes had gone by when there came a muffled shout to him down the hatchway. 'Zeppelin right overhead, sir!' Lightoller dashed back on deck and peered into the sky, but emerging from the brightness of his cabin into the darkness could not pick out anything at first. He could only hear it—the unmistakable drone of aircraft engines somewhere above them.

'There he is, sir!' exclaimed Ball the gunner in an excited whisper, fearing for some reason that a louder shout might alert the enemy. Then Lightoller began to make it out, a great black cigar, so fat and massive that it seemed almost to blot out the dim sky. But, big and juicy though the target was, it lay so directly overhead that the anti-aircraft gun had not quite enough elevation to bear on it. Lightoller promptly called up the engineer and asked for what steam he could raise without disturbing the fires and causing sparks from the funnels that might give away their presence. The tension on board was mounting to fever pitch as Lightoller moved the engine telegraph to Slow Ahead to manoeuvre 117 into a firing position. The screw slowly churned round and she nosed her way gently ahead with all attention now focused on the gunner, his eyes riveted to the telescope waiting for the sights to come on.

Then at last, 'Sights are on, sir!' he called.

'Fire!' On Lightoller's command 117's little anti-aircraft gun instantly burst into life and the shell, trailing its tell-tale tracer of fire, shot skywards.

It missed. Their first effort had gone over the target.

'Down fifty!' Lightoller barked while another three-pound shell clanked into the breech of the Hotchkiss.

'Fire!' The gun cracked a second time in response to the skipper's command with all watching breathlessly as another streak of fire flashed upwards at 2,000 feet per second towards the target. 'Hit!' The shot had gone right through the Zeppelin's tail. 'Fire!' boomed Lightoller again and a second hit in the tail was observed. The gun cracked once more and that too struck home on the target. And yet despite being apparently hit three times, that infernal great gas bag in the sky, instead of bursting into flames to come plunging down to its doom, remained stubbornly airborne, refusing to yield to the mortal damage that it must surely have suffered. Then suddenly they saw the tail begin to drop. 'She's coming down!' came the cry. But she was not quite. Instead, from out of the night sky came the unmistakable scream of bombs on their downward path—and, judging by the loud chorus, a large quantity of them. Everyone instantly dived for what meagre cover on the deck they could find and waited for the holocaust to arrive. Within a few seconds all hell was let loose as a rain of bombs came crashing down on the river. Surely one at least was going to hit as 117 lurched frantically under the impact of ten thousand pounds of destruction exploding in mountains of spray all round her. But by a blessing of fortune, though some must have landed only feet away, none found their mark. Then, as the terrifying blitz relented and the turmoil of erupting water died away there came the rumble of engines revving above. The Zeppelin having done its evil deed and lightened itself considerably in the act was turning away and making off giving Lightoller no further chance to have a go at it. As his adversary disappeared behind the blackness of the night sky he cursed his foul luck at being cheated out of the confirmed 'kill' which he was thoroughly convinced he had earned, as did all the rest of them. But at least he had the consolation of knowing that in being within an ace of getting blown out of the water himself, that was one sizable packet London was spared.

It would forever be a mystery to him how that Zeppelin managed to stay airborne and intact when he and a dozen other men had witnessed three shells thud into her. The answer was perfectly simple, although he would have taken some persuading to believe it. The Zeppelin was never hit at all. By a deceiving trick of the eye it had merely seemed that she was. All the worse for Lightoller because the airship he had fired on, which in return dumped its considerable rack of bombs on him, was no ordinary one. Unbeknown to him it was the newest and biggest Zeppelin ever to be despatched by Germany against England, L31, all 650 feet of her and by far the most formidable creation yet to emerge from the construction sheds at Friedrichshafen. Her captain, Heinrich Mathy, was regarded as Germany's foremost Zeppelin commander, who had inflicted widespread devastation on London in an earlier raid. If Lightoller had brought down Mathy and L31 the nation would indeed have had cause to be grateful. But instead Mathy flew off home undamaged, optimistic in the uncertain weather conditions that he had carried out a repeat of his previous success on London, though having encountered some very accurate anti-aircraft fire over the city which came rather too close for comfort. At the same time it would be a proud and happy crew that headed back to base in their torpedo boat in those early hours convinced, despite lack of confirmation, that this was one Zeppelin which would never survive the journey home. Lightoller would, however, still have something to show for his encounter. In recognition of his combat service he was awarded the Distinguished Service Cross. He was also promoted to a new command.

25

It was 1916, and the war was not going well for the Allies. At sea the only major battle to take place between the German and British fleets, the Battle of Jutland off the Denmark coast, had ended in victory being claimed by both sides, by the Germans because they inflicted more damage on the British fleet than they sustained themselves, and by the British because the Germans turned tail and would not show their faces in force at sea again for the rest of the war. As for the *Campania*, her seaplanes never did get the chance to have their day; the ship was turned back on her way to the battle by Admiral Jellicoe, who feared that she would be more of a hindrance than a help. It was later suggested that her seaplanes might have done enough to turn the battle into an outright victory for the Grand Fleet, but the chance was not taken.

However, the struggle for mastery of the seas would still go on, and perhaps the most crucial stretch of water was the Dover Straits, which carried the traffic of troops and their supplies of food, fuel, equipment and ammunition to the Western Front. To defend these waters a motley force was formed of old, worn-out destroyers, armed fishing vessels and a species of ungainly-looking one-gun battleship called monitors, that all added up to a miscellaneous fleet called the Dover Patrol—or Fred Karno's Circus as those who served in the Patrol had come to call it.

The Grand Fleet had monopolised all the newest and best ships of the Navy so the Dover Patrol had to make do with what was left. One of these was a torpedo-boat-destroyer called *Falcon*. Her Commander was Lieutenant C. H. Lightoller. This was his promotion and one which at first he had not readily welcomed, having been perfectly happy with HMTB *117*. He would have been more than content to see out the war with her and the Nore Defence Flotilla—particularly as he had got his family so conveniently housed and set up in the locality. But it was considered unthinkable that he should resist transfer to a destroyer command with the unique Dover Patrol!

So he had to go and the whole family, now totalling five children (Roger, Trevor, Mavis, Doreen and the latest addition, Brian) were on the move again following him faithfully to resettle at 8 East Cliffe, Dover, overlooking the harbour.

The Patrol had to be on guard around the clock to keep open the cross-Channel lifeline. The Germans had taken the two principal Belgian ports of Zeebrugge and Ostend further up the coast, while the Allies had managed to keep control of Calais, Boulogne and Dunkirk. It was imperative that they should. The loss of the Belgian ports had been a serious enough setback, but if the enemy were allowed to take the French ports as well, the troops already in the fighting would have been outflanked and cut off, leaving England wide open to invasion.

Although the Germans were being held back on land, there was the ever-present threat that they might try to take Dunkirk and Calais by sea. While the Dover-based fleet patrolled 'the Navy's front-line trench', German destroyers and U-boats out of Zeebrugge and Ostend were always looking for an opportunity to wreak havoc amongst the allied shipping. Their destroyers, never keen to get into a head-on fight, sneaked out mostly at night to come darting down the Channel firing off indiscriminately at any shipping in sight, usually steamers anchored in the Dover Straits or the drifters laying and tending the mines and anti-submarine nets. Within a few minutes it would be all over, with the attackers well on their way home leaving behind a trail of destruction before the Royal Navy had a chance to chase them and return fire. They persisted with these 'hit and run' tactics seemingly preoccupied with the fear of losing ships, even though their own were newer, faster and far better armed than any on the Dover Patrol—*Falcon* in particular.

A much bigger menace than the destroyers were the U-boats, which had to be watched not only for the damage they could do in the Straits with their torpedoes and the mines they laid across the shipping lanes, but because if they broke out into the English Channel, they were soon in the Atlantic where they could roam freely picking off shipping at random. The convoy system was yet to be introduced as not all the leading lights of the Admiralty were convinced it was the best method to protect shipping. In the meantime the Navy concentrated on laying mined nets at various points across the Channel in a bid to bar their way. This hampered their progress to a certain extent but it did not stop them, mainly because for a long time there were not enough mines available to make an effective barrier, and even as the minefields spread, the U-boats were still getting through on the surface under cover of darkness.

As the war went on Lightoller developed a bitter hatred of enemy submarines, all the more so after the sinking of the Cunard liner *Lusitania* off the coast of Ireland with the loss of twelve hundred lives. To him the sinking of the *Lusitania* was ruthless mass-murder, and he became increasingly obsessed with destroying enemy submarines. However, he would find this no easy ambition to achieve.

Like his previous command, *Falcon* was old and overdue for the breaker's yard. Built at the turn of the century, she was one of a dozen 'C' class torpedo-boat-destroyers on the Dover squadron known as '30-knotters'. In fact '30-knotter' was rather a misnomer as none of them were capable of that speed. '25-knotters' would have been more accurate. The most powerful of her collection of outdated guns was a single 12-pounder mounted just forward of the bridge. Adding versatility to her fire power she had two torpedo-tubes and for dealing with the under-water menace, a battery of depth-charge throwers. She was manned by a crew of 60. *Falcon* and the rest of the '30-knotters' worked in harness with the bigger 'Tribal' class destroyers forming the line-up of the incomparable Sixth Flotilla of Admiral Sir Reginald Bacon's Dover Patrol, and driven by him to the absolute limit.

Most of the skippers, like Lightoller, were men of the Royal Naval Reserve, formerly officers of merchant ships who had found themselves unexpectedly elevated to the responsibility of command to meet the demands of war. As in *117*, Lightoller continued as ever to stick doggedly to his Mercantile Marine attitudes, and once again, even though it was a bigger vessel manned by twice as many men, his system continued to work just as effectively, although he still raised a few Royal Navy eyebrows with some of his unorthodox ideas. One in particular was to keep every gun at all times loaded with a shell down the spout and the mechanism set up for instant firing if for instance an enemy periscope should suddenly appear above the surface. Any hand on the ship had permission to have a go in such circumstances, as one stoker did one day at a 'periscope' he spotted which turned out to be a porpoise.

It did not matter: he had done right. According to Lightoller's theory, if it had been a U-boat, the firing of the gun, even if ineffectual, was an instant alert to everyone on board that danger lurked; otherwise the man had to go through the motions of reporting it to a petty officer, who would then inform the bridge, and if Lightoller did not happen to be there, more critical minutes might be wasted locating him and sounding 'Action Stations'. By then the sub could have long since disappeared or, worse, had time to send a couple of torpedoes, targeted perhaps at *Falcon* herself.

Lightoller had never known such strenuously hard work as he found on the Dover Patrol. One day he might be carrying mails or escorting troop ships and ammunition barges across the Channel, the next tending drifters laying mines off the Belgian coast, sometimes under fire from the shore batteries; and then on another day protecting and laying smoke screens for the slow lumbering monitors as they sallied forth from the Patrol's forward base at Dunkirk up the coast to Zeebrugge and Ostend in hopes of inflicting some damage on the German navy. The results were rarely effective, as the monitors could not hope to outgun the shore batteries. If they hit anything of consequence it was more by good luck than by well aimed shooting. These exercises were more for the psychological effect, a way of returning some hate for the damage done by the Germans in their night raids, and to let them know the Dover Patrol still ruled the Channel. It was on one of these sorties up the Belgian coast earlier in the war that *Falcon*'s bridge was hit by a shell from the shore, killing eight including her commander, and seriously wounding ten others. From then on much more respect would be shown for the coastal gunnery.

Lightoller rarely got the chance for more than one night's rest in four, as he was required to keep steam up for seventeen days in succession, remaining on the ship even when in port, to be ready to get under way at ten minutes' notice. He was never more glad than when those seventeen days were up and it was time to stand down for three days' boiler cleaning.

The weather in the Channel could be cruel, every bit as bad as as he had known it in the Western Ocean, when the little *Falcon* would bury herself right up to the bridge. On reaching Dover harbour after battling home across the Channel through a mighty gale, his problems were not over. The port was the worst he had ever encountered for trying to enter in even the mildest blow. There was many a time he would curse the 'bright boys' who had decided to site such a badly laid out harbour in such an exposed spot. Dover had two entrances, one east and one west, and the sea during a bad storm would come rushing in at both inlets to meet in the middle and play havoc with vessels attempting to come in and tie up. It was a task difficult enough in daylight when there was a heavy sea running, but at night it was positively dangerous. The boom defences protecting the harbour, which included two old liners deliberately sunk for the purpose at the western end, should have helped to calm the vicious seas, but they made little difference. There would be times in a particularly bad south-west gale when he might try for an hour or more to get into the harbour and pick up his mooring buoy only to be forced to concede defeat and anchor outside for the night. So much for any hopes of grabbing a few hours' sleep those nights. Inevitably there were frequent collisions in the harbour, and *Falcon* herself would have her moments. On Falcon's first collision incident she was blameless, being moored at the time when another destroyer attempting to make her berth crashed into her stern. On the next occasion it would be *Falcon*'s fault, though not totally Lightoller's. He had concluded that the only way to enter Dover harbour during heavy weather was to take a run at the entrance, coming in at around 16 knots then, once inside, swing *Falcon* into a tight turn and, with a well rehearsed permutation of orders to the man on the bridge telegraphs, to bring his ship to rest right on her mooring. He was taking a leaf out of E. J. Smith's book, recalling his skill at handling the old *Majestic* at high speed round the South-West Spit into New York. However at Dover it was a manoeuvre that had to be judged to a nicety as the harbour was always busy with ships on the move in addition to those lying at their moorings. So it was that one day he came shooting in at his usual 16 knots to discover as he swung round towards his mooring that another ship had taken his spot. He ordered the helm hard over and called for full speed astern both engines. The bridge telegraphs had one engine on Half Speed Ahead and the other on Half Astern, but in panic the man standing at the handles, who happened to be doing the job for the first time, pushed them both to Full Ahead. Instead of slowing up, *Falcon* surged forward, heading straight for the obstructing vessel, a large solid troop transport called the *Accrington*. Although Lightoller dived for the telegraphs and jammed them over the other way it was already too late. *Falcon* crunched into the steamer, doing considerable damage to her own flimsy bows. He would have quite a job explaining to his superiors how it happened, but at the outset there would be no recriminations. Collisions had become an accepted hazard of Dover Patrol activities to the extent that Admiral Bacon allowed each of his skippers three accidents before ordering a full investigation into the man's competence to hold command. As for the poor Yeoman of Signals whose mental block on the telegraphs had ruined what hopes there were of avoiding the crash, after an initial 'what the hell did you think you were playing at?' from Lightoller he was forgiven.

While the loss of *Falcon* to have her damage repaired left the flotilla short-handed for a week, Admiral Bacon might grumble but at least Lightoller and his men got a short rest from the unyielding pressure and exertions under which they were living.

When on standby, *Falcon* would be one of four destroyers ready to steam out at short notice on warning of an enemy raid or of a U-boat sighted in the Channel. Lightoller would never get into combat with an enemy destroyer because of their reluctance to stay and fight, this despite being far superior to the likes of *Falcon*, who would not have stood a chance in the event. When they struck it was with devastating quickness, as one moonless night in October 1917 when four destroyers came out of Zeebrugge and down channel, sank three drifters and set a fourth one on fire. A '30-knotter' called *Flirt* came to investigate; she switched on her searchlight thinking that the drifters were firing on a submarine, but she too was met by an instant barrage of fire which sank her immediately. Only a handful of men from all the ships hit and sunk that night were saved, and it had all happened within ten minutes. Before *Falcon* and three other destroyers reached the scene the enemy had long since fled back to his lair.

Although storms were never welcomed, Lightoller would have been quite happy to settle for a Force 10 gale any day or night of the week instead of fog. This was the greatest dread of all the destroyer commanders working with the Dover Patrol, not merely because of the increased risk of collision with another vessel but because of the danger of straying out of the lanes and blundering into a mine-field—German or British. It was one evening at the end of a busy day escorting troop ships and ambulance ships across the Channel that Lightoller ran into a fog. He was on his way back from Folkestone to Dunkirk in company with another destroyer, *Racehorse*, which he was paired with at the time. Lightoller knew before he started out that a fog was imminent, but instead of choosing to stay in Folkestone for the night, with an early start for Dunkirk the following day, he decided to risk an immediate crossing so that he could have a full night's rest in port. Welch, the commander of *Racehorse*, decided to follow him. But they were not far out of Folkestone when the two ships ran right into as thick a fog as anything Lightoller had ever been through on the 'Grand Banks', with nothing but a claustrophobic grey murk in front of him. He decided to press on with *Racehorse* faithfully tagging behind, but instead of steering straight for Dunkirk, he put *Falcon* on a new heading for Calais further down the coast to avoid the possibility of running into the minefield surrounding the Haut Fond buoy, which guarded Dunkirk harbour. He would find the Calais green buoy about a mile outside the harbour then turn to port on a course ENE and feel his way from there along the coast to Dunkirk, threading *Falcon* through the gap between the shore and the mines. With the fog so thick he had nothing left to rely on but his dead reckoning, working out exactly when, at his speed of 20 knots, the Calais green buoy should appear. In typical mailboat fashion he was not letting any fog hold him up. Unfortunately, tonight as they reached the position where the Calais marker should have been it was not there. Confident that his navigation was not all that far out, he opted to make his turn anyway, certain that he was now heading up the French coast about a mile offshore and would soon be upon his next marker, the Gravelines Pile buoy midway between the two ports. The Gravelines buoy was at the southernmost tip of the Haut Fond minefield, and he should expect it to appear off his port bow. But as time went on it began to look as though he had missed this one too. Now he was getting concerned, less because of mines, than through fear of going aground. He was about to slow *Falcon* down to take a sounding when the cry came from one of the lookouts, 'There she is, sir!' It was a buoy all right, but as they examined it more closely in the beam of the searchlight it was not black as the Gravelines buoy should have been, but red. There was only one buoy in these parts that was red, the Haut Fond buoy—which lay right in the middle of the minefield! As Lightoller instantly looked aft and saw *Racehorse* merrily following his wake a lump of fear began to rise in his throat, as much for her as for his own ship. He had led her cheerfully trusting commander into this danger. There was nothing else to do but just keep going at the same 20 knots. After all, hitting a mine at 5 knots or at 20 would end with the same result. There was one small consolation. If he did not hit a mine, the ship behind ought not to either; he signalled *Racehorse* to stick to him like glue, thinking it better not to impart any further information at this stage. One thing Lightoller did at least know now was his exact position as he turned *Falcon* very gingerly so as not to cause unnecessary disturbance to the mines and headed for a lightship known as the Middle Dyck, which would take them by the shortest possible route out of the triangular field. All *Falcon*'s crew knew exactly what had happened as every man, Lightoller included, stood frozen to the spot, hair on end, knees trembling and breathlessly waiting to be blown to the heavens at any moment. A ship like *Falcon* hitting a mine would leave just so many scattered pieces to sink.

Then they saw something, a vague silhouette picked out in the spot of the searchlight reaching out towards them through the gloom. It was a lightship; not lit, but it was her all right, the beautiful Middle Dyck. They were out and in the clear. *Racehorse* was still totally unaware that she had just steamed through a minefield that had recently claimed five ships in as many weeks.

When they got into Dunkirk, Lightoller invited Welch aboard *Falcon* for dinner. 'Damn good course you made, "Lights",' said Welch cheerfully as he sat down to his meal. 'Oh yes? Did you see the buoys?' 'I didn't see Calais green, but of course I saw Gravelines.' 'That wasn't Gravelines, it was Haut Fond,' replied Lightoller with deliberate coolness, waiting for a reaction. 'Oh hell!' Welch's fork fell from his open mouth to the plate. He no longer felt all that hungry.

How many more times would Lightoller indulge his fancy for 'cracking on' and get away with it? There was to be one incident when Lightoller's enthusiasm for making his passage in the quickest possible time would land him in bother. *Falcon*'s 17 days of duty were up and he was taking her for the usual inspection and boiler clean. This time it would not be to Sheerness but to Portsmouth. It was his first visit to the naval base but he saw no reason to treat it any differently than Dover as he shot through the entrance at his customary 16 knots, unaware that the harbour had a strict 8-knot limit. He might well have got away with it but for a very high tide which resulted in *Falcon*'s wash sending waves cascading over the harbour wall and up the streets, much to the alarm and annoyance of the local citizens who happened to be walking there. The council complained to the Navy, and although it was some time before the culprit was tracked down, in the end Lightoller was collared and made to apologise to the city fathers for his irresponsible and careless behaviour in one of His Majesty's ships, and to give a solemn assurance that it would not happen again. As for his superiors, they were not so angry as he was led to believe, but he would never be allowed to share their amusement as the story went round.

261

Lightoller's reputation on the Dover Patrol as a 'cracker on' became quite notorious but never to the extent that anyone accused him of recklessness. An incorrigible merchant seaman, yes, a bad seaman he was never called. There was no one in the 6th Flotilla, they would say, who could handle a '30-knotter' better than 'Lights', even if at times he was just a little too daring with his cracking on. But then he had been a devoted student of the art for a long time, long before he ever came under the influence of E. J. Smith, John G. Cameron and all the rest of them bound by the 'Get On or Get Out' law of the Atlantic greyhounds. Yes, smokestacks apart, old Jock Sutherland would indeed have been mighty proud of his former pupil.

26

By the end of 1917 the Dover Patrol was proud to boast that it had escorted over five million troops across the Channel without the loss of a single man. The statistics would not prove to be so creditable once the men they were protecting during the sea phase of the journey reached their eventual destination at the front. The million wounded they escorted back to England in the hospital ships during the same period was evidence of that.

At Dover, Admiral Bacon was relieved by Admiral Keyes, who within a couple of months transformed the Patrol into a completely new operation. The Channel above and below the Straits was now effectively closed to the enemy as Keyes began putting into effect a more offensive policy, which included plans to launch a major attack on Ostend and Zeebrugge to knock the Germans out of their heavily protected bases.

Lightoller and *Falcon*, as it turned out, were not to be part of this operation, which was to rank in many eyes as second only to Jutland among the naval actions of the war. Instead they were moved, in February 1918, up to the North Sea Patrol to be based at Immingham on the Humber, and assigned to escort duty with incoming convoys on the final stage of their journey to Britain from Canada, the United States and Scandinavia. After much argument and doubt, convoys had finally been recognised as the most effective means of defending freighters against submarine attack. Now that the Channel had been virtually closed to the U-boats, they would need to take the longer route around the top of Scotland to get into the Atlantic, but it also meant that they would pose a bigger problem in the North Sea. The U-boat had become 'the gravest peril that ever threatened the population of the country as well as the whole Empire', as Jellicoe confirmed.

Having accounted for some 6½ million tons of shipping in the twelve months prior to Lightoller's transfer to the North Sea Patrol, it was beginning to look as though the U-boats alone could win the war for Germany. With corn reserves at one stage down to only 6 weeks' and the cutting off of reinforcements and essential supplies from overseas, the convoy solution presented itself as the last hope of warding off defeat through starvation. Moreover, it seemed to be working. The arguments that merchant captains could never be relied upon to keep station, and that many ships together would produce a much easier target for U-boat attack, turned out to be groundless. Concentrated into bigger groups, the ships were harder for enemy submarines to find, and once a convoy was tracked down, the escorting destroyers forced the U-boat commanders to keep their distance: firing their torpedoes at a greater range, they had less chance of scoring a hit.

Convoy work, Lightoller discovered, was no less taxing than his duties with the Dover Patrol. The weather in the North Sea could be as vile as anywhere. The little *Falcon* at her age was becoming less fit to cope with the rigours of heavy seas. Orginally built to last only five years, she was now almost twenty. Her thin hull was less resilient to the constant bouncing and buffeting of big seas as she battled to keep forty or so lumbering merchantmen together in their respective stations on a pre-arranged zig-zag course. On top of that, Lightoller had the constant worry that a U-boat could be stalking the convoy or lying in wait somewhere en route looking for the chance to pick off one of the stragglers. This was strain of a new kind, calling for the utmost in vigilance, forever watching for that tell-tale splash of a periscope or the dreaded whitened track of a torpedo lengthening out across the sea on its way to add one more to the tally of 5,000 merchant vessels which the U-boats had already sent to the bottom in this war.

He would not have to wait long for the first shock of hearing that ominous clanging explosion accompanied by a column of water erupting against the hull of a merchantman, and then to watch her heel helplessly over like some pole-axed animal and go down in a few minutes, knowing that many of her crew would not survive. The U-boat was away into the depths and gone before *Falcon* and the others shepherding the convoy could get back at it. Hydrophonic equipment was just being introduced but only into new destroyers, so all they could do was head at full speed for the approximate location of the submarine and blast away at the sea with depth charges in the hope, if not of destroying it, at least of giving it a good shaking up. Lightoller craved for the chance to finish one of them off and see positive proof of his kill. If he got that chance, it would not be in *Falcon*: she would not be in service much longer.

It happened soon after midnight on April 1st as *Falcon* was coming south to the Humber seeing a convoy in from Norway. Darkness was the most difficult time for convoy work: the escorts had to weave in and out of a large collection of ships steaming without lights on a constantly changing course, trying to keep in touch with them and make sure that all were present and accounted for. With winter now passed, they had known more adverse conditions than now in the North Sea, but it was still an unfriendly night—wet, cold and windy, with visibility difficult through the squalls and a heavy swell.

As midnight appoached Lightoller decided to leave the bridge and turn in for a while, leaving her in the charge of Sam Shonk the Gunner who had been an acting Officer of the Watch in *Falcon* since before she left the Dover Patrol. He had proved himself well capable of the job and Lightoller had grown to trust him. However on this night poor Shonk was to come unstuck while Lightoller was destined yet again to be lying in his bunk and slipping off to sleep at the critical moment.

When the terrific crash accompanied by a wicked jolt reverberated through the ship, Lightoller at first thought they had been struck by a torpedo, but when he dashed up onto the bridge the truth was evident at once: *Falcon* had collided with another vessel, the *John Fitzgerald*, an Admiralty trawler assisting with the escort. The trawler, apart from a nasty buckle in her bows, was still intact but *Falcon* was in a pitiful state. She had been struck just forward of the bridge with the result that her turtle-back bows had all but been severed as she wallowed helplessly in the North Sea swell. Her engines were now stopped as Lightoller quickly sized up the situation. Because of the way her two halves were concertinaed up out of the water, she was not filling up as rapidly as she might. The carpenter assured him she could remain afloat for a time provided that she stayed at that angle; if she developed a list, though, there was every chance she would capsize. Once the boilers were blown down and the fires extinguished Lightoller decided to get Cooper the Chief Engineer and the rest of the engineers and stokers away. There was little point in keeping them aboard as *Falcon* would be going nowhere under her own steam now. He had all thirty of them transferred to the *John Fitzgerald*, including one stoker who had been badly burned when a main steam pipe fractured on the impact. The man was in a bad way and Lightoller realised there was a risk that he might die. At least there was one thing in their favour. They were not far from the Humber and within a few hours the man would be in hospital.

Any hopes Lightoller had that reducing the ship's company by half would lighten *Falcon* enough to give her a better chance of surviving would not hold out for long. The after part of her was going down noticeably by the stern and it seemed only a matter of time before the two sections, rending and scraping as they swayed about independently in the sea, parted company completely. He decided the time had come to give the general order to abandon ship and the remaining half of the crew, except himself, the Gunner and Eric Gordon his First Lieutenant, went away in *Falcon*'s only pair of lifeboats. They were later picked up by *Peterel*, another '30-knotter' which had been working alongside *Falcon* on convoy escort and standing by since the accident.

It was not long after the boats had gone that *Falcon* gave a sudden upward lurch followed by a loud crack as the bows broke completely away and sank instantly. Lightoller was still determined to stick with her, as were the other two. Poor Shonk felt wretched: he was convinced it was his fault. Lightoller was characteristically philosophical, trying his utmost to console the man and persuade him that he ought not to blame himself. The trawler had suddenly appeared from out of the darkness, far too late to take avoiding action. Neither ship was any more to blame than the other. In night-time convoy work it needed only a slight misjudgement to cause a collision. They were regularly happening and the Navy was fully aware of the problems. But Shonk was still racked with guilt. Besides he had let the skipper down after he had shown trust in him.

Lightoller had for a time hoped there was still a chance that the remaining rear portion of *Falcon* could stay afloat and, come daybreak, be towed in. But since her bows had broken off she was beginning to tip further backwards through missing that extra weight forward which had been assisting her to maintain some balance. There was one small consolation in that the section laid open where the bows had once been was not taking water quite so heavily because of the way it was poised clear of the sea.

There was only one thing to do, Lightoller decided presently, as the forlorn trio sat huddled together in his cabin feeling cold, damp and miserable: make a fire, put the kettle on and wind up the gramophone. Shonk duly obliged and so they sat drinking hot tea, warming themselves by the fire and listening to Lightoller's well worn crackly sea-shanty records that periodically changed tempo with the rocking of the ship, while every now and again another book was wedged underneath the gramophone to keep it playing sweet and level. If ever there were three April fools, thought Lightoller as he woke up to the absurdity of the situation, it was he and his two loyal companions sitting around playing music and drinking tea in a broken ship floundering helplessly somewhere in the North Sea and threatening to go from under them at any moment. Yet he remembered it was not the first time he had listened to music being played on a ship in distress, and just now, as then, it was doing a power of good for morale.

They were all alone now. *Peterel* could not stay behind any longer as she had to catch up with the convoy and see it through on the last lap of the journey home. The three of them realised only too well that there were no boats left to take to if and when *Falcon* finally took the plunge, and as I a.m. came round there came with it an increasing awareness that the end might not be too far away. *Falcon* had reached an angle which Lightoller estimated to be about 30 degrees, with the sea beginning to swish over her stern. He knew she could not possibly remain afloat at that angle indefinitely. It was then that he was confronted with a new worry. Shonk, who had regularly been going below to check the situation in the stokehold and reporting back each time that the water level was 'still rising' returned with more disturbing news. Having just been out on deck to put all the depth charges on 'safe', he informed his commander that he was not fully confident that one of them had set properly. If his fears were confirmed, when the ship sank the depth charge would explode and more than likely set everything else off as well. Lightoller had by this time pretty well resigned himself to the prospect of sooner or later having to jump for it and there was nothing else they could do but hope that the Gunner's nagging doubts were unfounded. At least, he mused to himself, it would give them all a damn good start on the way. Perhaps that might be for the best rather than be left bobbing about in the sea for endless hours waiting in vain to be picked up. The water, he knew, would not be as cold as the last time he jumped into it from a sinking ship, but it would be cold and unpleasant enough. A trawler was on the way out to them from the Humber, but if *Falcon* went before it arrived, the crew would have the devil of a job spotting them in the water, particularly as she had since drifted a considerable distance away to the east of the original collision spot.

The worst part of it now for Lightoller was the feeling of utter helplessness, just sitting and waiting and wondering when she would finally go. At least when the *Titanic* was going down he was thoroughly occupied right up to the end. Here he had too much time to think, time for fear to start creeping up on him. He thought of Sylvia and the kids and how they would cope without him, but he had to fight such negative thoughts. Since the *Titanic* he was convinced he had found 'the Key'. 'Death is the Illusion', he must remember.

Without warning there was a tremendous crash down below followed by the noise of tons of water rushing into the ship. A bulkhead had given way. *Falcon*'s time had come: she was going and going fast. As the broken destroyer reared right up on end reminiscent of the *Titanic*, but in reverse, the three of them catapulted out of Lightoller's cabin to the rail and leapt overboard. As soon as they flopped into the sea they swam vigorously to get clear of the ship, not so much to avoid any suction as she went, but to get as far away as possible should that rogue depth charge decide to blow and take the others with it. There would be little hope for them if that happened, but they might as well give themselves a fighting chance. As Lightoller frantically swam away he began to hear that same rumbling roar he had heard once before which told him the ship was breaking up inside, not so thunderous this time as there was a significant difference between 400 tons and 45,000 tons of ship disintegrating, but still a very familiar sound. He paused for a moment in the cold water to look back and see the last of *Falcon* disappear stern first beneath the North Sea in a cloud of hissing steam. It was all too reminiscent of April 1912 as he realised she had gone at the same time of night almost to the minute—2.20 a.m. Six years on—and here he was again! He forgot any more about swimming, but let himself bob limply up and down in his lifejacket as the nightmare from the past came flooding back . . . the screams . . . the choking . . . the frantic splashing of people struggling in the water . . . the cries for help from a thousand dying throats . . . Suddenly a bigger wave than the others swept over him filling his mouth and nose with seawater and making him cough and choke as he fought for breath, half swallowing water, half spitting it out. It jerked him to his senses. This was the North Sea, not the North Atlantic and what of the depth charges? Too much time had passed for them to explode now. *Falcon* would be on the bottom by this time. It looked as though they were not to get that good start on the way after all.

He made contact with Shonk and Gordon and, grabbing onto some of the floating wreckage that had begun to appear around them, they braced themselves for a long gruelling night in the sea. This time, as he had anticipated, the temperature of the water was far more bearable than he had endured before and they should be able to survive some hours in it, certainly until daylight, before exposure started setting in. At the same time Lightoller was aware that on the previous occasion there had been some semblance of a craft beneath him, the sea was for the most part calm and there had always been the reassuring knowledge that help was rushing straight to them. Right now things in that respect were looking a good deal less certain. They could only hope that the wreckage scattered around them would attract the attention of a search ship when daylight broke.

Half an hour went by, and they intermittently broke into a chorus of shouting and whistling in faint hopes that some vessel might be near enough to hear them. Then they noticed it, the unmistakable thud of a ship's engine getting closer. With all their lung power they shouted and yelled, praying that they would be heard. It was heading towards them all right as out of the darkness the outline of a small ship loomed into view. It was a trawler but it showed no signs of slowing down, and worse, they realised it was steaming straight at them. This was cruel irony: a ship to run them down instead of picking them up! Then Lightoller remembered an old friend as he fumbled in his pocket and pulled out his officer's whistle that had rendered such good service once before. He tightened his numb lips around it and blew. The ship immediately veered off, just brushing by them and tossing them violently in its wash while they desperately struggled to swim clear of the propeller. But the propeller had stopped turning. The whistle had done its work as the trawler came to a stop and began feeling its way back to where the sound had come from. More shouting and blowing on the whistle to help her search-light pin-point the spot and she was soon up beside them with a rope ladder being flung over the side, and then the wonderful relief of many hands reaching out to help them aboard. The trawler turned out to be the one sent out to look for them. It had succeeded all right—almost a little too successfully Lightoller reflected as he sat back wrapped in blankets sipping a hot cup of cocoa.

He would certainly have another tale to tell Sylvia. But tremendously relieved though she would be that her husband was safe and well, she would not be so pleased to learn that in his latest shipwreck had gone every stick of furniture—gramophone included——which the family possessed, all on its way to their new home on Humberside. It had not been such a bright idea after all to utilise one of His Majesty's Ships as a removal van.

*

Within two weeks Lightoller was back at sea with a new command. The destroyer *Garry*, one of the so called 'River' class, was half as big again as *Falcon* and more heavily armed though, like her predecessor, having been built in 1905, she would have been a candidate for the breaker's yard or a foreign navy had the war not come along. She was assigned to the 7th Flotilla on the North Sea Patrol. But she still ranked as a commander's command, and as Lightoller was only a Lieutenant—and a Royal Naval Reserve one at that—it was some time before his appointment was confirmed. There was still the matter of the court martial over the loss of *Falcon*. Lightoller was encouraged that 'the brass' had seen fit to give him another ship before the case came up, a hint that they had already given him the benefit of the doubt as to his seamanship.

However, following the loss of a Royal Navy vessel, whatever the previously known circumstances, there would always have to be a court martial of the commander and other potential accessories, in this case Lieutenant Eric R. S. Gordon RNR and Gunner Samuel J. Shonk, to establish formally the cause of the wreck and whether any blame was attributable. Much to Lightoller's anguish the stoker, badly scalded by steam during the collision, died, putting a much more serious complexion on the whole thing.

In Lightoller's view the collision had been an accident pure and simple with no one party to blame. There was nothing to hide and if they stuck to the facts as they were, there would be little to fear. But at the same time he was only too well aware of what it could be like enduring a long and difficult cross-examination. On the previous occasion he had been a witness and that was bad enough. This time it was his own ship that had been wrecked and he really was on trial, as were Gordon and Shonk.

The court was an imposing affair conducted by a judge brought up specially to Immingham from the Admiralty Court in London, flanked by an equally stern and daunting array of high-ranking naval personnel heavily adorned with gold braid. If his fellow defendants were instantly awe-struck, not so Lightoller—he had been through this kind of thing before.

He decided to try a different approach this time, gathering together beforehand every possible piece of relevant information on the events leading up to the collision and all that happened subsequently, setting it down in a comprehensive statement with several copies to be put before the court. This method, though an unorthodox one, would, he hoped avoid much of the questioning they might otherwise be likely to face.

The judge himself proceeded to read out the statement in full, including the glowing report Lightoller had given the Gunner; a first-class seaman, a very capable and conscientious Officer of the Watch when called upon to act in that job, a man whose behaviour on the night of the wreck was exemplary especially in view of his decision to stay with the ship after being given leave to abandon it. Lightoller had even included as an afterthought what a good job the man did, keeping their spirits up, making tea and playing the gramophone—and found himself cringing when the judge read out that part of it too. Somehow it did not fit in with the rest of it, but it raised smiles all round. It was on the Gunner that the court would be concentrating, as he had been in charge on the bridge when the collision occurred. Lightoller was all too mindful of this and later in the hearing, in another unorthodox departure from regular court-martial procedure, he cross-examined Shonk himself to give him every opportunity to communicate to the court that despite this one costly mistake he could still be relied upon to hold a position of responsibility in one of His Majesty's ships.

And so the moment of truth arrived when the trio were summoned back into the room in turn to hear the verdict. The first thing Lightoller's eyes fell on was his sword, which had been taken away from him at the opening of the hearing. The hilt was pointing towards him. It meant that he was in the clear. So what about the others? He need not have worried. Not only were they all exonerated without censure, to the joy and relief of Shonk especially, but when the Judge launched into a eulogy for the courage they had shown to remain with their doomed ship until the end, it became almost embarrassing.

Shonk and Gordon were both promoted to new destroyers with the Grand Fleet while Lightoller went happily back to *Garry* and the North Sea Patrol with his appointment confirmed. He had undoubt-edly been helped by statistics which showed that out of 60 destroyers lost so far in the war, nearly half of them had sunk in collisions or due to some other cause not attributable to enemy action. Meanwhile he had his own personal statistic to dwell on. To experience four shipwrecks, one of them the worst in maritime history, *and* survive them all was surely some kind of record.

27

During April and May 1918 merchant-ship losses were reduced to a third of the catastrophic losses in the equivalent period of 1917; the net was finally closing on the U-boats. The number of U-boats destroyed had risen dramatically, a confirmed 25 being sent to their last account in those same spring months of 1918.

Life had become much tougher for the U-boat commanders, who were finding that where once they could pick off lone defenceless ships at random, convoys guarded by their destroyer escorts presented them with a far more difficult and risky target. They themselves had come to know the full meaning of being the victims of the hunt, with nerves on edge as they skulked in the depths under constant threat of vicious depth-charge attacks should they chance to reveal their periscope at the wrong moment. And there was no-one who delivered a depth charge attack with more ferocious determination than the commander of *Garry*.

Lightoller had yet to notch up a confirmed 'kill', though he was convinced on a few occasions that his depth charges has done more than enough to finish the job. He still lacked that material proof and until he could produce a body or some piece of identifiable wreckage his score sheet remained blank, though he still received commendation for his tenacity in driving off a number of U-boat attacks. He was now senior commander of his own little squadron of four destroyers, and during one spell brought home down the North Sea six consecutive convoys averaging forty ships at a time with only one loss. She was an ore carrier which blew up in a cloud of red dust and was gone in minutes. Only a handful of the crew were picked up. It may have been just one ship of hundreds sunk in the war but it was still one too many for Lightoller. She was part of his own convoy and he took it as a personal defeat. He was sure he had put paid to the U-boat responsible though, once again, he lacked that vital evidence.

He attributed his low convoy casualty record to his own particular escort strategy although it would put him constantly at loggerheads with the East Coast Commander-in-Chief, Admiral Nicholson. His promotion and the extra responsibility that went with it was a clear indication that Lightoller, despite his anti-Navy-establishment ways, had earned the regard of his superiors; but he was determined to stick to his own ideas whoever was telling him differently, and they had to admit he did produce the results to back up his theories.

The standard method devised by the Royal Navy for guarding a convoy with a four-destroyer escort was to have one destroyer a mile or so out at the head of the four lines of ships, with one each side halfway back, and one following up astern. In Lightoller's opinion that left the convoy far too exposed, the escort being limited enough as it was. His system was simply to have two at the front either side of the leading convoy ships, with the other two similarly deployed on each flank at the rear. That way, he argued, the U-boat had less time to get in a torpedo shot and escape. If he was not spotted by the leading escorts, those following up behind were well poised for seeing the enemy and making an effective attack.

Anti-submarine tactics were always the major topic of conversation in *Garry*'s wardroom when other destroyer commanders came aboard in port for a gin or two and a yarn with 'Lights'. The 'crack' was always that much better in *Garry* than other ships and it was like moths round a candle when she was in. They loved to listen to Lightoller holding forth, his deep sonorous voice dominating everyone else's, as he put forward with such conviction his own ideas on defence against the U-boats. Then, if they were lucky, he might start yarning about episodes in his past life—except when someone made a tactless joke about the *Titanic*, then the room went dead quiet and the subject was rapidly changed. Lightoller was flattered at being the centre of so much attention, though there were times when he wished they would go and drink somebody else's gin for a change as *Garry*'s supply forever seemed to need replenishing.

The truly orthodox Christian Scientist was not supposed to drink, but there were times when Lightoller found sticking to the rules difficult, and there was no doubt a gin or two with the tiniest dash of water never failed to go down well.

He continued to be just as popular with his men, particularly as those in *Garry* were the best fed in the whole flotilla. But there was a secret behind this which they had all been sworn to keep, otherwise the game would be up and mealtimes would never be the same again.

Having been frustrated by the failure of his depth charges to produce visible results against the enemy, Lightoller in the meantime found a very productive secondary use for them. His experience those years back down the Nitrate Coast had taught him how an explosive charge dropped in the right place could bring up a plentiful haul of fish, and now he was putting it into practice again to great effect. The North Sea was rich in good fishing grounds and, after a little bribery here and there with the odd bottle of gin to one or two trawler skippers he got friendly with, he learnt where the best spots were. But it all had to be done very furtively. If the Admiralty got wind that one of their commanders was using His Majesty's Depth Charges (at £400 a time) to catch fish for his crew a good few high-ranking eyebrows would be raised back at Whitehall. For obvious reasons he could never do it on escort duty, only when *Garry* was making her way north alone to pick up a convoy. He would arrive over a location where he had found out the fishing was good, and then suggest with tongue in cheek to his young Scots Number 1, Lieutenant Gillespie, that he was sure he had just seen the periscope of a submarine pop up. *Garry* would immediately go to 'Action stations' and the depth-charge 'attack' begin. 'This is for King George and Merry England!' the men would cry each time a charge was tossed over the stern and the sea shook to the blast. Two were usually enough to do the trick and then out went the boats with improvised nets to bring in the haul, while the cook looked on from the rail, shouting advice and encouragement and rubbing his hands at the fine mountain of cod that would soon be sizzling in his galley for breakfast. They had to be quick because the fish lying stunned on the surface soon came round and swam away. Equally important, it did not do to hang around for too long just in case an enemy submarine happened to be lurking in the vicinity.

On one occasion, however, Lightoller's clandestine fishing exercises were nearly rumbled. He had discovered a particularly good cod ground off Flamborough Head on the Yorkshire coast between Bridlington and Scarborough and, early one morning heading north to meet a convoy at the Firth of Forth, they decided to stop there for breakfast. The usual couple of depth charges were detonated and the boats lowered to scoop up the shoal of fish lying stunned on the surface. Unfortunately all this was happening in full view of the lighthouse keeper, who immediately contacted East Coast head-quarters to inform them of what he had seen. Some time later *Garry* received a signal from Admiral Nicholson requesting to know what her boats were doing in the water at 0700 on that particular date. As Gillespie delivered the message to Lightoller he realised that it was going to be a very tricky question to answer, particularly as he knew that his commander was a passionate believer in telling the truth, and besides he could hardly reply that they were using the boats to look

for a submarine. 'Don't look so worried, Gillie,' he said to his
Number 1. 'Make to Vice-Admiral East Coast: "Re your 0014.
Submit boats were examining objects in the water." ' It was no lie,
and nothing further was heard. That little incident told Alfred
Gillespie a lot about Lightoller and he never forgot it. Although his
commander was much older, the two developed a close friendship
that would last for life. Lightoller saw in this bright-eyed, alert young
spark from Dundee much of himself when he was that age. Like him
Gillespie was a merchant-service man, which meant that there was an
instant rapport between the pair.

They talked for many hours about anti-submarine tactics and how
Lightoller believed that every ship in the escort should be allowed to
work as an independent unit, within certain limits, acting first and
reporting afterwards, so that if a U-boat did appear no time was
wasted in going into the attack. Apart from the standard four
destroyers, the escort was usually backed up by half-a-dozen MLs,
which were small motor launches armed with one gun and depth
charges, the same number of trawlers of the Auxiliary Patrol similarly
armed, and sometimes a couple of spotter planes which Lightoller,
from past experience, was not surprised to find needed as much
nursing as the ships. Everyone in the escort, as far as he was
concerned, was free to pitch in and have a go at the slightest hint of
trouble, though on a couple of occasions, which in the event turned
out to be false alarms, things did almost get out of hand, with boats
tearing about dropping depth charges indiscriminately around one
another, threatening to collide, or worse, blow each other up.

Lightoller had by now become totally convinced that the only way
he was ever going to wipe out a U-boat and make absolutely certain of
it was by the good old-fashioned ram, then there could be no mistake.
There was one good omen. *Garry* had rammed and sunk a U-boat
earlier in the war, which proved she was capable of it and, more
encouraging, when her damaged bows were repaired they were
considerably strengthened to help her withstand it better in the event
of a repeat performance. Having witnessed what the U-boats could do
to merchant shipping, Lightoller reckoned that one submarine sent
to the bottom was worth ten destroyers. 'They rank lower than the
vilest of sharks, and I've met a good few of those in my time,' he
would say to Gillespie. For all his Commander's strong commitment
to Christianity, it did not appear to curb a desire to kill when it came
to U-boats.

275

Towards summer, 1918, the weather in the North Sea was slow to relent. Just when things looked like improving, the storms came back with a vengeance. The worst was having to heave to in the Firth of Forth and sit it out in a driving North-East gale, waiting to meet the ships as they neared the Scottish coast. It had been a long time since Lightoller felt seasick but there were moments in those situations when he wondered if his stomach was not going to let him down. Then, when the convoy arrived, there was little respite as they ploughed through heaving green mountains for the next couple of days, zig-zagging along at a painful 8 knots with the sea constantly lashing over *Garry*'s open bridge, keeping them permanently drenched to the skin. Although she was basically a good sea boat, *Garry* was just a bit too 'wet' for Lightoller's liking. Characteristic of many destroyers of her size and design, neither a hydroplane nor a submarine but intent on imitating the worst devices of both. Salt-water boils, like seasickness, he had thought were an evil of his sailing-ship past but as the wet oilskins chafed against his skin through endless stormy hours on the bridge, they came back as bad as ever he remembered. When the weather did ease up it usually waited until they were moored in the shelter of the Humber and then with the heat of the sun came the stench from the nearby fish-manure factory. At times it was overpowering, especially for those anchored closest to it, as *Garry* usually was, and then they were only too glad to get to sea again whatever the weather was like.

It was one such hot day in mid July that *Garry* received the by now familiar orders to get under way and proceed north to meet a convoy coming in from Norway and bring it down the east coast. As she nosed her way down the Humber to the estuary and headed northwards out round the Spurn the sea was smooth but for an easy swell with a breeze soft and warm. The weather on this trip should stay kind to them for a change, Lightoller and Gillespie agreed. But it would be ideal for others too, they realised; the arch enemy, when he was at his most accurate and deadly, and would most likely be waiting to strike.

Kapitän Leutnant Werner Fürbringer had been through a lean time since taking his brand-new submarine *UB 110* out of her base at Zeebrugge on a raiding cruise in the North Sea.

Life was not the same any more for Fürbringer compared with those earlier days of the war when it had all been so easy to chalk up thousands of tons of shipping sunk week after week with little fear of retaliation. *UB 110* should have returned to her Zeebrugge base by this time but because this, her first cruise, had turned out to be so disappointing, Fürbringer decided to stay at sea a few days longer than his scheduled return date in hopes of things improving. The persistent bad weather had been partly to blame for the lack of success, but when there had been opportunities to attack he failed to sink his prey. The nearest he had come to it was off Robin Hood's Bay when he torpedoed the oil tanker *Sprucol*, a single ship being escorted by three trawlers, but she did not go down, and was towed into port. The next time he attacked a ship almost a week later it was in convoy, and he only escaped by a whisker, missing his target completely as he dived to evade the attacking destroyers. He counted 26 depth charges exploding close to his vessel before he finally gave them the slip.

These days Fürbringer stayed submerged almost permanently apart from those few welcome hours during darkness when he came up to take in fresh air and recharge his batteries, then down again before dawn broke to resume what had become to him and his 30 crew an endless underwater journey with progressively diminishing results to show for it.

As *UB 110* crept stealthily along below the North Sea, a few miles off Hartlepool on that fine summer's day, July 19th, the mental and physical demands of life inside her had begun to drive Fürbringer and his crew to near breaking point. On the surface it was sweltering hot, one of the rare good days there had been so far that summer, but down in the submarine it was wretchedly cold and damp with nearly everyone suffering from bad colds and chills and heavily wrapped up. Fürbringer himself was clad in thick woollen sweater, scarf and three pairs of trousers and still felt cold.

It was around 1.30 p.m. that he decided to take his U-boat up to periscope depth to see if there was anything in the offing. As the periscope broke the surface and he swung it slowly round, his eyes lit up. There to the north, less than a mile away and steaming right into his lap, was a convoy of thirty ships at least. He observed that it was heavily guarded by destroyers and numerous other types of patrol vessels, but he had long since come to accept that in making an attack he would always have to run the gauntlet of the escort and trust to God and good fortune to escape unscathed. He had to choose his target quickly, fire all four bow torpedoes and then run for the deep as fast as he could. He picked out the biggest ship he could see in the van of the convoy and decided to go for that. But the heavy presence of protecting vessels was making it difficult to get into a good firing position. This convoy seemed to be escorted differently to the customary system employed. He noticed there was not a destroyer steaming way out at the head of the ships in the usual way. The escorts seemed to be in much closer attendance altogether, leaving fewer exposed gaps to take advantage of. He decided to wait. He watched the ships go by and then settled his attention on a freighter of about 3,000 tons bringing up the rear. She was not quite near enough yet, another minute, perhaps two, and then she would be nicely in his sights. He had another scan round through the periscope, jerking it to a sudden halt at the moment it was pointing directly aft. There coming up fast astern, only a hundred yards away, was a destroyer appearing to be heading straight for him. Had she seen him, Für-bringer wondered, or was it just coincidence? He opted to play safe, whipping down the periscope with an immediate order to the control room to take her down 20 metres. But Fürbringer had been seen.

A seaplane was the first to spot the U-boat, and a motor launch which picked up the pilot's Aldis-lamp alarm-signal was alerting everyone to the danger with repeated blasts on the hooter. Lightoller on the bridge of *Garry*, stationed at the back of the convoy, saw the periscope just as it was disappearing beneath the surface almost dead ahead and in response to his command 'Full speed ahead—Action stations!' she was now racing in to attack. As he observed the last of the periscope duck under the waves, the big question was, had he already fired his torpedoes and he waited for that dreaded clanging explosion and gout of water shooting up against the hull of yet another victim sent to the bottom by these devious, ruthless brutes. But Fürbringer had not fired. His main concern just then was whether he had been discovered. He was still hopeful that he had not and with *UB 110* now nearing the 20-metre mark the hydroplanes were set to level her out. The vibration of pounding propellers above became more pronounced until he could tell the destroyer was right overhead. He waited for the moment of truth. It was soon to arrive. On *Garry*'s bridge Lightoller pressed the firing bell for the depth-charge attack to commence. One . . . Two . . . Three . . . Four . . . Each blast that ripped through the sea in a straight line astern of *Garry* was followed a second later by a column of water leaping high into the air while the destroyer shook violently to the blast of the explosions. Primed up to the limit, and adrenalin running high, Lightoller ordered full helm to bring *Garry* round for another run. As she heeled over in a tight turn his eyes were fixed on the great patch of discoloured turbulence where the depth charges had been sown. He must have got him. He must have. He could not possibly have survived that.

Twenty metres down in *UB 110* the depth charges detonating in quick succession next to her hull had fractured the plates adjacent to the engine room, where the Chief Engineer was reporting to his Captain that they were starting to take water fast. At the same time the U-boat began to dip down by the stern, not from the effect of the sea coming in but because her hydroplanes had jammed in the depth-charge attack. *UB 110* was now refusing to dive in answer to Fürbringer's urgent command. He immediately gave the order to flood the trimming tanks and have every man sent forward to try and get her back on an even keel. It made no difference. Even worse he realised, not only was the submarine unable to go down, but it was beginning to rise and there was seemingly nothing that could be done to prevent it. As *Garry* circled the spot, lining up for her second attack, Lightoller remained glued to the area where the churned-up sea was beginning to subside, looking for just some sign: a patch of oil, a piece of debris, a sailor's hat, perhaps even a body, anything to confirm that he had done it this time.

'Flood! . . . Flood! . . . Open all tanks!' Fürbringer cried, but it was to no avail. *UB 110* was determined to keep rising. 'Have we flooded? . . . Are all valves open?' came his repeated desperate appeal. There was no response. His last hope of escape was in vain. He leapt to the periscope and saw to his horror as he peered through the eye-piece that it had gone above the surface.

'Submarine breaking surface on the port quarter, sir!' came the sudden cry from the look-out on *Garry*'s searchlight platform. But Lightoller had already seen it. Up came *UB 110* at a steep angle, first the bows and then the conning tower in a turmoil of gushing foam and spouting water vomiting from her casings; like a great ugly black fish that had found itself flushed from the deep and now lay wounded and exposed in all its loathsome wickedness, glinting in the heat of the afternoon sun.

'Hard a-starboard!' roared Lightoller, 'Submarine bearing red one-two–o. Five hundred yards. Open Fire!' As *Garry*'s smaller after guns opened up in response, Gillespie shoved 'Snotty' Kinman, the young Midshipman aside on the forward twelve-pounder and waited for the destroyer to swing her head round to port and bring her main fire power to bear. The wait was agony. Then at last his sights came on and he opened fire. He watched his first shot and then his second thud into the base of the U-boat's conning tower, while other escort vessels coming onto the scene joined in the shoot.

Inside the submarine the combined effect of all this fire power unleashed upon her was devastating. As Fürbringer and his petrified crew felt the shuddering impact of shots blasting the hull and conning tower they realised they were done for.

Gillespie, satisfied the twelve-pounder had done enough, hopped back onto the bridge and commandeered the helm. This was how it should be. He and Lightoller together at their moment of imminent triumph. 'We shall get him,' said Lightoller to Gillespie. 'We shall get him . . . Steady the helm Gillie . . . Now steer straight at him.' Fürbringer saw through his periscope the destroyer turning sharply towards him. He knew immediately what was coming. *Garry* cut through the sea, her bow wave dancing merrily as she sliced through the water towards the foe at her full 25 knots. Fürbringer watched her bearing down on him and warned his men to brace themselves for the shock. Four hundred yards . . . Three hundred yards . . . 'Prepare to ram!' bellowed Lightoller . . . Two hundred yards . . . One hundred yards . . . Fifty yards . . . Collision!

On the impact *Garry*'s bows lifted high into the air; inside the U-boat it was mayhem as it went right over on its beam ends and men were thrown in all directions. At first Fürbringer thought it was going to capsize but slowly it righted itself. Lightoller was certain that victory was now his, but he had a ruthless compulsion to crush out of existence this vile beast that had been the cause of so much death and suffering on the seas. The U-boat was severely smashed up, as were *Garry*'s bows, which were badly buckled and torn. She too was now in trouble but her commander was far too absorbed by his lust for the final kill to be distracted from his mission. 'Hard a-port!' he barked to Gillespie as he prepared to ram again.

Fürbringer realised that the commander of this destroyer was intent on giving no quarter. He had no choice left to him. 'Abandon ship!' he called out, telling Oberleutnant Löbell, his No. 1, to open the conning-tower hatch. But Löbell could not open it. Fürbringer ordered the Chief Stoker to try but he could not manage it either, so he decided to try himself, remembering it had certain peculiarities which only he understood. With a loud noise and a rush of escaping compressed air the hatch finally flew open, blowing Fürbringer's cap high into the air. Because his men were crammed up behind him he realised he would have to be first to climb out, but he stood over the hatch ushering them past him so that he could satisfy himself that as Captain he would be the last to leave the conning tower.

UB 110 was now listing 15 degrees to port because the diving tanks had been ripped open in the collision. Fürbringer peered over the top of the conning tower and for a moment felt like a spectator in some bizarre theatre. All around him there was turmoil with destroyers, numerous other vessels and planes too, blasting away at his ship. His friend Löbell was hit in the leg by a shell splinter but he could manage. He would have to. It was now every man for himself. *Garry* raced in again and Lightoller could now see men emerging from the conning tower of the U-boat, running forward and diving overboard. Her guns continued to blaze away killing some as they dashed for the sea. Fürbringer remained crouched in the conning tower watching the destroyer heading for him a second time. He left it to the very last and then, just as the crash was about to come, without waiting to see the last of his men out of the boat, dived into the sea. *Garry* ploughed once more into the U-boat, striking it amidships, smashing open the conning tower and pushing the boat over on its beam ends as before. Men were still inside trying to get out but many never would. Fürbringer hit the water and in the same instant saw one of his stokers leap to a ladder up the side of the destroyer and try to climb to the deck rail. He was met by a petty officer who smashed his clinging hands with the butt of a revolver making him cry out and fall back into the water.

UB 110 had received its death blow and in less than a minute sank to the bottom of the North Sea. *Garry* too was critically wounded as she lay still in the sea, stunned by the violent shocks she had received to her system, while men from the U-boat swam around waiting to be picked up. But to their dismay the opposite happened. Onto *Garry*'s deck came stokers carrying great lumps of coal which they started throwing down at the men floundering in the water and shouting: 'This is for the *Lusitania*!' Fürbringer saw his young batman hit on the head and drift away unconscious before he could reach him, then he heard the sound of gunfire open up again.

Lightoller on *Garry*'s bridge neither noticed nor cared what was happening to the men in the water. Why should he? They had been quite prepared to see thousands die in the execution of their wretched work. Let them get a taste of it themselves. Leave them for others to deal with. His job was done and the main concern now was his own badly crippled ship, and whether she could survive to reach port. One submarine was worth ten destroyers he had always maintained, but even better if he could score this victory and still save his own ship. Presently another destroyer, *Stour*, moved in to pick up those 15 members of the U-boat crew, Fürbringer and Löbell included, who had survived, while Lightoller on *Garry*'s bridge gave the order for Slow Ahead and began steering his ship towards the shore.

His first thought was that if she was destined to sink soon, better to make the beach first and run her aground with the hope that she could be salvaged to fight another day. Gillespie, who had been down to inspect the damage, returned to report that she was now three feet down by the head, with the forward mess-deck bulkhead in a bad way and threatening to cave in. It was being shored up with planks, which might help to hold it for a while, but with no long-term guarantees. If the bulkhead gave, her last wall of defence was gone and that would be the end of her for sure. One promising sign was that although the mess was flooded she did not appear to be taking in any more water, mainly thanks to the pumps. There was something else in their favour, too. The sea was almost flat calm and if the weather remained as it was there was a chance, just a chance, that they could make port—but which port? Lightoller knew there were any number within relatively easy reach along that Tyne–Tees coast, the most obvious one being a little to the north at Newcastle, with all the facilities to repair that kind of serious damage. But all the time something gnawed within him to try and get *Garry* all the way back home to the Humber, and then the job would be well and truly rounded off—but the Humber was over 100 miles away to the south.

Down below all was clamour and clatter as sailors laboured feverishly at the makeshift but crucial job of shoring up the bulkhead, banging and jamming timber props against it at all angles. When Lightoller came below to weigh up the situation for himself, to ordinary eyes it might have seemed a hopeless case, but to him, with his own approach to times of crisis, it looked just a little less than hopeless. Yes, it would be a gamble, but he was going to have a damn good go at it. The Humber it would be.

And so *Garry*, a ship which many a self-respecting ship surveyor would say could barely have steamed a hundred yards in her present condition, never mind a hundred miles, got under way for home. Lightoller's signal back to base at Immingham was dramatic in its simplicity: 'Returning under own power, stern first, 8 knots.'

As the full details of *Garry*'s encounter filtered back to her Immingham base, the Engineer Admiral, the man in charge of hardware, was beside himself with anxiety. It would be madness to try and steam all the way back. He could not possibly get this far. Yet despite all his efforts to persuade Admiral Charlton, the new Commander-in-Chief who had just taken over the East Coast operation, to order Lightoller to head for the Tyne, 'and he'll be damn lucky to reach there!' Charlton was adamant. He would leave Lightoller to follow his own judgement. 'The man's been at sea long enough to decide for himself what's best to do. Let him have a crack at it. Besides, here is where *Garry* belongs, not Newcastle.'

If Admiral Charlton had full confidence in his commander's decision, Lightoller himself was to question the wisdom of it a hundred times over during the long hours that followed, as he watched *Garry*'s smashed-up, wobbling stern sink lower and lower in the water, becoming more independent from her with every mile, while the protesting bulkhead on which so much hinged threatened to collapse at any time. It would be one of the most anxious, nerve-racking nights at sea he ever experienced, and he was no stranger to those in times past.

The sea stayed mercifully calm, calmer than it had been for weeks, and they prayed for their good fortune to hold. Any kind of swell building up would ruin their hopes for sure.

Throughout that interminable night, the hammering and battering at the rogue bulkhead broke out at regular intervals; a wardroom table banged in here, a piece of bunk propped up there. Now it was a case of commandeering anything in the ship which could be readily utilised to keep her afloat. Lightoller knew full well, having committed himself, that if *Garry* went now he would have to answer for his decision not to make for the nearest port when he had the chance, and so much the worse if lives were lost when she foundered. And there was no doubt if she went it would be quick. The boats were swung out ready but even so it was quite likely there would be no time to get men in and lower them.

He kept as close to the coast as his charts allowed, ready to turn for the beach should the dreaded moment come. At least in shallow water there was less chance of being ambushed by a U-boat and there was no ship more vulnerable to submarine attack just then than *Garry*, as she struggled gamely southwards along that monotonous stretch of Yorkshire coastline.

Whitby . . . Robin Hood's Bay . . . Scarborough . . . Filey Brigg . . . Each landmark she went painfully by meant they were that much closer to home—except that for the anxious crew of *Garry* the murky outline of a coast shrouded in wartime black-out offered little hopeful clue to the hour-by-hour progress of the stricken ship.

And then, with the rounding of Flamborough Head, the first shafts of daylight reached up over the eastern horizon. This was one morning they would not be stopping at their favourite fishing ground for breakfast. Nevertheless it was comforting to see that faint glow of early dawn appear. It meant they had at least made it through the night, though not so comforting when it revealed fully to Lightoller the true extent of *Garry*'s worsening condition.

The gap in her broken bows was so wide he was convinced that a bus could have driven through it. Down below, water was beginning to swill round men's legs as they toiled away to plug up the holes in the bulkhead where the sea was finding a way through at an ever increasing rate. It had sensed it was getting the advantage and now the situation was becoming a straightforward matter of time.

Then came a sight to behold as two jaunty little vessels came steaming up the coast towards them: they were *Joffre* and *Homer*, the Humber tugs. The lame-duck service had arrived to give poor *Garry* a helping hand home. Their timing could not have been better. *Garry*'s stern was now so high out of the water that the rudder was barely able to steer her. *Homer* would look after that problem as she nestled in under the stern while *Joffre* took the strain on the tow line aft. That was how *Garry* for those last few nail-biting miles, her bows hanging on by a thread and almost totally underwater made the final lap of her historic stern-first voyage home round Spurn Head, into the Humber estuary and dry dock—just! Fifteen hours had passed since her encounter with *UB 110* and now she looked a pathetic sight, but one that was bathed in glory. Those were wounds sustained in battle, a battle that brought her victory, not just against the Germans but against the last enemy of all, the sea.

For her commander it meant finding himself in the unexpected role of hero and he was feted accordingly with hearty congratulations all round, not least from the Admiral himself.

There would however be one question to cast a faint cloud over Lightoller's moment of triumph. Why had he not made more effort to pick up survivors? There had also been allegations from the U-boat commander that he and his men were fired on and coal thrown at them while they struggled in the water. Lightoller's answer was that he was far too preoccupied with his own stricken ship to be aware of what was going on around. The survivors, he knew, could be picked up by others, and as for the shooting he was sure no guns on *Garry* continued to fire once the U-boat sank, though he could not speak for other ships. There was so much going on at the time and everything was happening at once. If such a deplorable thing had occurred then he did not know of it.

The matter was quietly dropped. Lightoller got a bar to his DSC and was promoted to Lieutenant-Commander. And there would be more satisfaction to come. Divers who later went down to investigate the wreck of *UB 110* recovered code books and other information on U-boat movements in the North Sea which led to the sinking of several more in the same area. Some months later *UB 110* was secretly salvaged and brought into Newcastle.

As for *Garry*, within four weeks of nearly becoming Lightoller's fifth ship wreck, she was out of dry dock and back on convoy duty with brand new bows welded on and a fresh coat of paint leaving no scar of the terrible war wounds she had suffered. Lightoller, as it happened, did not go with her. For him there was the ultimate reward . . . a desk job. But the status of being appointed to a post as one of Admiral Charlton's right-hand men did not appeal to him as much as it might. All he wanted was to get back to sea, and he told the Admiral bluntly that if he was given stripes up to his elbows it would never be any substitute for a ship. Eventually after persistent bickering he got his way, being given command of a big new destroyer fitting out at Portsmouth. But he never got the chance to take her to sea. Shortly before she was due to be commissioned the war ended. The eleventh hour of the eleventh day of the eleventh month had arrived. The enemy was beaten and the armistice signed. From then on Lightoller saw no reason to stay in the fighting navy with all its pipes and bugles. He had to return to merchant ships where he belonged. It was time to get back on the old Western Ocean trail again, and the sooner the better.

PART FIVE
SMALL-BOAT SAILOR

There are many ships, both new and old, in
sea-girt Ithaca. I'll choose you out the best.

Homer, *Odyssey* II. 292

28

Within a few months of the Great War ending the White Star Line was back in business on the New York run. The Liverpool service, which in the years immediately preceding the war had become secondary to Southampton, was the first to reopen and Lightoller, having come out of the Royal Navy with the rank of full Commander, was appointed Chief Officer of the *Celtic*, the earliest of the old so-called 'Big Four'. She had been too slow for the Southampton service but an ideal workhorse on the less prestigious route out of Liverpool. After being torpedoed in the Irish Sea in March 1918, she had spent the rest of the war lying aground off the Isle of Man before being towed back to Belfast at the end of hostilities to have her damage repaired and undergo a complete overhaul. Being upgraded to Chief Officer from his pre-war rank of First was some consolation for being in a ship which could never match the speed and glamour of the thoroughbred Atlantic greyhounds he had known. But Lightoller knew it would not be long before Southampton was opened up again for passenger business, when he was sure to be put back into the mainstream.

For all his loyalty to the merchant service and its methods during his war years with the Royal Navy Lightoller still found the readjustment to his old calling tough going. He had become used to being in command of his own ship, however small, and now he had to answer to a captain again. That was the hardest part.

As the *Celtic* had been through an extensive overhaul prior to her re-entry into passenger service, he was preoccupied for the first few voyages in helping to get the ship organised and running smoothly in proper White Star fashion—not least her crew who, like him, took some time to make the readjustment and remember they were no longer in the Royal Navy and did not need to stand to attention and salute when an order was given. But in time things settled down into the old familiar routine and Lightoller once again became every inch the Western Ocean mail boat officer.

For his employers however the transition would be less straightforward. The main problem after the war was a shortage of ships. The *Oceanic* was no more, neither was the *Britannic*, the third big sister ship to the *Titanic* and the *Olympic*. She had been mined in the Aegean in 1916 and never lived to see the service she had been originally created for. As for the *Olympic*, she was still committed to trooping work repatriating Canadian and American forces, and then would go back to Harland and Wolff for her overhaul and refit.

When the Southampton service did restart some months after the *Celtic* had begun running from Liverpool, it was with two temporary ships, the *Adriatic* another of the original 'Big Four' and the *Lapland*, a liner borrowed from an American company. Meanwhile Lightoller was left kicking his heels in frustration at Liverpool but pinning his hopes on being transferred to the *Olympic* when she came back into service at Southampton. On paper there was no other officer in the company more experienced and better qualified than he to take on the job of Chief Officer in a ship that would be the show-piece of the White Star Line when she returned. Lightoller, now in his mid forties, was also thinking it could not be long before he was offered his own command: men younger than he had commanded White Star and Cunard liners. If not for the *Titanic*, Wilde and Murdoch would both have been in command of ships in their early forties and Arthur Rostron was even younger when given command of the Cunarder *Carpathia* which rescued all the *Titanic* survivors. Soon afterwards Rostron, 'The Electric Spark', was given the *Mauretania* largely as a token of his company's gratitude for what he had done on the night of the *Titanic*. He was to go on to become Commodore of the Cunard Line and receive that most coveted of accolades, a knighthood.

When the *Olympic* eventually made her reappearance on the trans-atlantic scene it was in grand style. After completing her £500,000 reconditioning at Harland and Wolff, which included conversion from coal to oil-fired boilers, she was opened to the Belfast public at half-a-crown a head, with the takings from the four thousand people who visited her over her two days on view going to charity. She then sailed for Southampton with a large party of VIPs on board as guests of Harold Sanderson, the man who had taken over the chairmanship of the White Star Line from the departed J. Bruce Ismay. At a dinner held on board, Sanderson made a speech in which he described the *Olympic* as 'the one ewe lamb of the White Star Line'.

As for Lightoller, he would never be offered a berth in her; nor would he ever set foot on either of the two new White Star liners that later joined her at Southampton, the 34,000-ton *Homeric*, the biggest twin-screw vessel afloat, and the 56,000-ton *Majestic II*, for the next ten years to be the biggest ship afloat and the fastest ever to sail under the White Star flag.

Lightoller was passed over: when the officers were chosen for the *Olympic* he was left out. For a time he was mystified by it and then gradually the message filtered through. An old ghost had come back to haunt him; in fact it had never really gone away.

The White Star Line under a new set of managers were anxious to make a brand new start. There was no place in their plans for officers connected with the disastrous *Titanic*. Never mind that he had defended the company so loyally during the inquiry. Far from feeling grateful to Lightoller, his employers now saw him as something of a black sheep left over from a disaster they wanted to forget. He realised all too clearly that he was not being held in the same high regard by his employers as he once had been. As an officer who had enjoyed regular promotion and at one time was earmarked to become one of the White Star Line's top commanders, perhaps even Commodore, it was hard to come to terms with the realisation that his career prospects had apparently come to a standstill as an officer in a second-rate ship. His very own ship, that greatest ambition of all, looked further away than ever. In fact he sensed now that he quite likely would never reach that treasured goal. Who in their right minds would give the command of a crack transatlantic liner to a man who had held a senior position in the *Titanic*? It would hardly be good for the image of the White Star Line at a time when they were trying so hard to rebuild their reputation.

They would not close the door on him: that would have been too obvious and they had no clear grounds. They were obliged to take him back and had even promoted him to Chief Officer, but then in the workaday sense he was a very useful man, particularly just after the war when experienced officers were in short supply. But not for long, and this was now as far as he would go, and not only in the White Star Line, but probably in any other company he tried to join, however long he stuck it out.

Even the surviving junior officers were to find the *Titanic* a millstone round their necks. Neither Boxhall, Pitman, nor Lowe would ever get their own commands. Of those three Boxhall was the one who stuck it out the longest, going right through to retirement age to finish his career as Chief Officer of the *Ausonia*, a small Cunarder.

Lightoller battled on for a while but his self confidence began to suffer woefully. The work, all that had ever really mattered to him in life, apart from his wife and family, ceased to be a joy any more and became an irksome bore. The zest and enthusiasm he had consistently shown in his job faded almost overnight. The sea, his old friend and foe, somehow just did not seem the same. The prospect of being Chief Officer of the *Celtic* indefinitely on the bread-and-butter run out of Liverpool—and oh how she rolled in heavy weather! —was a soul-destroying prospect, particularly after all the excitement he had known with his own commands in the war, which made his present dead-end seem that much more tedious.

His health too (though the Christian Scientist in him made him stubbornly refuse to admit it) was now beginning to suffer. The strain of slogging away at a job that made him more fed up and miserable with every day that went by was making him increasingly tired and run down.

There was only one answer. He would leave the White Star Line and his £38 per month salary and give up the sea altogether. Sylvia was relieved. She had noticed how in a matter of weeks her husband appeared to have aged ten years. Dark rings had appeared round his eyes, the lines on his face had become deeper, his tuft of hair had gone markedly thinner and so for that matter had he. It was almost as though everything he had been through during all those incident-packed and often traumatic years at sea had finally caught up with him.

The family also played a big part in the decision. Sylvia, although she coped admirably with her disability, was finding it harder to be left alone for long stretches coping with such a large family that was rapidly growing up. The two eldest boys were into their teens now and she felt it would be far better if their father was around more to keep a paternal eye on them.

And so Lightoller sat down in his cabin aboard the *Celtic* to write the hardest letter of his life, his resignation. As his mind drifted back through his eventful sea career spanning thirty-odd years, he recalled how as a young apprentice on the *Primrose Hill* swatting up for his Second Mate's Ticket he had gazed in awe so often at that picture of the old four-masted White Star Liner *Celtic* on the front of Todd and Whall's Manual of Seamanship. It was indeed ironic that he should be finishing his career in the later edition of that same ship he had looked upon in times long past as the very pinnacle of his ambitions—yet somehow not quite turning out now in the way the boy might once have envisaged.

But if Lightoller had been harbouring any second thoughts about his decision to leave the White Star Line, the company he had served with unwavering loyalty since the day he joined them over twenty years previously, these were at once dispelled when, at the end of his last voyage from New York, he arrived at head office to 'await the pleasure' of the managers. His letter of resignation had already been briefly acknowledged without a word of regret, and as he entered the room the man at the head of the table looked up and simply said with a wave of the hand: 'Oh, you're leaving us are you? Oh well, goodbye.' With that the door was held open for him, he was out, and that was the end of it.

As Lightoller strode out through the imposing portals of the White Star Line offices in James Street for the last time, a lump came to his throat and the water welled up in his eyes. He felt wretched. Not so much because he had made the break and buried the anchor, but for the way it had finally ended. All the years of service he had given to that company, and the man never even uttered a 'thank you'. It seemed as though they could not have cared less; why, almost as though they were relieved to see the back of him! It was humiliating.

Lightoller did not look back as he quickened his step down James Street and hopped on a tram to get home as fast as he could to Sylvia and the kids.

The first years ashore did little for 'Lights's' self-esteem. He set up a business importing Canadian furs, but soon ran out of cash and the venture folded. The family sold their Liverpool house and moved to London. Here Lightoller landed himself a job as British political correspondent to the *Christian Science Monitor* of Boston. This job came to an abrupt end when a boardroom *putsch* threw out the Editor who had hired him.

These were the years of the Depression, and he was only one of many who were knocking on doors applying for jobs, any jobs: Lloyd's insurers, cargo agents, shipping journals—every time he was told he was too old (he was now nearing fifty), or he lacked the right qualifications. With a wife and five children and a mortgage on a large house, he felt driven by sheer penury. His powers of survival at sea did not serve him so well on land. He was almost ready to give up the struggle.

It was Sylvia who saved the day. She opened their home in Pimlico as a guesthouse, which was soon fairly prospering—only Lightoller was now having to play Chief Officer (and stoker) to his wife's Captain. However, they were eventually in a position to realise a modest dream and buy a holiday home at Port Victoria on the River Medway. The sea now became not a task-mistress but a playground for 'messing about in boats'.

At about this time the family sold their guesthouse and put their money into property speculations. They moved to Putney, while keeping for a time their place at Port Victoria.

29

It was near Port Victoria, at Conyer, that Lightoller met a boat-builder, Charlie Cooper, in the summer of 1929, just when his urge to own a family-sized yacht had become an obsession. The problem was where to find it and how to pay for it. Charlie Cooper was the man to square the circle: he picked up a discarded Admiralty steam pinnace on the cheap and showed 'Lights' how it might be converted from a squat, ugly duckling into a beautiful sleek yacht in a couple of seasons' work. 'Sold!' cried his new client, and Cooper got to work gutting the pinnace down to its bare hull of solid, seaworthy teak, and rebuilding it according to the plans they had drawn up together.

His plans allowed for the extension of the original 55-foot hull to 60-foot with a counter stern. She would have a chunky but nicely proportioned wheelhouse with generous seating around its perimeter. Below, the after half was taken up with the spacious saloon connected further aft to the galley and up forward, the sleeping accommodation divided into three cabins, enough for six in comfort, though more could bed down in the saloon. Just aft of the sleeping area was the w.c. which included the luxury of a bath. The engine would go directly amidships, a petrol-paraffin Parsons 60 HP initially decided on to drive her single screw to a top cruising speed of eight knots, though Lightoller was later to change over to a more powerful 72 HP Gleniffer diesel, which would give her an extra two knots. To make her truly a motor yacht she would carry sails, one forward, one aft, as a Bermudan ketch.

When the launch day arrived, the yacht was lifted out of her cradle at Richardson's Old Wharf and sent down the slipway, christened in champagne by Sylvia, who named her *Sundowner* (an Australian word for 'wanderer'). A month later she was masted and rigged, and ready for her sea trials. From the day he took delivery of her *Sundowner*'s new owner could not keep away from her. In the years to come every holiday from spring to autumn was spent on the boat, going across to the Continent and calling in at ports all the way up the French, Belgian and Dutch coast on cruises lasting two and three weeks at a time. Le Havre, St. Valéry, Fécamp, Boulogne, Calais, Dunkirk, Ostend, Blankenberge, Flushing, Middleburg, the Hook of Holland and the Hague were to become regular ports of call for *Sundowner* in the early 1930s, with the occasional jaunt down the Dutch canals. On these voyages there would sometimes be as many as nine or ten aboard. To Lightoller the more the merrier within reason.

How good it felt to have a command again, even if his vessel was only a sixty-footer, and his crew were his wife and children and their friends. As in his Royal Navy destroyer days, relations between the bridge and the lower deck were both correct and informal, with mutual respect and tolerance. And the roasts, pies and hotpots that Sylvia unflaggingly turned out in the galley were a long, long way removed from the 'old horse' and ship's biscuit that 'Lights' had had to survive on as an apprentice those many years ago.

In 1931 Lightoller moved his large family from Putney to a quieter neighbourhood at Cockfosters in North-East London. He also was persuaded that money was to be made in the novel system of raising chickens—in batteries. He built up a poultry farm in the spacious grounds at the rear of his home and soon made himself something of an authority on chicken-raising. Meanwhile the family was growing up and leaving the fold, so that, by the late 1930s, *Sundowner* would often put to sea on her summer cruises with no-one aboard but 'Lights' and his wife. The days of the happy, boisterous gatherings which filled the yacht with a bustle of animated young people were, alas, passing.

So were the years of peace. Britain watched events in Germany with increasing suspicion and alarm. By July 1939 it seemed only a matter of time before Britain and Germany would be at war. In the midst of all this uncertainty the Admiralty realised to their great consternation that if any kind of assault from the sea or even a major sea-borne offensive on Germany should ever be planned, there was hardly any up-to-date information about the geography of its coastline. It was imperative to obtain more detail about its bays and inlets in order to evaluate the best places where assault troops could land. By this time it would hardly have been practicable to send a vessel of the Royal Navy to steam brazenly up and down surveying the German shores in full view of the imminent enemy. They had to find someone with an innocent-looking craft, one that would not arouse too much suspicion, but whose owner had an extensive enough knowledge of the waters and could be relied upon to do the kind of snooping job required. Through Naval Intelligence, which had recently come under the direction of Admiral John Godfrey, discreet inquiries were made at the yachting and cruising clubs around the South-East coast and eventually one man emerged as the perfect candidate, a retired Royal Naval Reserve commander by the name of Lightoller. It appeared there was no-one cruising regularly across the North Sea who knew the German coast better than he.

It was all very mystifying to Lightoller when, one stormy night towards the end of July, two men in raincoats, with trilbys pulled down over their eyes, turned up at the cottage and interrupted his bridge game. They said they were on government business and insisted that he accompany them there and then to their head-quarters. Why, this really was genuine cloak-and-dagger stuff, thought Lightoller to himself, enjoying the scent of adventure as they whisked him away in their car on a speedy, silent journey through the night that brought them eventually to a big, old, rambling house somewhere in the heart of East Anglia.

Once inside—after strange passwords and numerous other form-alities had been gone through at the gate and then again at the front door—the atmosphere was eerie and oppressive, with people con-versing in hushed tones and where it seemed a password was needed at every turn of a corner. In fact to Lightoller the whole business rapidly began to lose its initial thrill and lapse into a boring farce as he was kept sitting in a corridor waiting to find out what he was wanted for.

But at last he was ushered into a large office where the man sitting at the desk, his sleeves heavily adorned in gold braid, outlined the job they wanted him to do, and to do as soon as possible. Lightoller was only too glad to oblige, but wondered why it was necessary to go through all this mumbo-jumbo before getting to the point. It reminded him of something out of John Buchan, and at any moment he expected Richard Hannay to walk in through the door. This was another side to the Royal Navy he had not encountered before.

And so, briefed on this vital mission for his country, Lightoller in *Sundowner* was under way across the North Sea the following evening on course for the German coast. It was stormy, and Sylvia insisted she come too. She convinced him, besides, that with her along he would look far less suspicious.

During the next couple of weeks *Sundowner* worked her way systematically up the German coastline, dodging in and out of the

Frisian Islands, looking for all the world as though this was just an old man and his wife enjoying a summer cruise in their pleasure boat. But all the time Lightoller was hard at work photographing, sketching and making detailed notes at numerous strategic points along the way where in his limited military knowledge he considered a large-scale landing of troops could be made. Where possible he did all his work hidden below deck, taking his photographs through the portholes while Sylvia sat out on the stern either knitting or peeling potatoes, trying to look the perfect picture of shipboard domesticity and innocence.

Just as important as the lie of the land was to know the lay-out of the sea-bed going in towards the shore so at night Lightoller would get busy with the lead-line taking soundings. To be spotted in broad daylight doing that job really would have attracted interest from the land.

All the material that was gathered together, the notes, the sketches, the rolls of film and so on were stored away in a large, weighted canvas bag ready to be dumped over the side should any unwelcome visitor threaten to come aboard and investigate them. However only once, throughout that strange mission to what in a very short time was to become the enemy coast, did *Sundowner* attract any kind of close attention to make them nervous.

It happened as *Sundowner* was lying at anchor in Jade Bay a little up the coast from Wilhelmshaven. A patrol boat suddenly appeared round the headland and made straight for her. Sylvia, stationed as usual at her place out on the after deck pretending to do chores, shouted a warning to her husband, busy taking photographs below. Meanwhile the patrol vessel began circling inquisitively around with stern-faced men up on the bridge scrutinising *Sundowner* through their binoculars, while Sylvia waved and cooeed at them as idiotically as she could. Then through the loud-hailer came the repeated guttural call, '*Wo ist der Kapitän?*' '*Wo ist der Kapitän?*'

Presently 'der Kapitän' appeared, lurching out of the wheelhouse and on deck with a gin bottle in one hand and a glass in the other, looking to be rather the worse for the bottle he was clutching. Up went his glass towards the observers in a great demonstration of good cheer before putting it to his lips and tossing it back heartily. For a fleeting moment the granite faces of the German navy looked bemused but suddenly they creased into laughter at the sight of this drunken sailor weaving about the deck of his boat while his spouse looked on in apparent disgust and embarrassment. Then, bored with the joke, the intruders swung away towards the open sea and were gone.

Lightoller breathed a sigh of relief. Things were getting just a bit too hot in that quarter for his liking. It was time to weigh anchor and move on. But he was never troubled again, and a few days later, when *Sundowner* arrived back home at Burnham, where she now had her mooring, she brought with her a booty of highly useful data giving a fairly full survey of the coast she had visited, with photographs not just of the beaches and foreshore but also of shipping and other marine activity, gun emplacements and other defensive works which were being hastily prepared all along the German seaboard. Those people back at that citadel of intrigue in the East Anglian countryside would be very pleased with Commander Lightoller—even if, as it turned out, his survey would not be put to use.

A few weeks afterwards, Hitler marched into Poland and Britain and Germany were at war. Almost immediately, by a cruel stroke of luck, it brought tragedy to the Lightoller home. Brian, the youngest, who had gone into the RAF, was killed in a bombing raid on Wilhelmshaven on the very first night of the war, when the plane he was piloting collided with a barrage balloon. There had never been any favourites in the Lightoller family, but as Brian was the baby, his father had always harboured a soft spot for him. It was a terrible blow, and yet fate would have it that Brian, in an indirect way, would help to bring his father through another epic moment in his life that lay not many months off.

30

The ominous black plume of smoke reaching up before them cast a darkening shadow across the blue summer sky, while the roar of gunfire and thudding explosions in company with an incessant drone of aircraft drifted back over the smooth waters of the English Channel with increasing distinctness. With it came a smell, an unfriendly sickly smell, a mixture of spent high explosive and burning oil that were combining to form that evil, forbidding cloud.

Sundowner, her Gleniffer chuntering away with reassuring monotony, was getting closer to the war. Being a little faster than the other craft that had come out of Ramsgate with her, she had gradually left them behind and was now pushing on to Dunkirk alone. Her crew of three—Lightoller, his eldest son Roger, and the boy sea-scout Gerald—watched the sky and the sea warily.

Then Lightoller spotted it. 'Hard over!' he yelled to Roger at the helm; in instant reaction to his father's command, Roger spun the wheel to starboard as far as it would go while *Sundowner* in characteristic fashion swung violently to the sudden movement of her rudder. There, drifting by within feet of her hull, were the tell-tale horns of a mine bobbing menacingly about in the swell. It had been a near thing: their first encounter with danger. There was little Lightoller could do about that rogue mine except hail other vessels heading back the other way and warn them in hopes that a minesweeper could deal with it before some poor unfortunate ran foul of the thing.

A few minutes later three enemy fighters flying high looking for prey had spotted *Sundowner* and were sweeping down to attack. Lightoller prepared to take evasive action but just then racing up astern a destroyer overtook them, opening up with her anti-aircraft guns and drove the intruders off before they had a chance to attack the motor yacht.

It was that incident which made Lightoller first realise how vulnerable and exposed they were, without so much as a rifle or a tin hat on board to protect them. He had swopped his white-topped cap for a black beret. There was no point in posing an easier target than he already was.

They were approaching the thick of it. As the French coast drew nearer and the shores of Dunkirk became more clearly defined beneath that curtain of smoke which hung over the whole area, there appeared to be one unbroken wall of fire. It looked as though the whole place was ablaze. There was obviously one hell of a battle going on. Around the main body of the smoke the sky was pockmarked with bursting anti-aircraft shells and trails of tracer bullets whipping through the air in all directions, with the constant whine and snarl of aircraft darting around like angry wasps, and then the unrelenting whistle and crash of the bombs and shells while the sea all about was an unending, swirling turmoil of fountains erupting to the impact of continuous explosions.

So this was Dunkirk.

Lightoller spotted a motor cruiser broken down and on fire a little way off with its occupants desperately waving for assistance. He steered alongside to take off its anxious crew of two plus three naval ratings picked up at Dunkirk. As he was hauling them to the safety of his own craft the man in command of the stricken boat, a 25-foot motor cruiser called *Westerly*, warned him that she had 200 gallons of petrol on board which was about to go up at any moment. Lightoller needed no second hint. Barely were the men from *Westerly* aboard than *Sundowner* was parting company with all the revs her Gleniffer could muster, putting in every yard she could between herself and the blazing boat before it blew up. They were little more than a hundred yards off when there was a deafening blast and *Westerly* exploded in a great ball of flame and flying wreckage. That was the end of her Dunkirk—but alas, relieved though they were to get out of that certain crisis, it was not the end for the five men Lightoller had plucked just in time from her deck: after what they had been through, they would rather have been travelling the other way.

Then the Luftwaffe turned its attention again to *Sundowner*.

From out of the mêlée of planes filling the sky overhead, and none of them R A F, came the dreaded whine of two Stuka dive-bombers swooping down towards her—and this time with no friendly destroyer close by to ward them off. Lightoller, standing on the deck craning his neck skywards, fixed his eyes on the leading one and told Roger in the wheelhouse to stand by at the helm. Down came the plane making its deadly banshee scream, the familiar Stuka trademark of fear. He kept his eyes glued to it and then just as he sensed she was about to let go her package . . . 'Hard a-port!' he boomed. *Sundowner* heeled instantly in a sharp turn while the sea rose up in a mighty blast next to her hull, lashing her decks with a cascade of spray and nearly lifting her out of the water. The first had missed; the second was still coming. Lightoller followed his progress down in the same way. Roger at the helm waiting coolly for the command: 'Hard a-starboard!' yelled his father, thumping the wheelhouse with his fist. Again the sea, this time on the port side leapt up in a mighty column to the shock of the explosion, giving *Sundowner* another heavy shower as she lurched right over almost on her beam ends from the impact of the blast so close. The Stukas flew away in disgust. It was round one to *Sundowner* but Lightoller realised only too well there'd be plenty more before this day was out.

The merciless pounding that had been taken by the Dunkirk rescue ships that morning had been so costly, including two transports and four destroyers sunk with two more badly damaged, that it had been decided to call a halt to daytime sailings. After today the evacuation would be completed over the next two nights. June 1st had to be the last valiant effort to get as many men away in whatever was left floating before the Germans broke through the rear guard which was stubbornly defending the steadily shrinking area surrounding the port. At this stage more than 200,000 troops had already been plucked from the beaches but another 200,000 troops were still stranded and pinned down. Lightoller's younger son Trevor, a Lieutenant in the Royal Signals, had been among them but had been lucky enough to get away and was already back home in England. His father had at least got that to feel deeply thankful for, but there were many thousands of other sons still trapped there who deserved an equal chance.

Sundowner was almost at her destination, coming in on Route X, a course that brought her round in a wide sweep from the west past Gravelines with the sky as ever crowded with enemy planes supported by heavy shellfire from the German shore batteries on coastal territory lately won. The Stukas were continuously peeling off and screaming down to let go their bombs indiscriminately on ships and men, whatever took their choice. Either way the targets were easy: for the Luftwaffe Dunkirk was virtually a turkey shoot.

Then *Sundowner* was under attack again as a fighter was seen coming up astern of her. It was at that moment that Lightoller remembered Brian and certain things he had explained to his father about his bomber training on how to evade fighter attack; how the aircraft needed to elevate its guns to bring them to bear. He once again told Roger to stand by and waited as the Messerschmitt 109 closed low and rapidly on them over the sea. He must be patient. He must not make his move too soon. He must wait . . . wait . . . wait . . . the yellow nose lifted perceptibly. 'Hard a-starboard!' *Sundowner*, faithful to the helm as always, performed her pirouette while in that same moment the Messerschmitt's machine-guns and cannon opened up in a lethal chatter . . . but only to rake the empty sea where the target had been just a second before. The pilot, however, was not giving up as he circled round and lined up on his target again but Lightoller was coolly watching him . . . wait . . . wait . . . steady as you go . . . 'Hard a-port!' Once again as the bullets and shells straffed the water, *Sundowner* steamed on without even a chip out of her paintwork. The pilot did not bother to try again. There were plenty of other targets around far easier than this infernal one to go looking for. As he made off Lightoller thought of his late son and thanked providence. Brian could do his bit to to see them through this day yet. And *Sundowner*, the old girl, she was performing magnificently. What a boat she was proving herself to be! But Lightoller was soon to realise that she had not come through her baptism of fire quite so unscathed as he had at first assumed. Although the earlier bombs had not hit her, the force of the explosions so close to her hull had parted a couple of seams and she was beginning to take water. He started up the pump and was relieved that it was appearing to keep the leaks under control—which still left the crucial question of just how much more she was going to have to take.

Lightoller's original intention was to go right up to the beach where Trevor had been rescued two days previously and try to load troops there, but the men from *Westerly* informed him that the beaches were being cleared of soldiers and they were now embarking on the outer piers.

As he closed the harbour the true horror of it all unfolded before him. The whole area was strewn with wreckage. All the way along the roadstead small ships were on fire and sinking and the water was littered with the remnants of the scores of vessels that had already gone to their last account, decimated by the bombs and guns of the enemy; there were bits of furniture, broken wood and a mass of other debris all floating in one great sea of oil. *Sundowner* reduced speed and nosed her way through it all, including the spot where a big French transport had been bombed and sunk a short time earlier, revealing more than just wreckage: the yacht had to ease round a mass of bodies limply bobbing about in the swell. As young Gerald the sea-scout went to work with the boat-hook fending the corpses and other debris away in case the propeller got fouled, it was a sight he would not forget for as long as he lived. But today he was facing it as bravely as any man. A cursory nod and the slightest hint of a wink from the skipper told him so. For Gerald the most unnerving thing about it all was the colossal noise. It was that which he found most terrifying.

As *Sundowner* approached the West Mole at a cautious crawl, continuing to wade through the mass of destruction as she went, she was overtaken by a large two-funnelled, grey-painted transport. Immediately the dive bombers were upon her. As their bombs rained down on the ship she disappeared in a blitz of high explosive and smoke. 'She's gone!' exclaimed Lightoller in stunned astonishment. But then from out of the blanket of hissing fog she emerged, steaming serenely on towards the harbour, undamaged and undeterred, intent on getting on with her task. There was something about that incident which put new heart and confidence into Lightoller as he followed the transport in through the entrance of Dunkirk harbour.

Once inside it was an incredible, moving sight which met his eyes; troops, thousands and thousands of them lining both piers waiting patiently to embark and get away just as soon as their turn came, while the enemy continuously came down at them from above. Both moles were constantly under bombing and straffing and there was nothing that the soldiers could do but stand there and take it, completely exposed. But despite the destruction, the casualties, the heavy losses, the ships big and small kept coming and the soldiers in their thousands kept boarding. As one yachtsman who was also there on June 1st would later describe the scene: 'There is no separating naval vessel from tug, barge from motor-yacht, launch from Channel steamer. All through this day they are mingled together in an inextricable confusion of effort. The waters of the Dunkirk channels, the close passages of the harbour, the long swept approaches are a wild intermingling of movement and disaster . . .' (David Divine, *Dunkirk*).

Because it was Low Water in the harbour when *Sundowner* arrived, Lightoller realised it would be impossible to load up troops from the high quay down into his boat. He crossed over to the far pier, the East Mole, and made for the destroyer *Worcester* which he recognised as the one that had overtaken them en route and driven off that first attack. The destroyer could be used as a stepping stone down from the quay to *Sundowner*. They were almost alongside the lower after end of the warship, and Gerald was preparing to throw a line aboard when there was an almighty bang and a blinding flash. 'My God, I'm dead!' was the sea-scout's reaction. Then it happened again and he realised he was not dead after all. It was *Worcester*'s after 4-inch guns opening up on a new air raid coming in. Comforting, but unbearable on ears without protection.

Lightoller went aboard the destroyer where men were already embarking and rooted out her commander, Captain Allison, to offer his services.

'How many can you take?' asked Allison urgently. Lightoller remembered that day at the boat race when he had taken 21 on board, but he could manage a few more this trip. 'Oh, about a hundred!' he nonchalantly shouted back above the racket, hardly believing himself what he had just said. The Captain looked down at the little *Sundowner* and back at her owner with a look of amazement. 'Are you sure?' Lightoller was not sure but he would have a damn good try; he just nodded. Allison went off to consult with an army officer, then came back. 'All right,' said he with a chuckle, 'Go ahead and take them!'

Before leaving Cubitt's yacht basin at Chiswick, Lightoller, Roger and Gerald had worked all night stripping out everything remotely movable; bunks, seating, the saloon table, Sylvia's cooker and sink and even the masts, all to create that little bit of extra space that might mean room for one more man; also to make her lighter—and to have less on board that could catch fire.

The embarkation down to *Sundowner* commenced. Badly wounded soldiers were not put aboard but several coming down had nasty flesh wounds, mostly caused by shrapnel. On instructions from the skipper, Gerald immediately set up a dressing station on the roof of the wheelhouse and began tearing up sheets into strips for bandages —one part of *Sundowner*'s equipment Lightoller, with foresight, had decided not to leave behind at Cubitt's.

As the loading progressed they were under attack all the time from the air but *Worcester*'s guns kept up a perpetual barrage overhead in reply which seemed to be keeping the Luftwaffe at bay. There were prolonged gaps between the RAF's sorties, while destroyers like *Worcester*, which had been heavily relied on to fight off attacks hour after hour for the past days, were rapidly running out of ammunition. There had not been any time to rearm during the brief turn-arounds at Dover discharging troops before heading back across to Dunkirk to collect more. But Lightoller was relieved that she at least had enough shells remaining to keep the Luftwaffe at a respectable distance while *Sundowner* was moored to her, enabling him to concentrate on loading her up.

As previously arranged, Roger stationed himself below to pack the men down there first, using every available inch of space, while his father stood on the deck with a rating who was tallying them aboard. All were instructed to leave their equipment on deck and then once below to lie down flat in order to maintain the stability of the boat. It seemed that Roger was doing a remarkably good packing job. When the number below got to fifty his father called down 'How are you getting on?' 'Oh plenty of room yet!' came back the cheery reply.

As they filed aboard the little motor-yacht many were apologising for letting England down. Lightoller, knowing what his own son had been through, made it his business to persuade them otherwise. The way they had fought to the last, he assured them, every single one was entitled to the heart-felt thanks of their country.

At seventy-five Lightoller called below again to ask Roger how he was doing. 'It's getting a bit crowded,' he admitted; he had got two in the bath and one on the loo, he proudly declared. On hearing that, Lightoller came back with the immediate response: 'I hope the men in the bath haven't got their boots on!' Gerald Ashcroft wondered how a man caught up in the thick of all this could worry about boots in his bath. The boots, as it happened, were dutifully removed, as were everyone's boots, and helmets as well, when it was realised the amount of weight that could be saved if they were left behind—or thrown overboard as was the case. The same too would go for all the equipment which had been brought aboard, rifles included, as Lightoller, with seventy-five men below, began packing them on deck. Some were none too happy about parting with their rifles. Army discipline had drilled into them that not only was a soldier's best friend his rifle, but he would have to pay for it in the event of loss. It took some firm persuasion from the skipper to convince them that today was an exception. In short every rifle that had been brought aboard was obediently, if most reluctantly, tossed into the waters of Dunkirk harbour. By the time the number around the deck and in the wheelhouse was approaching fifty, *Sundowner* had gone noticeably lower in the water and Lightoller could feel her starting to get distinctly tender. He decided that was enough. Including the three-man crew and the five men rescued from *Westerly* she now had exactly

130 on board. It was impossible to believe but the count could not lie.
A mere sixty-foot yacht had somehow managed to find room for 130
men.

Sundowner cast off from *Worcester* and backed out of the harbour to
face the sea crossing, with no guarantees this time on how she would
handle. She was on her own, no comforting anti-aircraft guns to cover
her, and RAF air-cover all too little against the hordes of enemy
planes harrying the escapers. A number of other small craft similar in
size to *Sundowner* had earlier been turned back, such was the inten-
sity of the air raids. Meanwhile *Sundowner*, looking distinctly clumsy
under her load, edged out into Dunkirk roads again, weaving her way
in and out of the wreckage. So that Lightoller could concentrate more
on watching the steering and passing on commands to Roger at the
wheel, the men on their own initiative detailed look-outs to the stern,
the bow and on each beam to keep an eye out for enemy aircraft
showing special interest in *Sundowner*. She would not have to wait
long.

'Look out for this bloke, skipper!' came the alert from one of the
look-outs. A twin-engined Junkers 88 was coming in for a bombing
attack and it was definitely making for *Sundowner*. When the aircraft
was almost overhead Lightoller gave the by now well practised
command to Roger, 'Hard over!' The plane dipped low to unload its
present but *Sundowner*, despite all that weight she was burdened
with, swung on her helm as lightly as ever, laying her rail almost right
under in the process, her men, some crouched, some flat on their
bellies, clinging on desperately, while the bomb exploded in the sea a
few yards away. The bomber was coming back for another attempt.
This little boat packed with all those men was far too juicy a target to
pass up after one try. He came in for a second time but once again at
the critical moment his target suddenly altered course and the bomb
fell wide. He was just preparing to attack a third time when, to the joy
of everyone on the deck, a Spitfire appeared and latched onto his tail
and with a long decisive burst of its eight Browning guns sent the
Junkers diving down in flames. But the momentary pleasure provided by this for the spectators on *Sundowner* instantly turned to
terror. The stricken plane was about to crash on top of them, as
though in a last ditch suicidal effort to destroy once and for all its

elusive target. Then to their relief the flaming aircraft dipped its nose and plunged vertically down into the sea exploding in a spectacular burst of flame and spray fifty yards astern. A loud cheer went up round *Sundowner*'s deck. That bomber had been getting just a little too determined. But as *Sundowner* plodded on at a considerably reduced speed to her normal frisky ten knots, another fighter had espied her and was coming in to attack. Lightoller, having taken up a position at the bow watched it over the wheelhouse closing from the rear on a gliding run. *Sundowner* had already proved she could respond to the rudder, deep though she was in the water, but the guns of the Messerschmitt would put her to the acid test. Lightoller watched and waited, thinking again of his late son's words: 'When she lifts her nose, usually about ten to fifteen degrees, that's when she's going to open fire.' 'Stand by . . . steady as you go . . . Hard a-port!' *Sundowner* heeled right over as before, a streak of gunfire peppering the sea along her starboard side as she veered. The fighter followed through, roaring low over the top of her and turned. It looked as if he was coming back to try again. He did but with the same result. He tried for a third time but still without success. In the end like the other Luftwaffe pilots, he flew away in frustration as she forged on without so much as one bullet hole in her precious teak—and, more important, none in any of her passengers. She was performing like an ace. Time and again she was attacked. Sometimes a plane would try once, sometimes more, sometimes it was bombing and other times machine-gunning. It got to be all the same to Lightoller, standing up at her bow, totally exposed and unprotected, the soldiers pressing themselves as hard as they could to the deck at his feet, as he prepared yet again to give the vital order when he judged the moment was right. 'Hard a-port!' 'Hard a-starboard!' Roger reacted instantly to the commands while his father defiantly shook his fist and roared abuse at the 'Bloody Hun Swine!' trying to destroy his boat. Roger had rarely heard his father use bad language but this would be one occasion when he heard him use it a-plenty, and somehow it seemed to be helping. One thing Roger did realise, if ever he was lucky enough to get out of this his arms would be stiff for days. *Sundowner* may have been superb on the helm, but she had never been the easiest to turn.

Lightoller longed for just one machine-gun. On numerous occasions he was sure he could have given the antagonists plenty to think about. If not shoot one down, certainly give him a sore belly. This was

Lightoller of old. The years seemed to be falling away. He was going through hell and yet at the same time—even at the ripe age of 66—he was revelling in it. The Dunkirk spirit, they would call it in years to come. But this was also the Lightoller spirit, that old *Boy's Own* spirit that had seen him through so much danger and adventure in his earlier life, and it was still as much alive as ever. He was proud, too, of his son. The first time under fire and he was doing a grand job. It was the first time for young Gerald, as well, and the lad had never flinched once.

As time, and each nerve-racking mile, went slowly and painfully by the conditions down below became appalling. With everything battened down and not so much as a porthole or a skylight open, the atmosphere was wretched, a mixture of sweat, diesel fumes and a growing stench of seasickness, the sickness not because it was a rough day, far from it, but all the swerving and lurching about that *Sundowner* was doing was too much for the unaccustomed stomachs of exhausted men to stand. It was no place for claustrophobics and not knowing what was going on up top made it worse. But never a moan nor a grumble was heard. They all did their best to grin and bear it, obeying the instructions to remain lying down and under no circumstances to move. The only time when any doubts were expressed about their safety was when one young Tommy anxiously commented, ''Ere, some bloke told me the old skipper of this boat was on the *Titanic*. That's all the luck we need!' The retort from an older, wiser Tommy was pointed: 'Lad, if 'e was in that and came through it, 'e'll do you son, 'e'll do you.'

Sundowner battled on gamely across the Channel, ploughing a straight furrow for home, but dodging the air attacks when they came. Bombing and straffing were not her only problem: she was being continually buffeted by the wash of larger vessels going by in both directions which at times threatened to swamp her, because she was so deep in the water it would not have taken much of a sea to put paid to her and the whole effort. The pump was already fully stretched coping with the leaks she had. Each time she encountered the heavy wash from a passing troop ship Lightoller immediately hove to and put her head into it, letting her ride out the turbulence while down below a few more victims joined the growing list of seasick casualties. There would be a considerable—and somewhat unpleasant—cleaning up job to do when they got home. The wash of ships was one problem Lightoller had not bargained for. He had blessed his luck that this was one of the finest days he had ever known in the English Channel, which was why he was so confident about taking so many on board. He could handle the wash problem providing he got the boat stopped and turned into it in time, but there were those occasions when he could not avoid being caught beam on to the steep breakers thrown out by large ships speeding, which caused *Sundowner* to start rolling heavily. But then he was not without past experience for coping with this particular situation, and he got the men on deck to stand facing forwards and went into that old routine he had directed once before . . . 'Lean to the left! . . . Lean to the right! . . . Lean to the left! . . .' From the wheelhouse roof Gerald watched the skipper's arm signals and relayed them to the men aft, ensuring that all moved as one. The only trouble was, this was no healthy place to sit rocking about, with enemy aircraft always on the look-out for nice convenient targets. But good fortune here would be with them, and they were lucky enough not to attract any attention from the air during those anxious moments.

Beyond the halfway stage the Luftwaffe began to thin out. To reach midway by Route X, the route laid down, which was considerably longer than the normal Dunkirk route, had taken *Sundowner* some three nerve-wracking hours. None of the men who made the trip in her would ever forget the crossing from Dunkirk in that small boat, though few would ever remember her name, or her skipper's. By the finish Lightoller had lost count of how many times they were attacked. The odds on the leaky, overloaded boat making it through the repeated air attacks to arrive safely back at Ramsgate were never all that encouraging—but if *Sundowner*'s skipper had stopped to work out the odds . . . he might have stayed at home. Towards dusk they were off the Kentish coast and nearing home. It could only be that other unseen forces had been helping them safely through this day.

As they arrived outside the entrance to Ramsgate harbour, the time on that old grinning face of the ship's clock, which had ticked away serenely through it all, said ten—exactly twelve hours since *Sundowner* first headed out on her Dunkirk adventure. What a long, long day it had been—but this apparently was getting no sympathy from the man with the loud-hailer in the naval launch who told her to lie off and wait until she was given permission to enter. The harbour was just as active at the end of the day as it had been at the start, with craft like a colony of ants single-mindedly scurrying back and forth, intent upon their task regardless of how many of their numbers had been stamped on and crushed in the process.

After being instructed to wait outside Ramsgate harbour, Lightoller casually informed them he had 130 men on board. He did not need to say any more as permission to enter was immediately given.

Sundowner was just going through the harbour entrance when suddenly she heeled over to a terrifying angle. The soldiers below, learning that they had arrived in port, had all started getting to their feet. For the first time in her life *Sundowner* really was now in danger of capsizing, and what a time for it to happen! Immediately Lightoller boomed to them below 'Get down!' 'Get down!' 'Back as you were or we'll all be in the sea!' The message got through and slowly, oh so painfully, as the men on her deck clung on for dear life, *Sundowner* returned to an even keel. Lightoller gave strict instructions for nobody to move again until given the word.

Sundowner entered and nudged her way alongside a trawler at the quay and the disembarkation began. Lightoller realised that the harbour authorities had thought he was exaggerating about his 130 men, and that the men on deck were his full load; he relished the surprise he was about to reveal as the Chief Petty Officer on the quayside began to tally them off. As soon as the fifty on deck had been counted ashore and the Petty Officer was on the verge making off to attend to other business, Lightoller shouted the order, 'All right, come up from below!'

The man's eyes bulged as he watched a never-ending procession of soldiers just keep coming up through the forward companionway, the after companionway and through the doors on either side of the wheelhouse . . . 80 . . . 85 . . . 95 . . . 100 . . . 110 . . . 120 . . . When the procession stopped at 126 Lightoller was puzzled. There seemed to be one missing. Down below he scampered to find there, sitting on the loo, a young soldier, head slumped in his lap, totally dead to the world, having apparently slept through the whole thing. 'Come on son, come on. Wake up! You're home!' The head rose, the eyes blinked open and a rather confused but happy Tommy hauled himself to his feet to be last seen weaving a dazed and uncertain path down Ramsgate quay, wondering where his mates had got to.

'Gawd's truth, mate!' exclaimed the Chief Petty Officer to Lightoller. 'Where'd you put 'em?' Lightoller glanced down the quay towards the sleepy soldier he'd just woken up on the loo. 'You might ask . . . You might well ask!'

Lightoller had fully expected that he'd be asked to go back to Dunkirk and do it all over again and, despite everything he had gone through, he was quite resigned to going. He stood by with *Sundowner* at Ramsgate for two more days waiting to be called upon, but they were not to be required again. *Sundowner* had done her bit as had all the little armada, and it would now be up to the bigger ships to finish the job—though it would never be truly finished. On June 4th Dunkirk fell and the thousands of British and French troops who did not get away would find themselves prisoners for the rest of the war. However Lightoller could at least feel a personal satisfaction in knowing he had seen to it that there were a certain 122 Tommies who would go back to fight another day. That tally did not perhaps sound so many compared with the 64,000 in total that were brought back throughout that historic Saturday, and even less significant next to the 338,000 rescued during the whole nightmare of the Dunkirk evacuation. But there were few individual stories to come out of it afterwards to better the one they would tell of Commander C. H. Lightoller, D S C and Bar, R N R (retired) who, at the age of 66, took his 60-foot motor-yacht *Sundowner* over and brought back close on 130 men under constant fire.

June 1st 1940 was a great day for British seamen. For Lightoller, it was a very special day—as though he and his old mistress the sea had finally reached a complete understanding.

EPILOGUE

Dunkirk was not to be the end of Lightoller's war service. Although soon afterwards he joined up with the local Home Guard unit, the Royal Navy had more pressing work for him to do: he commanded scratch crews ferrying and delivering numerous types of small craft from port to port around the British coast, ranging from sailing vessels to auxiliary trawlers and naval supply tenders. The crews of the Small Vessels Pool, as it was called, were made up mostly of men who had not been called into active service owing to such reasons as age, health or other vital commitments to the war effort. Lightoller was engaged in his work with the Small Vessels Pool right up to the end of the war, when he was finally 'demobbed' in 1946 at the age of 72.

But as the beginning of World War II had brought tragedy with the loss of his youngest son Brian, it was with grievous irony that the last month would see the loss of his eldest son Roger, who had done such a fine job with him at Dunkirk. Roger had gone on to join the Royal Navy where he had later commanded Motor Gun Boats and was shot and killed while ashore during a German Commando raid on Granville on the North French coast. The war had been a costly one for the Lightollers.

However in his grief there would be one tiny consolation. Soon after the resumption of peace he got *Sundowner* back after she had spent the latter stages of the war in service with the army. It was perhaps not unpredictable that she should come through it all unscathed—except for her ugly coat of grey paint which was soon removed. On returning to her 'lawful occasions' she would be plying her way once again on those cruises to the Continent, though not going quite as far afield as she had done during her pre-war days.

The return to peace would also bring a new and greater involvement in the marine world for Lightoller. He wound up his chicken farm at Cockfosters, said goodbye to 'The Cottage', and moved to Twickenham to set up the one kind of business he had dearly wanted for years—a boatyard, which he called Richmond Slipways. He was at first in partnership, but would ultimately become the sole proprietor, running the business with the help of Trevor, his one surviving son, and living 'over the shop'. They specialised in motor launches and among the firm's biggest customers was the London River Police.

It was during one of those typical nights of heavy London fog that Captain Alfred Gillespie, his old friend and 'Number 1' in *Garry* of *UB 110* fame, received a telephone call from Sylvia Lightoller to say that 'Lights' wanted to see him. Despite the forbidding night Gillespie and his wife wrapped up and set off on a cold journey from their home in Regent's Park across London to 1, Ducks Walk, Twickenham, in answer to the summons. When they arrived it was to find an ailing old man, who had been battling with heart disease and bronchitis for some months, sitting by the fire in his dressing gown, with a rug wrapped round his knees quietly reflecting in the flicker of the flames. The man may have been unwell but the eyes were as blue and alert as ever. He just wanted to talk to his old friend, to share a few memories of the sea and a yarn or two of times past. The *Titanic* was not mentioned. Gillespie stayed with him for an hour or so and then, seeing that the old man was getting tired, he and his wife took their leave and headed back home.

Early the next morning Gillespie received a telephone call from Sylvia to break the news that her husband had passed away peacefully in the night. It was December 8th 1952. Three days later at a quiet and simple Anglican service Charles Herbert Lightoller was cremated at Mortlake Crematorium and his ashes scattered in the Garden of Remembrance.

He did not have that Viking's funeral after all on his boat as he had once suggested, and today, decades later, the motor-yacht *Sundowner* is still going strong, and as fine and sound a boat as the day she hit the water at Conyer on that sunny Easter in 1930. The last that was heard of her, she was under the caring ownership of Mr. John Sapsford, a retired engineer from Norwich. She had been through quite a few more adventures before coming into Mr. Sapsford's hands, but none that could ever match the one that is commemorated by a gleaming brass plaque screwed proudly to the front of her teak wheelhouse, bearing the simple inscription:

DUNKIRK

1940

SOURCES AND BIBLIOGRAPHY

Lightoller's own reminiscences, *Titanic and Other Ships*, which concluded with his departure from the White Star Line at the beginning of the 1920s, have given me an invaluable head start and have been a useful guide.

Other books consulted include:

Anderson, Roy: *White Star*, Stephenson and Son, 1962

Arnold, Sir Edwin: *Seas and Lands*, Longman, Green and Co., 1892

Bacon, Admiral Sir Reginald: *The Dover Patrol* (2 vols), Hutchinson, 1919

Beesley, Laurence: *The Loss of the SS Titanic*, Heinemann, 1912

Berton, Pierre: *Klondike!*, W. H. Allen, 1960

Bisset, Sir James: *Sail Ho!*, Angus and Robertson, 1958

Bisset, Sir James: *Tramps and Ladies*, Angus and Robertson, 1960

Boughton, Captain George: *Seafaring*, Faber and Gwyer, 1930

Bullen, Frank: *Men of the Merchant Service*, Smith Elder, 1900

Bywater, Hector: *Their Secret Purposes*, Constable and Co., 1932

Canham, Erwin D.: *Commitment to Freedom*, Houghton Mifflin, 1958

Chiang Yee: *The Silent Traveller in San Francisco*, Methuen, 1964

Clements, Rex: *Gypsy of the Horn*, Heath Cranton, 1924

Cooper, Commander E. G.: *Yarns of the Seven Seas*, Heath Cranton, 1927

Corbett, Sir Julian (and Newbolt): *Naval Operations* (5 vols) Longman, 1920–31

Coxon, Stanley: *Dover During the Dark Days*, John Lane, 1919

Craig, Gavin: *Boy Aloft*, Nautical Publishing Co., 1971

Divine, A. D.: *Dunkirk*, Faber and Faber, 1945

Divine, David: *The Nine Days of Dunkirk*, Faber and Faber, 1959

Dorling, Captain ('Taffrail'): *The Endless Story*, Hodder and Stoughton, 1931

Eddy, Mary Baker: *Science and Health* with *Key to the Scriptures*, Christian Science Publishing Company, 1875

Fell, Reverend James: *British Merchant Seamen in San Francisco 1892–98*, E. Arnold, 1899

Fox, Sir Frank: *Australia*, A. and C. Black, 1910

Fürbringer, Werner: *U-Boote in Kampf und Sturm*, Berlin, 1933

Gibbard-Jackson, G.: *Ships, Seas and Sailors*, Heath Cranton, 1933

Gracie, Colonel Archibald: *The Truth about the Titanic*, Mitchell, Kennerley, 1913

Grant, Robert H.: *U-Boats Destroyed*, Putnam, 1964

Grant, Robert H.: *U-Boat Intelligence*, Putnam, 1969

Greenhill, Basil: *The Life and Death of the Merchant Sailing Ship*, H.M.S.O., 1980

Harman, Nicolas: *Dunkirk*, Hodder and Stoughton, 1980

Hughes, Henry: *Through Mighty Seas*, W. and G. Foyle, 1939

Jane's Fighting Ships, Janes, 1914

Jones, H. A.: *War in the Air* (volume 2 of 5 volumes), Clarendon Press, 1926

Kipling, Rudyard: *Sea Warfare*, Macmillan, 1916

Lightoller, C. H.: *Titanic and Other Ships*, Nicholson and Watson, 1935

Lightoller, C. H.: *Testimony from the Field*, Christian Science Journal, 1912

Lord, Walter: *A Night to Remember*, Longman, 1956

Lord, Walter: *The Miracle of Dunkirk*, Allen Lane, 1983

Lubbock, Basil: *Around The Horn Before the Mast*, Brown, Son and Ferguson, 1902

Lubbock, Basil: *Last of the Windjammers* (2 vols), Brown, Son and Ferguson, 1927

Lubbock, Basil: *The Nitrate Clippers*, Brown, Son and Ferguson, 1932

Marcus, Geoffrey: *The Maiden Voyage*, Allen and Unwin, 1969

Martin, Simon: *The Other Titanic*, David and Charles, 1980

Masefield, John: *The Wanderer*, Heinemann, 1930

May, Robin: *The Gold Rushes*, Luscombe, 1977

Morell, W. H.: *The Gold Rushes*, A. and C. Black, 1940

Newbolt, Sir Henry (*also* Sir Julian Corbett): *Naval Operations* (5 vols), Longman, 1920–31

Newbolt, Sir Henry: *Submarine and Anti Submarine*, Longman, 1918

Oldham, W. J.: *The Ismay Line*, Journal of Commerce, 1961

Padfield, Peter: *The Titanic and The Californian*, Hodder, 1965

Robinson, Douglas: *Zeppelins in Combat*, G. T. Foulis, 1962
Rostron, Sir Arthur: *Home from the Sea*, Cassell and Co., 1931
Sattin, Donald: *Just Off the Swale*, Meresborough Books, 1978
Thayer, John B: *The Sinking of the SS Titanic* (1940), 7 Cs Press, 1974
Villiers, Alan: *Voyaging with the Wind*, H.M.S.O., 1975
Villiers, Alan: *Of Ships and Men*, Hodder and Stoughton, 1954
Wade, Wyn Craig: *Titanic, End of a Dream*, Weidenfeld and Nicolson, 1980
Young, Filson: *Titanic*, Richards, 1912

Lightoller's 1936 broadcasts on the BBC about the *Titanic*, and then in later programmes about Dunkirk have been also been most enlightening.

Numerous other sources have been referred to. The two most important are:

Report on the Loss of the *Titanic* (SS), H.M.S.O., 1912

The *Titanic* Disaster: Report of the Committee on Commerce, United States Senate.

The Public Records Office at Kew has supplied various useful items of information in both its Merchant Service and Royal Navy files. Other sources include: Adelaide Observer, Chorley Guardian, Christian Science Journal, Christian Science Monitor, Daily Herald, Daily Mirror, Dover Express, East Kent Gazette, Illustrated London News, Kent Messenger, Liverpool Daily Post, Marine Engineer, Mercantile Marine Association Reporter, Motor Boat and Yachting, Nautical Magazine, New York Times, Sea Breezes, Southampton Times, Sydney Morning Herald, Syren and Shipping, The Times, Washington Post.

The remaining sources for this biography are listed in the Acknowledgements at the front of the book.

INDEX

Accra (Gold Coast), 87, 88
Accrington, SS, 258
Adelaide, 53–7
Adriatic, RMS, 144, 200, 290
Africa, West, 86
Allison, Capt. (*Worcester*), 305
Amerika, SS, 152, 190–1
Andrews, Thomas (Harland & Wolff), 165
Antillian, SS, 152
Apprenticeship, 5–7, 8–9, 11, 14–15, 29, 63–5
Argentina, 14, 69, 71–5
Aspinall, Butler, 206
Astor, John Jacob and Mrs., 145, 174, 180, 187
Athabasca, River, 100–2, 106
Athenai, SS, 152
Atlantic Daily Bulletin (Titanic), 152
Ausonia, RMS, 291
Australia, Australians, 53–7, 60, 118–27

Bacon, Adm. Sir Reginald, 256, 258 263
Bahia Blanca, 69, 71, 74, 75
Bailhache, Mr Justice, 224
Baltic, RMS, 152
Barker (Assistant Purser, *Titanic*), 174, 188
Bell (Chief Engineer, *Titanic*), 162, 171, 186, 188
Benin (Nigeria), 88
Billings Frederic, USS, 79
Binoculars, *see* Glasses

'Black Gang', The, 130, 162, 182
Blair, David (White Star Line), 144, 148, 237–40, 243
Blue Riband, 134
Board of Trade (Certificates), 63–5, 143, 189, 207, 218, 222, 223, 224, 231
Boer War, 118–19, 121–2, 125
Boulogne, 255, 295
Bowyer, George (Pilot, Southampton), 146–7
Boxhall (Fourth Officer, *Titanic*), 144, 153, 154, 164, 168, 185, 187, 291
Brazil, 14, 26–30
Bride (Wireless Operator, *Titanic*), 152, 158, 166–7, 176, 182
Britannic, RMS, 289
Brown, Mrs J. J. 'Molly', 145, 170
Bundey, Mr Justice, 57–9
Burnham, 299
Butt, Maj. Archibald, 145, 187

Calais, 255, 260, 295
Calcutta, 30, 31, 61, 63–5, 66
Californian, SS, 201–3
Callaghan, Adm. 249
Cameron, Capt. John G. (*Oceanic*), 130–1, 133, 242, 262
Cammell, Laird Co., 244
Campania, HMS, 244–9, 254
Canada, 97–110
Cape Coast, (Gold Coast), 87, 88
Cargo, 11, 23, 25, 53, 66, 68, 77, 79–80, 91, 114, 149
   Discharging by surf boat, 86–8